ALASTAIR SAWDAY'S

Special
places to stay

BRITISH BED & BREAKFAST

Edited by Jackie King

Typesetting, Conversion & Repro: ..... Avonset, Bath

Design: .... Caroline King
& Springboard Design, Bristol

Mapping: .... Springboard Design, Bristol

Maps: .... Maps in Minutes ™ 1999
© Crown Copyright, Ordnance Survey 1999

Printing: .... Stige, Italy

UK Distribution: .... Portfolio, Greenford, Middlesex

US Distribution: .... The Globe Pequot Press,
Guilford, Connecticut

Published in October 2001

Alastair Sawday Publishing Co. Ltd
The Home Farm Stables, Barrow Gurney, Bristol BS48 3RW
Tel: +44 (0)1275 464891 Fax: +44 (0)1275 464887
E-mail: info@specialplacestostay.com Web: www. specialplacestostay.com

The Globe Pequot Press
P. O. Box 480, Guilford, Connecticut 06437, USA
Tel: +1 203 458 4500 Fax: +1 203 458 4601
E-mail: info@globe-pequot.com Web: www.globe-pequot.com

Sixth edition

Copyright © October 2001 Alastair Sawday Publishing Co. Ltd

A catalogue record for this book is available from the British Library.

Alastair Sawday has asserted his right to be identified as the author of this work.

ISBN 1-901970-19-1 in the UK

ISBN 0-7627-1245-7 in the US

Printed in Italy

The publishers have made every effort to ensure the accuracy of the information in this
book at the time of going to press. However, they cannot accept any responsibility for any
loss, injury or inconvenience resulting from the use of information contained therein.

ALASTAIR SAWDAY'S

Special

places to stay

Pennard Hill Farm, no. 378

BRITISH BED & BREAKFAST

"A home is not a mere transient shelter,
its essence lies in the personality of the people who live in it."
H L Mencken 1880-1956

The
Globe
Pequot
Press

Guilford
Connecticut, USA

Alastair Sawday Publishing
Bristol, UK

Contents

Contents

Quick reference indices - places which are: wheelchair-friendly, good for people of limited mobility, good for singles, child-friendly, good if you have no car, pet-friendly and places which use mostly organic or home-grown produce.

What is Alastair Sawday Publishing?

www.specialplacestostay.com

Alastair Sawday's Special Places to Stay series

Order forms

Report form

Index by surname

Index by place name

Exchange rate table

Explanation of symbols

Acknowledgements

This is so much more than a guide to Bed and Breakfast. It is a vast and complex project wherein a very special collection of people throughout the UK undertake to welcome strangers to their homes - unreservedly. That is a great commitment on their part. Jackie King has had to arrange and co-ordinate inspections, and liaise constantly with owners, in a year made difficult for many by Foot and Mouth. Then every detail has to be kept on a data-base, checked, double checked and confirmed, before the writing, editing and proof-reading begins. It is a task that might faze a team; Jackie does it on her own, with kindness, sound judgement and good humour. Most importantly, she maintains the high standards and integrity of this remarkable book. I owe her much and I am grateful, too, to her family, David, Alex and Oliver.

Many are the inspectors upon whom Jackie depends and is indebted to, and I hope I'll offend nobody for singling out Jonathan Goodall for special thanks. He has, simply, done an enormous amount - and has done it all in the most equable and amiable way. That makes such a difference to a project that is so very 'human'. David Griffiths, too, has been a solid support. So too has Bridget Bishop, in the often unsung area of accounting.

My particular thanks go, as with all our books, to Julia Richardson and Annie Shillito. Julia makes the projects metamorphose into books; Annie looks over it all with a kindly eye and administers morale-boosters at crucial moments. They are a powerful duet.

Alastair Sawday

Series Editor:................... Alastair Sawday

Editor:............................ Jackie King

Managing Editor:............ Annie Shillito

Production Manager:...... Julia Richardson

Administration:............... Rachel Brook, Laura Kinch

Accounts:........................ Bridget Bishop

Additional writing:.......... Jo Boissevain

Photo of Alastair Sawday: Mark Bolton

Inspections:..................... Fredena Burns, Annie Coates, Mary Dolman, Trish Dugmore, Jonathan Goodall, David Griffiths, Juliet Harkness, Joanne Macinnes, Auriol Marson, Rosemary Piper, Caroline Portway, James & Petrina Pugh, Sheila & Peter Sorrell, Robert & Mary Stevenson, Stephen Tate

Special thanks, too, to those people not mentioned here who visited often at short notice - just one or two houses for us.

A word from Alastair Sawday

Why are these books such a roaring success? I'm sure it is because there are a lot of people who share my distress at the way so much of that which we once considered precious is going, or gone. Small, locally-owned shops are an endangered species. Butchers who sell real meat, bakers who appreciate texture and taste, eggs fresh from the chicken and milk fresh from the farm - you need to ferret to find them. The same is true of good B&Bs. In many the rooms are mean and towels wafer thin. At breakfast you sit, hushed, at your own table self-consciously studying the packets. The sausages are for 'caterers', the tomatoes from tins, and the eggs from imprisoned chickens.

But let us be your ferret. We devote vast energy to finding, inspecting, describing and publicising the special places we have found. They deserve it, for they stand ready to receive you with open arms, in the houses they love, and feed you like royalty (or rather better!). Not only that but you'll see little that is ugly, never be exposed to unexpected noise, never suffer pompousness or coolness. (If you do, please tell us!)

If you are canny you'll have realised that this book - like all our guides - is much more than a reference book. It is a wonderful resource. It is a catalogue of potential friends and contacts. It is full of experts on their area, people who will help you, bail you out in a disaster and then celebrate with you. It is a magnificent compendium of holiday possibilities, short and long. With it you can plan your Scottish walking week, your cycling in the Dales, your bird-watching jaunt in Wales, your church-carving research, your family holiday in Cornwall - whatever. It is marvellous for singles, too - you can enjoy the company of your hosts - and for parents who need kindness and even support when travelling with children.

A final clarion call, a blowing of trumpets: we're working hard to promote organic and locally-produced food. So look for the symbol 🐝 that denotes that the owner is making a real effort and play your part in this exciting food revolution. Even better, join the Soil Association; there's an application form at the back of this book. It is battling to promote the organic and rural regeneration movement. It campaigns against antibiotics in animal feed, GM crops, pesticides in your food, the closure of local abbatoirs, the destruction of our countryside. With this book you can play your part and have more fun that you imagined possible!

Alastair Sawday

Introduction

How do we choose our Special Places?

A Special Place doesn't have to have magical architecture, a grand garden, masses of antiques and hot and cold running luxury. Many of the houses in this book have all that - and more - but many others are special in different, equally important, ways, too.

At the heart of each of our choices is a host. We like those who are generous - a drink before dinner, the offer of a lift to a pub, a simple, early supper for your children, help in planning your day. Many of them will go out of their way to be flexible. We know that an encounter with genuine kindness and an easy welcome live longer in the memory than any amount of poly-starred 'facilities'.

Thus, among the houses that ooze elegance and history, we include more modest homes, all providing much more than basic comfort: an atmosphere that induces contentment and the loveliest of people to look after you.

We have sifted out the B&Bs that we know wouldn't quite fit. Many offer more 'facilities' than you should ever hope for and may have spent a lot of money smartening up their houses for guests, but are simply missing out on old-fashioned generosity, perhaps, or may have become a bit jaded.

A host who is prepared to knock about a beautiful old room to satisfy the Tourist Board demand for 'en suite' bathrooms is probably not for us. Nor are those who feel that if they have the 'right' number of hooks on the backs of doors, the 'right' curtain rails and the 'right' hospitality trays no one could fail to be impressed.

We like to include people who are at ease with themselves, who enjoy sharing their family life and their home with you. We try to weed out those who want you to feel privileged to be staying in their historic, beautiful home, or those that have succumbed to 'Creeping Guest House Syndrome'.

Creeping Guest House Syndrome

What are the signs of this syndrome? 'Private' signs on doors leading to 'their' part of the house, tourist pamphlets in the hallway, a surfeit of Fire Exits, laminated information telling you how the house is run, large exterior signs proclaiming professional affiliations, strict timetables for meals or arrivals or departures, separate dining tables...

Of course, some rules have to be set and some of the above may be sensible measures, but CGHS occurs when there's a subtle shift away from dealing with practicalities oneself and handling guests without apparent effort. We hope that our B&Bs are homes first and businesses second.

Introduction

What most sets us apart is that we set no objective criteria for inclusion. We like the immeasurable: style, generosity, a genuine welcome, a lovely setting and an easy atmosphere.

What to expect

You will be staying in someone's home and, however simple or grand it may be, we want you to enjoy it and to be enriched by the experience. Your hosts are 'real' people who have families, sometimes other jobs, pets, friends, gardens or farms to look after. We choose them all because we know that they will look after you, too - in spite of the usual pressures of family life. We hope that they will also spoil you, at least a little.

Most houses run on well-oiled wheels but occasionally there will be a spanner in the works - maybe a power cut, a family trauma, a need to help a neighbour, all of which may mean that you are less well looked after, even thrown into a touch of chaos. Most of you are probably extremely tolerant and understand that these 'things' happen. But if your needs aren't being met - simple things such as not enough towels, or covers on the bed, or toast at breakfast - please do ask. Your host would far rather put things right there and then than have you leave unhappy.

Many of our owners are un-selfconsciously easy about having guests around and won't set strict rules about arrivals and departures; others have their own very good reasons for needing to impose the odd rule. But in all houses, do remember that you are embarking on a bed and breakfast 'contract' and anything more shouldn't be taken for granted. Time in the garden or in the pool, or early or late breakfasts, needs to be discussed with the owners.

Another thing: all of these houses are homes, not hotels. So please don't expect your bags to be carried for you, your wet towels to be picked up off the bathroom floor, beds to be made or drinks to be brought to your room. By the same token, you are right to expect to feel more like a 'human being' than a 'hotel guest'.

Finding the right place for you

If you read between the lines and are are canny about interpreting our descriptions and symbols, you'll end up in a place that you will like and that will suit your friends, be they spouses, children, dogs or horses. If a house isn't what we led you to expect, do write and tell us so that we can chat about your comments with owners and maybe adjust the copy.

Introduction

Ask your host about things that matter to you: we have only 100 words to tell a story, but a phone call can fill in the gaps. If traffic noise, walks from the house, bedding, bathing arrangements, meal times or other guests matter to you, don't be afraid to say so.

Quick reference indices

At the back of the book we give easily digested information to help you find the right place. We categorize those owners:

- with single rooms or those that charge no single supplement
- willing to host your pet
- that accept children of any age
- willing to collect you from local train or bus stations
- with houses suitable for wheelchair users or for those of limited mobility

How to use this book

Map

Look at the map in the front of the book first, find the area you want to visit and look for the nearest houses. Don't focus on counties as this can be misleading - you may be heading for a wedding in Perthshire but the ideal place for you may be just over the border in Stirling. London houses are not placed geographically, so check individual entries for their position.

Rooms

We tell you if rooms are double, twin, single and, sometimes, if beds are king-size or four-poster. If a bathroom is 'en suite', it's off the bedroom and we tell you if it has a bath or a shower.

A private/shared bathroom means that it is not 'en suite': it has a wc, basin and either a bath or shower; the former you will have to yourself, the latter may be shared with other guests or family members.

Many hosts will provide foldaway beds for children in your room: ask at the time of booking if this is possible and what it will cost.

Prices

We give the price per person. A full, cooked breakfast is included unless we say it is not. Some owners - particularly in London - will give you a prodigious Continental breakfast instead.

If there is not a single room, we show how much you'll have to pay for sleeping in a double room on your own and mention either 'single supp.' (the price to be added to the p.p. price) or 'single occ.' (total price payable).

Introduction

Some owners put up their prices during the year. Check how much your particular room will be.

Symbols

On the very last page we explain our symbols. Use them as a guide, not as a statement of fact. If an owner welcomes pets or children, there may nevertheless be times when they feel that they won't fit with other guests; equally, owners without the symbols that you are looking for may occasionally bend their own rules.

Abbreviations

SSSI stands for Site of Special Scientific Interest (often rich in flora and fauna) and AONB stands for Area of Outstanding Natural Beauty.

Types of houses

We hope you'll find value for money in all of our houses - even the most expensive ones. Price, of course, should give a clue as to how lavish your surroundings will be.

If you are staying in a sprawling, old, country house, expect the odd draught. Town houses or working farms may be noisy at times, so ear plugs may be a good idea for light sleepers. Some houses have rooms in converted stables, annexes or garden cottages. If it matters to you, check exactly where you will be sleeping.

Practical matters

Meals

We give you prices per person for packed lunch, lunch, supper, dinner, if available. Please say in advance if you want any of these meals and tell your hosts about any dietary requirements; let them know too if you want a vegetarian breakfast. Many of our hosts are wonderful cooks and an increasing number, we are delighted to say, source local or organic produce. So eat in if you can - at the end of a day's driving it is so much more relaxing to amble downstairs to a table especially set for you than to get in the car again. (Ask the owner if you may bring wine; some state B.Y.O. wine on their entry and many others will give you a glass with your meal.)

Seasons and public holidays

Book early if you want a specific room - the best ones usually go first. Many of our houses are booked up well in advance - early worms and birds... etc.

Bookings

Most of our owners take bookings by phone, fax or email. The phone has the advantage of enabling you to 'get the feel' of people and place.

Introduction

Do get written confirmation of the room booked and the price that you will pay for B&B and for meals. Confirm roughly what time you will arrive as most hosts will want to welcome you personally.

Promptness is important if you have booked dinner; delays happen, but a phone call to explain the situation can avert spoilt dinners and spilt tempers. Owners vary hugely in their insistence upon arrival and departure times generally. Do ask when booking; the house rules may not suit you.

Requests for deposits vary, too - some are non-refundable, especially in our London homes, and some homes may charge you for the whole of the booked stay in advance (see below).

Cancellations

If you have to cancel your booking, phone the owner as soon as possible. It is likely you will lose your deposit and, in many cases, will have to make at least part-payment of the total cost of your stay. Some owners will charge you the total cost if you cancel at short notice.

We have steered clear of fixing a cancellation policy as dictating terms is not our style. Different hosts operate different booking systems and the contract is between you and them. We advise you to agree these things when booking.

If an owner holds your credit card details, they may deduct a (widely varying) cancellation fee from it and may not contact you to discuss this. This is rare, but you need to be aware of the legalities of this in the eyes of your credit or debit card company.

Payment

All of our owners take cash and cheques with a cheque card. If they also take credit cards, we have given them the appropriate symbol. If you have an obscure one, confirm that it is acceptable.

Children

If an owner accepts children of any age they have the 'Child Welcome' symbol. We do not presume that they have cots, high chairs or other paraphernalia, so this must be discussed. If an owner welcomes children, but only with age restrictions, they will not have the 'Child Welcome' symbol, but will have a defining section of text at the end of their entry.

Many owners love having children to stay, knowing that parents will do their best to keep them under control and to encourage 'best' behaviour.

Introduction

Dogs

We have many dog-loving owners, most of them with the 'Pets Welcome' symbol. This doesn't mean that they will definitely accept your dog - or any other pet - or that it will be able to sleep in the house. It simply means that they MAY let your pet stay, too. Discuss arrangements beforehand and be honest. If your animal is an excitable Rottweiler, then say so.

Smoking

A 'No-Smoking' symbol means no smoking anywhere in the house. Where there is no symbol, you should, of course, still ask the owner where you may smoke and ask other people if they mind.

Owners and non-smoking guests usually can't stand the smell of cigarette smoke in bedrooms; they spot it at twenty paces, even if the window has been opened!

Tipping

Owners do not expect tips. If you have been treated with extraordinary kindness, a letter of thanks is much appreciated. Do write to tell us of your good fortune, too; we love to hear your comments.

Environment

We try to reduce our impact on the environment where possible by:

- planting trees to compensate for our carbon emissions (as calculated by Edinburgh University): we are officially a Carbon Neutral® publishing company. The emissions directly related with the paper production, printing and distribution of this book have been made Carbon Neutral® through the planting of indigenous woodlands with Future Forests.

- re-using paper, recycling stationery, tins, bottles, etc.

- encouraging staff use of bicycles (they're loaned free) and encouraging car sharing.

- celebrating the use of organic, home- and locally-produced food.

- publishing books that support, in however small a way, the rural economy and small-scale businesses.

- encouraging our owners to follow recommendations made to them by the Energy Efficiency Centre to make their homes more environmentally friendly.

We also publish The Little Earth Book, a collection of essays on environmental issues as diverse as Cod, Chaos and Global Warming.

Introduction

Subscriptions

Owners pay to appear in this guide. Their fee goes towards the high production and publishing costs of an all-colour book.

We only include places and owners that we find special. It is not possible for anyone to buy their way into our guides so these are not advertisements and the fee is not a bribe.

www.specialplacestostay.com

Our web site has online entries for many of the places featured here and in our other books, with up-to-date information and with direct links to their own email addresses and web sites. You'll find more about the site at the back of this book.

Disclaimer

We make no claims to pure objectivity in choosing our *Special Places to Stay*. They are here because we like them. Our opinions and tastes are ours alone and this book is a statement of them: we hope that you will share them.

We have done our utmost to get our facts right but apologise unreservedly for any mistakes that may have crept in. Sometimes, too, prices shift, usually upwards, and 'things' change. We should be grateful to be told of any errors or changes that you encounter on your travels, however small.

Finally

Do let us know how you get on in these houses. We rely on research and inspectors to find the right places. A third vital source of information is YOU - we need your feedback (ideally on every place that you visit) so that we can stay up to date and share it with owners, whether it's good or bad.

In your hand you hold a wonderful selection of houses and owners. We hope to introduce you to much of what is best about Britain: varied architecture, wonderful gardens, unspoiled countryside and massively interesting people. I hope you enjoy it.

Jackie King

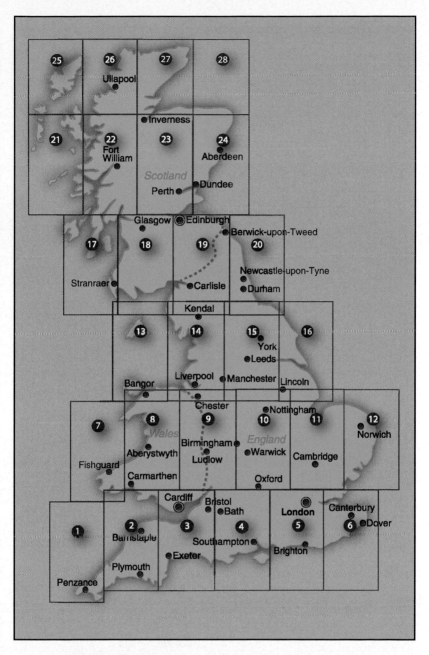

Guide to our map page numbers

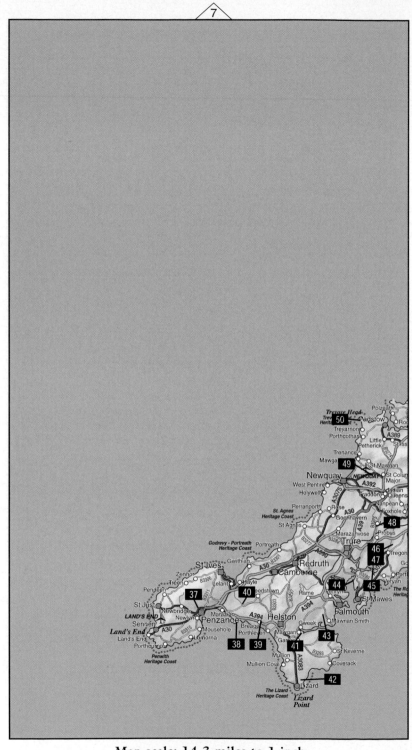

Map scale: 14.3 miles to 1 inch

Map 1

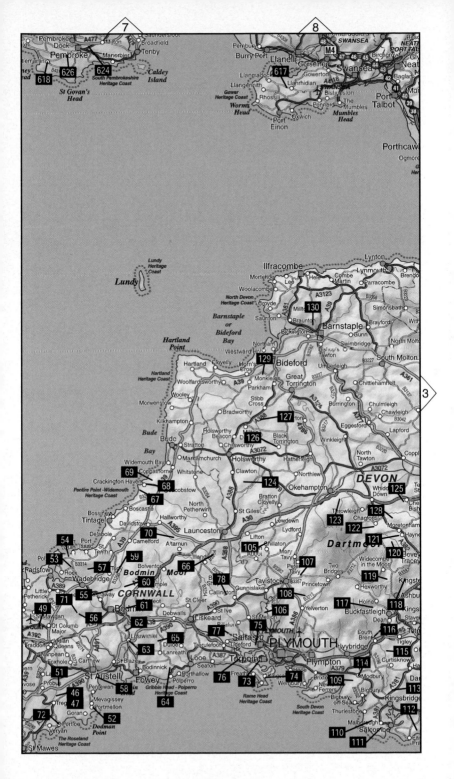

Map 2

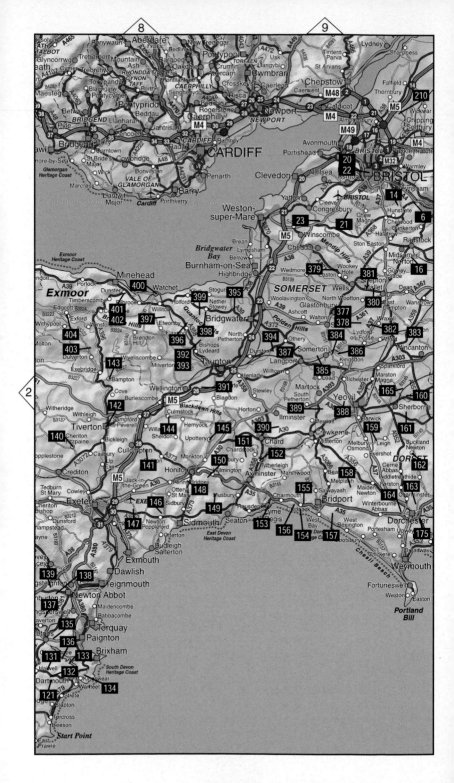

Map 3

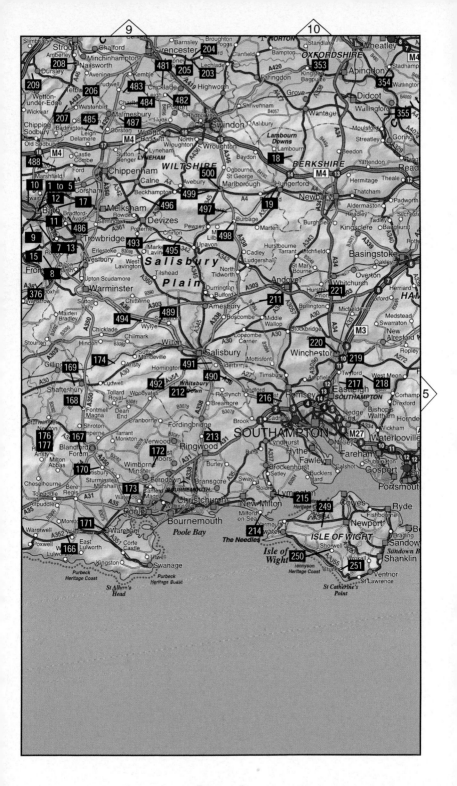

Map 4

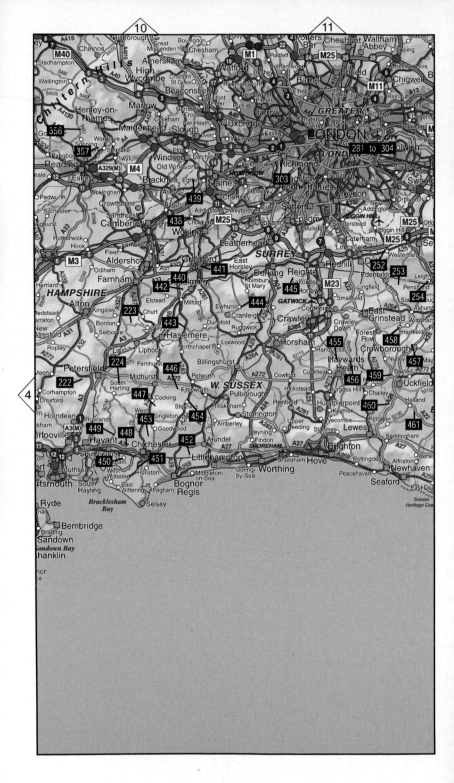

Map 5

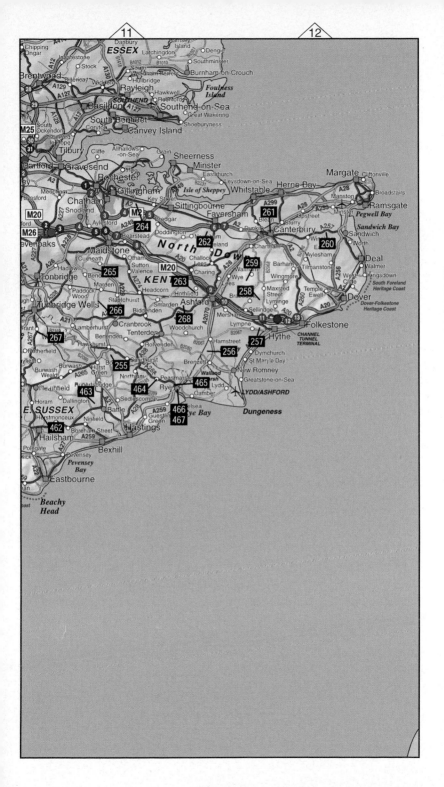

Map 6

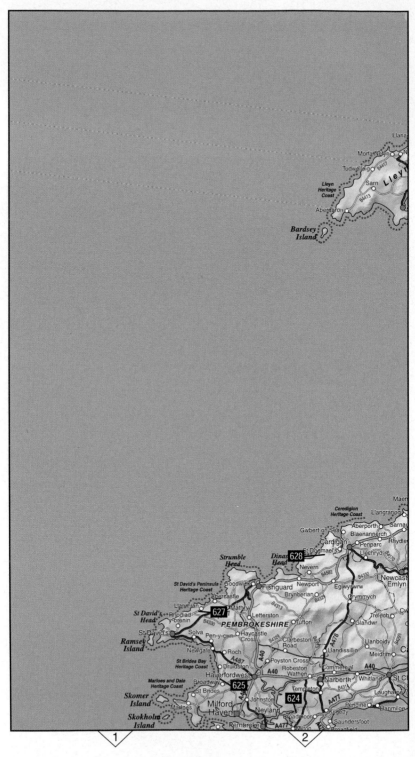

Map 7

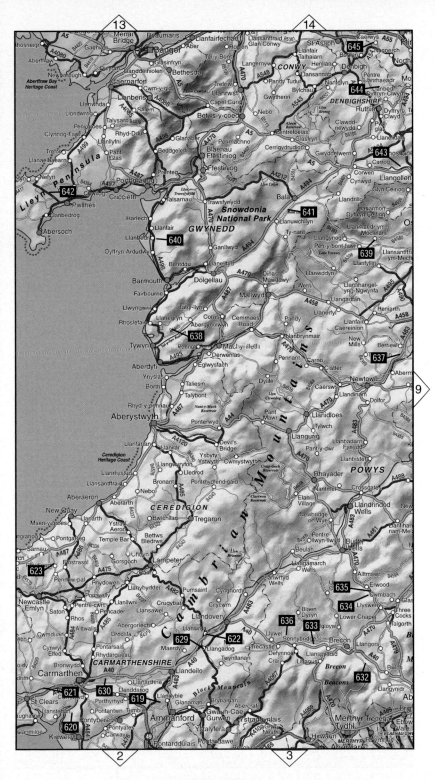

Map 8

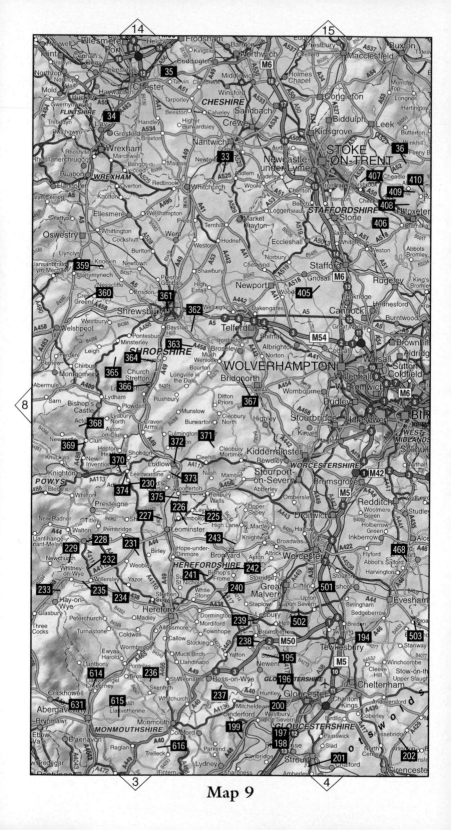

Map 9

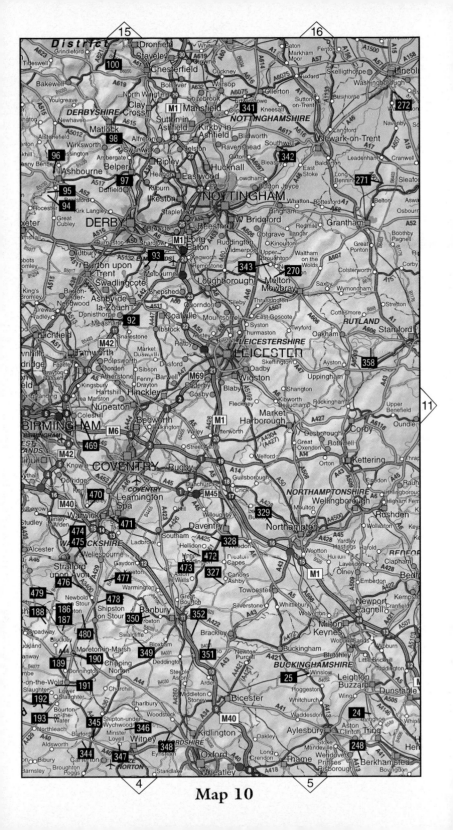

Map 10

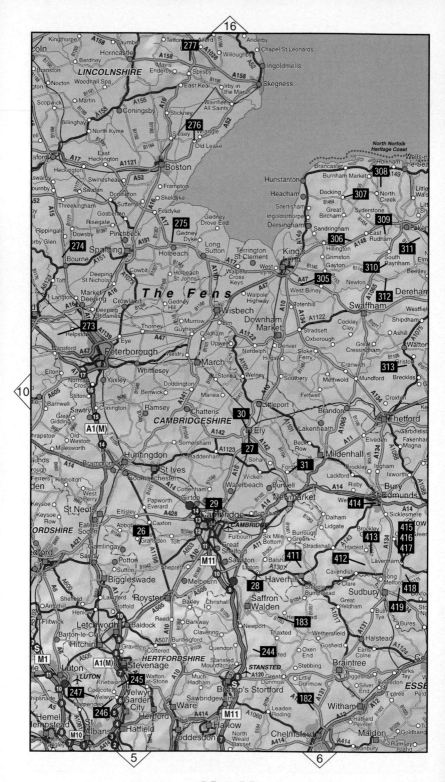

Map 11

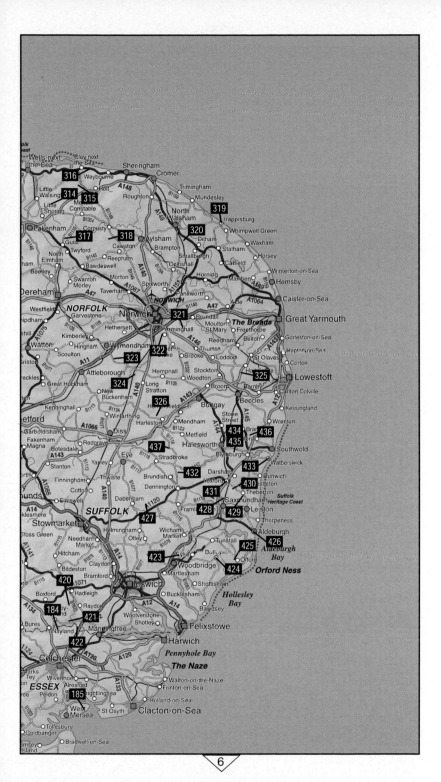

Map 12

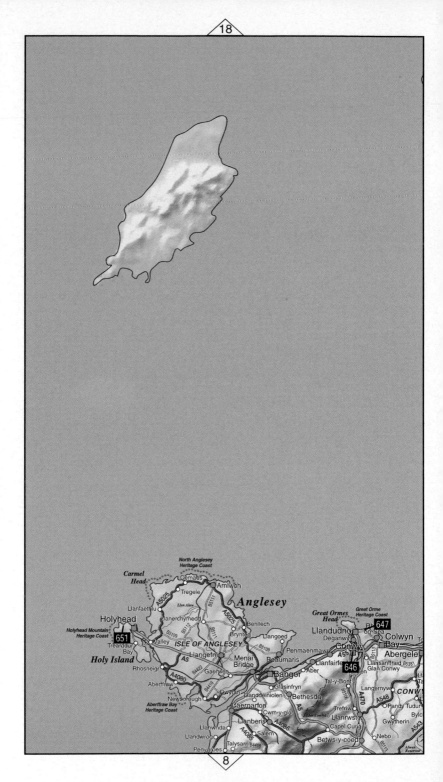

Map 13

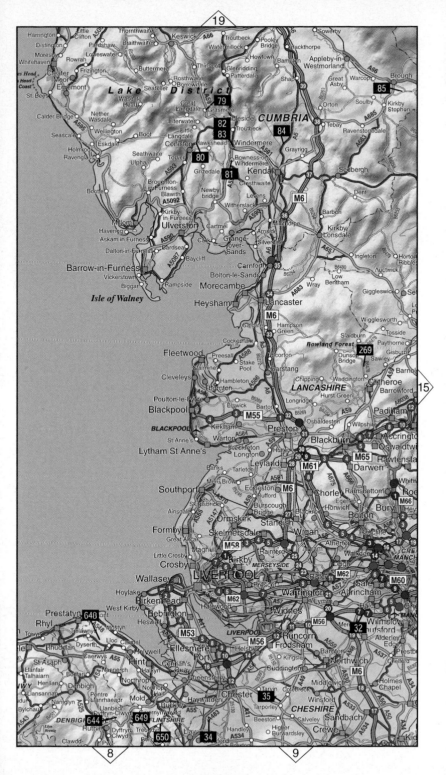

Map 14

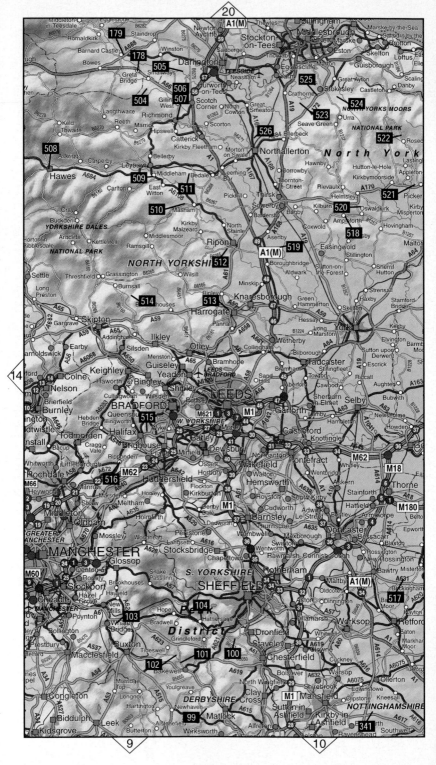

Map 15

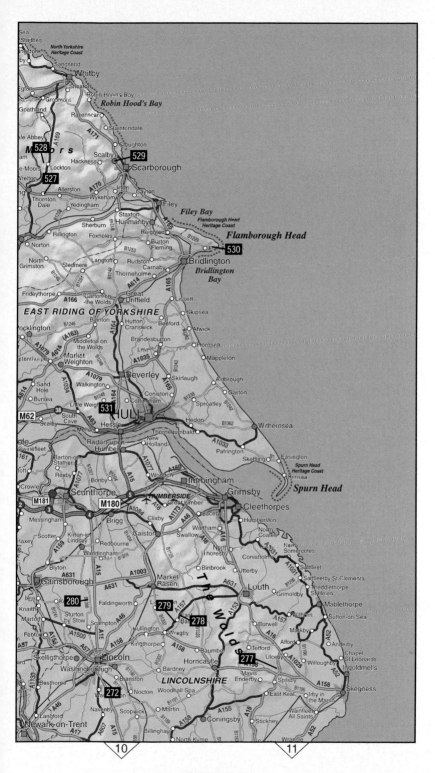

Map 16

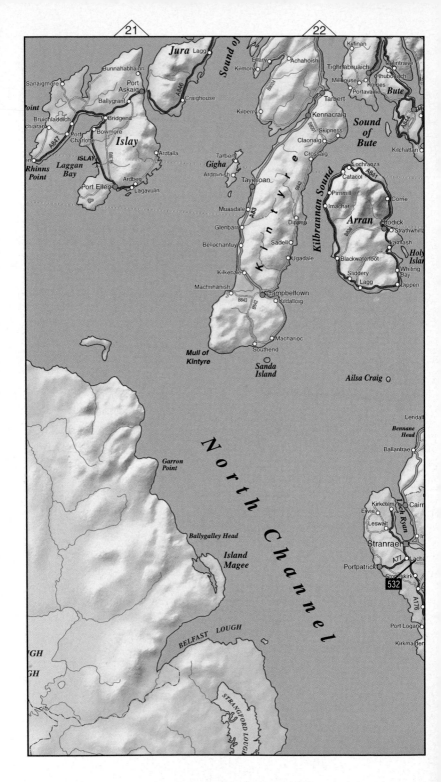

Map 17

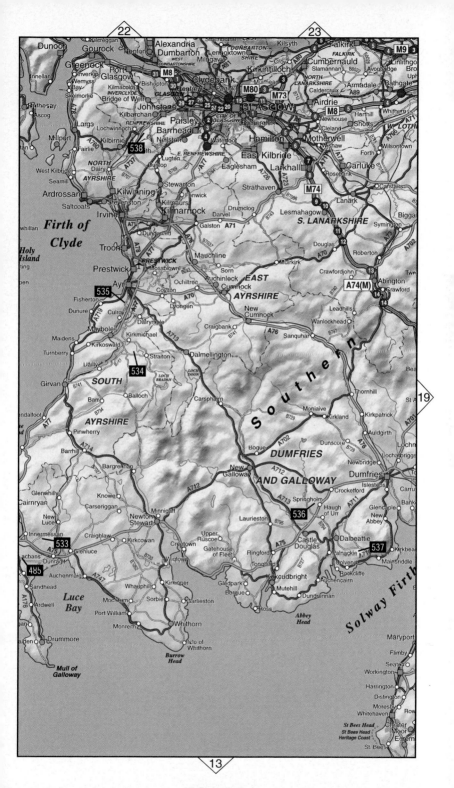

Map 18

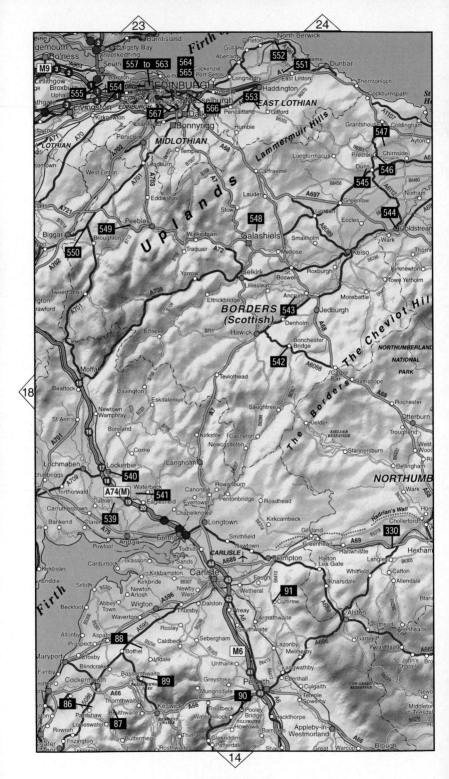

Map 19

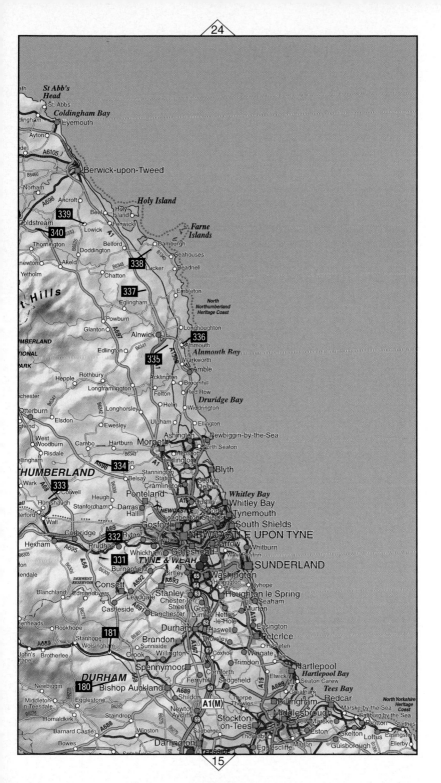

Map 20

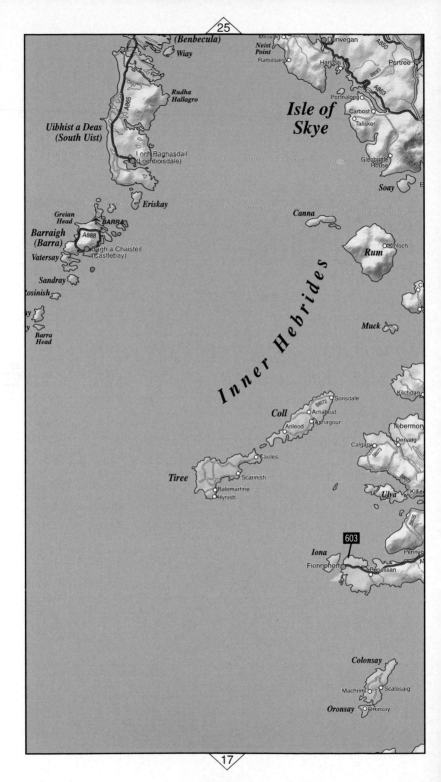

Map 21

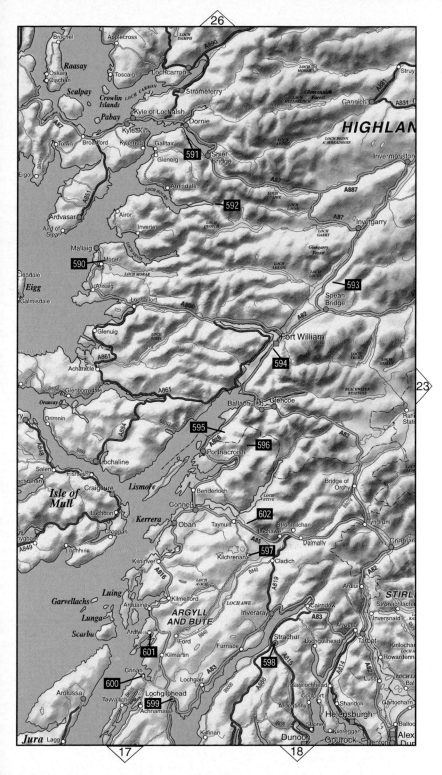

Map 22

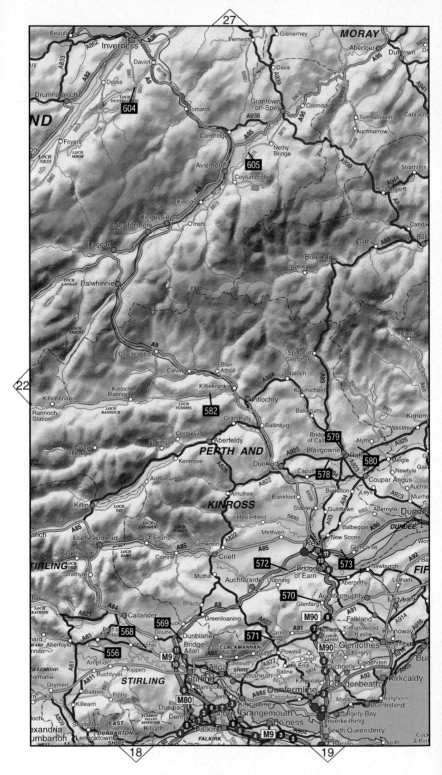

Map 23

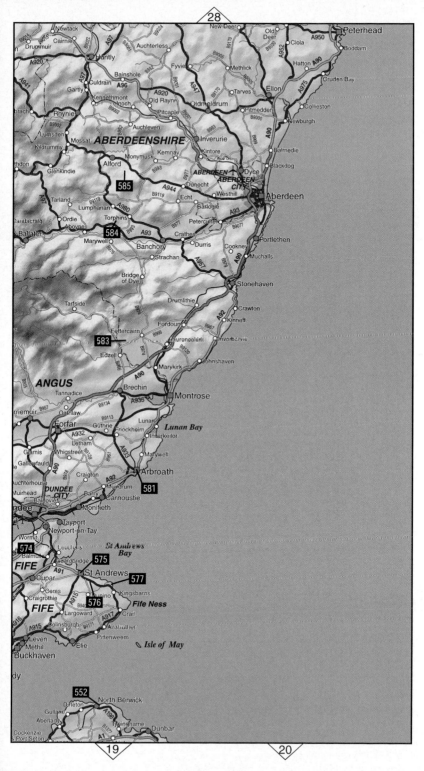

Map 25

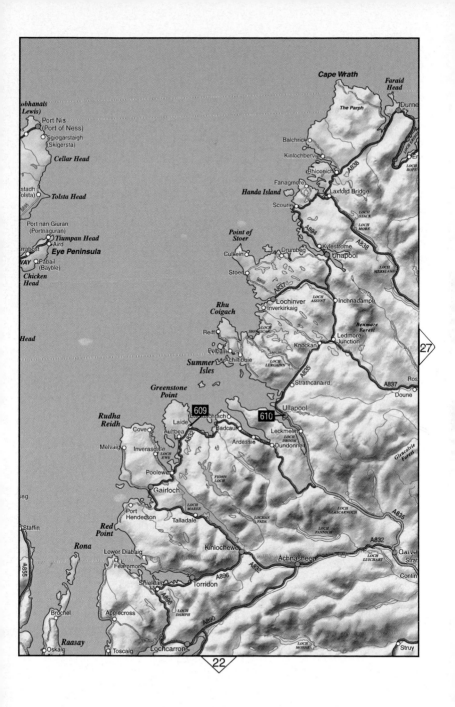

Map 26

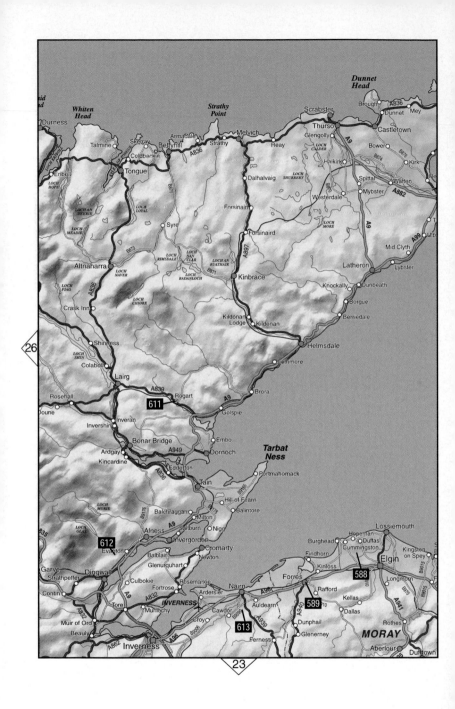

Map 27

Map 28

England

England is the paradise of individuality, eccentricity,
heresy, anomalities,
hobbies, and humours.

George Santayana

Need a lift to/from the station? Maria or Derek will oblige with memorable good humour and kindness. They love their 1778 Georgian city home and have decorated the rooms with colours authentic to the era, restored the veranda at the front to its former glory and collected period furniture. There is road noise in the two front bedrooms, but there is also a quiet room overlooking the rear garden and many guests have stayed here happily. A 20-minute canal-side stroll takes you to the centre of Bath and all its wonders. *Minimum two nights stay. Children over 10 welcome.*

Rooms: 2 doubles, both en suite (shower); 1 twin with private bathroom.

Price: £30-£37.50 p.p. Single occ. £45-£55.

Meals: Breakfast times flexible. Dinner available locally.

Closed: Sometimes at Christmas.

On A4 (London Road), towards city centre, near junc. of A46. Opposite Bath Rugby Club training ground.

Derek & Maria Beckett
Cedar Lodge
13 Lambridge, London Road
Bath
Bath & N.E. Somerset BA1 6BJ
Tel: 01225 423468

The peace suggests rural retreat but the views of the floodlit Abbey remind you that you are in Bath. Simone's home is well loved; it is luxurious with embroidered cotton bed linen, fluffy towels and excellent bathroom fittings. Haitian Simone spoils guests and does it with cross-cultural colour - breakfast here is Caribbean with fresh fruit, yogurt and cereals. The garden looks French and formal, with box parterre, lavender and roses. The rooms have views across the canal to the city or across National Trust land, yet it's less than 10 minutes to the city centre. *Babies and children over 10 welcome.*

Rooms: 1 double, en suite (bath/shower); 1 twin, 1 single, both with private bathrooms.

Price: From £33 p.p.

Meals: Breakfast 7.30-9am. Dinner available close by.

Closed: Christmas Day.

From Bath centre follow signs to American Museum. Pass Mercedes garage (300 yds up Bathwick Hill on right). 1st road on right after garage. House 300 yds down on right.

Mrs S. Johnson
42 Sydney Buildings
Bathwick Hill
Bath
Bath & N.E. Somerset BA2 6DB
Tel: 01225 463033/461054
Fax: 01225 463033
E-mail: sydneybuildings@bigfoot.com

Built in 1820 and with lovely views over the city, this is a truly fine Bath stone 'residence'. It is beautifully furnished with pieces accumulated over the years; it feels evolved rather than designed. Mrs Bowman gives her guests the freedom to come and go and they also have the run of the large living room with French doors. Open these and step out onto an exceptional walled garden that she largely manages herself. In one bedroom there are a bow-fronted mahogany chest, a bureau, an arched alcove bookshelf and a bathroom across the hall. The second looks over the north lawn. *Children over 12 welcome.*

Rooms: 2 twins, both with private bathroom (bath/shower).

Price: £25 p.p. Single supp. £3.

Meals: Breakfast times flexible. Dinner available locally.

Closed: Christmas & New Year.

The Bath stone of this Georgian replica will soon be swathed in rambling roses and who wouldn't have chosen this spot to build? It is close to the centre of Bath, yet wonderfully secluded in its elevated grounds and the views are tremendous. The house, named after one of Andrew's illustrious forbears, is pristine with handsome furniture and family portraits in gilt frames. Your lovely hosts enjoy entertaining and will spoil you with an excellent dinner from the Aga – Philippa is an experienced *Cordon Bleu* cook. *Children over 12 welcome.*

Rooms: 1 twin/double, en suite (bath/shower); 1 twin/double with basin & private shower room.

Price: £35 p.p. Single supp £10.

Meals: Breakfast until 9.30am; dinner, 4 courses, £25; light supper £14; by arrangement.

Closed: Occasionally.

From Bath centre, 15-minute walk. Quarter way up Bathwick Hill. Pass Cleveland Walk on left, house one of big ones on right.

A4/A46 Bath, then ring road clockwise, signed A4, for Bristol. Left at sign for Claverton Down just before White Hart. 0.5 miles up Widcombe Hill on left.

Mrs Elspeth Bowman
9 Bathwick Hill
Bath
Bath & N.E. Somerset BA2 6EW
Tel: 01225 460812

Philippa & Andrew Gordon-Duff
Blantyre House
Widcombe Hill
Bath
Bath & N.E. Somerset BA2 6AE
Tel: 01225 480682
Fax: 01225 789543
E-mail: blantyrebath@aol.com

Entry No: 3   Map no: 4

Entry No: 4   Map no: 4

Step inside and forget the bustle of the city - a serenity pervades the Smith's Grade I-listed Bath apartment. A Chinese lantern with handpainted silk, a fascinating mix of furniture and pottery, framed embroideries and pictures from all over the world hint at the Smith's life of travel; he was with the British Council and both are charming and multi-lingual. The calm bedroom - pale walls, pretty Delft chandelier, cream counterpanes - has a collection of books on art/tea/opera; take one and wander into the courtyard garden where the colourful pots are arranged as artfully as the treasures in the house.

Rooms: 1 twin/double, en suite (bath).

Price: £30 p.p. Single supp. £15.

Meals: Breakfast: Until 8.45am. Dinner available locally.

Closed: Christmas & New Year.

A46 into Bath, then A4 signed city centre. Left onto A36 over Cleveland Bridge; follow signs to Holburne Museum. Gt Pulteney St is opp. museum. Down steps to basement. Parking available: £1 per day.

Chan Loo Smith
Apartment One
60 Great Pulteney Street
Bath
Bath & N.E. Somerset BA2 4DN
Tel: 01225 464134
Fax: 01225 483663
E-mail: chanloosmith@aptone.fsnet.co.uk

Entry No: 5   **Map no:** 4

The Addicotts have given over a generous swathe of their farm to the creation of a natural habitat for indigenous wildlife and achieved a Countryside Award to boot. Utterly committed to the environment, they use flax from the vibrant blue linseed crops to heat their sturdy listed house. There are stone mullion windows, dressers with old china, Chinese rugs on wooden floors, open fires, a smattering of Africana and big bedrooms with all mod cons. Your affable hosts manage the mix of B&B-ing and farming with easy-going humour.

Rooms: 1 double, en suite (bath); 1 twin, en suite (bath), 2 doubles sharing bathroom/shower.

Price: From £26 p.p. Single occ. £32.

Meals: Breakfast until 9am. Dinner available locally.

Closed: Christmas & New Year.

From A4 W of Bath, A39 through Corston. 1 mile on, just before Wheatsheaf Pub (on right), turn right. Signposted 200 yds along lane on right.

Gerald & Rosaline Addicott
Corston Fields Farm
Corston
Bath
Bath & N.E. Somerset BA2 9EZ
Tel: 01225 873305
E-mail: corston.fields@btinternet.com
Web: www.corstonfields.com

Entry No: 6   **Map no:** 3

Bath & N.E. Somerset

200 years ago, it wasn't so much 'messing about in boats' - it was more a way of life; canals were the arteries of the burgeoning Industrial Revolution. This lock-keeper's cottage was built in 1801 by the Somerset Coal Canal Company. The Wheeldons own the stretch of water running through the garden that carries brightly-coloured narrow boats. There's a peaceful towpath walk to the local pub and to a café/restaurant. You can hire an electric launch for a day's pootling, or a bike. The Wheeldons will set you off on a safe, scenic route.

Rooms: 1 double, 1 twin/double, both with private bath & shower.

Price: £25-£27.50 p.p. Single supp. by arrangement.

Meals: Breakfast until 9am. Dinner available nearby.

Closed: Christmas & New Year.

5 miles south of Bath just off A36, 50 yds north of BP garage. Entrance at an oblique angle, so turn into garage & approach entrance from south.

Tim & Wendy Wheeldon
Dundas Lock Cottage
Monkton Combe
Bath
Bath & N.E. Somerset BA2 7BN
Tel: 01225 723890
Fax: 01225 723890
E-mail: dundaslockcottage@freenet.co.uk

Entry No: 7   Map no: 4

Meandering lanes lead you to this 17th-century cottage; quintessentially English with roses round the door, a grandfather clock in the hall and an air of genteel tranquillity. The cottage charm has been updated with Regency mahogany and sumptuous sofas. Bedrooms have long views over farmland and undulating countryside; behind is a conservatory and sloping, south-facing garden with pond and benches. Bath is 20 minutes away and Julia knows the city well.

Rooms: 2 king-size doubles, both with en suite (bath & shower), let only to members of same party; 1 twin, 1 single, both en suite (bath & shower).

Price: £30 p.p., less for long stays. No single supp. Family suite (two rooms) from £80 per night.

Meals: Breakfast until 9.30am; dinner, 3 courses, £18, by arrangement.

Closed: Christmas Day.

From Bath, A36 to Woolverton. Opposite Red Lion pub, turn for Laverton. 1 mile to x-roads, & continue towards Faukland. Downhill for 80 yds. House on left, just above farm entrance on right.

Mrs Julia Naismith
Hollytree Cottage
Laverton
Bath
Bath & N.E. Somerset BA2 7QZ
Tel: 01373 830786
Fax: 01373 830786

Entry No: 8   Map no: 4

"Yes, yes, yes", quoth the inspector. She loved the way it manages to combine elegance with a sense of cosiness. Logs burn in the fire, the colours are warm, the dresser is Welsh, the stones are flagged. The kitchen - Aga and terracotta tiles - is beamed and easy around the cherry wood refectory table. There is peace and comfort among the quirky internal touches, the winding stairs and old bread-oven. Angharad is an aromatherapist (treatment available). The bedroom is "pure magic", with gorgeous furniture. *Children over five welcome.*

Rooms: 1 double, en suite(shower), 1 single with separate bathroom (bath).

Price: £25 p.p. Single supp £30.

Meals: Breakfast times flexible; light supper, from £10, by arrangement. Good local pubs.

Closed: Never.

From Bath A367 Exeter rd. After 3 miles, left opp. Strydes Inn, signed 'Wellow 3 miles'. Park in square by the Fox & Badger pub. House 2 doors down in Railway Lane.

Angharad Rhys-Roberts
Honey Batch Cottage
Railway Lane, Wellow
Bath
Bath & N.E. Somerset BA2 8QG
Tel: 01225 833107
E-mail: angharad@waitrose.com

Entry No: 9   **Map no: 4**

What a gorgeous, mullion-windowed, rambler-rose-strewn home. It sits in 450 acres with views to Bristol on a clear day. Graham runs the farm (converting to organic status and he makes Bath soft cheese – "delicious", said our inspector), and helps the sweet, sunny Gabrielle run the B&B. Quiet guest bedrooms are in their own wing; they overlook the village gardens and are carpeted, cottagey and decorated in soft colours. You can breakfast beside the inglenook fireplace, or in the garden on a warm summer's day. The guest book overflows with praise for Gabrielle's cooking – and her welcome.

Rooms: 1 double, en suite (bath/shower); 1 double, en suite (shower).

Price: £25 p.p. Single occ. £35.

Meals: Breakfast times flexible. Dinner available locally.

Closed: Occasionally.

A431 out of Bath (Upper Bristol Rd.), signposted Bitton. Kelston 2.5 miles. 1st left into 1st turning in village by cul-de-sac sign. House 1st on right.

G.P. Padfield
Park Farm
Kelston, Bath
Bath & N.E. Somerset BA1 9AG
Tel: 01225 424139
Fax: 01225 331601
E-mail: parkfarm.b.b@amserve.net
Web: www.parkfarm.co.uk

Entry No: 10   **Map no: 4**

Duchy of Cornwall farmland stretches as far as the eye can see - the views from this neatly-converted, open-plan barn are magnificent by any standards, but remarkable considering you are so close to Bath. There's much wildlife, too: sparrowhawks nest in the gable end and Giles 'converses' with owls. Spruce guest rooms with houseplants and excellent beds are painted in pale colours. For breakfast Sue, competent and kind, offers kippers or croissants on the terrace if it's fine. And the glories of Bath are just a short ride away - by bus or car.

Rooms: 1 twin, en suite (bath); 1 double with private shower.

Price: £27.50-£30 p.p. Single supp. £10.

Meals: Breakfast times flexible; packed lunch by arrangement. Dinner available locally.

Closed: Christmas & New Year.

An easy stroll into Bath and, hill station-like, above the fray, with fine mature trees all around, a croquet lawn and summer house. Your very affable, well-travelled, well-informed hosts' Victorian family home is smartly decorated: pale fitted carpets, ruched curtains, Regency stripes. Peaceful, big-windowed bedrooms are comfortably decked out with space to sit, original fireplaces and cosy touches. *Albert* has views of Bath Abbey - wonderful illuminated in the distance at night; *Palmerston* its own baby grand, which you're welcome to play. Dining room breakfasts always include fresh fruit served on family china. *Children over 12 welcome.*

Rooms: 1 twin/double, 1 double both en suite (shower); 1 double with private bath & shower room.

Price: £30-£35 p.p.

Meals: Breakfast 8am-9am. Excellent choice of restaurants in Bath.

Closed: Christmas.

From Bath, south on A367. Right onto B3110. 1.5 miles on, left after Culverhay School to Englishcombe. Right again & follow road behind church to Barn.

A36 (Warminster road) from Bath. At boundary Bath/Bathampton, right on to North Rd (signed Bath Golf Club), pass Golf Club entrance on left, house 200 yds further on right.

Sue & Giles Barber
Manor Farm Barn
Englishcombe, Bath
Bath & N.E. Somerset BA2 9DU
Tel: 01225 424195
Fax: 01225 427434
E-mail: info@manorfarmbarn.com
Web: www.manorfarmbarn.com

Patrick & Hilary Bryan
Ravenscroft
North Road, Bathwick
Bath & N.E. Somerset BA2 6HZ
Tel: 01225 461919
Fax: 01225 461919
E-mail: patrickbryanr@cs.com
Web: www.ravenscroftbandb.co.uk

Entry No: 11   **Map no: 4**

Entry No: 12   **Map no: 4**

Bath stone from Combe Down was trundled down the hill to build all that celebrated Regency elegance. We defy you not to be hit by the 'wow' factor when you stand in the gorgeous garden and see the steep valley stretching out before you. The Sticklands are in our *Garden Bed & Breakfast* book, too, and do a professional job, with a personal touch that has brought guests back time and time again. Organic eggs and proper bacon for breakfast, fluffy towels and a range of teas in the bedrooms. A peaceful retreat from city bustle.

Rooms: 2 twins/doubles, 1 family, all en suite (shower).

Price: From £30 p.p. Single occ. £35. £5 supp. per room for single night stays.

Meals: Breakfast 7-9.30am; dinner £18-£22 (for 4 or more, only). Also excellent places nearby.

Closed: Christmas.

From A36 about 3 miles out of Bath on Warminster road, take uphill road by lights & Viaduct Inn. 1st left (approx. 100 yds) signed Monkton Combe. After village (0.5 miles on) house 1st on left.

Jane & Anthony Stickland
Grey Lodge
Summer Lane
Combe Down, Bath
Bath & N.E. Somerset BA2 7EU
Tel: 01225 832069
Fax: 01225 830161
E-mail: greylodge@freenet.co.uk

Entry No: 13　　**Map no: 4**

An exceptional house in a quiet, secluded hamlet, yet minutes from Bath and Bristol. Julia exudes warmth and enthusiasm and is utterly natural. Both she and Patrick love their garden - immaculate lawns, deep herbaceous borders, croquet lawn, masses of roses and clematis, burgeoning fruit and vegetable garden and views to the Mendips. "I could hardly tear myself away," wrote our inspector. On warm days breakfast is served on the terrace and guests have exclusive use of the drawing room. Julia has deep local knowledge. *Children over 12 welcome.*

Rooms: 1 twin/double, with extra single bed, en suite (bath & shower).

Price: £30 p.p. No single supp.

Meals: Breakfast times flexible; dinner £15-£20, by arrangement. Good food available locally, too.

Closed: Mid-December-mid-January.

From Bath, A4 west. At r'bout by Globe Inn, left onto A39 towards Wells. Through Corston (ignore Burnett sign), after 0.5 miles take B3116, SHARP right. After 1 mile left signed Burnett & next right. House 100 yds on left.

Patrick & Julia Stevens
Brooklands
Burnett
Keynsham
Bath & N.E. Somerset BS31 2TF
Tel: 0117 986 8794
Fax: 0117 986 8794

Entry No: 14　　**Map no: 3**

Bath & N.E. Somerset

So much to delight the eye - a Georgian corner cupboard, mellow elm floors, pottery, pictures and coloured glass within and, without, the quaintly symmetrical front elevation with Venetian windows. Built in 1760, the house was sold for £400 in 1920 when it became a police house. Today a cottagey charm reigns - bedrooms are pretty and simple with cushions piled on patchwork quilts and the bathroom has new pine panelling. This is a fascinating village that oozes history; there are two famous pubs nearby – The George, where Judge Jeffrey held court, and the Fleur de Lys, where the worst of his villains were hung.

Rooms: 1 double with private bathroom and 1 single let only to same party.

Price: £25 p.p.

Meals: Breakfast times flexible. Dinner available locally.

Closed: Christmas.

From Bath, Norton St Philip is signed (A366) off A36, approx. 7 miles south of Bath. After village sign, house soon on left. If you come to The George, you have gone too far.

Judy Jenkinson
The Old Police House
Town Barton
Norton St. Philip
Bath & N.E. Somerset BA3 6LN
Tel: 01373 834308
E-mail: judy.jenkinson@lineone.net

Entry No: 15   **Map no: 4**

Interesting, child-friendly hosts who are entirely natural and un-businesslike make this place special - and it's excellent value, too. The large old Mendip-style 'long cottage' with mullioned windows and beams made of ships' timbers is fronted by a vineyard and temptingly close to Babbington House, the treasures of Bath and Wells, the gardens and concerts at Stourhead and Gregorian chant in Downside Abbey. Bedrooms are simple and unfussy, with fresh flowers and family furniture. No sitting room, but tea in the beautiful walled garden is rich compensation.

Rooms: 1 twin/family, en suite (shower); 1 small double/single with shared/private bathroom.

Price: £17-£20 p.p.

Meals: Breakfast times flexible. Dinner available locally at excellent pubs.

Closed: Never.

From Bath A367 Wells rd through Radstock. After 3 miles, at large r'bout, B3139 for Trowbridge. 1.1 miles on, right up drive. House at top, visible from road.

Virginia & Hugh Pountney
Melon Cottage Vineyard
Charlton, Radstock
Nr. Bath
Bath & N.E. Somerset BA3 5TN
Tel: 01761 435090
E-mail: pountney@pountneyb.freeserve.co.uk

Entry No: 16   **Map no: 3**

Breakfast on the terrace and gaze over the honey-coloured collage of Regency Bath below, a stunning spectacle from this lofty vantage point. Much-travelled Anne's Cotswold stone house is an oriental excursion, enriched by batiks, silk paintings and other Malaysian memorabilia. Exotic plants and hand-painted pots fringe the garden pond that shimmers with fish. Anne, once a Far East head-hunter, now channels her considerable vitality and energy into caring for guests.

Rooms: 1 twin/family, en suite (shower); 1 double, en suite (bath & shower); 1 double/single with private shower room.

Price: From £25-£33 p.p. Single occ. £38.

Meals: Breakfast times flexible. Excellent pub within walking distance.

Closed: Occasionally.

M4 exit 18, A46 A46 joins A1, then left for Chippenham. At r'bout, A363. Under bridge, bear left at Crown pub into Bathford. 1.5 miles uphill, left after Swan pub (Lower Kingsdown rd). Bear right at bottom, house 300 yds on left.

Anne Venus
Owl House
Kingsdown, Nr. Box
Bath & N.E. Somerset SN13 8BB
Tel: 01225 743883
Fax: 01225 744450
E-mail: venus@zetnet.co.uk
Web: www.owlhouse.co.uk

Entry No: 17   **Map no:** 4

If you want to swim, there's an indoor heated pool, if you want to walk, there are 650 acres of farmland and a dog to keep you company. Both hosts are multilingual and enjoy their guests: Henry works less on the farm now and has turned his hand to breakfasts; Mary cooks the evening meals which include home-grown produce. Some of the guest rooms date back to the 16th century and are bright, airy, simply and attractively decorated and have views of garden and fields. There are books and a fire for you in the sitting room.

Rooms: 3 twins/doubles, 2 en suite (bath/shower), 1 with private bathroom.

Price: £26-£30 p.p. Single occ. £35-£50.

Meals: Breakfast usually until 9am; dinner, £18, only by prior arrangement. Good pub nearby.

Closed: Never.

From M4 junction 14, A338 north towards Wantage. After 0.5 miles, 1st left (B4000). House on 1st farm road on right after Pheasant Inn.

Mary & Henry Wilson
Fishers Farm
Shefford Woodlands, Hungerford
Berkshire RG17 7AB
Tel: 01488 648466
Fax: 01488 648706
E-mail: mail@fishersfarm.co.uk
Web: www.fishersfarm.co.uk

Entry No: 18   **Map no:** 4

The welcome is the same, the house is new - and what a place! The Welfares moved here from another *Special Place* and Pevsner has described this as "The most ambitious house in Hungerford". A classic town house with a Queen Anne façade and, inside, wood panelling and beams, wonky floors, period furniture and family portraits. Bedrooms are just right, and so is breakfast in the 18th-century dining room. Antique shops to the front and a walled garden with cordon-trained fruit trees to the rear. *Children over eight welcome.*

Rooms: 1 double, 1 twin/double, both en suite.

Price: £29 p.p. Single supp. £10.

Meals: Breakfast until 9am (Mon-Fri); flexible (Sat-Sun); packed lunch £5. Dinner available within walking distance.

Closed: Christmas.

Junc. 14 from M4. Turn off A4 at Bear Hotel onto Salisbury road (A338). Over canal bridge into High St. Wilton House 200 yds past Town Hall on right.

Deborah & Jonathan Welfare
Wilton House
33 High Street, Hungerford
Berkshire RG17 0NF
Tel: 01488 684228
Fax: 01488 685037
E-mail: welfares@hotmail.com
Web: www.wiltonhouse.freeserve.co.uk

Entry No: 19   **Map no: 4**

Unabashedly 1920s mock-Tudor with an oak-panelled hall and a great engraved fireplace. This is a generous house on the edge of the Bristol Downs, perfectly placed for country quiet in the evening after city bustle in the daytime. Light from the garden floods in and Philippa, with long experience of five-star hotels, revels in doing a proper job. The breakfast menu is mouth-watering and the morning papers come with it. The guest rooms are 'fully-equipped', pastel-decorated and eminently comfortable; your hosts are affable and interested. *Children over seven welcome.*

Rooms: 1 twin, en suite (bath); 4 doubles, en suite (shower) & private wc; 1 single with private bathroom.

Price: £31 p.p. Single occ. £45-£48.

Meals: Breakfast times flexible. Dinner available locally.

Closed: Christmas & New Year.

From M5, exit 17 onto A4018. At 4th r'bout 3rd exit into Parry's Lane. Left into Saville rd. 3rd right into Hollybush Lane. 1st left immed. after 2nd road hump into Downs Edge. Drive to end.

Alan & Philippa Tasker
Downs Edge
Saville Road
Stoke Bishop
Bristol BS9 1JA
Tel: 0117 968 3264
Fax: 0117 968 3264
E-mail: downsedge@sbishop99.freeserve.co.uk

Entry No: 20   **Map no: 3**

Smothered in clematis, jasmine, roses and honeysuckle - the scent wafts delectably through the bedroom window - it's hard to believe that Spring Farm, with its beautiful walled garden and lush meadow of wild flowers, is only a few miles from Bristol. Plump beds and lovely linen in light, airy bedrooms decorated with elegant country simplicity. Laze in the garden, lulled by the sound of summer bees. In winter, breakfast by an open fire, enveloped by the friendly, generous atmosphere of the Gallannaughs' impeccable English farmhouse with its Aga, terracotta tiles and antique pine.

Rooms: 1 large double, en suite (bath); 1 double with private bathroom; 1 single (sharing bathroom if in same party).

Price: £20-£25 p.p. No single supp.

Meals: Breakfast until 9am; packed lunch £5. Dinner available locally.

Closed: Christmas.

From Bristol A38 for airport. 5 miles out, left on B3130 towards Winford. On leaving village, bear right up Regil Lane. After Regil Stone, farm 5th on right.

Judy & Roger Gallannaugh
Spring Farm
Regil
Nr. Winford
Bristol BS40 8BB
Tel: 01275 472735
Fax: 01275 474445
E-mail: bookings@springfarm.swest.co.uk

Entry No: 21   **Map no:** 3

An easy-going house and hostess - there's enough of a family feel to make you feel at home in the city and enough privacy to ensure a peaceful stay. Anne enjoys meeting guests and has furnished rooms carefully with flowers, books, pretty china and good linen - the twin beds each have a double duvet to make them extra snug. Some strong colours - jade green in the double's shower room and terracotta in the dining room, where breakfast (as organic as possible) is served. It's a short walk to Clifton village and the Suspension Bridge and to the thriving harbourside. Excellent value for city convenience.

Rooms: 2 doubles, 1 twin, all en suite (shower).

Price: From £26 p.p. Single occ. £38.

Meals: Breakfast times flexible. Dinner available locally.

Closed: Christmas Eve.

From M5 SW, junc. 18. Follow A4 signs to Bristol West & airport. Under Suspension Bridge & follow city sign painted on road. Follow lane signed Clifton. Left into Clifton Vale just before church. 1st right into Camden Terrace. House on right.

Anne Malindine
14 Camden Terrace
Clifton Vale
Bristol BS8 4PU
Tel: 0117 914 9508
Fax: 0117 914 9508
E-mail: anne@amalindine.freeserve.co.uk

Entry No: 22   **Map no:** 3

Cool and uncluttered, with wooden floors, a piano and open fires. They are interesting people, he ex-business in Africa, she an English (EFL) teacher - with small, well-behaved children. The house is Grade II-listed and has lovely views across the Vale of Wrington. The bedrooms are in a wooden-floored wing (built long and low, around 1760, for rope-making); it looks onto a paddock and a copse. You feel very private here. The bed is huge, made specially for them in Africa, with the best linen and there's a large bathroom with an old pine dresser stacked with books. *Only five minutes from Bristol airport.*

Rooms: 1 king-size room, en suite.

Price: £25 p.p. Single supp. £10.

Meals: Breakfast 8-10am; supper from £12.50.

Closed: Christmas & New Year.

With a church across the way and gracious, comfortable rooms, this is a lovely house, built by the Rothschilds in 1865 when they bought the village of Mentmore. Guests can use the large drawing room and gaze out on lovingly-tended gardens and spectacular, unspoilt countryside over breakfast. Bedrooms are peaceful, airy and big (one overlooks the swimming pool). Waddeson Manor is nearby; London is less than an hour away, by car or train. A charming family and a big welcome.

Rooms: 1 twin, en suite (bath); 1 double, en suite (shower).

Price: £27.50 p.p. Single supp. £5. Children under 12, £10 when sharing.

Meals: Breakfast 7.30-9am. Dinner available locally.

Closed: Occasionally.

From Bristol A38. 4 miles past airport, right to Lower Langford. 200 yds on, 5th, pink, house on left.

At Cheddington r'bout, left for Mentmore. Pass gates to Mentmore Towers. House on right opp. church.

Rebecca Wimshurst
Dring Cottage
Lower Langford
Bristol BS40 5BW
Tel: 01934 862243
Fax: 01934 862670
E-mail: wimshurst@dringcottage.fsnet.co.uk

Charles & Susie Kirchner
The Old Vicarage
Mentmore
Buckinghamshire LU7 0QG
Tel: 01296 661243
Fax: 01296 661243
E-mail: susie.kirchner@tesco.net

Entry No: 23   **Map no: 3**

Entry No: 24   **Map no: 10**

This is a one-off. Sarah's conversion, architectural rather than religious, has turned a fascinating church into a fascinating home, complete with tower and spiral staircase, original stained-glass and stone-mullion windows. It has a charm all its own - the Winnie the Pooh mural in one bedroom and the fish swimming around the bathroom walls are amusing touches. Each of the bedrooms is compact but each has its own church window. The old schoolroom is now a kitchen/dining room - impressively big and a great place for breakfast. Sarah is ease personified and this is good value.

Rooms: 1 twin, 1 double, 1 single, sharing 1 bathroom & 1 shower room.

Price: £22.50 p.p. Single, £30.

Meals: Breakfast times flexible. Excellent restaurants & pubs nearby.

Closed: Never.

One cosy yet large and very private bedroom is up its own spiral staircase - a lovely conversion and sure winner of 1st prize in any Loo With A View competition. In the main house is a fresh blue and white bedroom; those that like their independence will be happy in either room as the Barlows relaxed 'take-us-as-you-find-us' approach pervades the whole house. There are fruit trees and bees and home-made jam and honey for breakfast and, although this is now an arable farm, sheep still graze the land. Perfectly quiet, and surprisingly close to Cambridge.

Rooms: 1 double, 1 family, both en suite (shower).

Price: £22.50 p.p. Single occ. £25.

Meals: Breakfast until 9.30am. Dinner available locally - good pubs nearby.

Closed: 22 December-2 January.

From Aylesbury, A413 towards Buckingham. On reaching Winslow centre, left into Horn St between Bell Hotel & The George. Church on left.

Turn off A1198 at Longstowe onto B1046. House on right after 3 miles, before reaching Little Gransden.

Sarah Hood
The Congregational Church
15 Horn Street
Winslow
Buckinghamshire MK18 3AP
Tel: 01296 715717
Fax: 01296 715717

Sue Barlow
Model Farm
Little Gransden
Cambridgeshire SG19 3EA
Tel: 01767 677361
Fax: 01767 677883
E-mail: bandb@modelfarm.org.uk
Web: www.modelfarm.org.uk

Entry No: 25   **Map no:** 10   **Entry No:** 26   **Map no:** 11

Cambridgeshire

You are in the middle of an ancient market town with narrow streets and medieval buildings, yet have a beautiful one-acre garden to wander in with lawns, shrubbery, orchard and vegetable garden. The Friend-Smiths have retained the original Edwardian garden design. The feel in the bedrooms is traditional English with good quality linen and country antiques and you have lovely views of the garden and Cathedral. Sheila serves locally-baked bread and home-made marmalade at the long mahogany dining table. The Cathedral is just five minutes' walk away and Cambridge 15 miles.

Rooms: 1 double with private bathroom; 1 twin, en suite (bath).

Price: £25 p.p. Single supp. £10-£16.

Meals: Breakfast until 9.30am. Dinner available locally.

Closed: Christmas & New Year, & for annual holiday.

A happy combination of elegance and a bustling family atmosphere in a large 1840 Regency-style home. The former school house hugs the bend of a river on the edge of the quiet, historic village of Linton and the rooms overlook the large gardens and the river. The conservatory, draped with a mimosa tree, is exceptional and a wonderful spot for summer breakfasts, while in winter one repairs to the dark green dining room. Bedrooms are large, so are the beds, and are stocked with books. This is exceptional value, and so close to Cambridge, too.

Rooms: 2 doubles, both en suite (bath).

Price: £30-£35 p.p. Single supp. £27-£30.

Meals: Breakfast 7.30-9.30am. Dinner available locally.

Closed: Never.

From Cambridge, A10. Entering Ely, left at lights by Lamb Hotel. Left at next lights, after 200 yds into Egremont St. House last on left. Off-street parking just beyond.

A1307 from Cambridge, left into High Street. 1st right after The Crown (on left) into Horn Lane. House on right next to chapel & before ford.

Sheila & Jeremy Friend-Smith
Old Egremont House
31 Egremont Street
Ely
Cambridgeshire CB6 1AE
Tel: 01353 663118
Fax: 01353 614516

Judith Rossiter
Springfield House
14-16 Horn Lane
Linton
Cambridgeshire CB1 6HT
Tel: 01223 891383
Fax: 01223 890335

Entry No: 27   Map no: 11

Entry No: 28   Map no: 11

Just 10 minutes' walk from King's College Chapel - services during term time - No 46 is, among the whooshing bicycles and swishing gowns, an oasis of peace and good taste. The feel is of a mews cottage: small but smart. You may not have the run of the house and there is no sitting room, but there is every comfort in your room: good quality carpets and furniture and, in one bathroom, a power shower. Over breakfast Alice will help you plan your day. Off-street parking is a real plus. *Children over 12 welcome.*

Rooms: 1 twin/double with private bathroom; 1 double, en suite (shower).

Price: £35 p.p. Single occ. £50.

Meals: Breakfast until 9am. Dinner available locally.

Closed: Never.

A Grade II-listed house whose period elegance clearly encourages long stays – it has had only three owners since a doctor built it in the 1800s. Lots of original features - high ceilings, tall windows, wood floors, cast-iron baths, an enormous log-burning fireplace - yet it all feels open and light; white prevails, fresh and bright. Breakfast is at the old pine farmhouse table where the food is "brilliant". Robin and Jenny slipped the leash and left London for the Isle of Ely, where everything, everybody, slows down. Join them, and see one of England's loveliest Cathedrals, too. *Minimum two nights stay at weekends. Children over 10 welcome.*

Rooms: 1 double suite, 1 family suite, 1 twin, all en suite (bath).

Price: From £30-£35 p.p. Single occ. from £40. Short break rates available.

Meals: Breakfast 8.30-9.30am, or by arrangement. Good restaurants nearby.

Closed: Christmas & New Year.

From M11, exit 12. Right at r'bout into Fen Causeway, right at T-junc. into Trumpington rd & 1st left into Bateman St. Panton St is 1st on left.

House 75 yds down from Tourist Information Centre, in centre of Ely, near Cathedral.

Alice Percival
46 Panton Street
Cambridge
Cambridgeshire CB2 1HS
Tel: 01223 365285/568305
Fax: 01223 461142

Robin & Jenny Farndale
Cathedral House
17 St. Mary's Street, Ely
Cambridgeshire CB7 4ER
Tel: 01353 662124
Fax: 01353 662124
E-mail: farndale@cathedralhouse.co.uk
Web: www.cathedralhouse.co.uk

Entry No: 29   **Map no: 11**

Entry No: 30   **Map no: 11**

It's a racing cert - you'll find an engaging style running alongside the most delicious of breakfasts here in the wistful *Waterland* world of Graham Swift's novel. (Malcolm's an equine buff). We cannot overstate the quality of the locally sourced fresh produce, soft cheese, hams, black puddings, kippers, haddock. Jan, formerly an illustrator, cooks and attends to the décor - old pine, huge cushions, handsome wallpapers and fresh flowers. A Georgian home, croquet lawn and conservatory - a winner! *Minimum two nights stay in high season.*

Rooms: 1 twin/double, 1 single sharing bathroom; 1 double, en suite (shower).

Price: Double from £25 p.p. Single occ. £30-£40.

Meals: Breakfast times flexible. Dinner available locally.

Closed: Never.

David designed some of the furniture, including the vast bed that needs nine pillows. The rooms are sumptuous (TV and video hidden in wooden cabinets) and have great country views - you are on a quiet country lane with the village pub at the end of the drive and Dunham Massey Deer Park five minutes' walk away. David was a professional snooker player. Good value so close to the city (Manchester and its airport are six minutes away), yet so rural. Great hosts, too. *Children over 12 welcome.*

Rooms: 1 7ft 6in bed, en suite (shower); 1 four-poster, en suite (bath & shower), 1 double with large, private bathroom.

Price: From £30 p.p. Single occ. from £47.

Meals: Breakfast until 9.30am. Dinner available locally.

Closed: Christmas & New Year.

A142 Newmarket to Ely road, through Fordham & right at Murfitts Lane; at end, right into Carter St & Queensbury 200yds on left next to Fordham Moor Rd.

A556 NE to Manchester, then left on A56 towards Lymm. At 1st pub, right down Park Lane. House next to The Swan With Two Nicks.

Jan & Malcolm Roper
Queensbury
196 Carter Street
Fordham, Ely
Cambridgeshire CB7 5JU
Tel: 01638 720916
Fax: 01638 720233

David & Janice Taylor
Ash Farm Country Guest House
Park Lane, Little Bollington,
Nr. Altrincham, Cheshire WA14 4TJ
Tel: 0161 929 9290
Fax: 0161 928 5002
E-mail: jane@ashfarm97.fsnet.co.uk
Web: www.ashfarm.co.uk

See how that ground-floor window bulges to meet the green sward, and the front door is off-set from the square to reflect the jagged, unconnected shapes of the whole house. There are, admittedly, odd touches – like the exaggerated, almost Germanic, dormer and the over-exuberant determination to emphasise the age of the house. But it is a splendid old house, fit for the discerning, historically literate, readers of this book. If you have the courage to attempt a stay here you will be rewarded with the musty emptiness so appropriate to the era, the well-eaten floorboards and sagging joists that you should properly expect.

Rooms: 1 open-plantk, bunk-bedded dormitory for 8.

Price: Pay the price.

Meals: Fish and chipboard.

Closed: Woodworm Sunday.

From the A4 left and left again at the Dutch Elm Inn.

Mr Alf Timber
Rickety Cottage
Sward Lane
Leaning
Cheshire ELM4 2BB
Tel: 01560 27272
E-mail: timber@weird-angle.co.uk
Web: www.weird-angle.co.uk

Entry No: 33   **Map no:** 9

Rachel is delightful, warm and friendly. This is Britain at its best with rare trees planted in 1860, flowers everywhere, a pond and a fruitful vegetable garden. The Victorian house is furnished in elegant and traditional style, with garden views from every angle. The proportions of the light-filled drawing room and the big, high-ceilinged dining room feel just right. The bedrooms are inviting, bright and large with attractive fabrics, art, lovely furniture, new mattresses and bedheads. This is a haven for garden buffs, walkers and birdwatchers and there's tennis, too. *Children over 12 welcome.*

Rooms: 1 double, 1 twin/double, both en suite (bath); 1 twin, en suite (shower).

Price: From £25 p.p. Single supp. by arrangement.

Meals: Breakfast before 10.30am; dinner, £18, on request, B.Y.O. wine. Good pubs within walking distance.

Closed: Christmas & New Year.

From Chester, A55 west, then A5104 to Broughton. Through Broughton & over A55. 1st left to Kinnerton down Lesters Lane. On right, opp.Mount Farm.

Jonathan & Rachel Major
The Mount
Higher Kinnerton
Chester
Cheshire CH4 9BQ
Tel: 01244 660275
Fax: 01244 660275
E-mail: major@mountkinnerton.freeserve.co.uk

Entry No: 34   **Map no:** 9

A wonderful farmhouse atmosphere, with two extremely friendly hosts. Very quickly you get the feel of Roughlow, planted in its leafy hillside - it is solid, authentic, and greatly loved. The cobbled entrance yard is a treasure box of carefully-nurtured flowering trees and shrubs. From the terrace you can see for 40 miles. Large bedrooms and bathrooms are furnished with artistic flair; the suite is vast. Sally, once an interior designer, has an eye for colour and has created a calming, uncluttered space. There's a tennis court and they both collect art.

Rooms: 2 doubles, both en suite (bath), 1 with sitting room; 1 twin/double en suite (shower).

Price: £25-£40 p.p. Single supp. £10.

Meals: Breakfast 8-9am. Good pubs & hotels nearby.

Closed: Never.

Set off on a bike - you can hire one - to enjoy easy, scenic rides; you could even cycle the four miles to Chester to visit the 900-year-old Cathedral. Back at the farm you have 250 acres to explore and geese, sheep and, maybe, otters to watch - parts of the farm are cared for under the Countryside Stewardship Scheme. Bedrooms are 'stylish farmhouse' with lovely fabrics, and best of all is the relaxed, family atmosphere created by the Hills. There are touches of luxury - huge bath towels and excellent breakfasts, cooked by Prue Leith-trained Clare.

Rooms: 2 doubles, 1 twin, all en suite (bath).

Price: From £25 p.p. Single occ. £30.

Meals: Breakfast times flexible. Lunch & dinner available locally.

Closed: Never.

A51 from Chester. Cross r'bout at Tarvin & take A54 to Manchester (not Tarporley). Pass Total garage. Take 2nd right & follow signs to Willington. Straight over x-roads & up Chapel Lane. On right at top.

From Chester, A51 west towards Tarvin for 4 miles. Just before BP garage on left, right down Cotton Lane. At T-junc., left along Plough Lane. Farm on right.

Sally & Peter Sutcliffe
Roughlow Farm
Willington
Tarporley, Cheshire CW6 0PG
Tel: 01829 751199
Fax: 01829 751199
E-mail: sutcliffe@roughlow.freeserve.co.uk
Web: www.roughlow.freeserve.co.uk

Clare & Nigel Hill
Cotton Farmhouse
Cotton Edmunds
Chester, Cheshire CH3 7PG
Tel: 01244 336616
Fax: 01244 336699
E-mail: info@cottonfarm.co.uk
Web: www.cottonfarm.co.uk

Flowers, fruit and firewood await your arrival in these 200-year-old converted barns where you self-cater. Sally and John in the main house are easy-going and kind and will instantly put you at your ease. Exposed granite, wooden beams, stencilled walls, pieces of local art and a refreshing simplicity set the tone in your holiday home. You have your own patio, but can play in the main garden, too; and there's a barbecue for summer evenings. High beds, comfy sofas, views of wooded hills and distant sea. Good beaches nearby, yet you feel insulated from the bustle of Penzance.

Rooms: 2 self-catering cottage suites for 2-4 people.

Price: Cottage from £200-£300 p.w. Short breaks available October-March.

Meals: Self-catering.

Closed: Never.

Take Penzance bypass for Land's End. Right at r'bout to Heamoor. Through village, right at x-roads signed to Gulval, 1st left signed Bone Valley/New Mill. House on right after 0.5 miles.

Sally Adams
Tremearne
Bone Valley
Penzance
Cornwall TR20 8UJ
Tel: 01736 364576
Fax: 01736 364576
E-mail: sally@threesfilms.com

Entry No: 37   Map no: 1

Roomy, artistic interior and stunning coastal setting. Set foot in the slate-flagged hallway of this converted barn and feel calmed by the whitewashed stone walls and honey-coloured timbers. Your hosts - busy and efficient - are horsey people. Richly-coloured rugs and Liberty sofas piled high with cushions coax you into comfortable decline; there are fresh flowers, fruit and toiletries and a four-poster, too. From your private terrace, the wild blue yonder and views across the sea to St. Michael's Mount.

Rooms: 3 doubles, 2 en suite (bath/shower), 1 en suite (bath).

Price: £27.50-£35 p.p. Single occ. £45-£60.

Meals: Breakfast until 9am. Dinner available within walking distance.

Closed: Christmas.

From A30 after Crowlas r'bout, A394 to Helston. 0.25 miles after next r'bout, 1st right towards Perranuthnoe. Ednovean Farm drive on left, signed.

Christine & Charles Taylor
Ednovean Farm
Perranuthnoe
Nr. Penzance, Cornwall TR20 9LZ
Tel: 01736 711883
Fax: 01736 710480
E-mail: info@ednoveanfarm.co.uk
Web: www.ednoveanfarm.co.uk

Entry No: 38   Map no: 1

Built of sturdy granite from two, or even three, 200-year-old miners' cottages, this home in a quiet hamlet is a typically Cornish blend of inglenooks, narrow staircases, low ceilings, stripped pine doors with touches of unpretentious, flowery decoration and needlework. Moira, a retired midwife, has a passion for gardening - Goff, a potter, is currently creating a potager for her and there's a petanque pitch to play on. Flowers are fresh, sheets are crisp and cotton, and beds have patchwork and quilted bedspreads. Goff and Moira are immensely kind.

Rooms: 1 double, en suite (bath/shower); 1 twin/double with private bathroom; 1 double, en suite (shower).

Price: £20-£25 p.p. No single supp.

Meals: Breakfast times flexible; packed lunch, from £4.50 and evening meal, from £12.50, by arrangement.

Closed: Christmas & New Year.

From A394 Helston to Penzance, 2nd right after Ashton Post Office for Tresowes Green. After 0.25 miles, sign for house (with 3 chimneys) on the right.

Moira & Goff Cattell
The Gardens
Tresowes
Ashton, Helston
Cornwall TR13 9SY
Tel: 01736 763299
E-mail: goff.and.moira@amserve.net

Entry No: 39   **Map no: 1**

You'll feel spoilt. Bedrooms are luxurious - the four-poster has pretty *toile de Jouy* wallpaper, a powerful shower and fat pillows. Complimentary afternoon tea is laid out in the huge farmhouse kitchen. A roaring fire burns in the sumptuous sitting room. Everywhere there are fascinating artefacts and curios from Gill's travels, designer fabrics and antique pieces. The road ends at Ennys, so the rural bliss is entirely yours. Walk down to the river and along the old towpath, or simply stay here, play tennis, or swim in the heated pool sunk deep into the tropical gardens. *Children over three welcome.*

Rooms: 1 twin, en suite (bath); 2 four-posters, en suite (shower); 2 family suites in barn; 3 luxury self-catering apartments sleeping 2-4.

Price: £30-£40 p.p. Single supp. from £15. Self-catering: £225-£800 p.w.

Meals: Breakfast until 9.15am. Dinner available locally.

Closed: November-January.

2 miles east of Marazion on B3280, look for sign leading down Trewhella Lane between St. Hilary & Relubbus. Keep going to Ennys.

Gill Charlton
Ennys
St. Hilary
Penzance, Cornwall TR20 9BZ
Tel: 01736 740262
Fax: 01736 740055
E-mail: ennys@ennys.co.uk
Web: www.ennys.co.uk

Entry No: 40   **Map no: 1**

What a stunning position! The house sits in a secluded spot at the top of a wooded valley, just minutes from the coast and the Helford River. The Leiths are attentive and charming hosts who want you to leave feeling refreshed and well looked after. The Georgian rectory, restored with enormous care and style, is both elegant and comfortable with lots of space, light and views. Breakfast, all organic from the farm shop, is served in the beautiful turquoise dining room – the magnificent table is a family heirloom. Bedrooms are exceptionally comfortable with lovely colours and great views.

Rooms: 2 twins/doubles, both en suite (bath & shower).

Price: £35 p.p. No single supp.

Meals: Breakfast 8.15-9.15am. Dinner available locally.

Closed: Occasionally.

All is immaculate: the vegetable garden, the decoration, the flower arrangements - and run like clockwork by Marion, who loves this special place. The views to the sea are heart-stopping and the ever-changing light casts a spell over the landscape. The dining room is illuminated by fire and candle; the yellow drawing room, with wooden floors and deep sofas, is perfect. Good linen, a regal four-poster and a luxurious half-tester - the bedrooms are exquisite. Ask if you may swim in the sheltered pool, or plan a day taking in the remarkable coastline - the sea is a three-minute walk away.

Rooms: 1 four-poster, 1 half-tester, 1 twin/double, all en suite (bath & shower).

Price: £40-£46 p.p. Single supp. £10.

Meals: Breakfast until 9.30am; dinner, 3 courses, £26, by arrangement.

Closed: Christmas.

From Helston, A3083 for the Lizard. Left onto B3293 for St. Keverne. Left at Mawgan Cross, past post office, & right into tiny slip road. Pass Old Court House pub, house 2nd on right.

From Helston, A3083 south. Just before Lizard, left to Church Cove. Follow signs for about 0.75 miles. House on left behind blue gates.

Susan Leith
The Old Rectory
Mawgan
Helston
Cornwall TR12 6AD
Tel: 01326 221261
Fax: 01326 221797
E-mail: leith@euphony.net

Peter & Marion Stanley
Landewednack House
Church Cove
The Lizard
Cornwall TR12 7PQ
Tel: 01326 290909
Fax: 01326 290192
E-mail: landewednack.house@virgin.net

Entry No: 41   **Map no: 1**

Entry No: 42   **Map no: 1**

We love this place and the Fords share their beautiful house with ease. Parts are 13th century and there are unchanged sweeping views beyond the old granite walls to the distant Helford river. Country house elegance entwines with a higgledy-piggledy lived-in feel, warm woods, lots of antiques, dark oak and fireplaces. You eat either in the vast family kitchen or in the candlelit dining room; the drawing room, with French windows, has creamy silk curtains. Bedrooms are stocked with good books, jugs of fresh water and home-made biscuits. Judy makes her own bread and preserves.

Rooms: 2 doubles/twins, both en suite (1 bath & shower, 1 bath). Self-catering cottage available.

Price: £30 p.p. Single supp. in high season, £15.

Meals: Breakfast until 10am; dinner, 4 courses, with wine, £20.

Closed: Christmas.

From Truro, Falmouth Rd (A39). At Hillhead r'bout follow sign to Constantine. 0.5 miles after High Cross garage left to Port Navas. House opposite granite mushrooms.

Judy Ford
Treviades Barton
High Cross, Constantine,
Nr. Falmouth, Cornwall TR11 5RG
Tel: 01326 340524
Fax: 01326 340524
E-mail: treviades.barton@btinternet.com
Web: www.treviades.co.uk

Entry No: 43   **Map no: 1**

Trelissick Mansion, next door, was bought by the Copeland family in 1920; the gardens were developed by Peter's grandparents, who then gave the whole lot to the National Trust in the '50s. The estate's bailiff used to live here at Trevilla - and what a stunning position; the Fal Estuary, the sea and the peninsula wrap around you. You have a small sitting room next to your bedroom; the high, antique basketwork twin beds have French polished frames - nothing frilly, but entirely comfortable and with sea views. Jinty and Peter are special and the King Harry Ferry will take you to the Roseland Peninsula.

Rooms: 1 twin with basin, private bathroom and small private sitting room. Can sleep 3rd person.

Price: £25 p.p.

Meals: Breakfast until 9.30am. Dinner available locally.

Closed: Christmas & New Year.

A390 to Truro, left onto A39 to Falmouth. At double r'bout with Shell garage, left off 2nd r'bout (B3289). Pass pub on left. At x-roads, left (B3289). 200 yds on, fork right to Feock. Continue to T-junc., then left. House 1st on right.

Jinty & Peter Copeland
Trevilla House
Feock
Truro
Cornwall TR3 6QG
Tel: 01872 862369
Fax: 01872 870088
E-mail: jinty@trevilla.com

Entry No: 44   **Map No: 1**

Cornwall

Annabelle and Graham moved for the lifestyle, to bring up their sons, to sail, to escape the city. They do everything themselves, but have time to chat too; a great sense of fun echoes around Polsue. Rooms are huge with stacks of relaxed style; wooden floors and rugs in the dining room, a crackling fire in the sitting room. Bedrooms have country eiderdowns, comfy beds and spotless bathrooms. Take the footpath from the garden to a lovely sandy beach, the coastal path and miles of bracing walks. The Eden project and many National Trust gardens are also nearby.

Rooms: 4 doubles/twins, all en suite (bath).

Price: From £35 p.p.

Meals: Breakfast until 9.30am. Dinner available locally.

Closed: Never.

A3078 south from Tregony. In Ruan High Lanes, 2nd right (signed Philleigh & King Harry Ferry). House 1 mile up on left.

Graham & Annabelle Sylvester
Polsue Manor
Ruan High Lanes
Truro
Cornwall TR2 5LU
Tel: 01872 501270
Fax: 01872 501177

Entry No: 45   **Map no:** 1

Lally and William have transformed a jungle into one of Cornwall's loveliest gardens. Secret paths lure you into the dappled woodland. Set deep in tranquil countryside there's a comforting sense that all is well in England's green and pleasant land. Inside the lovely 1730s house shimmering wooden floors are covered with Persian rugs and light pours into every elegant corner. The large guest rooms are furnished with antiques and exude taste and breakfast in the large dining room often turns into an early morning house-party, such is Lally's sense of fun and spontaneity. *Children over eight welcome.*

Rooms: 3 twins/doubles, 1 en suite (bath/shower), 2 with private bathrooms.

Price: £30-£35 p.p. Single supp. by arrangement.

Meals: Breakfast until 9.30am. Dinner available locally.

Closed: Christmas & New Year.

From St. Austell, A390 to Grampound. Just beyond clock tower, left into Creed Lane. After 1 mile left at grass triangle opposite church. House behind 2nd white gate on left.

Lally & William Croggon
Creed House
Creed
Grampound, Truro
Cornwall TR2 4SL
Tel: 01872 530372

Entry No: 46   **Map no:** 1

Your stunning bedroom leads onto a pretty private garden with banked lawns - take your breakfast tray and revive yourself gently in the morning sun. The house has been in the family since the 1600s and the young Croggons have renovated this barn extension with such flair and attention to detail: Floris soap, pretty china, squashy sofa, Colefax & Fowler fabrics, seagrass matting, sofa in the huge bedroom, and lovely greys and greens everywhere. Annabel stocks your fridge with chopped exotic fruits, walnut bread, jams and yogurts, to be eaten when you want. Cooked breakfasts are available sometimes, too. A perfect hideaway.

Rooms: 1 suite with double/twin and breakfast room.

Price: £30 p.p.

Meals: A tray will be laid out for breakfast. Dinner available locally.

Closed: Christmas, New Year & Easter.

From Truro, A390 for St. Austell. 6 miles on, through Grampound; on leaving village, at top of hill, right at speed limit sign into Bosillion Lane. House 150 yds on left.

Jonathon & Annabel Croggon
Bosillion
Bosillion Lane, Grampound
Truro
Cornwall TR2 4QY
Tel: 01726 883327

Entry No: 47   **Map no: 1**

Barbara is genuinely keen on doing B&B; their previous house was a glorious, old listed farmhouse and they have built Oxturn specifically for welcoming guests. The interior is all beiges and creams, fitted furniture, impeccable modernity. Don't expect anything rustic or quaint - you come for Barbara herself who is a true Cornishwoman, for the excellent breakfasts, for the views, for the care and attention to detail and comfort. Nothing whacky, eccentric or old here, just B&B of the best kind, in a good position above the village. *Children over 12 welcome.*

Rooms: 1 double with private bathroom; 1 twin/double, en suite.

Price: £23-£27 p.p. Single supp. by arrangement.

Meals: Breakfast 8-9am. Good food in village pub.

Closed: December & January.

From A30, B3275 south to Ladock. There, turn opposite the Falmouth Arms & follow road uphill for 200 yds. Right 70 yds after 'End 30mph' sign. House on right.

Ian & Barbara Holt
Oxturn House
Ladock
Truro
Cornwall TR2 4NQ
Tel: 01726 884348
Fax: 01726 884248

Entry No: 48   **Map no: 1**

Jacqui used to be head chef for the National Trust and she now specialises in cooking local produce - her breakfasts and dinners are excellent. You are in tranquil countryside, yet the drama of the sea is close by; Watergate bay is popular with surfers. This is a solid, cosy, farmhouse B&B with antique and pine furniture, watercolours, dried flowers, four-posters, big bathrooms and good china. You eat at separate tables in the guests' dining room. Best of all is John and Jacqui's kindness - and the Eden Project is less than an hour away.

Rooms: 2 doubles, 1 family, all en suite (1 shower, 2 bath/shower). 1 children's room.

Price: £24 p.p. Single supp. by arrangement.

Meals: Breakfast 8-8.30am; dinner from £14.

Closed: Never.

A3059 west to Newquay. 0.5 miles on, follow signs to Tregaswith. Farm is 2nd on right.

John & Jacqui Elsom
Tregaswith Farmhouse
Tregaswith
Nr. Newquay
Cornwall TR8 4HY
Tel: 01637 881181
Fax: 01637 881181
Web: www.tregaswithfarm.co.uk

A homely refuge with family furniture and oil paintings and so intimately close to the sea that you might spot dolphins or a lazy basking shark. You are almost at sea - crashing surf and Atlantic winds in a stunning Daphne du Maurier setting; this is rugged North Cornwall and there are surfing beaches all around. The cottage, in the family for four generations, was once a 'fish cellar' for processing catches. There's a woodburner in the drawing room and the bedrooms are very simple and unfrilly, but it will be the views that rivet you. Excellent choice for families.

Rooms: 2 twins, both en suite. A single can be added to one to make a family room.

Price: From £22.50 p.p. Single supp. by arrangement.

Meals: Breakfast times flexible; packed lunch from £5; dinner from £12.50.

Closed: Never.

From St. Merryn, right for Trevose Head. Over sleeping policemen. After toll gate ticket machine right through farm gate. On towards sea; cottage gate at end, on right.

Phyllida & Antony Woosnam-Mills
Mother Ivey Cottage
Trevose Head
Padstow
Cornwall PL28 8SL
Tel: 01841 520329
Fax: 01841 520329
E-mail: woosnammills@compuserve.com

Entry No: 49   Map no: 1   Entry No: 50   Map no: 1

Cornwall

Surrounded by a lovely garden which is open to the public once a year under the National Gardens Scheme, this classical late Regency English country house has the occasional hint of Eastern promise. In the drawing room, where tea is served, a beautiful Chinese cabinet occupies one wall and, in the dining room, there's a Malaysian inscribed silk-screen - a thank-you present from the Empire days. Upstairs the comfortable bedrooms have antique furniture, views onto the glorious garden and generous baths. The Eden Project and Heligan are nearby. *Children by arrangement.*

Rooms: 1 four-poster, 1 twin, en suite (bath); 1 double with private bath.

Price: £30-£38 p.p. Single supp. £10.

Meals: Breakfast until 9.30am; dinner, 4 courses, £24, by arrangement; B.Y.O. wine.

Closed: Christmas & Easter.

A30 towards Truro, then left for Grampound Rd. After 3 miles, right onto A390 towards Truro. After 200 yds, right where double white lines end. Pass between reflector posts towards house, 200 yds down private lane.

Alison O'Connor
Tregoose
Grampound
Truro
Cornwall TR2 4DB
Tel: 01726 882460
Fax: 01872 222427

Entry No: 51   Map no: 2

Sir Henry de Bodrugan lived here - he was a renowned host and, 500 years on, Tim and Sally uphold the tradition with sackfuls of enthusiasm. Everything's freshly decorated, there are family antiques, the promise of home-made bread and good food. In the dining room, even with sofas, woodburner and piano, you could turn a cartwheel. An ancient lane flanked by flowers leads you to Colona Bay: small, secluded and full of rock pools where Robin, their son, catches 'blemmies' by hand. It's blissful. There's an indoor heated pool and sauna, too. Heligan and the Eden project are nearby.

Rooms: 1 large double, 1 twin, both with private bathroom; 1 double, en suite (shower).

Price: £25-£30 p.p. No single supp.

Meals: Breakfast until 9.30am. Packed lunch from £3.50; supper/dinner, £15/£25 by arrangement.

Closed: Christmas & New Year.

From St. Austell to Mevagissey. Through village, up steep hill & down into Portmellon. Up steep hill, left-hand bend, entrance 100 yds on.

Sally & Tim Kendall
Bodrugan Barton
Mevagissey
Cornwall PL26 6PT
Tel: 01726 842094
Fax: 01726 844378
E-mail: bodruganbarton@ukonline.co.uk

Entry No: 52   Map no: 2

Cornwall

Tea in the garden or the drawing room when you arrive; the grandeur is so soft and Sarah and her family so natural that you'll feel at home immediately. The Empire sofa, good oils, faded rugs on wooden floors, lovely lamps and an oak chest are just what you might hope for. They, and Sydney the polar bear, all sit beautifully in the 1780s, creeper-clad vicarage. Good period furniture, fresh flowers and quilted bedspreads in the bedrooms: in one a Napoleonic four-poster. The children's room, off the twin, with its miniature beds is charming. *Children over five welcome.*

Rooms: 1 four-poster, 1 twin with children's room, 1 suite, all en suite (bath).

Price: £20-£30 p.p. Single supp. £5.

Meals: Breakfast until 10.30am. Dinner available locally.

Closed: Christmas Day.

From Wadebridge, B3314 towards Rock & Polzeath. After 3.5 miles, left signed St. Minver. In village, left into cul-de-sac just before Four Ways Inn. House at bottom on left.

Graham & Sarah Tyson
The Old Vicarage
St. Minver
Nr. Rock
Cornwall PL27 6QH
Tel: 01208 862951
Fax: 01208 863578
E-mail: g.tyson@virgin.net

Entry No: 53   Map no: 2

The Bloors strike the balance between being kind and helpful and unobtrusive. "They are doing a perfect job," said our inspector. The converted barn hunkers down in its own secluded valley and a path leads you through the woods to delightful Epphaven Cove. It's elegantly uncluttered and cool; seagrass contrasts with old oak and the downstairs bedrooms have fresh flowers, quilted bedspreads and doors onto the garden. The shower room - a mixture of rusty reds and Italian marble - is magnificent. Jo's daughter is an aromatherapist - book an appointment. *Children over 12 welcome.*

Rooms: 1 double, 2 twins sharing 1 bathroom & 1 shower room.

Price: £28 p.p. Single supp. by arrangement.

Meals: Breakfast times flexible. Dinner available locally.

Closed: Never.

A39 to Wadebridge. At r'bout follow signs to Polzeath, then to the Porteath Bee Centre. Through Bee Centre shop car park, down farm track; house signed on right after 150 yds.

Jo Bloor
Porteath Barn
St. Minver
Wadebridge
Cornwall PL27 6RA
Tel: 01208 863605
Fax: 01208 863954
E-mail: mbloor@ukonline.co.uk

Entry No: 54   Map no: 2

A place for peaceful time away. You have your own entrance at the side of the farmhouse (14th century in parts) to two bedrooms, a dining room and a sitting room with an open fire and bread oven. There's also a *loggia* for summer breakfasts. The feel is traditional, with antiques and quilting; the Hurleys are keen for you to feel happy, yet they are unobtrusive. Their adorable black Labradors will give you the most enthusiastic welcome. Rock is just 15 minutes away - the Hurley's cottage for six, with Aga, is here, too. *Children by arrangement.*

Rooms: 1 double with private bathroom; 1 double available to same party.

Price: From £25 p.p. Single supp. £5. Cottage for 6 £350-£600 p.w.

Meals: Breakfast until 9.30am; packed lunch from £5; supper from £12.50; dinner from £17.50, by arrangement.

Closed: Occasionally.

A30 towards Bodmin. 6 miles after Jamaica Inn, right for St. Breward. Follow signs for St. Mabyn, left over bridge. House 2.5 miles on, on right, on bend with trees, before B3266.

Heather & George Hurley
Penwine Farmhouse
St. Mabyn
Nr. Bodmin
Cornwall PL30 3DB
Tel: 01208 841783
Fax: 01208 841783
E-mail: penwine@faxvia.net

Entry No: 55   **Map no:** 2

At the head of the beautiful Ruthern Valley, there are stunning views, grassy fields and grazing cattle and horses all around this 450-acre dairy farm. Lie back in the garden hammock to take in the undulating view and drink in the peace. Gelda has decorated the house with flair and attention to detail. Swathes of designer fabrics hang in thick folds at the windows, bathroom towels are large and fluffy and sofas are satisfyingly squishy. Breakfast can be served in the garden in summer. *Children by arrangement.*

Rooms: 2 doubles, both with private bathroom.

Price: £25-£35 p.p. Special rates available.

Meals: Breakfast times flexible; dinner, £15-£20, by arrangement.

Closed: Never.

From M5, A30 to r'bout south of Bodmin. Continue on A30 towards Redruth. 2.2 miles on, right to Withiel. Through Withiel (do not fork right), down hill, over bridge, left at T-junc., signed Wadebridge. Drive on right, 0.5 miles on.

Gelda & Michael Madden
Higher Tregawne
Withiel
Bodmin
Cornwall PL30 5NS
Tel: 01208 831257
Fax: 01208 831257

John Betjeman and A.L. Rowse, the historian, both loved 15th-century Bokelly and often wrote about it. The Elizabethan tithe barn, your hosts and the garden are absolutely marvellous, too, and a tennis court, croquet lawn and a folly add to the magic. The house is relaxed and is beautiful - easily so. There's an exhilarating mix of the exotic (a papier-mâché ship used in a film that Lawrence directed) and the familiar (squishy sofas and traditional carpets). You have your own drawing room with open fire; the Eden Project and surfing beaches are nearby. A special place indeed.

Rooms: 1 double, en suite (bath); 1 double, with private bathroom.

Price: From £30 p.p.

Meals: Breakfast times flexible; dinner, first night only, £15.

Closed: Never.

On A39, 7 miles south of Camelford at St. Kew Highway, right through village on Trelill Rd (Do not go to St. Kew.) 1 mile on, pass white cottage on right, left over cattle grid past white bungalow, house 0.25 miles down drive.

Maggie & Lawrence Gordon Clark
Bokelly
St. Kew
Bodmin
Cornwall PL30 3DY
Tel: 01208 850325

Entry No: 57   **Map no:** 2

Step from the bedroom balcony and throw a stone into the sea - you are that close. "I can't believe how lovely this is," wrote our inspector. The house was to be Georgian but things took so long to arrive from London that it slid into Regency. You eat in a Tuscan pink kitchen; wooden floors shine, there are pictures, deep sofas to curl up in - all flooded with natural light. Beds are big with generous swathes of material at the windows. Walk barefoot from the heavenly garden onto the sandy beach and swim or launch a boat. Idyllic, and the Harveys are lovely. *Children by arrangement.*

Rooms: 1 twin/double with private bathroom; 1 twin/double, 1 double, both en suite (bath) and with sitting room.

Price: £30-£38 p.p. Single supp. by arrangement.

Meals: Breakfast times flexible; dinner occasionally available.

Closed: Christmas & New Year.

From A390 beyond St. Austell, left for Mevagissey & Pentewan, past Mount Edgecombe Hospice. Left signed Porthpean Beach. Down narrow lane, 2nd big house at bottom.

Christine & Michael Harvey
Tredeague
Porthpean
St. Austell
Cornwall PL26 6AX
Tel: 01726 72142
Fax: 01726 73084
E-mail: tredeague@amserve.net

Entry No: 58   **Map no:** 2

From January to October you can only come if you have a child under five! This is an unpretentious, jolly haven for families. Your children can collect eggs, climb in the garden, visit the animals or miniature farmyard, watch a video. Nursery teas begin at 5pm (you can have a cream tea in the garden) and Lucy will babysit while you slink off to the local pub – the highest in Cornwall. One bedroom is jolly with new pine, the other two more traditional. Celtic crosses in the garden and original panelling hint at the house's 500-year history.

Rooms: 3 family, all en suite (baths or showers).

Price: From £44 per room. Special breaks available.

Meals: Breakfast times flexible; packed lunch £5; nursery tea £3.50; supper £8; evening meal £12.50.

Closed: Christmas.

From Launceston, A395, then A39 through Camelford. Left onto B3266 to Bodmin. 4 miles on, left (signed Wenfordbridge Pottery). Over bridge, past pottery & on brow of hill, left into a lane. House at top.

Lucy Finnemore
Higher Lank Farm
St Breward
Bodmin
Cornwall PL30 4NB
Tel: 01208 850716

Entry No: 59   **Map no: 2**

One of the most exquisite houses we've seen - parts are 15th century and the setting is magical. There are 30 acres with ancient woods, an unrestored water garden, three Celtic crosses and a holy well; the scent of the wisteria is heady. The magic continues inside. Catherine - the loveliest of ladies - has matched fabrics, antique pieces, colours and bed linen with enormous care and flair. One of the bedrooms was part of the old chapel and has ancient stone lintels - all are sunny and have proper bathrooms with lovely old baths. The guest sitting room has a piano, books, beautiful art and fresh flowers. There's a heated outdoor pool, too. *Children over 10 welcome.*

Rooms: 1 twin, en suite (bath); 2 doubles, both with private bathroom.

Price: £35-£40 p.p. No single supp.

Meals: Breakfast times flexible; dinner £25, by arrangement.

Closed: Occasionally.

From A30, take turning for Blisland. There, past church on left & pub on right. Take lane at bottom left of village green. 0.25 miles on, drive on left (granite pillars & cattle grid).

Christopher & Catherine Hartley
Lavethan
Blisland
Bodmin
Cornwall PL30 4QG
Tel: 01208 850487
Fax: 01208 851387
E-mail: chrishartley@btconnect.com

Entry No: 60   **Map no: 2**

Cornwall

See the world in writer-explorer Robin's 18th- and 19th-century manor house, chock-a-block with exotic artefacts and Louella's sumptuous hand-stencilled fabrics and furniture. Rich, dark colours, wonderful quilts, cushions and rugs, old beams, and books floor-to-ceiling. A sensuous mix of old-English country life, the 'global village' and atelier - with comfort that swaddles you. Here on the edge of Bodmin Moor, wild boar roam; closer to home there is a splendid conservatory looking onto elegant lawns, gardens, a tennis court and views to make your heart leap - and an opera house in a converted barn at the bottom of the garden.

Rooms: 1 double en suite (bath); 2 doubles, 1 twin, sharing 2 bathrooms.

Price: £30 p.p. No single supp. Reduced rates for children.

Meals: Breakfast times flexible; packed lunch from £5; dinner, 3 courses, £18, by arrangement.

Closed: Christmas & New Year.

6 miles after Jamaica Inn on A30, left signed Mount. Straight on, ignore Cardinham sign. After 2.5 miles, left to Maidenwell. House 400 yds on right.

Robin & Louella Hanbury-Tenison
Cabilla Manor
Nr. Mount
Bodmin
Cornwall PL30 4DW
Tel: 01208 821224
Fax: 01208 821267
E-mail: robin@cabilla.co.uk

Entry No: 61   **Map no: 2**

Doorway to Eden - and a family home now, full of laughter. The Black Prince owned this land in the 12th century and the Crusaders sailed from here to France. The kitchen is homely and the Aga has hatched many a bantam's egg. Rob, a retired Admiral, was in command of the Royal Yacht Britannia; Restormel is his new ship. Bedrooms are traditional, not frilly - three doubles in the house and two doubles and a bunk room in the self-contained wing. Views are to the salmon and trout river below. Many fine gardens and churches to visit; the Eden Project just 7 miles away; good fishing, walking, bicycle trails and beaches too.

Rooms: 1 double/family room, en suite (shower); 2 doubles sharing private bathroom. Self-catering also available, sleeps 4/6.

Price: From £25 p.p. No single supp. Self-catering from £250 p.w. Short breaks available.

Meals: Breakfast times flexible; packed lunch from £5. Dinner available locally

Closed: Never.

Into Lostwithiel on A390, follow signs to Restormel Castle. Stone gateposts on right 1 mile on. Follow drive to back of house.

Roz Woodard
Restormel Manor
Lostwithiel
Cornwall PL22 OHN
Tel: 01208 873444
Fax: 01208 873455

 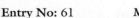

Entry No: 62   **Map no: 2**

A tall Georgian 18th-century farmhouse with intriguing round windows and an unspoilt farmyard; the buildings are still used for sheep. Chickens strut, scratch and lay eggs; this is very much a working farm with all the family involved. Anne, who sells dried flowers all over the country, has a magnificent eye for colour and her sons - two sculptors and one designer - are artistic, too. The super bedrooms are on the second floor, with fine views and there is a lovely calm little drawing room for guests. Good walks all around and the Eden Project is nearby.

Rooms: 2 twins with connecting bathroom, let to one party only.

Price: £30 p.p. Single supp. by arrangement.

Meals: Breakfast times flexible. Dinner available nearby.

Closed: Christmas & Easter.

From Plymouth, A38 then A390 west. 1 mile before Lostwithiel, 2nd left after garage to Lerryn. Before bridge, left for Couch's Mill, then 1st left into cul-de-sac, up hill for 0.25 miles.

Anne & Iain Mackie
Collon Barton
Lerryn
Lostwithiel
Cornwall PL22 0NX
Tel: 01208 872908
Fax: 01208 873812

Entry No: 63   **Map no: 2**

You are at the head of the old smuggling route and an ancient right of way leads you to Polperro's little harbour. The Macartneys have breathed new life into the 14th-century Grade II*-listed hall house with enormous passion and style and the ancient charm blends perfectly with added comforts. There are three dressing gowns in descending order of size and you have your own cosy, timbered A-frame sitting room with woodburner, candles, wild flowers - it's memorably special and good value, too. Food is organic and free-range where possible. This is a favourite among guests.

Rooms: 1 double, 1 single with shared use of private bathroom and sitting room.

Price: £25-£32 p.p.

Meals: Breakfast times flexible; dinner, £12.50-£19.50, by arrangement. B.Y.O. wine.

Closed: Never.

A387 through Looe & approx. 3 miles beyond, then B3359 signed Pelynt. Just less than a mile on, 2nd of 2 turnings on left. After 0.5 miles, left at T-junc., then fork left, signed.

Michael & Ann Macartney
Penellick
Pelynt
Nr. Looe
Cornwall PL13 2LX
Tel: 01503 272372
Fax: 01503 272372
E-mail: penellick@hotmail.com

Entry No: 64   **Map no: 2**

Down a wild-flowered drive in a hidden fold, inland from the Fowey river, this is a treasure house, a charming synthesis of style, stone, wood and colour. A Shaker simplicity is sprinkled with pretty touches such as flowers, candles and printed fabrics. There's a settle by the Rayburn and espressos can be brought to you in the garden where goats, chickens and ducks potter happily. Helen is an aromatherapist and reflexologist (you can book a treatment); she and Richard are young, enthusiastic and gentle. Bedrooms are gorgeous. Organic breakfasts, home-made biscuits and fresh fish dinners - wonderful.

Rooms: 1 double, 1 twin (small double bed plus single bed) both with basins, sharing bathroom.

Price: £25 p.p. Single supp. by arrangement.

Meals: Breakfast times flexible; packed lunch, cream teas and drinks available; dinner including wine, £20-£30.

Closed: Occasionally.

Leave Liskeard on A38. At Dobwalls take left fork, A390 signed St. Austell. After East Taphouse, left onto B3359 signed Looe. After 2 miles, right signed Botelet.

The Tamblyn Family
Botelet
Herodsfoot
Liskeard, Cornwall PL14 4RD
Tel: 01503 220225
Fax: 01503 220225
E-mail: stay@botelet.co.uk
Web: www.botelet.co.uk

Entry No: 65   **Map no: 2**

The garden has seats positioned to catch the evening sun: perfect for relaxing after a day exploring the gardens and beaches of Cornwall. The peaceful house is named after the hill and you have utter privacy and a private entrance to your fresh, roomy suite: a twin-bedded room and a large, square, high sitting room with double doors giving onto the wooded valley. There's a CD player, plus music, chocolates and magazines. Jos, a kitchen designer, and Mary-Anne really want you to enjoy your stay; you will. Local produce and free-range eggs for breakfast.

Rooms: 1 twin, en suite (bath/shower) with sitting room and adjoining single for child if needed.

Price: £30 p.p. Single supp. £10.

Meals: Breakfast times flexible; dinner, 3 courses, £18, by arrangement. B.Y.O wine.

Closed: Christmas.

From Launceston, B3254 towards Liskeard. Through Daw's House & South Petherwin, down steep hill & last left before little bridge. House 1st on left.

Jos & Mary Anne Otway-Ruthven
Hornacott
South Petherwin
Launceston
Cornwall PL15 7LH
Tel: 01566 782461
Fax: 01566 782461
E-mail: otwayruthven@btinternet.com

Entry No: 66   **Map no: 2**

Cornwall

You get the peace and privacy of self-catering, yet can eat in the farm's award-winning restaurant. Samphire House feels mediterranean with two open plan sitting rooms and a balcony overlooking its swimming pool. There are equally large sitting rooms, and a huge garden, in Samphire Cottage; Eastwood Cottage, a converted barn, is a charming retreat with an oak staircase and gallery. Walk along the donkey path - two moorland ponies will probably follow you - to National Trust coastline, Strangles beach and High Cliff. You can get married here, too.

Rooms: Samphire House & Cottage each sleep 10. Eastwood sleeps 4.

Price: Samphire House from £850 p.w. Samphire Cottage from £650 p.w. Eastwood Cottage from £350 p.w.

Meals: Breakfast self-catering, so any time! Dinner available in farmhouse restaurant.

Closed: Never.

The Domesday-listed property of Duke William's half-brother sits in the most glorious garden with manicured lawns and immaculate outbuildings - the setting is stunning. Inside there is sober luxury and Muriel runs the house with irreproachable efficiency. If you stay in to eat, you meet fellow guests for drinks before dining in dinner party style; Muriel plans her menus with care. There are fine paintings, stone-silled windows onto garden views, carefully decorated rooms. Your hosts pride themselves on running an immaculate, peaceful, totally English home.

Rooms: 3 twins/doubles, en suite (1 bath, 2 showers).

Price: £30 p.p. Single occ. £40.

Meals: Breakfast 8.30am; dinner £18.

Closed: Christmas Day.

From Crackington Haven follow coastal road keeping sea on right. Up hill & right signed Trevigue. Farm 1.5 miles on left on top of cliffs.

From Wainhouse Corner on A39, follow sign to Crackington Haven. At beach, turn inland for 1 mile, left into Church Park Road & 1st right into lane.

Gayle Crocker
Trevigue
Crackington Haven
Bude
Cornwall EX23 0LQ
Tel: 01840 230418
Fax: 01840 230418
E-mail: trevigue@talk21.com

Muriel Knight
Manor Farm
Crackington Haven
Bude
Cornwall EX23 0JW
Tel: 01840 230304

Entry No: 67   Map no: 2

Entry No: 68   Map no: 2

Cornwall

The road twists and turns, the driveway falls through the spring-fed wooded valley and, suddenly, the secret is yours. The former vicarage - part 16th-century with Georgian and Edwardian additions - is beautiful and within its intriguing garden you are neighbour only to sea, coastal path and fields; nearby are sandy beaches. Lots of light, sea views, seagrass matting, paintings, comfy sofas, pretty fabrics and the feel of a family home. Perfect. Bedrooms are fresh and peaceful, bathrooms charming. What's more, Jane and Anthony share their house without fuss. *Children over five welcome.*

Rooms: 1 double, 1 twin, both with basin and private bathroom; 1 further twin let to members of same party; 1 small single for child.

Price: £22-£30 p.p. Single supp. £10.

Meals: Breakfast times flexible; simple supper or dinner, 3 courses, from £12, by arrangement.

Closed: Christmas.

Leave A39 at Wainhouse Corner, south of Bude, signed St. Gennys Church. 2 miles on, fork right by white cottage signed St. Gennys Church. Before church, right into lane/drive.

Anthony & Jane Farquhar
St. Gennys House
St. Gennys
Bude
Cornwall EX23 0NW
Tel: 01840 230384
Fax: 01840 230537

Entry No: 69   **Map no: 2**

A Grade II-listed, slate-hung Georgian farmhouse in 30 acres of pastoral loveliness with its own (ancient) Holy Well – can you resist? Your immensely likeable hostess Gillian is full of enthusiasm for her new home where guest rooms have beautiful antique bedspreads and glorious views. (Bask in the morning sun with your head on your pillow.) The vegetable garden is her passion; the freshest produce ends up on the supper table in the Moroccan look dining room. A sitting room is available for guests. The perfect spot on the way to surf, sand and the Eden Project. *Children over five welcome.*

Rooms: 1 double, en suite (shower); 1 double with w.c., 1 twin sharing bathroom.

Price: £25 p.p. £23 p.p. for more than one night.

Meals: Breakfast until 10am; dinner, £12.50, by arrangement.

Closed: Easter & Christmas.

Heading west, right off A30 onto A395 towards Wadebridge. Through Pipers Pool & 3rd left signed Laneast. Left again, through village. House has wooden gates on left.

Gillian & Anthony ffrench Blake
Laneast Barton
Laneast
Launceston
Cornwall PL15 8PN
Tel: 01566 880104
Fax: 01566 880103
E-mail: affb@totalise.co.uk

Entry No: 70   **Map no: 2**

Charlie was on the tube when he saw an ad for a grandfather clock business in Cornwall; he convinced Fiona to leave London, bought the company and returned to his roots. They found land, built their house and have the space and peace that townies dream of. It's not finished yet, but the lilac and pink kitchen with cream Aga, the huge sitting room with open fires and the bedroom with painted Victorian bedsteads and fresh white and blues bode well. There's an organic/eco slant and you bathe in the softest Cornish rainwater.

Rooms: 1 twin with en suite bathroom (bath).

Price: £25p.p. Single supp. £5.

Meals: Breakfast until 10.30am; dinner, £10-£20, by arrangement.

Closed: Christmas & New Year.

At end of Bodmin bypass; Innis Downs r'bout A30 exit; immediate 1st right to Lake view. Crossroads straight over, left 2nd crossroads to Ruthern Bridge; 1st right; 1st left to Withiel. House on left & signed.

Fiona Turner
Trebois
Withielgoose Mills
Bodmin
Cornwall PL30 5NN
Tel: 01208 832901
Fax: 01208 75699
E-mail: cjtfht80@aol.com

Entry No: 71   **Map no:** 2

What a treat! Catch a tantalising glimpse of the sea from your B&B and wake to the sound of a bubbling stream. Clare's generous and sunny nature is reflected in her lovely home, with its shelves of books, rose-strewn wallpapers and delicious smells of beeswax and baking. She used to run an excellent restaurant and is a superb cook who loves to treat guests to locally-caught fresh fish. Bedrooms are sunny: an elegant double/twin and a sweet double with that glimpse of the sea. All this, a garden full of birdsong and a (real) fishing village 500 yards below. *Children by arrangement.*

Rooms: 1 king-size/twin, en suite bath/shower; 1 double with private bathroom.

Price: £35 p.p. Single supp. by arrangement.

Meals: Breakfast times flexible; packed lunch £7.50; dinner, 2/3 courses, £20/£25.

Closed: Occasionally.

From Tregony, A3078 to St. Mawes. After 2 miles at Esso garage on left, left to Portloe. Through village until Ship Inn. Immediate right fork after pub car park. Cottage on left between white gate posts.

Clare Holdsworth
Pine Cottage
Portloe, Truro
Portloe
Cornwall TR2 5RB
Tel: 01872 501385
Web: www.pinecottage.net

Entry No: 72   **Map no:** 2

Cornwall

Although Button and Clive look after you with a deft professionalism and attention to detail, their personal touch makes your stay special. The 1744 house sits at the top of a tidal creek where 200 years ago the Navy tested their cannons; now you hear only wildlife. The quietly elegant bedrooms - *Aqua*, *Oyster* and *Cranberry* - have wonderful views. You are brought scones in a sitting room alive with colour and light, and you eat your morning kippers and free-range eggs from a walnut table that cleverly conceals a snooker table.

Rooms: 1 four-poster, 1 twin/double, both en suite (shower); 1 double with private bath.

Price: £32.50-£47.50 p.p. (for 2 night stays). Single person/single night supp. from £15.

Meals: Breakfast until 10.30am. Dinner available locally.

Closed: Occasionally.

A38 over Tamar Bridge. After 7 miles, A374 left towards Torpoint at Ring O'Bells pub in Antony. Right round back of pub, then 1st left to St. John. Left at small green. House 1st on right.

Clive & Button Poole
The Old Rectory
St John-in-Cornwall
Nr. Torpoint
Cornwall PL11 3AW
Tel: 01752 822275
Fax: 01752 823322
E-mail: clive@oldrectory-stjohn.co.uk

Entry No: 73   **Map no:** 2

Ann is huge fun and a natural entertainer - you'll feel at ease. This is a wonderfully comfortable house with touches of luxury and matchless views over Plymouth Sound. It is at the top of a steep hill overlooking a charming seaside village of 600 souls. Ann cooks superb meals with wholefood ingredients and local produce and makes her own muesli, bread, yogurt and ice-cream and can even cater for vegans. Bring your own music... there's a 'boudoir grand' to be played as well as a music centre you can use. There's a superb first floor drawing room with sea views.

Rooms: 1 twin/double, 1 twin, both en suite (shower); 1 double, en suite (bath).

Price: £22 p.p. Single supp. by arrangement. Reduction for 3 nights or more.

Meals: Breakfast until 9.30am, or by arrangement; dinner £20; light supper £9.

Closed: Never.

B3247 towards Mount Edgcumbe. Right before school, signed Kingsand. Down hill to right, left fork on bend into Kingsand, 2nd left, then left again. House on left with yellow door. Avoid single track road.

Ann Heasman
Cliff House
Devonport Hill
Kingsand
Cornwall PL10 1NJ
Tel: 01752 823110
Fax: 01752 822595
E-mail: chkingsand@aol.com

Entry No: 74   **Map no:** 2

All of our inspectors have been bowled over by this house. The approach, surrounded on three sides by tidal estuaries, makes your heart leap. The Grade II-listed manor has its own chapel in which a 14th-century fresco clings to the walls. Its many rooms are filled with thousands of books, pictures and some slightly worn, but massively stylish, fine furniture. Guy is eccentric, funny and passionate about horses - bring your own, or some may be available to competent riders. Rooms, reached via four staircases, are simple and bright with old rugs and scattered books. *Children over 12 welcome.*

Rooms: 1 twin with private bathroom; 2 doubles, both en suite (bath).

Price: £35 p.p. Single supp. £5.

Meals: Breakfast until 9.30am; dinner £20; B.Y.O wine.

Closed: Never.

From Plymouth A38 & cross Tamar Bridge. Through bypass tunnel over r'bout. On top of next hill left to Trematon; through village to Elmgate. Take road to right of white house with letter box, shoulder hard on left.

Guy Bentinck
Erth Barton
Saltash
Cornwall PL12 4QY
Tel: 01752 842127
Fax: 01752 842127

Entry No: 75   **Map no: 2**

This is 'Cornwall's Forgotten Corner', in gorgeous countryside. The house is opposite the church, rooted in time and space; the massive walls echo their 400 years of history. There's great style everywhere, with farmhouse charm in the kitchen - Aga, pine chairs, chequered tablecloth, Welsh dresser - and sheer elegance in the flagstoned sitting room, with Farrow and Ball Library Red walls contrasting with heavy calico curtains, off-white sofas and church candles. Bedrooms have crisp cotton and great comfort. Your hosts are easy and relaxed and there is a games room, too, with bar billiards and table tennis. Excellent value.

Rooms: 1 king-size with extra single, en suite (shower), 1 double, en suite (bath & shower); 1 double with private bathroom.

Price: £22 p.p. Single supp. £5.

Meals: Breakfast times flexible. Dinner available locally.

Closed: Christmas & Boxing Day.

To Sheviock on A374. House opposite church.

Carol & Tony Johnson
Sheviock Barton
Sheviock
Torpoint
Cornwall PL11 3EH
Tel: 01503 230793
Fax: 01503 230793
E-mail: thebarton@sheviock.freeserve.co.uk

Entry No: 76   **Map no: 2**

The setting will bowl you over, and so will the Walkers' warmth and talent (Nicky is an artist who will share her studio or give you lessons). This lovely old Georgian farmhouse has breathtaking views over undulating countryside, streams and wooded valleys - wander along a track beside the leat. Delicious breakfasts in the walled garden in summer, log fires, a good collection of books and two grand pianos inside. Lantallack is an inspiration for musicians, artists or anyone wanting to combine fun with peace and tranquillity. A cottage with stunning views for self-catering, too.

Rooms: 1 double, en suite (shower); 1 twin with basin, with private bathroom next door. Cottage: sleeps 6.

Price: £25-£27.50 p.p. Single supp. by arrangement. Cottage £255-£600 p.w.

Meals: Breakfast times flexible. Good pubs and restaurants nearby.

Closed: Never.

A38 through Saltash & on for 3 miles. At Landrake 2nd right signed New Barton. After 1 mile, left at white cottage signed Tideford. House 150 yds on, on right.

Nicky Walker
Lantallack Farm
Landrake
Nr. Saltash, Cornwall PL12 5AE
Tel: 01752 851281
Fax: 01752 851281
E-mail: lantallack@ukgateway.net
Web: www.lantallack.co.uk

Entry No: 77   **Map no: 2**

An old corn mill with the original water wheel now in the kitchen and with views down the garden to the salmon/sea trout river from the bedrooms. Richard is a keen fly fisherman and can fix up rods for visitors. Mariebel is a professional portrait painter who taught for many years; she's still happy to teach individuals or groups. Bicton is informal, comfortable and relaxed. Meals are eaten in the huge farmhouse kitchen or in the impressive slate-floored dining/sitting room. The Lynher Valley is unspoilt and enchanting, with lovely walks all round. *Children by arrangement.*

Rooms: 1 double, en suite (shower); 1 double with private, adjacent bathroom & wc.

Price: £25-£30 p.p. Single supp. by arrangement.

Meals: Breakfast times flexible; dinner £18, by arrangement.

Closed: Never.

On A388 Callington-Launceston, left at Kelly Bray (opp. garage) to Maders. 400 yds after Maders, left to Golberdon & left at x-roads. After 400 yds, right down unmarked lane. Mill 0.75 miles by bridge.

Richard & Mariebel Allerton
Bicton Mill
Bicton
Nr. Liskeard
Cornwall PL14 5RF
Tel: 01579 383577
Fax: 01579 383577

Entry No: 78   **Map no: 2**

A Victorian Lakeland house, all set about with gables and chimney stacks and light-filtering bay windows, in three supremely peaceful acres on the edge of Grasmere. Rooms are pristine, big and comfortable, with some new pine furniture, matching floral wallpapers and cushions and brass bedside lamps - from two you can see the lake across the wildflower meadow cultivated by the Kirkbrides. There's a payphone, and a boot-and-drying room, too. Walk from the house, row round the lake or make a pilgrimage to Wordsworth's cottage and grave. *Children over 10 welcome.*

Rooms: 1 four-poster, en suite (bath/shower); 2 doubles, en suite (1 bath & 1 shower). Self-catering cottage also available.

Price: £32.50-£37.50 p.p. Single occ. £47.50. Check for price of cottage.

Meals: Breakfast until 8.45am. Dinner available locally.

Closed: November-February.

Bonnie Prince Charlie rested here. The River Rothay flows by (you cross it on a private bridge to reach the house) and the scenery is glorious. Riverside is without a doubt a guest house - far more so than most homes in this book - but it is the the sweet and down-to-earth Alan and Gillian that add the specialness. There's a clothes' drying-room for walkers, a small sitting room and small dining room, too. The bedrooms are modest and most have views of the river - there's also a self-catering cottage for two.

Rooms: 5 doubles, all en suite (3 bath, 2 shower).

Price: £30-£35 p.p. Single occ. not available.

Meals: Breakfast until 9am. Dinner available locally.

Closed: Occasionally.

Enter Grasmere from A591, turn opposite St. Oswald's church. After 100 yds, right into Langdale road. House on left.

From Ambleside, A593 Coniston road to Rothay Bridge (approx. 500 yds). Cross bridge & immed. into entrance.

Lyn & John Kirkbride
Ryelands
Grasmere
Cumbria LA22 9SU
Tel: 015394 35076
Fax: 015394 35076

Alan & Gillian Rhone
Riverside Lodge
Nr. Rothay Bridge
Ambleside
Cumbria LA22 OEH
Tel: 015394 34208
E-mail: alanrhone@riversidelodge.co.uk
Web: www.riversidelodge.co.uk

Entry No: 79   **Map no: 14**

Entry No: 80   **Map no: 14**

Cumbria

Guests have been very happy here in this big, light house where you'll find a smiling welcome and not a hint of stuffiness - the Broughtons have a great sense of fun. Bedrooms have big, comfy beds - there is lots of attention to detail - and the suite is a lovely hideaway in the loft. You'll find it easy to relax by the fire in the winter with a glass of wine, or in the garden in summer - it's sunny and secluded. After a splendid cooked breakfast - there's organic home-made bread and Aga pancakes, too - walk to the lakes, fells and village, all a mere five-minute stroll away.

Rooms: 1 family suite (1 double, 1 twin), en suite (bath); 1 twin/double, en suite (shower).

Price: £28-£30 p.p. Single supp. £10. Half-price for children.

Meals: Breakfast 8.30-9.30am. Dinner available locally.

Closed: Christmas & New Year.

From Kendal, A591 to Windermere & follow signs to Bowness. There, bear left at bottom of hill & 1st left opposite church. Follow road past garage on left. House 50 yds on, on right.

Louise & Steve Broughton
Low Fell, Ferney Green
Bowness-on-Windermere
Cumbria LA23 3ES
Tel: 015394 45612
Fax: 015394 48411
E-mail: lowfell@talk21.com
Web: www.low-fell.co.uk

Entry No: 81   **Map no:** 14

You won't find another B&B like this in the Lakes. Splashes of colour - Barbie pink, lime, lemon, peppermint - give a fresh, exciting feel to the house. Blinds, no frills, modern art, black-and-white checked hallway and the odd Conran piece set it apart from other B&Bs on Windermere's busy 'Golden Mile'. The dining room in the conservatory is café-style, but fun; there are lots of places nearby for dinner. The lovely terraced garden at the rear leads to a stream and, beyond that, woodland protected from development. Pat and David are a super, hospitable couple.

Rooms: 5 doubles, all en suite (shower).

Price: From £27 p.p. Single supp. £10.

Meals: Breakfast times flexible; light evening meals, £10, by arrangement.

Closed: Never.

A591 to Windermere. Left by Tourist Information & through village. House on right after less than 0.5 miles, opposite modern church.

Pat Downes & David Linnell
The Coach House
Lake Road
Windermere, Cumbria
Tel: 01539 444494
Fax: 01539 443476
E-mail: info@coachhouse.net1.co.uk
Web: www.lakedistrictbandb.com

Entry No: 82   **Map no:** 14

Cumbria

"Such lovely, gentle people," wrote our inspector. The Grahams hold huge passion for conservation, their house and for the rich wildlife which populates the 14 acres of private woodland and grounds. The 1903, Edwardian Arts & Craft-style house has been built with great attention to detail: beautifully-made oak doors with wooden latches, motifs moulded into plasterwork, local stone fireplaces, green Lakeland slate roof and great round chimneys. Bedrooms, reached via a spiral staircase, are simple and, like the panelled sitting room, allow the architecture to breathe. Distant views of mountains and lakes are stupendous. *Babies and children over six welcome.*

Rooms: 1 double, en suite (shower); 1 twin, en suite (bath).

Price: £27.50 p.p. Single supp. £7.50.

Meals: Breakfast times flexible.

Closed: Christmas & New Year.

From M6, junc. 36, B5284 signed Hawkshead (via ferry) for 6 miles. After Golf Club, right signed Heathwaite. Bear right up hill past Nursery. Manor next drive on right. Gillthwaite Rigg is central part.

Rhoda M. Graham
Gillthwaite Rigg, Heathwaite Manor
Lickbarrow Road
Windermere
Cumbria LA23 2NQ
Tel: 015394 46212
Fax: 015394 46212
E-mail: tony_rhodagraham@hotmail.com

Entry No: 83   Map no: 14

Alison's and Philip's welcoming smiles and great love of Low Jock make this house very special. The Scar in the name refers to the wall of rock on the far side of the stream. You're immediately wrapped in the Midwinters' enthusiasm, just as Low Jock Scar itself is folded into the valley. This is a spotless country guest house. From the conservatory you are lured out to ramble in the flourishing gardens, the pride of your hosts. Listen out for the burbling beck and rest on its banks in the evening to recover from the five-course feast at dinner.

Rooms: 1 twin, 2 doubles, all en suite (2 with bath, 1 with shower); 1 twin, 1 double sharing bathroom.

Price: £23.50-£29 p.p. Single supp. £10.

Meals: Breakfast until 9am. Packed lunch £3.50; dinner £17 by arrangement,

Closed: 31 October-mid-March.

From Kendal, A6 to Penrith. After 5 miles, Plough Inn on left, turn into lane on left after 1 mile.

Alison & Philip Midwinter
Low Jock Scar
Selside
Kendal
Cumbria LA8 9LE
Tel: 01539 823259
Fax: 01539 823259
E-mail: philip@low-jock-scar.freeserve.co.uk

Entry No: 84   Map no: 14

Cumbria

"I wish it were mine," said our inspector. This is a Victorian folly with a panelled hall, vast drawing room, grand piano, great tumbling curtains and rugs galore on wooden floors. The bold, south-facing bedrooms elaborate the fantasy. As for the wardrobes - look in the turrets. Huge pillows, excellent linen, handmade chocolates, sherry, scented hot water bottle covers and massive tubs. And take in the gilded, vaulted ceilings, the oak panelling, the soaring stained-glass windows. Meals are informal feasts and, remarkably for a house of this size, there's a real happy, family feel.

Rooms: 2 four-posters, 3 twins/doubles, all en suite (bath & shower).

Price: £40-£50 p.p.

Meals: Breakfast times flexible; dinner £22.50, by arrangement.

Closed: Never.

M6 junction 38, then A685 through Kirkby Stephen. Just before Brough, right signed South Stainmore & house signed on left after 1 mile.

Simon & Wendy Bennett
Augill Castle
Brough
Kirkby Stephen, Cumbria CA17 4DE
Tel: 017683 41937
Fax: 017683 41936
E-mail: augill@aol.com
Web: www.augillcastle.co.uk

Entry No: 85　　**Map no:** 19

Rare wild flowers line the bank and salmon splash in Sandy Beck, the SSSI stream at the bottom of the garden. Water, hills, mountains and wildlife surround you and after a day's exploring you can slip into a state of oblivion - Janet is an aromatherapist and reflexologist. Cooking is imaginative - red onion and pepper quiche with cheese pastry; smoked haddock and parmesan omelette - and the Wright's advice informed. Bedrooms are beamed with new pine furniture and white-tiled bathrooms with charming handmade pottery basins. *Children over five welcome.*

Rooms: 1 family, en suite (Continental bath); 1 double, en suite (shower).

Price: From £26 p.p. Single supp. £8.

Meals: Breakfast 8.30-9.30am; packed lunch £3.50; dinner, 3 courses, from £16.50.

Closed: Occasionally.

From A66, A5086, signed Egremont, at r'bout just outside Cockermouth. After 1 mile left at x-roads by school. 1st right signed Brandlingill. House on right after 1 mile.

Mike & Janet Wright
Toddell Cottage
Brandlingill, Nr. Cockermouth
Cumbria CA13 0RB
Tel: 01900 828696
Fax: 01900 828696
E-mail: toddell@waitrose.com
Web: www.eden-bandb.co.uk

Entry No: 86　　**Map no:** 19

Hazel's family are hoteliers - she knows what she is doing and will do a professional job of looking after you. Beds are hotel-big, too, and a dish of fresh fruit is placed in each room. Oak beams, flagged floors and stone fireplaces have been preserved in this 1650s house. The views are such that each of the five bedrooms is named after the mountain view that it has; Swinside brings the house its own spring water. Next door is a converted milking parlour where you can take lunch or tea. *Children over six welcome. Self-catering also available in the valley.*

Rooms: 2 doubles, 3 twins/doubles, all en suite.

Price: £40-44 p.p. Single supp. up to £15.

Meals: Breakfast times flexible; packed lunch £6.50; dinner £22. There are tea rooms next door, open April-October.

Closed: Never.

From M6 junc. 40 west on A66. Past Keswick & continue on A66 for Cockermouth. Left at Braithwaite onto B5292, Whinlatter Pass. Through forest to Lorton. Left onto B5289 to farm, 1.5 miles on.

Hazel Thompson
New House Farm
Lorton, Cockermouth
Cumbria CA13 9UU
Tel: 01900 85404
Fax: 01900 85404
E-mail: hazel@newhouse-farm.co.uk
Web: www.newhouse-farm.co.uk

Entry No: 87   **Map no:** 19

The setting of this lovely old house could hardly be more beautiful. Many of its rooms face south and have superb views of peaceful countryside with the mountains and fells of Lakeland beyond. The house dates from c.1360 but bedrooms are sumptuous and large and the mood is of a tranquil, elegant, country way of living almost forgotten. Anthony, a tenor soloist, and Kathleen, a talented flower arranger, love sharing their home. Their food is legendary and, with a list of over 60 fine wines, dining in the 17th-century oak-beamed dining room is a memorable experience.

Rooms: 3 doubles, 2 en suite (shower), 1 with private bath.

Price: £40-£42 p.p. Single supp. £10.

Meals: Breakfast 8.30-9am; dinner £20.

Closed: Christmas & New Year.

From M6, junc. 41, B5305 for Wigton. At A595, left, signed Cockermouth. After 6 miles, left for Boltongate: up & down hill & left at bottom to Ireby. Out of village & down hill, between 2 white buildings & left into drive after 50 yds.

Anthony & Kathleen Peacock
Boltongate Old Rectory
Nr. Ireby
Cumbria CA7 1DA
Tel: 016973 71647
Fax: 016973 71798
E-mail: boltongate@aol.com
Web: www.boltongateoldrectory.com

Entry No: 88   **Map no:** 19

You look across rooftops towards the towering mass of Skiddaw, the Lake District's third highest mountain. Here is a cottage garden with sweet peas, herbs, veg and flowers... all perfectly rambling. Roy and Chris have kept most of the original features and there is wood everywhere. Dried flowers, cast-iron tubs, antique linen and patchwork quilts, a collection of Christening gowns - all set against a background of wooden floorboards, high bedroom ceilings and a palpable keenness to make it work. Television is delightfully absent, classical music plays. The Beatys are lovely.

Rooms: 1 double, 1 twin, both en suite (bath).

Price: £22-£25 p.p. Reduction for weekly booking. Single supp. £10.

Meals: Breakfast until 9am. Dinner available locally.

Closed: 18-28 December.

From Keswick A591 to Carlisle (approx. 6.5 miles). Right at Bassenthwaite Chapel into village (0.5 miles). Straight on at village green for 170 yds.

Roy & Chris Beaty
Willow Cottage
Bassenthwaite
Keswick
Cumbria CA12 4QP
Tel: 017687 76440

Entry No: 89   **Map no: 19**

Wordsworth's brother-in-law lived here and the great man visited frequently. The views that he enjoyed, over to Barton Fell, are as glorious as ever. The mood is genuine and uncomplicated country hospitality at its best, with communal dining and no ceremony. Much of the atmosphere comes from Mary herself; she is great fun, down-to-earth and friendly, a real farmer's wife. The home-made biscuits in the rooms are a typical gesture. The bedrooms are simple and unfussy, with bathrobes for you, and with those views. There are 300 acres, 850 sheep and a lovely walled garden... all in the National Park.

Rooms: 2 twins/doubles, both en suite (shower) each with extra single. Further bathroom available.

Price: £22.50 p.p. Single supp. £1.

Meals: Breakfast until 8.30am unless previously arranged. Dinner available locally.

Closed: 1 December-28 February.

From M6 junc. 40, A66 west. At r'bout left on A592. Follow signs to Dalemain house, through car park into courtyard ignoring 'No car' signs. Right for 0.5 miles & right again, at farm building.

Mrs Mary Milburn
Park House Farm
Dalemain, Penrith
Cumbria CA11 0HB
Tel: 01768 486212
Fax: 01768 486212
E-mail: park.house@faxvia.net
Web: www.eden-in-cumbria.co.uk/parkhouse

Entry No: 90   **Map no: 19**

The house echoes the enthusiasm and love poured into it by the Duffs. Built in 1753, it has a classic Georgian façade built from mellow Eden sandstone. Many original features remain, including the ornate ceiling in the dining room. Find the secret door to the billiard room, draw a chair up to the fire, play tennis, or settle on the terrace for a sun-downer. Bedrooms and bathrooms are large and freshly painted with far-reaching views; there's a super walled garden, too. Shooting, fishing, golf, sailing or riding can be arranged for you. *Children over eight welcome.*

Rooms: 2 doubles, both en suite.

Price: £30 p.p. Single supp. £10.

Meals: Breakfast times flexible; dinner £25 inc. wine, by arrangement.

Closed: Christmas & New Year.

From M6 junc. 41, A6 to High Hesket, right to Armathwaite & follow signs to Newbiggin. There left at T-junc. 0.5 miles on, right into Cumrew. House straight ahead.

Roddy & Isabel Duff
Cumrew House
Cumrew, Heads Nook
Brampton, nr. Carlisle
Cumbria CA8 9DD
Tel: 01768 896115
E-mail: rabduff@aol.com
Web: www.countrysport-lodge.com

Entry No: 91   **Map no: 19**

A former monastery dating from 1642, this Grade II* rambling family house is set in 18 acres of rolling lakeside gardens and woodland. Rooms are large but cosy, spotless and flower-filled with views over the gardens and surrounding countryside. Bold chintzy fabrics complement the classic English furniture, and bathrooms have Victorian claw-footed baths. Meals are eaten in the linen-fold panelled dining room overlooking the gardens where you may stroll, play croquet or just relax and enjoy the friendly, peaceful atmosphere. Can you resist?

Rooms: 1 twin with private bathroom; 2 doubles, both en suite (bath).

Price: From £28-£32 p.p. Single £32-£38.

Meals: Breakfast until 10am; packed lunch, from £3-£5; dinner, £17.50 or light suppers, by arrangement.

Closed: Christmas & New Year.

M42, junc. 11, A444 for Burton on Trent for 2 miles, left immed. before Cricketts Inn signed Netherseal. Gate is 0.5 miles on right at end of long red brick wall.

Clemency Wilkins
The Old Hall
Netherseal, Swadlincote
Ashby de la Zouch
Derbyshire DE12 8DF
Tel: 01283 760258
Fax: 01283 762991
E-mail: clemencywilkins@hotmail.com

Entry No: 92   **Map no: 10**

Derbyshire

They are the kindest, most gracious hosts. Robert races vintage cars and Patricia tends the beautiful garden and anticipates your needs. Their splendid Georgian mansion, listed by Pevsner, was 'improved' in 1850 with pillars and again later with a high Victorian conservatory where breakfast, overlooking the beautiful garden, is not to be missed. Shutters, antique furniture and fine country or garden views sit well with the elegant Georgian proportions. The bedrooms are in keeping, with plenty of space, traditional quilts and excellent bathrooms, too.

Rooms: 1 twin, en suite (shower); 2 doubles, en suite (bath/shower).

Price: £32-£35 p.p. Single occ. from £45.

Meals: Breakfast until 9.15am; dinner, 3 courses, £20, by arrangement.

Closed: Christmas.

A lush greenness surrounds the house which is up a tiny country lane with long views over the Dove Valley; there's a fine garden, too. An ancestor of Peter was Lord Mayor of London in 1681, hence the memorabilia; Cynthia is Australian. They are a delightful and genuinely friendly couple. Although elegant, the house is a home and guests are treated as friends - no off-limits, although there is a small, book-lined sitting room just for you. The hall sets the tone: white tiles, Indian rugs, woodburning stove and ancestral paintings. The bedrooms are impeccable. *Children over 12 only.*

Rooms: 2 doubles, 1 en suite (bath), 1 with private bathroom.

Price: £25-£27 p.p. Single occ. £35.

Meals: Breakfast times flexible. Good local pubs & restaurants nearby.

Closed: Christmas.

Leave M1 at junc. 23a. At Isley Walton, right to Melbourne. Left in centre of village, then on Ashby road. Right at Melbourne Arms on to Robinsons Hill.

From Ashbourne, A515 Lichfield road. After 4 miles, right onto B5033. After approx. 1 mile, 2nd lane on right. Rose Cottage is about 0.5 miles on, on right.

Robert & Patricia Heelis
Shaw House
Robinsons Hill
Melbourne
Derbyshire DE73 1DJ
Tel: 01332 863827
Fax: 01332 865201
E-mail: robert.heelis@onetel.co.uk

Peter & Cynthia Moore
Rose Cottage
Snelston
Ashbourne
Derbyshire DE6 2DL
Tel: 01335 324230
Fax: 01335 324651
E-mail: pjmoore@beeb.net

Entry No: 93   **Map no: 10**

Entry No: 94   **Map no: 10**

Rose walkways, a brook and lawns that open onto fields - a lovely setting for afternoon tea; the teapot will be silver, the cakes home-made. Sue's competence has not overshadowed her sense of humour; she's frank and friendly. Guests have the run of the downstairs - two sitting rooms, stacks of books and oriental and antique pieces. The twin has mahogany beds and a Regency chair; the double has rose-patterned, cotton fabrics and a deep cast-iron bath next door. Fruit platter and scrambled eggs and smoked salmon will tempt you to get out of bed.

Rooms: 1 twin, 1 double, both with private bathrooms. Coach House for 4.

Price: From £32 p.p.

Meals: Breakfast times flexible; dinner, £20 including wine, by arrangement.

Closed: Christmas & New Year.

From Ashbourne A515 towards Lichfield. 3 miles on, right to Snelston. Follow road for 1.25 miles to centre of village. House opposite War Memorial. Drive to rear.

Edmund & Sue Jarvis
Oldfield House
Snelston
Ashbourne
Derbyshire DE6 2EP
Tel: 01335 324510
Fax: 01335 324113
E-mail: suejarvis@beeb.net

Entry No: 95   **Map no: 10**

A fine gentility here that's enhanced by the delicate Georgian architecture. Gateposts topped with stone pineapples (symbols of hospitality) and huge copper beeches lead to the glorious house set in 50 acres with grass terraces leading to the River Dove - Dove Dale, Chatsworth and the potteries are all close by. Polished floors and attractive carpets, but still very much a family home; one bedroom has a four-poster with golden coverlet, another a French bed and pale peach walls. Your host is a keen country sportsman and can arrange fly-fishing. A magnificent house with the kindest of hostesses. *Minimum stay two nights at weekends.*

Rooms: 1 twin, 1 four-poster, 1 double, all with private bathrooms.

Price: From £35 p.p. Single occ. from £40.

Meals: Breakfast times flexible. Many good local pubs & restaurants.

Closed: 1 December-1 January.

From Derby on A52 take Ashbourne bypass, direction A52 Leek. Right after Queen's Arms to Mappleton. Through park, over bridge & left out of village. House on right with white gate.

Cedric & Rosemaré Stevenson
Hinchley Wood
Mappleton
Nr. Ashbourne
Derbyshire DE6 2AB
Tel: 01335 350219
Fax: 01335 350580

Entry No: 96   **Map no: 10**

Derbyshire

You'll be hit by the wow factor. One of the four-poster rooms is HUGE, decadent, lavish - over-the-top, even - but you'll revel in the generosity of it all. Soft white robes, masses of pillows, a chandelier and a vast bathroom with an enticing tub sitting right in the middle. The generosity extends to the price, too; this is good value. New-laid eggs for breakfast, fresh fruits and home-made breads accompany the full monty. The solid Victorian farmhouse sits in 370 peaceful acres and Kedleston Hall park with its Robert Adam masterpiece provides a stunning backdrop. *Children over eight welcome.*

Rooms: 2 doubles, en suite (1 bath/shower, 1 shower); 1 double with private bathroom.

Price: £30-£35 p.p. Single supp. £10.

Meals: Breakfast times flexible. Good food available locally.

Closed: Christmas Eve & Day.

From A52/A38 r'bout west of Derby, A38 north. 1st left for Kedleston Hall. House 1.5 miles past Park on x-roads in Weston Underwood.

Linda & Michael Adams
Park View Farm
Weston Underwood
Ashbourne, Derbyshire DE6 4PA
Tel: 01335 360352
Fax: 01335 360352
E-mail: enquiries@parkviewfarm.co.uk
Web: www.parkviewfarm.co.uk

Entry No: 97   **Map no:** 10

On a steep hillside between the Dales and the Peaks, this converted chapel has enormous views; you can eat on the balcony and much of the food is organic. The top floor is open-plan, loft style with huge leaded windows with distinctive coloured panels around the edges. The feel is simple/contemporary - wrought iron light fittings, woodburner, candelabras, very large beds; each bedroom has garden views. Outside: wooden decking, pretty terraces and a small lily pond. It's easy, fun and without pretension; Fay is a delight and committed to her guests.

Rooms: 1 family with twin/king-size and sofa bed, en suite (shower); 1 twin/king, en suite (bath & shower).

Price: £27.50 p.p. Single occ. £32.50. Children under 2 free, then £7.50-£10. Discounts for longer stays.

Meals: Breakfast times flexible; dinner, 3 courses, £18.50.

Closed: Christmas & New Year.

From junc. 26 on M1 A610 towards Ripley. At Sawmills, right under railway bridge, signposted Crich. Right at market place onto Bowns Hill. Chapel 200 yds on right. Can collect from local stations.

Fay & Steve Whitehead
Mount Tabor House
Bowns Hill
Crich
Derbyshire DE4 5DG
Tel: 01773 857008
E-mail: mountabor@email.msn.com

Entry No: 98   **Map no:** 10

This house hasn't always had such easy-going hosts; in 1821 its owner was involved in the last fatal illegal duel in England. Entering the 16th-century mellow limestone house, one feels the warmth of the beamed sitting room with its unusual Derbyshire stone fireplace and part-flagged floor. The elegant dining room looks out to the walled country garden and you can dine on Marsha's freshly prepared breakfasts, with farm-cured bacon. Large bedrooms look down the conservation village towards the National Trust market hall. Freshly renovated bathrooms have a William Morris theme.

Rooms: 1 double, en suite (bath/shower); 1 double, 1 twin, both with large private bathrooms.

Price: £35-£37.50 p.p. Single occ. £50-£52.50.

Meals: Breakfast times flexible; packed lunch £3.75. Dinner available locally.

Closed: Christmas & New Year.

3 miles from Matlock on A6 towards Bakewell. Left on B5057 signed Winster for 3 miles. House at end of Main Street.

John & Marsha Biggin
The Dower House
Main Street
Winster
Derbyshire DE4 2DH
Tel: 01629 650931
Fax: 01629 650932
E-mail: fosterbig@aol.com

Entry No: 99   **Map no: 15**

Explore the new 'jungle garden' or the two acres of herbaceous beds, kitchen garden, lovely terraces of stone walls, hidden patios and even sculptures and streams. This is garden heaven. Hens, ponies and doves animate the charming, old stable yard and, inside the 1783 house, Margaret has created more magic. Her fine eye for detail has brought together perfect colours, fabrics and pieces of furniture to create a thoroughly inviting whole. Breakfast is served in the old schoolroom - organic eggs, honey, home-made jams and, of course, garden fruit. Glorious setting... and place. *Children over five welcome.*

Rooms: 1 double, en suite (bath/shower); 1 family, 1 twin sharing bathroom & separate wc.

Price: £23-£25 p.p. Single supp. from £4.

Meals: Breakfast until 9am. Dinner available locally.

Closed: 23 December-4 January.

M1, junc. 29, A617 to Chesterfield, then B6051 to Millthorpe. Horsleygate Lane 1 mile on, on right.

Margaret Ford
Horsleygate Hall
Horsleygate Lane
Holmesfield
Derbyshire SI8 7WD
Tel: 0114 289 0333

Entry No: 100   **Map no: 15**

Elisabeth, immensely kind, is an avid gardener and bird lover and has designed her garden to encourage wildlife; it works. She also bakes bread, buys 'best local' and has generally made this big country house a real pleasure to visit. The double bedroom has walnut furniture, chintz, silk flowers and a superb view; you bathe in a cast-iron bath. The twin shares the fabulous view and its Victorian/Edwardian furniture fits with the period of that part of the house; the rest is 150 years older. Great walking all around and Chatsworth is 10 minutes away.

Rooms: 1 double with private bathroom; 1 twin with private shower room.

Price: £25 p.p. Single occ. £40.

Meals: Breakfast until 9am. Dinner available locally.

Closed: Christmas & New Year.

On A6, 1.5 miles from Bakewell, right to Ashford-in-the Water. Right to Monsal Head & right at Monsal Head Hotel into Little Longstone. Pass Pack Horse pub on left. House almost opposite.

Elisabeth Chadwick
The Hollow
Little Longstone
Bakewell
Derbyshire DE45 1NN
Tel: 01629 640746

Entry No: 101   **Map no:** 15

You are on the precipice of a spectacular limestone gorge - on some days, cloud is at window level. This is a former mill owner's house, a magnificent William IV property with truly panoramic views over the River Wye and to the green hills beyond. Don't be surprised if you see Len in the sky - he is famed for his hang-glider landings in the 30 acres of parkland. Inside, bedrooms are simple but sympathetic renovation is ongoing; the orangery has just been completed. The Hall buzzes with family life - four generations live here and dynamic Bobby is central to it all.

Rooms: 2 doubles, 1 twin, all en suite (bath & shower).

Price: From £32.50-£47.50 p.p.

Meals: Breakfast times flexible; packed lunch & dinner by arrangement.

Closed: Christmas & New Year.

From Ashford-in-the-Water, B6465 to Monsal Head. Left at Monsal Head Hotel, follow valley to Cressbrook Mill, fork left. Left, at lodge building with white fence & 'Private Drive' sign.

Bobby & Len Hull-Bailey
Cressbrook Hall
Cressbrook, Nr. Buxton
Derbyshire SK17 8SY
Tel: 01298 871289
Fax: 01298 871845
E-mail: stay@cressbrookhall.co.uk
Web: www.cressbrookhall.co.uk

Entry No: 102   **Map no:** 15

Derbyshire

Views every which way and farmhouse life at its luxurious best in the heady surroundings of the Peak District. Water from the spring, breakfasts with eggs and fruit from the farm, local sausages, oat cakes and home-made preserves. The farmhouse was built by the family in 1880 and has been deftly and smartly decorated - all rooms are closely carpeted and well lit and have elaborate window treatments. Bedrooms are pristine yet homely and one takes in views of the Peaks. Pam, South African, capable and welcoming, serves home-made cake and tea on arrival.

Rooms: 2 doubles, en suite (1 shower, 1 bath); 1 twin/double room, en suite (bath/shower).

Price: £24-£32 p.p. No single supp.

Meals: Breakfast times flexible. Plenty of local pubs & restaurants.

Closed: December-February.

From A6 follow Chinley signs. At Squirrels Hotel leave B6062, over bridge, left into Stubbins Lane. After 0.25 miles, left fork onto farm road, over cattle grid & almost 0.5 miles into farmyard.

Pamela & Nick Broadhurst
Cote Bank Farm
Buxworth
High Peak
Derbyshire SK23 7NP
Tel: 01663 750566
Fax: 01663 750566
E-mail: cotebank@btinternet.com.

Entry No: 103   **Map no: 15**

People come from far for the magic of this beautifully restored farmhouse. Such are the views of moor, valley and heather from the bedrooms that guests rarely use the curtains. It is deeply cared for, from the yellow hall with ticking grandfather clock to the pretty drawing room with sky-blue walls and clouds of cream damask at the windows. Flowers everywhere, oak furniture, fine rugs and ancestral bits and pieces, Chippendale chairs and a Louis XV rosewood bed. The terraced garden is a fine place for star-gazing. Drink - even bathe in - pure spring water; it is delicious. Mary is a delight and the house emanates a nourishing peace.

Rooms: 1 double, 1 four-poster, both en suite (shower).

Price: From £30 p.p. Single occ. from £45.

Meals: Breakfast until 9am. Dinner available locally.

Closed: Christmas.

From Sheffield A625 into Hathersage. Right into School Lane. After 100 yds, left fork up 'Church Bank'. 50 yds on, right fork, then 0.5 miles. Over cattle grid. Signed.

Mary Bailey
Carrhead Farm
Hathersage
Hope Valley
Derbyshire S32 1BR
Tel: 01433 650383
Fax: 01433 651441

Entry No: 104   **Map no: 15**

Luxury touches at every turn – as if the rare solitary stream-side setting of this longhouse wasn't enough. Maureen pampers you imaginatively: champagne on occasions, toiletries, bedside bags of truffles, soft towels and robes in huge bedrooms - one with its own conservatory, the other two with private terraces. Outdoors, a swimming pool is colourfully lit at night. Renowned for inspired vegetarian and traditional cooking, Maureen serves breakfast in the (fountained) sunroom. She is gregarious yet unobtrusive. Moors, not fairies, at the bottom of the gardens. But there is magic here... *Minimum two nights stay.*

Rooms: 3 garden rooms: 2 doubles, 1 twin/double, all en suite (bath or shower). Each has private garden or conservatory.

Price: £57.50 p.p. Single occ. £89. Special winter breaks.

Meals: Breakfast until 9.30am. Restaurant nearby.

Closed: Christmas & New Year.

In Chillaton keep pub & P.O. on your left, up hill towards Tavistock. After 300 yds, right (Bridlepath sign). Cottage at end of lane.

Maureen Rowlatt
Tor Cottage
Chillaton
Nr. Tavistock, Devon PL16 0JE
Tel: 01822 860248
Fax: 01822 860126
E-mail: info@torcottage.co.uk
Web: www.torcottage.co.uk

Entry No: 105   **Map no: 2**

Fascinating! The Tamar is magnetic and there's a mine count house from the days when lead and silver were mined here. The lovely Trish makes bread and will procure beef and lamb for your supper, or salmon fresh from the river below. Martha, the donkey, reluctantly helps Trish win the battle with nature but prefers to have her front feet in the kitchen. Sail in - through the SSSI and AONB - there are moorings and a jetty, or book in for a writing or poetry course. It's glorious, characterful, fun, charming. Local branch line connects with Plymouth. *Ask about courses.*

Rooms: 1 double, en suite (bath); 1 twin/double, en suite (bath) with extra single/dressing room.

Price: £23-£25. No single supp.

Meals: Breakfast times flexible; packed lunch £5; supper £12.50; dinner £15; all by arrangement.

Closed: Never.

Into Bere Alston on B3257, left for Weir Quay. Over x-roads. Follow Hole's Hole sign, then right for Hooe. Fork left for South Hooe Farm. 300 yds on, turn sharply back to your left & down track.

Trish Dugmore
South Hooe Mine
Hole's Hole
Bere Alston, Yelverton
Devon PL20 7BW
Tel: 01822 840329
E-mail: trish@weirquay.com

Entry No: 106   **Map no: 2**

An enchanted guest wrote: "If your life is full of stress, there is no better place to recover". Everything is geared to your comfort: enticing four-poster and half-tester beds in cottagey rooms and deep, free-standing baths. It is Joanna and Graham, though, who give that extra something. A lovely Devon couple, they have worked hard to restore the former gardener's bothy; Graham made much of the furniture. The guest sitting room has a slate floor, pine Victorian fireplace and leather sofas. There's a thriving organic vegetable garden, ponds, a stream and Nelson, newly retired from the rigours of the Pony Club.

Rooms: 1 four-poster, 1 half-tester, both with private bathroom (bath/shower); further single available.

Price: From £25 p.p.

Meals: Breakfast times flexible; dinner, 3 courses, £12.

Closed: Never.

From Tavistock B3357 to Princetown. 0.25 miles on, after Mount House School, left. Drive past lake to house.

Mr & Mrs G.H. Moule
Mount Tavy Cottage
Tavistock
Devon PL19 9JL
Tel: 01822 614253
Web: www.mounttavy.freeserve.co.uk

History oozes from every cranny of this Devonshire manor farmhouse which predates the Domesday Book! Granite mullioned windows, slate floors and beamed ceilings are all impressive. Ros gives a big welcome - it's clear that she loves her ancient smallholding with chickens and a carthorse; if you're looking for utter peace - and privacy - you'll be smitten. Guest bedrooms have their own entrance and a lovely feel: pretty fabrics sofa in the double; apricot walls and crocheted bedspreads in the twin. Stabling and grazing for your horse – this is beautiful walking and riding country.

Rooms: 1 double with private bathroom; 1 twin with private shower room.

Price: From £23 p.p.

Meals: Breakfast until 9.30am; packed lunch £5; dinner £12.50.

Closed: Never.

From Tavistock B3357 towards Princetown. At 1st x-roads, right towards Whitchurch Down. Next x-roads 'Warren's Cross', left for Sampford Spiney. 2nd right at national speed limit sign, past 1 cottage on left. Manor next house on left.

Ros Spedding
Samford Manor
Sampford Spiney, Yelverton
Tavistock, Devon PL20 6LH
Tel: 01822 853442
Fax: 01822 855691
E-mail: manor@sampford-spiney.fsnet.co.uk
Web: www.sampford-spiney.fsnet.co.uk

The woodpecker comes at 8.10 every morning; this is a haven for wildlife. Even the cat enters the mood, keen to join you in your room, and there is a goat to take for a walk. The 1860s house was part of the Flete estate - 5,000 acres which run from the South Hams to the sea - and has big, bright bedrooms with velux windows and cheerful colours. Carol and Peter couldn't be nicer - they are clearly happy in their chosen spot. Cream tea if you arrive before 5pm, gin and tonic after. *Children over 10 welcome.*

Rooms: 2 doubles, 1 twin/double, all en suite (bath & shower).

Price: £25 p.p. No single supp. Reduction for 2 nights or more.

Meals: Breakfast times flexible; packed lunch £5; dinner, £15, by arrangement.

Closed: Never.

From Modbury, A379 towards Plymouth. After 1.5 miles, left to Orcheton. Right after 50 yds (Flete estate sign). Cottage 3rd on right.

Peter Foster & Carol Farrand
Goutsford
Ermington
Nr. Ivybridge
Devon PL21 9NY
Tel: 01548 831299
Fax: 01752 601728

Entry No: 109   **Map no: 2**

A cottage and a bakery used to sit side-by-side - 200 years later, the dividing walls have gone. You are less than a mile from the coastal path at Hope Cove (smugglers used to use this as a den) and local materials have been sourced in the renovation - beams made from wood from Plymouth docks and panelling in the bedrooms from Dartmouth church. You have breakfast in a small book-filled, geranium-scented conservatory. There are stripped pine doors, a tongue-and-groove panelled bathroom and some lovely oak and pine furniture; bedrooms are cosy and low ceilinged. Paddy and Griselda, who used to run a restaurant in Salcombe, are delightful.

Rooms: 2 doubles, both en suite (bath); 1 twin, en suite (shower).

Price: £20-£24 p.p. Single supp. £10.

Meals: Breakfast times flexible. Dinner available locally.

Closed: Christmas.

From Kingsbridge on A381, right to Hope Cove. In Galmpton, cottage is 200 yds on left, past village sign.

Paddy & Griselda Daly
Rose Cottage
Galmpton
Salcombe
Devon TQ7 3EU
Tel: 01548 561953
Fax: 01548 561953
Web: www.rosecottagesalcombe.co.uk

Entry No: 110   **Map no: 2**

The house is one of the few remaining thatched Devon longhouses in the area and sits at the head of its own valley with wonderful walking and beaches nearby. More like an hotel than a private house, you will be pampered. Lots of attention to detail – a fridge for drinks, Molton Brown toiletries in the bathroom, boxed stationery, lavender-scented linens and tea on arrival. Every window is dressed with swags, tails and tie-backs. Breakfast will be free-range, organic, local and seasonal. Bread is baked daily and jam and muesli are home-made. *Children by arrangement.*

Rooms: 1 king-size twin/double, 1 double, both en suite (shower); 1 four-poster, en suite (bath).

Price: £40-£55 p.p.

Meals: Breakfast until 10am or by arrangement; dinner, £30, minimum of 6 people, by arrangement.

Closed: Christmas.

In Marlborough, take turning opp. Texaco garage into Collaton Rd. Approx. 0.3 miles on, left signed Collaton. Keep left at grass island, signed Higher Collaton. House at end of private lane.

Mark Andrews
The Yeoman's Country House
Collaton
Salcombe, Devon TQ7 3DJ
Tel: 01548 560085
Fax: 01548 562070
E-mail: yeomanshouse@easicom.com
Web: www.yeomanshouse.co.uk

Entry No: 111   **Map no: 2**

We defy you not to wax lyrical over the setting. The house clings to the hillside before the manicured fields give way to shallow, grassy cliffs, a private beach and tennis court. From the balcony in the four-poster room you can take in the National Trust land that wraps around this stretch of coastland and the views towards Lannacombe Bay. There is no sitting room for guests, but the bedroom has easy chairs. There's a heated indoor swimming pool and sauna that you can use and share with up to 16 self-caterers *Children by arrangement.*

Rooms: 1 four-poster, en suite (bath).

Price: From £35-£45 p.p. Single supp. by arrangement.

Meals: Breakfast times flexible; packed lunch from £5, by arrangement. Dinner available locally.

Closed: Never.

From Kingsbridge, A379 for Dartmouth. In Frogmore, right over bridge. Follow signs to East Prawle. On entering village, left by school. Continue to phone box & turn left. Right 200 yds on, & follow sign down very steep drive to house.

Sally & Peter Barber
Maelcombe House
East Prawle
Kingsbridge
Devon TQ7 2DE
Tel: 01548 511521
Fax: 01548 511501
E-mail: barber.maelcombe@talk21.com

Entry No: 112   **Map no: 2**

You can walk through the pretty garden, past seats strategically placed to soak up the sun, to your own entrance and private terrace just outside your bedroom door. The bedroom is large, with wooden floors, an extremely comfortable brass bed and pieces of Spanish pottery dotted around; there are biscuits on the tea tray for you. It's an immaculate, homely place, just above the rural town of Modbury and only three miles from the sea - the Ewens are friendly and easy company; their two spaniels will enjoy welcoming you. Generous breakfasts are served in the oak-beamed dining room. *Children over 10 welcome.*

Breakfast, served at a table by the sitting room's French windows, is a hearty affair with own free-range eggs and home-made marmalade and jam. The bright, spotless bedrooms have sofas and super bathrooms, one a double-sized shower and the other a luxuriously large corner bath. Scented roses and climbers flourish on the local stone walls of this pleasing barn conversion and you cross a primrose-banked stream to an old orchard; Petrina and Kevin, easy and friendly, harvest apples for cider which they sell at the local farmer's market.

Rooms: 1 double, en suite (shower); 1 twin/double, en suite (bath).

Price: £28-£32 p.p. Single supp. £5.

Meals: Breakfast times flexible. Excellent pub in village.

Closed: Christmas & New Year.

Rooms: 1 double, en suite (shower).

Price: £22.50 p.p. Single supp. £7.50.

Meals: Breakfast times flexible. Dinner available locally.

Closed: Christmas.

From M5, A38 for Plymouth, A384 for Totnes, then A381 for Kingsbridge; through Harbertonford, Halwell & The Mounts. 0.25 miles on, right for Grimpston Leigh. On left at end of lane.

A379 from Plymouth towards Modbury. On reaching Church St at top of hill, before Modbury, fork left at Palm Cross, then 1st right by school into Back St. Cottage 3rd on left, past village hall.

Petrina & Kevin Frost
Lower Grimpstonleigh
East Allington
Totnes, Devon TQ9 7QH
Tel: 01548 521258
Fax: 01548 521258
E-mail: grimpstonleigh@ukgateway.net
Web: www.grimpstonleigh.com

Maureen Ewen
Orchard Cottage
Palm Cross Green
Modbury
Devon PL21 0QZ
Tel: 01548 830633

Devon

Arrive before 5.30pm and you're offered tea and cakes; arrive later and it may be something stronger. Andrew and Janice, young and relaxed and full of zip, want you to enjoy their corner of softest Devon as much as they do. The long, beamed kitchen/dining room is colour-washed yellow; there's a fireplace at one end, and jade green, painted woodwork. A real candle chandelier hangs over the scrubbed pine table. Bedrooms, private and up a separate staircase, are fresh and vibrant - muslin or checked cotton curtains, bright blues, sunny yellows and views to Dartmoor and its ever-changing sky.

Rooms: 1 twin, 1 double, sharing private bathroom.

Price: From £20 p.p. Single supp. by arrangement.

Meals: Breakfast times flexible; packed lunch £5, by arrangement. Dinner available locally.

Closed: Never.

From A38, south on B3272 for South Brent. After petrol station & humpback bridge, immed. right for Diptford. There, follow road to left. House 100 yds on, on left. Parking opposite.

Andrew & Janice Gordon
Hedgehog House
Diptford
Totnes
Devon TQ9 7NZ
Tel: 01548 821115
E-mail: hedgehog.house@virgin.net

Entry No: 115   **Map no: 2**

Be pampered! Brenda and Alan have restored this large courtyard barn with confidence and panache. The mood is set by the sand-and-earth colours of Africa (their home for 15 years), coir carpeting, cane furniture, sunlight and space. Bedrooms are luxurious but not fussy: sensuous materials, fat pillows, an antique French brass bed, a new Lloyd loom chair – even bathrobes and hot water bottles. Brenda is an interior designer and runs courses from home. Stay for dinner - your hosts are friendly, dynamic and genuinely love meeting people. The food's good, and beaches are nearby.

Rooms: 1 twin, 1 double, both en suite (bath/shower); 1 double, en suite (shower).

Price: £30-£35 p.p. Single supp. by arrangement.

Meals: Breakfast times flexible; packed lunch by arrangement; dinner £22.

Closed: Occasionally.

Plymouth exit from A38, take A385 South Brent turn off. At 1st r'bout take S Brent turn. 2nd r'bout, take sign for Avon Down. At x-roads right to Harbourneford. Granary on left as you enter hamlet.

Brenda & Alan Willey
The Granary
Harbourneford
South Brent, Devon TQ10 9DT
Tel: 01364 73930
Fax: 01364 73930
E-mail: granary@ic24.net
Web: www.granary.ic24.net

Entry No: 116   **Map no: 2**

You come for the glory of the setting and the unpretentiousness of it all, not for huge luxury or sterile scrupulousness. The 17th-century longhouse has a gorgeous cobbled yard (laid by Judy), a bridge across to the island (shades of Monet) and goats. The family produces its own moorland water, all its fruit and vegetables and they even make cheese. The rooms are simple country-style, the attitude very 'green' (hedge-laying, stone wall-mending) and the conversation fascinating. You can wander through two acres of young woodland, too. *Minimum two nights stay.*

Rooms: 2 twins, 2 singles, all with basins, sharing 1 bathroom.

Price: £25 p.p. Children under 2 free, under 5 half price in parents' room.

Meals: Breakfast times flexible; evening meal occasionally available, £10; also good pub.

Closed: Christmas.

Leave A38 at 2nd Ashburton turning; follow signs for Princetown. After 2 miles, fork left to Holne. Pass inn & church on right. After 240 yds, right; after another 150 yds, left to Michelcombe. Over bridge & left. Farm 200 yds on right.

Judy Henderson
Dodbrooke Farm
Michelcombe
Holne
Devon TQ13 7SP
Tel: 01364 631461

Restoring Bagtor House has been a labour of love; the family feel a deep attachment to their "friendly, happy" house. The kitchen and the breakfast room are tangibly ancient - 14th-century - and the latter contains an inglenook fireplace and oak panelling. Among this ancient beauty - where dramatist John Ford was born - there is no stinting on comforts; bedrooms, beds and bathrooms are big. You breakfast on home-laid eggs and here, in a leafy, lush spot of the Dartmoor National Park, you can watch fat sheep graze, wander in the garden or walk to Bagtor, just behind the house.

Rooms: 1 double and 1 king-size (with extra single), both with private bathroom.

Price: From £25 p.p. Single supp. by arrangement.

Meals: Breakfast times flexible. Dinner available locally at excellent pubs.

Closed: Christmas.

From Bovey Tracy, B3387 for Widecombe in the Moor. After 2.5 miles, left for Ilsington. After 0.75 miles, fork right to Bickington. Next right to Bagtor. House on right 0.75 miles on.

Nigel & Sue Cookson
Bagtor House
Ilsington
Newton Abbot
Devon TQ13 9RT
Tel: 01364 661538
Fax: 01364 661538
E-mail: sawreysue@hotmail.com

Entry No: 117   Map no: 2

Entry No: 118   Map no: 2

Pure ancient magic! Ann is kind and helpful so, too, is William. She has restored this listed Devon longhouse with its Bronze Age foundation, keeping the shippon end (where her gentle giant shire horses live) and creating an engagingly chaotic haven for innumerable furry friends and the B&B guests she so enjoys. Simple but snug bedrooms, one with a four-poster. Their shire horses will pull you in a wagon to discover the secret lanes and picnic spots of the Dartmoor they know and love so deeply. The house is right by the Two Moors Way footpath. *Children over 10 by arrangement.*

Rooms: 1 four-poster, 1 twin, sharing private bathroom.

Price: £20-£25 p.p. No single supp.

Meals: Breakfast times flexible; packed lunch by arrangement. Dinner available locally.

Closed: Christmas.

From A38 2nd Ashburton turn towards Dartmeet & Princetown. In Poundsgate pass pub on left & 3rd signposted turning right towards Corndon. Straight over x-roads, 0.5 miles further, farm on left.

Ann & William Williams
Corndonford Farm
Poundsgate
Newton Abbot
Devon TQ13 7PP
Tel: 01364 631595

Entry No: 119   **Map no:** 2

A little green lane goes up beyond this cottage to the moor and Easdon Tor - this is a great place for walking and riding. A great place to relax, too. Liza and Hugh both have such an easy, calm manner. They are also vegetarian and dedicated users of organic produce, some of which is home-grown. The large, comfortable rooms in the cottage and the barn, which is also let for self-catering, have a successful mix of pictures, oriental rugs, books, plants, granite walls and some handsome Victorian finds, like the bath. *Children by arrangement.*

Rooms: 1 twin/double, en suite (bath). In barn, double with sofa bed and bunk, with private bathroom.

Price: £24 p.p. No single supp. Barn from £160-£270 p.w.

Meals: Breakfast, times flexible; supper £10, by arrangement.

Closed: Christmas & New Year. Barn open all year.

A38 SW from Exeter, A382 to Bovey Tracey. Left at 2nd r'bout in Bovey for Manaton. Through Manaton &, 2 miles on, right at Heatree Cross, signed Moretonhampstead. 0.5 miles on, cottage sign in hedge. Cottage up track, to right.

Liza & Hugh Dagnall
Easdon Cottage
Long Lane
Manaton
Devon TQ13 9XB
Tel: 01647 221389
Fax: 01647 221389

Entry No: 120   **Map no:** 2

Through the reigns of 25 monarchs, Gate House has stood solidly on this beautiful corner of Dartmoor. Unusually for a 15th-century hall house, a brightness finds its way inside, making everything gleam. You dine by candlelight off crisp white table linen and have your own sitting room with a vast, granite fireplace. There's a pool in the large, secluded gardens that overlooks woodlands and the moor. John and Sheila love having guests and take such care with everything that you will feel truly spoiled.

Rooms: 2 twins/doubles, both en suite (1 bath/shower, 1 shower); 1 twin/double, with private bathroom.

Price: £28 p.p. Single supp. £7.

Meals: Breakfast times flexible; packed lunch available; dinner, 4/5 courses, £16, by arrangement. B.Y.O wine.

Closed: Never.

A charming small terraced cottage full of 16th-century nooks, crannies and beams worth ducking. The setting is exquisite - the garden leads into fields of sheep and the Dartmoor Way goes through the town and the Two Moors Way skirts it. Shelagh, a lovely lady, gives guests their own sitting room with a fire - lit on cool nights; breakfasts, served in the cosy dining room, are fresh and free-range. Up the narrow stairs and into the flowery bedrooms - a small double and a tiny twin. A perfect house and hostess - and a perfect village, with its pubs, fine restaurant and delicatessen for picnickers.

Rooms: 1 double with private bathroom; 1 twin, en suite (shower).

Price: £20-£22 p.p. Single supp. £2.

Meals: Breakfast until 9.30am. Meals available locally.

Closed: Christmas & January.

25 yds off North Bovey's village green, down Lower Hill past village inn.

In Chagford leave church on left & take 1st right beyond The Globe Inn. House 150 yds on right in New Street.

John & Sheila Williams
The Gate House
North Bovey
Devon TQ13 8RB
Tel: 01647 440479
Fax: 01647 440479
E-mail: gatehouseondartmoor@talk21.com

Shelagh Weeden
Cyprian's Cot
47 New Street
Chagford
Devon TQ13 8BB
Tel: 01647 432256
E-mail: shelagh-weeden@lineone.net

Entry No: 121   **Map no:** 2

Entry No: 122   **Map no:** 2

This 14th-century, Grade II-listed, thatched Dartmoor longhouse, within Dartmoor National Park, was recently home of author Doris Lessing. Its history goes on and on... enchantingly pervasive in the architecture, interiors, gardens - and atmosphere. Sleep resplendent in four-posters in low-ceilinged, beamy rooms, all with views of the very English country garden, whence come copious fresh flowers. Your hosts are adventurously well-travelled and interesting. There's a petanque pitch outside and just one field away lies the moor with all its wild treasures.

Rooms: 3 four-posters, 2 en suite (1 shower, 1 bath), 1 with private shower room.

Price: £35 p.p. Single supp. £10.

Meals: Breakfast until 9.30am. Excellent places for dinner nearby.

Closed: Christmas & New Year.

From M5, A30 for Okehampton. After 23 miles exit to Belstone. Left, pass garage & immed. right opp. lay-by into lane. After 1 mile, left at T-junc. Gate on right after 50 yds.

John & Maureen Pakenham
Tor Down House
Belstone
Okehampton, Devon EX20 1QY
Tel: 01837 840731
Fax: 01837 840731
E-mail: info@tordownhouse.co.uk
Web: www.tordownhouse.co.uk

Entry No: 123   **Map no: 2**

Sonia and Geoffrey are wonderful, natural hosts; they have lived all over the world and are now tangibly happy in their converted mill in this corner of Devon. You can walk, ride or sail on or around nearby Roadford Reservoir or set off with Sonia, a keen landscape painter, to capture the natural beauty of your surroundings. You'll be folded in human warmth, offered a glass of wine in their large, homely kitchen and be given plenty of ideas for exploring the area. *Children by arrangement.*

Rooms: 1 twin, en suite (bath & shower) with sitting room. Camp beds in studio available, too.

Price: £25 p.p. Studio available when twin is full, £15 p.p. Variable rates for children.

Meals: Breakfast times flexible; light supper £10 (not on Sundays).

Closed: Christmas & New Year.

From Launceston-Holsworthy road (A388), east towards Ashwater. There, 1 mile north, at Thorney Cross, continue for 100 yds & take 1st drive to left, then right down driveway 70 yds from road.

Geoffrey & Sonia Archer
Renson Mill
Ashwater
Devon EX21 5ER
Tel: 01409 211665
Fax: 01409 211665
E-mail: soniaarcher@globalnet.co.uk

Entry No: 124   **Map no: 2**

Only 900 years old and still humming with life: there's a goat in love with a goose, a pony in the rambling gardens, dogs, cats, guinea fowl, rabbits and foxes. Sally-Anne is artistic, slightly zany and adventurous, as is her family. The farm is in the Domesday Book and is steeped in history; huge flagstone fireplaces, interesting contemporary art, books, pianos and wellies by the front door where you leave your stress on arrival. The BBC twice filmed here for *Down to Earth* - reinstating the place afterwards to its former glory. Not a road in sight, perfect quiet, sweeping views.

Rooms: 1 twin, 1 double, sharing bathroom.

Price: £25 p.p. Single occ. £30.

Meals: Breakfast times flexible. Dinner available nearby.

Closed: Christmas & New Year.

A30 to Okehampton. After 10 miles left exit into Cheriton Bishop, 2nd left between 2 cottages. Down & up hill. Road turns sharp left. Down lane; signed.

Sally-Anne Carter-Johnson
Higher Eggbeer Farm
Cheriton Bishop
Nr. Exeter
Devon EX6 6JQ
Tel: 01647 24427

Stewart & Jennie gave up working in London to take over the estate that has been in the family for 900 years. They look after the house (Georgian with Victorian façade) and 150 acres almost single-handedly. You'll find a real country home with history oozing from every stone, painting, piece of furniture and panelling. The large, newly-decorated guest room has padded headboards, piped covers and a big bathroom. The breakfast room is lined with ancient books; the snooker room has a grand piano and an open fire. Walk along the old carriage drive to Black Torrington or fish on the river which runs through the estate.

Rooms: 1 twin, en suite (bath).

Price: £26 p.p. Single supp. £4.50.

Meals: Breakfast times flexible. Dinner available locally.

Closed: Christmas & New Year.

From Okehampton, A386 towards Hatherleigh. There, left onto B3072 towards Holsworthy. After 4 miles, through Highampton, then right to Black Torrington. Left at Post Office. Entrance 750 yds on right.

Jenny & Stewart Coham-MacLaren
Coham Manor
Black Torrington
Beaworthy, Devon EX21 5HT
Tel: 01409 231514
Fax: 01409 231514
E-mail: maclaren.4@cwcom.net

Rolling fields and gentle hills stretch up to Dartmoor and there's hardly another house to be seen. Everything feels exactly right – fresh flowers, shiny silver, comfy sofas, lovely oak furniture. The bedrooms are just as good – white, crisp cotton duvets, soft chairs and books. The views are unbeatable and you are midway between Bideford and Holsworthy. The façade is Georgian, but the house's origins are 16th-century. Valerie loves gardening and is retrieving this pretty garden from its former ignored state. She is fun and delights in having guests. A great place to escape from it all. *Children over 12 welcome.*

Rooms: 1 king-size double, 1 twin, sharing private bathroom.

Price: £25 p.p. No single supp.

Meals: Breakfast times flexible; dinner £12.50, by arrangement.

Closed: Never.

From Holsworthy, A388 for Bideford. Through Milton Damerel & past Woodford Bridge Hotel on left, then right to Newton St. Petrock. 1 mile on, nr church, straight on signed Shebbear. House round bend in lane on left.

Mrs Valerie Lampen
The Old Rectory
Newton St. Petrock
Holsworthy, Devon EX22 7LR
Tel: 01409 281225
Fax: 01409 281225
E-mail: vlampen@netscapeonline.co.uk
Web: www.members.netscapeonline.co.uk/vlampen

Entry No: 127 **Map no: 2**

A winding, high-hedged Devon lane leads to Great Sloncombe - a working Dartmoor farm with milking cows and a pedigree Aberdeen Angus herd. There are few traces of its 13th-century origins - the house is listed - but there are pieces of old oak and granite everywhere, to which the Merchants have added their own antiques and old photographs. Doorways are tiny, bedrooms are country-style cosy - one has a pine four-poster - and all have views to meadows teeming with wildlife. Trudie, who is very involved with carriage driving, cooks dinners of home-grown meat and vegetables.

Rooms: 1 twin, 1 double, 1 four-poster, all en suite (shower).

Price: £23-£25 p.p. Single supp. by arrangement.

Meals: Breakfast times flexible; dinner £13.

Closed: Never.

From Bovey Tracey A382. After Moretonhampstead, look for signs to farm.

Trudie Merchant
Great Sloncombe Farm
Moretonhampstead
Devon TQ13 8QF
Tel: 01647 440595
Fax: 01647 440595
E-mail: hmerchant@sloncombe.freeserve.co.uk
Web: www.greatsloncombefarm.co.uk

Entry No: 128 **Map no: 2**

The bleat of a lost lamb was the only sound we heard at the 16th-century traditional Devon farmhouse. Ann and Richard - vastly talented and artistic - have worked in harmony to restore it all. Ann has laid brick paths, stencilled, stitched and painted with striking Jane Churchill colours; Richard, a restoration builder and carpenter, has renovated brass beds, made the dresser and uncovered everything of ancient beauty. The beds are so inviting that you can't resist the urge to collapse into them, and there's a garden room for breakfast.

Rooms: 1 double, en suite (shower); 1 twin, en suite (bath/shower).

Price: £25 p.p. Single supp. £5.

Meals: Breakfast times flexible; dinner, 2 courses, £12.50, by arrangement.

Closed: 20 December-5 January.

The Bradiford Valley is pretty and lush and runs down to glorious beaches. The deceptively big, creaky, comfortable 17th-century home is wrapped in the most lovely garden that stretches up the hill. Old rugs give a warm passage over slate floors, and chintz and pretty wallpapers add to the rural charm. One bathroom, with a huge bath under a long sloping ceiling, has views of a hilltop crowned with trees, the handsome main bedroom has wiggly walls and wicker furniture and there's a drying room downstairs for wet walkers' gear. Very nice, easy and unstuffy people. *Children over 12 welcome.*

Rooms: 2 doubles, 1 twin, all with basins, sharing bathroom and shower room.

Price: £17-£20 p.p. No single supp.

Meals: Breakfast until 9.30am. Good pubs nearby for dinner.

Closed: Christmas & New Year.

From A39, left into Bideford, round quay, passing old bridge on left. Follow signs to Torrington. 1.5 miles on, right at Crystal Centre, signed Buckland Brewer. 2.5 miles on, left, also signed. House on right, 0.5 miles on.

From Barnstaple, A361 towards Braunton. At 2nd set of lights, right signed Bradiford. Next T-junc., sharp left, over bridge, up hill for 50 yds, 2nd lane to right. House 1st on left.

Ann & Richard Dorsett
Beara Farmhouse
Buckland Brewer
Bideford
Devon EX39 5EH
Tel: 01237 451666

Jane & Tony Hare
Bradiford Cottage
Halls Mill Lane, Bradiford,
Barnstaple, Devon EX31 4DP
Tel: 01271 345039
Fax: 01271 345039
E-mail: tony@humesfarm.co.uk
Web: www.humesfarm.co.uk

Entry No: 129   **Map no:** 2

Entry No: 130   **Map no:** 2

The exterior is newly painted and Jackie is planning more improvements; the interior is as lovely as ever. The Coopers have unleashed their arty, bohemian taste and created a magnificent backdrop of colour for interesting artefacts, huge sofas and wood and slate. They are interesting people, green-leaning farmers who produce their own organic range of soups and sauces. Jackie's breakfasts - platters of fruits and meats *and* the full English - are quite something. Gorgeous bathrooms, large bedrooms and a heated outdoor pool - come for a wonderful, informal time.

Rooms: 2 king-size beds, 1 double, all en suite (bath/shower); 1 twin with basin and private jacuzzi bath.

Price: £40-£50 p.p. Supp. for one night £5 p.p. Children in same room, £10. Single supp. by arrangement.

Meals: Breakfast times flexible; dinner in summer, from £18-£25, by arrangement.

Closed: Christmas.

A3122 from Totness towards Dartmouth. Left at Forces Tavern, then follow signs to Cornworthy. At Tideford Cross, house opp. with wooden fence. Turn right then left into drive over cattle grid.

Jackie Cooper
Higher Tideford
Tideford Cross, Cornworthy
Totnes
Devon TQ9 7HL
Tel: 01803 712387
Fax: 01803 712388

Entry No: 131   **Map no: 3**

From a narrow decorative window you see a charming vignette of Devon: a winding country lane edged by fat hedgerows, the hillside dotted with sheep. The 18th-century former gamekeeper's cottage is folded into Devon's gentle green softness. Bedrooms are fresh and charming, the drawing and dining rooms formal and immaculate with fine furniture. Tim and Sally - gentle and new to B&B - serve tea and home-made cake on arrival; they used to run a clematis nursery and the terraced garden is lovely. An excellent pub and the sea are nearby; at night you can see the beam from Start Point lighthouse.

Rooms: 1 double, 1 twin/double, both en suite (shower); 1 double, en suite (bath).

Price: From £25 p.p. Single supp. by arrangement.

Meals: Breakfast 8.30-9.30am; packed lunch £5. Dinner available locally.

Closed: Christmas & January.

A381 from Totnes to Halwell, then A3122 towards Dartmouth. After Dartmouth Golf Club, right at sign to house & Blackawton. 0.5 miles before Blackawton, cottage on right.

Tim & Sally Adams
Woodside Cottage
Blackawton
Totnes, Devon TQ9 7BL
Tel: 01803 712375
Fax: 01803 712757
E-mail: woodside-cottage@lineone.net
Web: www.woodside-cottage-devon.co.uk

Entry No: 132   **Map no: 3**

Yachts bob at anchor on the sparkling Dart estuary below this 18th-century home, renamed The White House by American soldiers during World War II. The maritime theme plays throughout, with pebble collections and a flotilla of model ships. In one of the bright, cheerful, flower-filled bedrooms you can gaze snugly down at the Dart from the warmth of your double bed. You have your own sitting/breakfast room with an open fire, comfortable chairs and French windows opening onto the terrace. The views are magical and Hugh and Jill revel in having guests. *Children by arrangement.*

Rooms: 2 doubles, 1 en suite (bath & shower), 1 with private bathroom.

Price: £30-£32.50 p.p. Single occ. £35-£45.

Meals: Breakfast 8-9am. Dinner available locally.

Closed: Christmas.

Coming downhill into Dittisham, sharp right immed. before Red Lion Inn. Along The Level, up narrow hill & house entrance opposite at junc. of Manor St & Rectory Lane.

Hugh & Jill Treseder
The White House
Manor Street
Dittisham
Devon TQ6 0EX
Tel: 01803 722355
Fax: 01803 722355

The view from Nonsuch is staggering. From the conservatory or the lovely terraced garden you watch the ever-changing scene of boats sailing up and down the estuary. The delights of Kingswear and Dartmouth are linked by a little ferry that will take you and your car across the water in a matter of minutes. But Nonsuch does not rest on its natural laurels; everything about it is captivating. The guests' sitting room has its own balcony, there are great fresh breakfasts, large and extremely comfortable bedrooms, top quality bathrooms and views and more views. *Children over 10 welcome.*

Rooms: 5 twins/doubles, 2 en suite (bath), 1 with private bathroom, 2 en suite (shower).

Price: From £40 p.p. Single supp. by arrangement. Special winter breaks available.

Meals: Breakfast 8.30-9.30am; dinner, 3 courses, £21.50, cheese course, £3.50.

Closed: Never.

2 miles before Brixham on A3022, take A379. After r'bout, fork left (B3205) downhill, through woods, left up Higher Contour Rd, down Ridley Hill. Nonsuch at hairpin-bend.

Christopher Noble
Nonsuch House
Church Hill, Kingswear,
Dartmouth, Devon TQ6 0BX
Tel: 01803 752829
Fax: 01803 752357
E-mail: enquiries@nonsuch-house.co.uk
Web: www.nonsuch-house.co.uk

Devon

William of Orange sailed into England in November 1688 and is said to have held his first parliament here. The ancient, rambling, thatched house has blossomed with the attention to detail that you'd expect from two designers. Wallpapers, napkins, *toile de Jouy* - they're all Carole's own design; fresh whites and plain, painted wood are the perfect backdrop for the many pretty touches. Cooked breakfast, along with home-made marmalade, fruits and yogurt, is served on pretty china. Bedrooms are supremely comfortable - one with a cast-iron fireplace and hand-stencilled paper and the garden, with many enchanting corners, is a joy.

Rooms: 1 twin/super king-size, 1 double, both with private bathroom. 1 single sometimes available.

Price: From £25 p.p. No single supp.

Meals: Breakfast times flexible. Dinner available locally.

Closed: Occasionally.

From Totnes, A385 Paignton road. 2 miles on, look for South Hams Motors on right. Turn right. House 1st on right. Just past house to parking area on right.

Carole & Harry Grimley
Parliament House
Longcombe
Totnes
Devon TQ9 6PR
Tel: 01803 840288

Entry No: 135   **Map no: 3**

Your generous host has given over the best room in the house - your bedroom opens onto a large terrace high above the spectacular garden: 11 wondrous acres of rhododendron, magnolia, fuchsia, a lily-strewn pond, lawns and paths that dip and rise through wild flower areas. Richard is a gifted gardener and the archetypal gardener's modesty and calm have penetrated to the house itself. It is uncluttered, serene and comfortable. There's a sheltered corner for breakfasts and you are welcome to find a spot to read or simply sit and absorb the tranquillity.

Rooms: 1 twin, en suite (bath).

Price: £25 p.p. Single supp. £5.

Meals: Breakfast times flexible. Excellent pub in village for dinner.

Closed: Never.

From Totnes follow signs to Kingsbridge (A381) for 1 mile. Left, signed Ashprington. Into village then left by pub (Dead End sign). House 0.25 miles on right.

Richard Pitts
Avenue Cottage
Ashprington
Totnes
Devon TQ9 7UT
Tel: 01803 732769
Fax: 01803 732769

Entry No: 136   **Map no: 3**

You can feel that this elegant, Devon farmhouse (part 14th century) has always been a happy family home. Sarah is capable and jolly and she and husband Michael clearly enjoy guests. The two bedrooms are large - the linen has that lovely, fresh, garden-dried smell - and each has a tray with pretty china, two types of tea, coffee and local spring water. By the bed you'll find a thoughtful selection of bedtime reading but sleep comes too easily for you to get through much of it. There's a pond, orchard and hens that give breakfast eggs and excellent food in the pub just up the road.

Rooms: 1 king-size, en suite (bath/shower); 1 twin with private bathroom.

Price: £24-£26 p.p.

Meals: Breakfast until 9.30am; packed lunch £3-£4; dinner £12-£15, both by arrangement.

Closed: Christmas.

From Newton Abbot, A381, signed Totnes. After approx. 2.5 miles, right for Broadhempston. There, village sign faces you as lane turns sharp right. Down hill & 2nd left. Pass pub on right & left 170 yds on into courtyard.

Sarah Clapp
Manor Farm
Broadhempston
Nr. Totnes
Devon TQ9 6BD
Tel: 01803 813260
Fax: 01803 813260
E-mail: clappfamily@members.shines.net

Entry No: 137   **Map no:** 3

Clough Williams-Ellis (of Portmeirion) designed this elegant country house, set in five acres of wooded gardens in the Dartmoor National Park; test his genius yourself. It works: the spaces, the light and the soft, warm colours, the all-embracing atmosphere of elegant homeliness. There's comfort at every turn, antiques and heirlooms, and chats with well-travelled Madeleine and Mike are full of fun and a broad perspective. Enjoy the views of the Devon hills from the enchanting gardens and play tennis on the all-weather court.

Rooms: 1 twin/double with private bathroom; 1 double with private shower.

Price: From £25 p.p. Single supp. by arrangement.

Meals: Breakfast times flexible. Dinner available locally.

Closed: Never.

A38 west to Plymouth, A382 turnoff, & 3rd turning off r'bout, signed Bickington. There, right at junc. (to Plymouth), right again (to Sigford/Widecombe). Over top of A38. Penpark 1st entrance on right.

Madeleine & Michael Gregson
Penpark
Bickington
Newton Abbot, Devon TQ12 6LH
Tel: 01626 821314
Fax: 01626 821101
E-mail: gregson.penpark@ukgateway.net
Web: www.penpark.co.uk

Entry No: 138   **Map no:** 3

Devon

The seductive charm of this hideaway miner's cottage will soothe even the most stressed souls. At the end of a long track criss-crossed by bridal paths, you find a lush oasis carved out of woodland. Mary, gently-spoken, loves to see guests unwind; both she and Dick have a finely-judged sense of humour. There's a pretty American patchwork quilt on the brass double bed and a small bathroom off it (this also leads to a twin room). The sound of the river (they have their own water supply) and birdsong fill each room. Local sausages and bacon for breakfast, excellent dinners, easy company, a pool and 12 acres to explore – you'll want to return.

Rooms: 1 double en suite (bath/shower), 1 further twin.

Price: From £22 p.p.

Meals: Breakfast times flexible; supper £10, by arrangement. B.Y.O. wine.

Closed: Never.

From A38, A382 at Drumbridges for Newton Abbot. 4th left at r'bout for Bickington. There, down hill & past garage on left. Right for Haytor. Under bridge, 1st left & down long, bumpy track, past thatched cottage to house.

Mrs Mary Lloyd-Williams
Hooks Cottage
Bickington
Nr. Ashburton
Devon TQ12 6JS
Tel: 01626 821312
E-mail: hookscottage@yahoo.com

Entry No: 139　　　**Map no: 3**

You go down a very long lane and, more than likely, will wonder if you have lost your way. But what reward for your adventurousness! Mediterranean, surprising, bright, fresh, vibrant - Jellicoe's is an exceptional find. Michael is widely-travelled, he cooks all kinds of food with passion and only copper pots and pans separate the master at work in his kitchen from your dining area; his three-course meals must be the best value food in this book. Bedrooms are exceptional with polished wooden floors and whitewashed walls and bathrooms are rag-rolled and fluorescent (lime green, for example). Come for restorative peace and excellent value.

Rooms: 2 doubles, en suite (shower); 1 twin/family room, en suite (bath).

Price: £22 p.p. No single supp.

Meals: Breakfast 7.30-9.30am. Packed lunch £2.50; dinner, 3 courses, £12.

Closed: Rarely. Please check.

Leave A396 at Bickleigh, right for Crediton, then immediate right again for Cadeleigh. Through Cadeleigh. Left at 'Post Box Cross', & right signed Upham. House 2nd on left.

Michael Jellicoe
Jellicoe's, Higher Holn
Upham, Cheriton Fitzpaine
Crediton, Devon EX17 4HN
Tel: 01363 866165
Fax: 01363 866165
E-mail: enquiries@jellicoes.co.uk
Web: www.jellicoes.co.uk

Entry No: 140　　　**Map no: 3**

Fay puts masses of thought into looking after her guests. Large panelled bedrooms have lots of little extras - hairdryers, sewing kits, mints, bathrobes, stationery - and floral curtains and matching duvets. The Downs' great love in life is breeding and racing horses and there are 180 acres of organic farm, parkland and views around the 300 year-old house. Breakfast, with home-made marmalade and fresh fruit, is served in the oak-panelled dining room which has a conservatory leading from it... look for the recently revealed inscription dated 1760. Within a short walk is a lovely lake for fishing.

Rooms: 1 twin, 1 double, both en suite (shower); 1 double, en suite (bath). Another bath & shower available.

Price: £20-£25 p.p. Single supp. £2.

Meals: Breakfast times flexible. Great pubs within 2 miles.

Closed: Christmas.

M5, junc. 28, head for Cullompton, then left for Broadclyst. Through town & left at Sports Centre sign. Right at T-junc. Cross over m-way bridge. Next left (signed Plymtree). House next lane on left.

Fay Down
Upton House
Cullompton
Devon EX15 1RA
Tel: 01884 33097
Fax: 01884 33097

Entry No: 141   Map no: 3

The top of a steep hill seems an odd place for a coaching inn – the horses must have toiled. Now reap the panoramic rewards over the Exe valley. High ceilings and large windows bring light and space to this unpretentious family house. Barbara is an efficient, kind, no fuss hostess. Dining room and drawing room have a subdued grandness. One flowery bedroom has a Victorian four-poster; another on the ground floor opens onto the gardens. A good place for breaking a journey or for those on business in Tiverton. *Children over 12 welcome.*

Rooms: 1 double, en suite (shower); 1 four-poster with private bathroom/shower; 1 twin with private bathroom (bath/shower).

Price: From £22 p.p. Single occ. £25.

Meals: Breakfast until 9am; dinner, 3 courses, £12.50, by arrangement.

Closed: Never.

At junction 27 (M5), A361 for approx. 4.5 miles. Turn off at Gornway Cross, for Grand Western Canal. At Canal Hill, 1st right into Exeter Hill. House at top on left.

Barbara Pugsley
Hornhill
Exeter Hill
Tiverton, Devon EX16 4PL
Tel: 01884 253352
Fax: 01884 253352
E-mail: hornhill@tinyworld.co.uk
Web: www.hornhill-farmhouse.co.uk

Entry No: 142   Map no: 3

This Bampton-stoned, slate-roofed house was once the town mill - it dates back to the early 1600s. The expected beams, inglenook fireplaces and stream are still here, along with a fully co-ordinated look. The bedrooms are cosy, not large, and you may find a teddy on your bed. Kathy puts a lot of thought into creating a memorable breakfast and uses as much local, organic and home-grown produce as she can. The garden slopes down to the River Batherm and you are welcome to fish for trout. *Children over 12 welcome.*

Rooms: 1 four-poster, 1 king-size double, 1 twin, all en suite (shower).

Price: £22-£25 p.p. £147 p.p. p.w.

Meals: Breakfast times flexible. Dinner available locally.

Closed: Never.

From Tiverton, A396/B3227 to Bampton. There, right just before bridge over river. Cream house is opposite.

Chris & Kathy Ayres
Manor Mill House
Bampton
Devon EX16 9LP
Tel: 01398 332211
Fax: 01398 332009
E-mail: stay@manormill.demon.co.uk
Web: www.manormill.demon.co.uk

Entry No: 143   **Map no: 3**

"An Irish attitude to life dominates this house," says Charlotte – that means friends, family and guests mingle naturally. There's plenty of company and activity (friendly family, polo ponies – tuition available – fishing, the garden to explore) or enjoy the privacy of your room. Sit and catch the morning sun in the dining room. Bedrooms have handsome, traditional furniture, fat pillows, new mattresses, cotton linen and a tray with whisky decanter, mineral water and biscuits. For breakfast, home-reared organic sausages and bacon, and home-grown melon in season. Delicious. Your horse is welcome, too. *Children over six welcome.*

Rooms: 1 double, 1 twin, both en suite (bath). In the wing, an adjoining double and twin, en suite (bath), let only to members of same party.

Price: £20-£35 p.p. Single supp. £10.

Meals: Breakfast until 9.30am; picnic lunch £15; dinner £25.

Closed: Christmas & New Year.

From M5, junc. 26 or 27, A38 towards Exeter for 6 miles, then left to Culmstock. There, over bridge, 1st right into Silver St. Last drive on right.

Roger & Charlotte Horne
Woodhayne Barton
Culmstock
Devon EX15 3JG
Tel: 01884 840708
Fax: 01884 841479
E-mail: rogercharlotte@hornewoodhayne.demon.co.uk
Web: www.hornewoodhayne.demon.co.uk

Entry No: 144   **Map no: 3**

The Buxtons look after hundreds of guests each year - lots of them stopping off en route to Cornwall. They enjoy what they do and have it down to a fine art. They love their bit of Devon surrounded by the Blackdown Hills. The kitchen is vast, with terracotta tiles and an Aga which Rosalind uses to produce her generous Devon farmhouse breakfasts. The bedrooms are bright and airy. Fresh flowers and lovely views and a chance to sample the many French wines which Bob imports.

Rooms: 1 family (for 4), 1 double, 1 twin, all en suite (shower).

Price: From £20 p.p.

Meals: Breakfast 8.30am, or by arrangement. Dinner from £12.

Closed: Christmas.

Unwind in a home that perfectly matches its owners: friendly, gentle, charming. This old cottage has had many facelifts over the years, hence the delightfully varying ceiling heights. Nurse-turned-reflexologist Joanna wants you to feel at home – play the piano, browse through the family's books (lots of Dickens), try her home-made elderflower cordial. Your creamy coloured bedroom has pine furniture and watercolours by Joanna's father; its garden-to-hillside views are super and there's a Victorian tub in your small bathroom. This is a designated AONB full of wildlife, especially birds. Your sleep should be deep.

Rooms: 1 double with basin, private bath & separate wc.

Price: £20 p.p. Single supp £5.

Meals: Breakfast times flexible; packed lunch £3. Dinner available locally.

Closed: Christmas & New Year.

At M5 junc. 25 A358 to Ilminster then A303 towards Honiton. After A30 merges from left, farm is 0.5 miles ahead on right (directly off A30).

From junc. 30 off M5, A3052 to Sidmouth through Newton Poppleford. Take 1st left to Harpford.

Rosalind & Bob Buxton
Courtmoor Farm
Upottery
Nr. Honiton
Devon EX14 9QA
Tel: 01404 861565
E-mail: courtmoor.farm@btinternet.com
Web: www.btinternet.com/~courtmoor.farm

Hendrik & Joanna Vollers
Otter House
Harpford
Nr Sidmouth
Devon EX10 0NH
Tel: 01395 568330
E-mail: jovollers@btinternet.com

Entry No: 145   **Map no:** 3

Entry No: 146   **Map no:** 3

The round-headed oak door frame in the back bedroom hints at this Grade II-listed farmhouse's 16th-century origins – James will tell you all about its history. Orchards, paddocks and ponds outside; homeliness and comfort in. You'll want for nothing with Sîan (once a nurse) your attentive yet unobtrusive hostess. Bedrooms are whitewashed and simple, with charming old windows and deep sills. The odd beam to be ducked, a soppy black Lab to be fussed over... a delightful place. Only eight miles from Exeter and a dream for walkers, too. *Children by arrangement.*

Rooms: 1 double, en suite (bath); 1 twin, en suite (shower); 1 double with private bath.

Price: £23-£26 p.p. Single supp. £5.

Meals: Breakfast until 9.30am; packed lunch £3. Dinner available locally.

Closed: Never.

From your free-standing bath you can look straight onto the church; a fine view from a fine bathroom. Floors slope and the peace hums. The house is part of the Combe estate (Grade II*) with magnificent thatch and cruck beams, a 1600 date-stone and a 17th-century extension. It's full of colour and imagination, flowers and music, and the Hills - artistic, fun and hugely welcoming - will look after you with the same attention to detail that was lavished on the renovation of the house. The drawing room is very pretty, with shutters and leaded windows.

Rooms: 1 double, 1 twin, sharing bathroom.

Price: £25 p.p. No single supp.

Meals: Breakfast times flexible; supper, £15, by arrangement.

Closed: Christmas.

From A30 B3180 for Exmouth. 0.75 miles on, right at x-roads signed Marsh Green. House 1st on left on entering village.

A30 through Honiton, & follow signs to Gittisham. In village, right over bridge; large house, last on left.

Mr & Mrs J.B. Wroe
Lower Marsh Farm
Marsh Green
Exeter
Devon EX5 2EX
Tel: 01404 822432
Fax: 01404 823330
E-mail: lowermarshfarm@talk21.com

Andrew & Meriel Hill
Town House
Gittisham
Honiton
Devon EX14 3AJ
Tel: 01404 851041
Fax: 01404 851289

Entry No: 147　　　**Map no: 3**

Entry No: 148　　　**Map no: 3**

Ian, a solicitor, has recently retired to concentrate on looking after his prize-winning Berkshire pigs and guests - he likes both equally! He and Maggie will give you the full Devon B&B experience - home-reared, additive-free sausages and bacon with newly-baked bread for breakfast. 'Combe' means valley and the downstairs bedroom with pink-flowered duvet and valance has a heart-healing view up the valley - it also has its own living room. Upstairs there is another pretty double room, plus a family suite of two adjoining rooms. Both enjoy the same lovely views and there is a large sitting and dining room, too.

Rooms: 1 twin, 1 double, 1 family suite, all en suite (bath/shower). Self-catering option for the suite (kitchen attached). Two self-catering barns.

Price: £22-£25 p.p. Single supp. £5.

Meals: Breakfast times flexible; packed lunch £3; dinner £12.50.

Closed: Never.

From Honiton High St, turn into New St by Lloyds Bank. At mini-r'bout, left, then 1st right. Up hill to golf course & on towards Colyton. 3rd left signed Slade. Farm in bottom of valley on right.

Maggie Todd
Smallicombe Farm
Northleigh
Colyton, Devon EX24 6BU
Tel: 01404 831310
Fax: 01404 831431
E-mail: maggie_todd@yahoo.com
Web: www.smallicombe.com

Entry No: 149   **Map no: 3**

After a lot of travelling, these ex-TV producers had a clear vision of what made a perfect place to stay: privacy, stylish comfort and peace in stunning surroundings. Here you have it. Each bedroom is self-contained and has a private 'deck' dotted with pots; the woodland views are glorious. No expense has been spared: chrome shower heads are the size of dinner plates, the beds new and firm, the linen luxurious. They have used local craftsmen and much local material in the renovation. Judging by Frank's take on Jamie Oliver's nut torte, his breakfasts will be excellent. Valley, woodland and bluebell walks start from your terrace.

Rooms: 3 king-size, en suite (shower).

Price: £32.50 p.p. 10% discount for 3 or more nights.

Meals: Breakfast times flexible; packed lunch from £7.50. Restaurants in Honiton, 3 miles away.

Closed: Christmas.

Offwell is 3 miles from Honiton & signed off A35 Honiton-Axminster road. In centre of village, at church, go downhill. Farm 0.5 miles on.

Frank & Carol Hayes
West Colwell Farm
Offwell
Honiton, Devon EX14 9SL
Tel: 01404 831130
Fax: 01404 831769
E-mail: stay@westcolwell.co.uk
Web: www.westcolwell.co.uk

Entry No: 150   **Map no: 3**

Devon

You come for the gardens and for the food: organic and local, traditional and delicious. Up to 16 can eat at separate tables. Outside, nine acres with an orchard of damson and cherry trees; then ghinkos, meta sequoia, magnolia, jacaranda and Chinese shrubs. There are even ponds and a bamboo valley, and sheep, ponies, geese and free-range hens. The house is mainly Georgian but parts date back to 1332 and, set on a gentle southern slope, the views are wonderful. Sparkling cottage suites have stripped pine, Laura Ashley-style linen and curtains and oak kitchens.

Rooms: 1 twin/double, en suite (bath). Two cottage suites available.

Price: £28-£30 p.p. Single supp. £3.50-£5 in high season. Gourmet packages available for special occasions.

Meals: Breakfast until 8.45am; dinner, inc. aperitif, £19.50.

Closed: Mid-November-Christmas Eve; 3 January-12 February

From Chard, A30 Honiton rd for 0.25 miles. At top of hill fork left. After 3 miles, right after animal sanctuary. Follow signs for Furley. At T-junc., left to Ford, then bear right. On left.

Robert & Pat Spencer
Goodmans House
Furley
Membury
Devon EX13 7TU
Tel: 01404 881690

Entry No: 151   Map no: 3

A self-contained hideaway for nature lovers - with terrific views. At last Katrina has the opportunity to do B&B, and has converted the stone and slate "garden shed" into a comfortable two-bed cottage with sitting room for guests. Eat the best bacon and eggs for breakfast – all locally produced – on your private patio with those glorious views. Perfect as a couple's hideaway or for families: Katrina has three children of her own and offers babysitting and high tea. The Axe Valley is a designated AONB and the walks are all you'd expect them to be.

Rooms: 1 double, 1 twin sharing bathroom.

Price: £22.50 p.p

Meals: Breakfast times flexible; packed lunch £3; children's high tea £3. Dinner available locally.

Closed: Never.

A358 from Chard to Axminster. Through Tytherleigh & 1st right to Alston. Through village & bear left towards Holy City. House down 4th drive on left.

Katrina Felgate
Beaconhill Cottage
Chardstock, Axminster
Devon EX13 7LB
Tel: 01460 220065
Fax: 01460 220065
E-mail: katrina_felgate@btinternet.com
Web: www.beaconhillcottage.co.uk

Entry No: 152   Map no: 3

Years of travel and naval lifestyle lie behind the Normans' meticulous and old-fashioned hospitality; they have settled happily here in this large 1920s house. Rooms are thoroughly comfortable and the dining room refurbished in keeping with the period of the house; when the weather is fine you can enjoy breakfast on the balcony. You can see clear across Lyme Bay and along the Dorset coast for 30 miles - it is spectacular. Two of the guest rooms are large with wonderful coastal views, the third more cottagey; all have chairs, a writing desk and fresh flowers. *Children over eight welcome.*

Rooms: 1 family, 2 twins, all en suite (bath).

Price: £22-£27 p.p. Single occ. £33-£40.

Meals: Breakfast until 9am; supper tray on first night, £9.50, by arrangement.

Closed: Mid-November-early March.

On A3052 to Lyme, house 1st left after 'Welcome to Lyme' sign on right. From Lyme up Sidmouth Rd, past Morgan's Grave & Somers Rd, & enter 1st drive on right, opp. junc. sign.

Tony & Vicky Norman
The Red House
Sidmouth Road
Lyme Regis
Dorset DT7 3ES
Tel: 01297 442055
Fax: 01297 442055
E-mail: red.house@virgin.net

Entry No: 153   **Map no: 3**

What stunning views! Catch them from the bedrooms, the gardens, the patio (a summer breakfast spot). This handsome '50's house stands in a glorious position overlooking the sea and National Trust land - up and away from the summer crowds. Jane and Adrian, good company and well-travelled, have created a hugely comfortable home and B&B. Polished furniture and books in the main rooms, connected by an arch; bedrooms with colour-washed walls, pretty fabrics and dressing-gowns. You are a five-minute walk from Seatown beach and the Anchor Inn. *Children over eight welcome.*

Rooms: 1 double, with private bathroom; 1 twin, en suite (shower). Further single available let only to members of the same party.

Price: £25 p.p. Single supp. £5.

Meals: Breakfast 7.30-9am; packed lunch, £4.50; dinner, £15, by prior arrangement.

Closed: Christmas & New Year.

Into Chideock on A35, take Bridport/Honiton road. Left at sign to Seatown, then right fork. On reaching top of hill take access road on right hand side. House signed on right.

Jane & Adrian Tamone
Seahill House
Seahill Lane, Seatown
Chideock, Dorset DT6 6JT
Tel: 01297 489801
Fax: 01297 489526
E-mail: jane@seahill.co.uk
Web: www.seahill.co.uk

Entry No: 154   **Map no: 3**

The Royal Commission included this house in its inventory on Historical Monuments in England. Dorset, with its softly-folding hills and leafy lanes, is the perfect backdrop for the listed, 17th-century house. There's stacks of atmosphere – original beams, flagstones, window seats, numerous family treasures, books and pictures. The bedrooms have been generously furnished with fine pieces as has the guests' own sitting room. There is a lovely garden, an orchard leading to a stream and the sea is 1 mile away. Mrs Tennant is a quiet, thoughtful hostess.

Rooms: 1 double with private bathroom; 1 twin sharing bathroom, let only to members of same party.

Price: £35 p.p. 3 nights or more, £30 p.p. Single supp. by arrangement.

Meals: Breakfast times flexible. Many pubs & restaurants nearby.

Closed: Christmas & New Year.

From Bridport, A35 into Chideock. Right at church. 0.75 miles up 'No Through Road' to T-junc. Turn right, house 7th on right (thatched with 2 porches). Drive to end of house, through gate to car park.

Mrs M. Tennant
Champ's Land
Brighthay Lane
North Chideock, nr. Bridport
Dorset DT6 6JZ
Tel: 01297 489314

Entry No: 155   **Map no: 3**

In the parlour, deep sofas pulled up to the woodburner and piles of magazines urge you to rest. This is a thatched dream surrounded by 80 acres of bio-dynamic farmland on which the Bells graze Aberdeen Angus cattle, Portland sheep and Tamworth Pigs (they supply Nigella Lawson, no less). Two large guest rooms have fluffy duvets, comfy armchairs and views of Golden Cap – the South Coast's highest point – so-called because the sun illuminates its peak as it rises over the sea. Beaches nearby and wildlife and wildflowers all around. *Children and horses by arrangement.*

Rooms: 2 large doubles & 1 single, all sharing bathroom (bath and hand-shower)

Price: £50p.p. Single supp. £50.

Meals: Breakfast flexible; hampers and packed lunch from £15; dinner, 3 courses, from £20.

Closed: Occasionally.

Directions given at time of booking.

Denise & Ian Bell
Shedbush Farm
Muddy Ford Lane, Stanton St. Gabriel
Lyme Regis
Dorset DT6 6DR
Tel: 01297 489304
Fax: 01297 489531
E-mail: heritageprime@aol.com

Entry No: 156   **Map no: 3**

Sydney and Jayne couldn't be nicer and they share a gift for unwinding stressed souls. Here are 10 acres of orchard, valley and wooded hills, wrapped in peace and quiet and, inside, 17th-century stone walls, low-beamed ceilings and a warm French flair. Bedrooms have antique French beds, bold colours and crisp linen; in the sitting room are books, an open fire and soft, deep chairs. Jayne makes compotes from the orchard fruit; you'll see them at breakfast with cured ham, *pain au chocolat* and American pancakes. Cliff walks, beaches and fields are yours, too.

Rooms: 1 twin, 3 doubles, all en suite (bath).

Price: £32.50-£40 p.p. Single occ. (weekdays only), £15 off room price.

Meals: Breakfast 8.45-9.30am; dinner, 3 courses, £17.50; hot supper tray for late arrivals, £13.50.

Closed: October, Christmas & New Year.

From Dorchester A35 towards Bridport. After 13 miles 2nd road signed left to Shipton Gorge & Burton Bradstock. 1st left to farmhouse.

Sydney & Jayne Davies
Innsacre Farmhouse
Shipton Gorge
Nr. Bridport
Dorset DT6 4LJ
Tel: 01308 456137
Fax: 01308 456137
E-mail: innsacre.farmhouse@btinternet

Entry No: 157   **Map no:** 3

Stand on the cowslip and orchid-strewn ramparts of Eggardon's hill fort and you gaze across a valley to this enchantingly secluded farmhouse. The house is set in a maze of paths through ancient wildflower meadows and medieval woodland. Follow the sleepy flower-decked lanes to the former shooting lodge with its enormous flagstones, stripped floors, chunky studded doors and exposed beams. The tranquillity of the bedrooms complements Rosie's vibrant paintings. Explore the enchanting secret valleys and bumpety hills of West Dorset or the spectacular Heritage coast.

Rooms: 1 twin, en suite (bath); 1 double/family, en suite (bath/shower).

Price: From £22.50 p.p.

Meals: Breakfast times flexible. Award-winning pubs within short drive.

Closed: Occasionally.

On A37, then A356 from Dorchester, left at 1st sign for Toller Porcorum. Through village & up hill for approx. 1 mile. At tiny x-roads, right signed Powerstock, under r'way bridge. Track to farm 0.5 miles on left, opp. unmarked lane. House at end, on left.

Rosie & Roger Britton
Grays Farmhouse
Toller Porcorum
Dorchester
Dorset DT2 0EJ
Tel: 01308 485574
E-mail: rosieroger@freenetname.co.uk
Web: www.farmhousebnb.co.uk

Entry No: 158   **Map no:** 3

You are deeply in Hardy Country here; the bedrooms are traditionally pretty and beamy with fresh flowers everywhere. There is an inglenook fireplace in the dining room with log fires that are coaxed into flame at the faintest hint of cold. Anita and André have travelled widely and Anita is very knowledgeable about health food; she loves this work and can produce almost anything you want for breakfast. There is a small sitting area in the dining room if you want to be private, with ample books, or a very pretty garden to sit in.

Rooms: 1 twin, 1 double, both en suite (bath); 2 singles, sharing bathroom. Cot bed & extra bed available on request.

Price: £25 p.p. Single £18 p.p.

Meals: Breakfast 8-9.30am. Dinner from £14 by special request.

Closed: 20 December-3 January.

From Holywell Cross (midway between Yeovil & Dorchester on A37) turn towards Batcombe; 50 yds on, left into lane to Chetnole. On for 0.75 miles. House on right.

André & Anita Millorit
Brambles
Woolcombe
Melbury Bubb, nr. Dorchester
Dorset DT2 0NJ
Tel: 01935 83672

Entry No: 159   **Map no: 3**

Jorgen and Anthony fled London for Wessex peace. Their refuge is this imposing, hydrangea-clad mock Gothic house - built by the Lord of the Manor for a vicar son - where excellent food and a striking mixture of décor dramatically blend east and west. At weekends, a chef from an acclaimed local restaurant prepares dinner. The open, light drawing room is a melange of sofas, oriental antiques and heavy, traditional curtains. Upstairs, design is at its showiest in the Chinese room where half-tester bed and furniture are black and gold lacquer. *Children over five welcome.*

Rooms: 3 twins, 3 doubles, 1 single, all en suite (bath/shower).

Price: £27-£48 p.p. Single occ. £37-£60.

Meals: Breakfast until 10am; dinner, £17.90-£23.50, Fri & Sat only.

Closed: January.

From Sherborne A30 to Milborne Port. House 2nd on right on entering village.

Mr Anthony Ma & Jorgen Kunath
The Old Vicarage
Milborne Port
Sherborne
Dorset DT9 5AT
Tel: 01963 251117
Fax: 01963 251515

Entry No: 160   **Map no: 3**

The Benjamins worked in the States and have imported the country's high standard of B&B. Bedrooms are more 'le grand luxe' than cottagey and the beds are big and of the finest quality; the four-poster has steps up to it. Lovely *toile de Jouy* curtains throughout and a feeling of opulence. State of the art bathroom fittings, power showers (of course) and generous, fluffy towels. The garden was professionally designed and there is much of interest. Sylvia's other passion is antiques - you can buy some of her finds if you wish - and they run bridge, art and pampering weekends.

Rooms: 4 doubles, 2 twins, all en suite. Studio: foldaway double, campbeds, cot, kitchenette & shower room, suitable for families.

Price: £32.50-£42.50 p.p. Single supp. £10. Studio from £65-£75 for 2; extra beds £15 each.

Meals: Breakfast times flexible. Dinner available locally.

Closed: Never.

From Sherborne follow signs to A3030, then to Alweston, 2 miles on. There, past Post Office on right, "P" for parking sign on left, & next left into Munden Lane. House behind Oxford Bakery.

Sylvia & Joe Benjamin
Munden House
Alweston
Sherborne, Dorset DT9 5HU
Tel: 01963 23150
Fax: 01963 23153
E-mail: sylvia@mundenhouse.demon.co.uk
Web: www.mundenhouse.demon.co.uk

Entry No: 161   **Map no:** 3

Breakfast by the log fire in the elegant dining room in winter; you'll enjoy a memorable feast of free-range eggs, home-made jams and marmalades. There is a walled half-acre garden and herbaceous border (Tia's passion). All rooms are beautifully decorated - lovely prints, many lamps - and have stunning views. After a day out or a good walk, sit beside the fire with a pile of their books in the large drawing room. On a quiet road, this is a fabulous old house, comfortable and easy, and the Labrador Holly is as welcoming as her owners.

Rooms: 1 twin/double en suite (shower); 1 double, 1 single both with private bathrooms.

Price: £22.50-£25 p.p.

Meals: Breakfast until 9am; supper tray, £8 on first night by arrangement.

Closed: Christmas.

From Dorchester, B3143 into Buckland Newton over x-roads; Holyleas on right opposite village cricket pitch.

Tia Bunkall
Holyleas House
Buckland Newton
Dorchester
Dorset DT2 7DP
Tel: 01300 345214
Fax: 01305 264488
E-mail: tiabunkall@holyleas.fsnet.co.uk

Entry No: 162   **Map no:** 3

Wild deer frolic on the hillside and the Cerne Abbas Giant intrigues not only archaeologists... The house is the oldest one in this pretty village where Ann Winzer, nursing heroine at Waterloo, lies buried in the churchyard. The Adeneys are particularly nice people who have renovated their home and converted stable block with enormous care; they are very keen to do a good job of caring for you. There is just one room in the house, with white walls, exposed beams and antique furniture; others (unfinished when we visited) are in the stable block. Breakfast is served in the dining room in the house.

Rooms: House: 1 twin, en suite (bath). Stables: 4 doubles/twins, all en suite (1 shower, 3 baths).

Price: £25 p.p. Single supp. £7.50.

Meals: Breakfast until 9.30am. Packed lunch from £3 p.p. Dinner available locally.

Closed: Christmas & New Year.

From Dorchester, A35 towards Bere Regis for 1 miles. B3143 left to Piddlehinton. Through village. house on left 100 yds after Thimble pub.

Robin & Liz Adeney
White Dairy House
Piddlehinton
Dorchester
Dorset DT2 7TD
Tel: 01300 348386
E-mail: robin.adeney@care4free.net

Entry No: 163   **Map no: 3**

Breakfast, with newspapers, is served in the large, beamed kitchen, and in summer in the walled courtyard. The well-travelled Jackie and David make light of the practicalities of looking after guests; they and their 200-year-old cottage have bountiful character and charm. One immaculate twin bedroom has fresh blue and white checks and access to the garden, another has attractive chintz. The sitting room has pretty pink sofas, an inglenook fireplace and window seats. The River Frome - a chalk stream favoured by local fishermen - is within 150 yards of the grounds. Convenient for the A35, yet peaceful.

Rooms: 2 twins - one with (downstairs) en suite shower and 1 twin sharing bathroom with single room.

Price: £24-25 p.p. Single supp. £10.

Meals: Breakfast until 9am. Good selection of restaurants nearby.

Closed: Easter & Christmas.

From r'bout at top of Dorchester, west on B3150 for 100 yds. Right onto Poundbury Rd (before museum). 1 mile on, over another road, then 2nd concrete track on right beyond Whitfield Farmhouse sign. Cottage set back from road.

Jackie & David Charles
Whitfield Farm Cottage
Poundbury Road
Nr. Dorchester, Dorset DT2 9SL
Tel: 01305 260233
Fax: 01305 260233
E-mail: dc.whitfield@clara.net
Web: www.dc.whitfield.clara.net

Entry No: 164   **Map no: 3**

This rambling, rose-clad Georgian farmhouse is English to the core. Rooms are stylishly cluttered with lovely old pieces, paintings and prints - books, delightful objects and flowers at every turn. Bedrooms under the eaves are deliciously cosy - and chic, with matching curtains and bedheads in creamy chintz. Breakfast is served in the farmhouse kitchen - amid copper pans and colourful plates picked up on Jenny's travels - and under the vine-strewn loggia in summer. The garden overflows with honeysuckle and roses. A Dorsetshire dream. *Children over 12 welcome.*

Rooms: 1 twin, 1 double (only let to one party), with private bathroom.

Price: £27.50 p.p. Single supp. £5.

Meals: Breakfast until 9.30am; packed lunch £3; dinner £15-£20.

Closed: Christmas & New Year.

Thomas Hardy and his brother were so taken by the neighbouring 12th-century church that they helped restore it; Hardy's home, Max Gate, is nearby. This 300-year-old thatched cottage hugs the church boundary and has been diligently restored. Sink into comfy mattresses on king-size beds - bedrooms are simple, serene and softly lit. The village is truly quaint and there's a local pub that does excellent food a short stroll away. Good breakfasts with local, free-range eggs, honey and home-made yogurt and preserves. Renee also offers reflexology.

Rooms: 1 double/twin, 1 double, both en suite (bath and shower).

Price: £25-£30 p.p. Single supp. £10.

Meals: Breakfast until 10am. Dinner available locally.

Closed: Christmas & New Year.

From Wincanton, A357 towards Templecombe. 2nd right to Stowell opposite entrance to Horsington House. Down hill past church. 0.5 miles on. House on left immed. after phone box.

A352 Wareham road from Dorchester by-pass. Left at signe to West Knighton, or continue to Broadmayne & left signed West Knighton at x-roads.

Jenny Gold
Windrush Farm
Stowell
Sherborne
Dorset DT9 4PD
Tel: 01963 370799
E-mail: jennygold2@hotmail.com

Renee East
Church Cottage
West Knighton
Dorchester
Dorset DT2 8PF
Tel: 01305 852243
E-mail: info@church-cottage.com
Web: www.church-cottage.com

Entry No: 165   **Map no: 3**

Entry No: 166   **Map no: 4**

An encapsulation of much that is charming about Dorset - a soft, delightful, thatched cottage in an enviable rural setting. Sandy and Paul have poured love into this Grade II-listed farmhouse and garden, the latter bursting with lupins, poppies, cornflowers, foxgloves, clematis, delphiniums... Sandy is very welcoming; Paul, brought up in South America, is full of stories and fluent in Spanish, Portuguese and French. Excellent bedrooms with good prints, pretty bedheads and lovely pieces of furniture. The garden room with exposed flintstone walls, has its own door to the garden. Very special indeed. *Children over 10 welcome.*

Rooms: 1 ground-floor twin, 2 doubles, all en suite (shower).

Price: £25 p.p. Single supp. £5.

Meals: Breakfast until 9am; packed lunch, from £5, by arrangement.

Closed: Christmas & New Year.

Leave Blandford towards SW, cross river Stour. Hard right after Bryanston school, signed Winterborne Stickland (4.5 miles). There, down North St, right signed W'bourne Houghton. House 150 yds on left with 5-bar gate.

Sandy & Paul Crofton-Atkins
Stickland Farmhouse
Winterborne Stickland
Blandford Forum
Dorset DT11 0NT
Tel: 01258 880119
Fax: 01258 880119
E-mail: sticklandfarmhouse@sticklanddorset.fsnet.co.uk

Entry No: 167   **Map no: 4**

Lucy and Tim are tangibly happy in this converted forge; it dates back to the 1700s and the wheelwright and carriage-builder from the local estate used to work here. They enjoy entertaining guests and share their space with ease; Tim is a classic car restorer and has rebuilt a 1934 Lagonda and Lucy rides long-distance on her Arab horse. The attic bedrooms are snug, with Lucy's quilts, country antiques and sparkling bathrooms. Breakfasts include organic sausages and bacon and eggs from the Kerridges' free-ranging chickens and ducks. The Downs beckon keen walkers; warm corners invite readers. A lovely setting.

Rooms: 1 double/family room, en suite (shower); 1 double, 1 single (let to same party) sharing bathroom. 2 self-catering cottages for 2 and 3.

Price: £22.50-£25 p.p. Single £40. Supp. for single night's stay £2.50 p.p.

Meals: Breakfast until 9am. Good food available locally.

Closed: Never.

From Shaftesbury, A350 to Compton Abbas. The Old Forge 1st property on left before Compton Abbas sign. Turn left; entrance on left through 5-bar gate.

Tim & Lucy Kerridge
The Old Forge, Fanners Yard
Compton Abbas
Shaftesbury
Dorset SP7 0NQ
Tel: 01747 811881
Fax: 01747 811881
E-mail: theoldforge@hotmail.com

Entry No: 168   **Map no: 4**

Dorset

It's a short stroll into the centre of town and so quiet, thanks to the magnificent one-acre walled garden which is open to the public once a year. With delicate, decorative details, the house is a Regency gem and there are many of them in this historic town. Have tea in the garden on arrival and, in the morning, take full English breakfast there with black pudding, kippers, home-made jams, eggs every way... There's an elegant drawing room for you and one bedroom has views of the church and Melbury Hill and a vast and luxurious bathroom. A delight.

Rooms: 2 twins, both en suite (bath).

Price: £27.50-£30 p.p. Single occ. £40-£45.

Meals: Breakfast until 9.30am. Good restaurants locally.

Closed: Christmas Day.

Below is the River Stour which winds through the valley and under the medieval, nine-arched bridge; above is an Iron Age hillfort; between is Crawford House. Soft and pretty, the house has floor-length windows in the sitting room and dining room that allow sun to stream through in the most uplifting way. Bedroom colours are neutral and calm, offsetting floral curtains. One room has charming four-poster twin beds with chintzy drapes. Downstairs, there are lovely oils on the walls and Andrea brings you breakfast in the pale green dining room. Ferry ports are 25 minutes' away.

Rooms: 1 double/twin, en suite (bath); 2 twins, sharing bathroom.

Price: £25 p.p.

Meals: Breakfast times flexible. Dinner available locally.

Closed: Mid-October-mid-April.

From Shaftesbury, B3091 towards Sturminster Newton. After 0.25 miles down St. John's Hill, house 1st on right, with parking next to garage.

1st gateway on left after x-roads (B3075) on A350 going north after entering Spetisbury.

Diana Pow
Cliff House
Breach Lane
Shaftesbury, Dorset SP7 8LF
Tel: 01747 852548
Fax: 01747 852548
E-mail: dianaepow@aol.com
Web: www.cliff-house.co.uk

Andrea Lea
Crawford House
Spetisbury
Blandford
Dorset DT11 9DP
Tel: 01258 857338
Fax: 01258 858152

Entry No: 169   **Map no: 4**   **Entry No: 170**   **Map no: 4**

The mood is of restrained luxury and uncluttered, often beautiful, good taste. Bedrooms are painted cream with mahogany furniture, sloping ceilings, beams, a radio and armchairs. There's a large drawing room and good paintings are all around. The Hipwells are easy; the house, and the garden, are a refuge. Views are soft and lush yet you are in the main square of this attractive town; the house was rebuilt in 1762 after a great fire, on the foundations of a 13th-century goldsmith's house. *Children over 10 welcome.*

Rooms: 3 twins/doubles, all with private bathroom.

Price: £25-£27.50 p.p. Single occ. £30-£35.

Meals: Breakfast times flexible; dinner £10-£12, available in winter, by arrangement. Many good restaurants nearby.

Closed: Christmas & New Year.

From A35, A351 to Wareham. Follow signs to town centre. In North St, over lights into South St. 1st left into St John's Hill & house on SW side.

Anthea & Michael Hipwell
Gold Court House
St. John's Hill
Wareham
Dorset BH20 4LZ
Tel: 01929 553320
Fax: 01929 553320

Entry No: 171   Map no: 4

Puzzle no more... a 'hard' is an area of firm ground for landing boats; 'lytchett' is a strip of land. The delights of this 1935 house include a 1662 court cupboard, home-grown just about everything, a telescope for bird and deer watching and excellent beds. In good weather, breakfast on the stone terrace or perhaps in the conservatory with its exotic and fragrant plants. The gazebo is the perfect spot for enjoying the garden with its shimmering view across Lychett Bay and the heathland fringe. The Collinsons are easy going and friendly.

Rooms: 1 king-size four-poster, en suite (bath & shower); 1 twin, en suite (bath); 1 small double, en suite (shower).

Price: £21-£33 p.p. No single supp. in small double. 10% discount for 3 nights, 15% for a week.

Meals: Breakfast times flexible; dinner, £12-£18, by arrangement.

Closed: Hardly ever.

From Upton x-roads (0.5 miles S.E. of A35/A350 interchange), west into Dorchester Rd, 2nd left into Seaview Rd, over Sandy Lane into Slough Lane, then 1st left into Beach Rd. House 150 yds on, on right.

David & Elizabeth Collinson
Lytchett Hard
Beach Road
Upton, Poole
Dorset BH16 5NA
Tel: 01202 622297
Fax: 01202 632716

Entry No: 172   Map no: 4

A large house kept in pristine condition by Sara and John - the huge and enchanting garden comes in for the same careful treatment, too. Furnishings are sedate, some newer pieces are well mixed with family antiques. The twin, with patterned carpet, has a good collection of books and the double is double aspect; garden views are never far away in this house. Sara pays attention to detail, such as a new toothbrush for the forgetful, linen table napkins and a choice of teas. Every view is into green Hardy Country. Bring your racquets - there's a tennis court.

Rooms: 1 double, 1 twin, 1 single sharing 2 bathrooms. Possible use of private bathroom.

Price: From £22 p.p.

Meals: Breakfast until 9.30am. Good food available locally.

Closed: Never.

From Wimborne B3078 to Cranborne. Right to Holt. After 2 miles Thornhill on right, 200 yds beyond Old Inn.

John & Sara Turnbull
Thornhill
Holt
Wimborne
Dorset BH21 7DJ
Tel: 01202 889434
E-mail: sct@gardener.com

Entry No: 173   **Map no: 4**

A new house that will soften with age and Ella has great plans for the garden, including a breakfast terrace (in her former Special Place she had a vineyard that produced wonderful wine). In the dining room there's a large collection of books, and dining chairs sporting Ella's tapestry work, designed to match the curtains. Thoughtful extras in the comfortable bedroom - spring water and fresh flowers - and an antique mahogany chair and towel rail. This is a quiet spot in an AONB; there's a pub and a church in the charming village. *Children over 10 welcome.*

Rooms: 1 twin, with private bathroom.

Price: £25 p.p. Single supp. £10.

Meals: Breakfast until 9.30am. Dinner available locally.

Closed: Never.

From Shaftesbury, A30 east. Through Ludwell, then left at bottom of hill signed The Donheads. At T-junc. follow sign to Donhead. Pass Foresters Inn on right, fork left after 150 yds. House on right after 300 yds.

Ella Humphreys
Oakdale House
Donhead St Andrew
Shaftesbury
Dorset SP7 9EG
Tel: 01747 828767
E-mail: oakdale@eurolink.ltd.net

Entry No: 174   **Map no: 4**

Solid, Elizabethan grandeur in this magnificent 1590s Grade-I listed manor. At every turn your eye is delighted by views to the lake, huge and impressive antique, carved beds, enormous staircases, beautiful rugs on stone and wood floors and excellent fabrics which perfectly suit the period. Pevsner described the Manor as being 'refined to a point of perfection'. The splendours are varied and the grounds live up to the house. Andrew and Mulu will feed and pamper you in great style; Mulu can even give you a massage/beauty treatment in the salon. *Children over 12 by arrangement.*

Rooms: 1 four-poster, 1 twin, both en suite (bath), 1 double, en suite (shower) and/or with private bathroom.

Price: £40-£55 p.p. Single supp. £15.

Meals: Breakfast times flexible; dinner, 4 courses, £23.50, by arrangement.

Closed: Mid-December-mid-February.

At r'bout on A35, 1 mile NE of Dorchester, follow sign to Kingston Maurward gardens & animal park. Once in grounds, follow signs to house.

Andrew Thomson
The Old Manor
Kingston Maurward
Dorchester, Dorset DT2 8PX
Tel: 01305 261110
Fax: 01305 263734
E-mail: thomson@kingston-maurward.co.uk
Web: www.kingston-maurward.co.uk

Entry No: 175   Map no: 3

Across the road the water meadows descend to the river that winds round Sturminster Newton. Australian Margie is fun and easy-going and the house is reassuringly homely; you'll feel at ease surrounded by their attractive, convivial clutter. There's a huge fireplace in the hall and a smaller one in the snug sitting room with its matted carpet and jolly rugs. Bedrooms are big, spotless and attractive with plain Wilton carpets; one of the bathrooms has pretty handmade tiles. Breakfasts, served from the vast and friendly kitchen, are feasts of local sausage, home-made marmalade and fruit salad. A wonderful house.

Rooms: 1 double, en suite (bath); 1 double with private bathroom; 1 twin, 2 singles sharing bathroom and wc.

Price: From £25 p.p.

Meals: Breakfast times flexible; packed lunch, from £3, on request. Good pub within walking distance.

Closed: Christmas.

On A357 Sherborne to Blandford road. House 0.25 miles west of Sturminster Newton Bridge, on south side of road.

Charles & Margie Fraser
Newton House
Sturminster Newton
Dorset DT10 2DQ
Tel: 01258 472783
Fax: 01258 473235
E-mail: carolinepass@lineone.net

Entry No: 176   Map no: 4

Dorset & Durham

A magical place. Complete peace: the garden runs down to the River Stour and has uninterrupted views over the water meadows. The millhouse, 16th-century and Grade I-listed, is as warm and interesting as the owners. The inside is no surprise: an original moulded plaster ceiling, half-tester bed in one room, a real four-poster in another, rich decoration and large table in the dining room. There is no sitting room for guests, but the rooms are big and who cares when the house is so magnificent? *Children over 12 welcome.*

Rooms: 1 double, en suite (bath); 1 double, 1 four-poster sharing bathroom.

Price: £22.50-£30 p.p. Single occ. from £30.

Meals: Breakfast times flexible. Dinner available locally.

Closed: Never.

We loved this place – the cobbled courtyard that evokes memories of its days as a coaching inn (Dickens stayed here), the River Greta that runs through the estate, the lovely garden and potager, the fine breakfasts (kipper and smoked haddock). Above all, Peter and Mary, your kind, unstuffy and dog-adoring hosts. Every creature comfort has been attended to in the cosy, Beatrix-Potterish bedrooms: crisp linen, soft lights, embroidered pillows, and, in the bathrooms, big soft towels and heated rails. A perfect, rural, stepping-stone to Scotland - or the south.

Rooms: 1 double/twin, en suite (bath & shower); 1 double/twin with private bathroom.

Price: £32 p.p. Single supp. £13.

Meals: Breakfast times flexible; packed lunch £5; dinner, 3 courses, £20, by arrangement.

Closed: Never.

House on A357 between Sturminster Newton & Blandford. Look for well-marked turning on north side between Lydlinch & Fiddleford.

Mr & Mrs A & J Ingleton
Fiddleford Mill
Fiddleford
Sturminster Newton
Dorset DT10 2BX
Tel: 01258 472786

A1(M) to Scotch Corner. A66 west until Greta Bridge turn-off. House on left just before bridge.

Peter & Mary Gilbertson
The Coach House
Greta Bridge
Barnard Castle
Durham DL12 9SD
Tel: 01833 627201
E-mail: info@coachhousegreta.co.uk
Web: www.coachhousegreta.co.uk

Entry No: 177   Map no: 4

Entry No: 178   Map no: 15

Sarah-Jane, with energy and good humour, is breathing new life into her 10-bedroomed, seven-bathroomed Regency house. There's a large guest sitting room with two enormous sofas; murals remind you that this doubles as a nursery for the little ones when no-one is visiting. Fresh flowers in the bedrooms, which have plain emulsioned walls and pretty floral curtains. The mature gardens envelop the house and merge with a buttercup field. Explore the rose garden and parkland and delight in finding the many rare plants in the woods.

Rooms: 1 double, en suite (shower); 2 twins, 1 en suite (bath), 1 with private bathroom.

Price: £22.50-£27.50 p.p. Single supp. £5.

Meals: Breakfast until 9.30am. Dinner available locally.

Closed: Christmas & New Year.

From A1, at Scotch Corner, A66 for Barnard Castle. 7 miles on, approaching 1st section of dual carriageway, 1st right for Barnard Castle to traffic lights. Right over bridge. At T-junc. left for Barnard Castle Town. Pass school & museum & through iron gates on left.

Sarah-Jane Ormston
Spring Lodge
Newgate
Barnard Castle
Durham DL12 8NW
Tel: 01833 638110
Fax: 01833 638110
E-mail: ormston@telinco.co.uk

Entry No: 179   **Map no: 15**

A walker's paradise, with pure air, birds, deer, and woodpeckers. The Georgian shooting lodge is in an open glade with views of the moors - you drive for two miles through the forest to get to 5,000 acres of woodland, moors, becks, rivers and ancient trees. The Art Nouveau furniture and fittings are a refreshing change from traditional furnishings and there are some dramatic touches, such as the shocking pink bathroom. Big downstairs rooms, small bedrooms, open fires and books. Helene is an exceptional cook and has lived here all her life. *Children over eight welcome.*

Rooms: 2 doubles, en suite (bath & shower); 1 twin, en suite (shower).

Price: £26.00-£32.50 p.p. Single supp. £10 (May-Sept & Easter).

Meals: Breakfast until 9am; packed lunch £4; dinner £22.50.

Closed: 20 December-3 January.

A68 from Darlington, left to Hamsterley. On for 2 miles (ignore forest signs) in village, then right, signed The Grove, then left. Right (signed), after 3 miles, over stone bridge, house faces you.

Helene Close
Grove House
Hamsterley Forest, Bishop Auckland
Durham DL13 3NL
Tel: 01388 488203
Fax: 01388 488174
E-mail: xov47@dial.pipex.com
Web: www.come.to/grovehouse

Entry No: 180   **Map no: 20**

Durham &Essex

Just 12 miles from Durham, one of England's jewels, and one of only 20 similarly listed farmhouses in the county. It is way off the beaten track in magical scenery, a Grade II* early 17th-century building with later additions, with huge charm. The kitchen has the original bread oven and Marguerite produces mouth-watering meals - and enjoys doing so. It is also sybaritically comfortable, with deep sofa and armchairs below beams in the sitting room and before the open fire in the dining room. Higgledy-piggledy and comfortable - perfect.

Rooms: 1 twin with sitting room and bathroom in own wing.

Price: £32 p.p. Single supp. £10.

Meals: Breakfast times flexible; dinner, 4 courses, £24, by arrangement.

Closed: Occasionally.

Floors slant and the old elm creaks – this timber-framed, 13th-century, Grade II* listed Essex hall house is tangibly ancient. You have your own drawing room with stunning silk curtains and can be a cherished only guest, or things can be moved around to accommodate a larger group. Strong (Designers' Guild) colours in the twin bedroom and a fresh blues and white in the large double. Stansted airport is 20 minutes away, Chelmsford 12, yet this is very rural: the tennis court is hard by open fields and there are ponds, an island and tame ducks.

Rooms: 1 double, 1 twin, sharing private bathroom.

Price: £28-£35 p.p.

Meals: Breakfast times flexible; dinner, £20, by arangement.

Closed: Occasionally.

Going west on A689, approx. 1 mile west of Wolsingham, left opp. brown caravan sign. Over bridge, sharp left over disused railway line. 0.5 miles up track, fork right through ford. House 200 yds further.

From Stansted, A120 east, then right onto A130. After Ford End, right at r'bout to Gt. Waltham. There, right at Beehive Pub into Barrack Lane. 1.3 miles on, right down track in between 2 cottages. Left through 5-bar gate just before barn.

Anthony & Marguerite Todd
Coves House Farm
Wolsingham
Weardale
Durham DL13 3BG
Tel: 01388 527375
Fax: 01388 526157

Mrs Roslyn Renwick
Fitzjohns Farmhouse
Mashbury Road
Great Waltham, Chelmsford
Essex CM3 1EJ
Tel: 01245 360204/361224
Fax: 01245 361724
E-mail: rosrenwick@aol.com

Entry No: 181   **Map no:** 20

Entry No: 182   **Map no:** 11

An Elizabethan jewel in a superb rural setting! Exposed timber ceilings, open fireplaces, endless nooks and crannies: this 'farmhouse' trumpets its history at every turn. The two-acre garden has old-fashioned roses and a pond that attracts many birds. The Wordsworths (yes, they are related to the poet) are engaging and solicitous people, who delight in their guests. Anne, an excellent cook, serves home-grown organic vegetables with dinner and the hens and bantams provide organic eggs for breakfast served in the Aga-warm kitchen. The perfect retreat from London and so close to Stansted airport, Cambridge and Duxford.

Rooms: 1 double, en suite (bath/shower); 1 twin with private bathroom.

Price: £37.50 p.p.

Meals: Breakfast times flexible; supper/dinner £15-£22.50. B.Y.O wine.

Closed: Never.

From Saffron Walden B1053 (George Street) to Radwinter. Right at church & 1st left after 1 mile (at grass triangle on sharp right-hand bend). Farm signed.

Antony & Anne Wordsworth
Little Brockholds Farm
Radwinter
Saffron Walden
Essex CB10 2TF
Tel: 01799 599458
Fax: 01799 599458
E-mail: as@brockholds99.freeserve.co.uk

Entry No: 183   **Map no: 11**

The cattle seem perilously close; it is the ha-ha that does it, a dominant feature of the garden with its pond, lush greenery and tennis court. The entrance hall is surprisingly large and elegant for a '60s house; the drawing room is traditionally furnished and has fine windows looking over the garden to Dedham Vale. The walls are soft yellow, the carpet blue-grey. The dining room has a parquet floor, open fire and terracotta walls, hunting prints and candlelit dinners. Play the baby grand piano, let your conversation range wide with two delightful and widely-travelled people.

Rooms: 1 family, 1 twin, both en suite (bath/shower).

Price: From £24-£30 p.p. Single occ. £35.

Meals: Breakfast times flexible; packed lunch £7; dinner £22.50, by arrangement. B.Y.O wine.

Closed: Never.

From A134 (Colchester/Sudbury road), at Great Horkesley, take Boxted Church Road for 2 miles east. House 200 yds beyond turning to church.

Jeremy & Mary Carter
Round Hill House
Parsonage Hill
Boxted, Colchester
Essex CO4 5ST
Tel: 01206 272392
Fax: 01206 272392
E-mail: jermar@appleonline.net

Entry No: 184   **Map no: 12**

The house is minutes from wild walking; the island of Mersea is secluded, surprising; the sea murmurs across the saltings where the Brent geese wheel and the great Constable skies stretch. The house began in 1343, a hall house nearly as old as the exquisite church. The Georgians added their bit, but the venerable beams and uneven old construction shine through. It is a sunny, comfortable, beautiful house. There is a snug, book-filled, sitting room, a terracotta-floored conservatory and much wood and soft colours. It is a privilege to stay here, among such nice people.

Rooms: 1 double, 1 twin, both with private bathroom.

Price: £25 p.p. Single occ. £25-£30.

Meals: Breakfast until 9am. Restaurant 1 mile away, pub within walking distance.

Closed: Never.

Once you've arrived in this quintessentially English village, you can forget about your car; walks on the Cotswolds Way and cycle rides start from your front door. For supper, visit the famous Churchill Inn next door. Bedrooms are charming - one terracotta with a star pattern and the other creamy with floral curtains; there's an antique free-standing bath and wooden floors in the bathroom. Your breakfast room opens onto the garden. Clare runs an interesting craft shop with an unusual collection of artefacts in the converted gallery next door.

Rooms: 2 doubles, 1 en suite (shower), 1 en suite (bath).

Price: £30 p.p. Single supp. £5.

Meals: Breakfast times flexible. Dinner available in the village.

Closed: Never.

From Colchester B1025, over causeway, then bear left. After 3 miles, pass Dog & Pheasant pub. Take 2nd right into Bromans Lane. House 1st on left.

From Chipping Campden, B4035. 1.5 miles on, right to Paxford & right at T-junc. Left at Churchill Inn; cottage on left.

Ruth Dence
Bromans Farm
East Mersea
Essex CO5 8UE
Tel: 01206 383235
Fax: 01206 383235

Clare Shaw
Vine Cottage
Paxford
Chipping Campden
Gloucestershire GL55 6XH
Tel: 01386 593266
Fax: 01386 593266

Entry No: 185   **Map no:** 12

Entry No: 186   **Map no:** 10

Robin has added curves to his handcrafted furniture so that it hugs the floorboards where they bow with age. It's homely, comforting and exquisitely cottagey, yet stylish and not at all claustrophobic. There's huge attention to detail and things of interest everywhere - like the compelling view up the stairs: a forest of beams, timber posts and bannisters. A split-level bathroom, Tudor bricks, honey-coloured stone windows with seats and more lovely furniture crafted by Robin in his workshop; the whole is captivating. You'll feel at ease with this small family.

Rooms: 2 doubles, 1 en suite (bath), 1 with basin and private bathroom.

Price: £30 p.p. Single supp. £5.

Meals: Breakfast until 9.30am. Dinner available at acclaimed inn opposite.

Closed: Christmas & New Year.

In centre of Paxford opposite church.

Lisa & Robin Knott
Wells Farmhouse
Paxford, Chipping Campden
Gloucestershire GL55 6XH
Tel: 01386 593429
Fax: 01386 593693
E-mail: lisa@clockrobin.co.uk
Web: www.wellsfarmhouse.co.uk

Entry No: 187   **Map no:** 10

The Kettle sits snugly besides St James church. You can see the ancient place of worship from the guest sitting room and through an open skylight while you shower! The Kettle has been an inn, brewery, grocer's shop and pottery and now Susie has a small antique shop downstairs. The mood is set by stripped doors, coir matting, beams, leaded windows, antiques, white linen and the prettiest murals. Yogurt and berries for breakfast, then glazed tomatoes, crispy bacon and eggs. There's a lovely terraced roof garden, too: you could almost be in France. *Minimum 2-night stay.*

Rooms: 2 doubles, en suite (shower); 2 twins sharing bathroom.

Price: £35 p.p. Single occ. £50.

Meals: Breakfast until 9am (Mon-Fri), until 10am (Sat-Sun). Excellent restaurants nearby.

Closed: Mid-January-mid-February.

A44 (Oxford-Evesham Rd). Turn off to B4018 for Chipping Campden, approx. 2 miles. House at top of village on right heading towards Stratford-on-Avon.

Charles & Susie Holdsworth-Hunt
The Kettle House
High Street, Chipping Campden
Gloucestershire GL55 6HN
Tel: 01386 840328
Fax: 01386 841740
E-mail: bed&breakfast@kettlehouse.co.uk
Web: www.kettlehouse.co.uk

Entry No: 188   **Map no:** 10

Ample space for everyone to feel at ease - and you do so in luxury and style. You are on the site of an extinct medieval village that is mentioned in the Domesday book: until 1610 this was the village church. The hall and ground floor are stone-flagged, with rugs for colour, and there are delightful touches of exotica everywhere. One bedroom is massive. The gardens, set in 37 acres, are simply beautiful, with a trout lake, tennis court, pool and wonderful views. John and Camilla are wickedly funny and easy-going. Our inspector didn't want to come home. *Children over seven welcome.*

Rooms: 2 doubles, both en suite (bath); 1 single with private bathroom.

Price: £38 p.p. Single supp. £10.

Meals: Breakfast until 9.30am; supper by arrangement £24. Excellent pub and restaurant nearby.

Closed: Christmas.

Astonishing! It feels palpably old - Elizabethan even - with superb mullioned windows, gables and extensive stoned slated and thatched roofs with those unexpected corners which make old buildings so fascinating. Yet unbelievably, it was started in 1951. Cecil, a retired builder, and his family have thrown their home open to guests, with huge generosity and bonhomie. There's an outdoor swimming pool flanked by a folly, an all weather tennis court, croquet, a snooker/billiards room, a superb prize-winning garden and a 10-acre arboretum with almost 300 species of trees. It's immaculate and sumptuous, but fun and rather special.

Rooms: 2 doubles, both en suite (bath); 1 double with private bathroom.

Price: £40 p.p. Single supp. £20.

Meals: Breakfast times flexible. Good pub up road.

Closed: Never.

4 miles north of Moreton-in-Marsh on A429, left to Aston Magna. At 1st building, immed. right. House 0.75 miles on right, up drive.

From Stow-on-the-Wold on A424 for 2 miles. Opposite Coach & Horses pub, right by postbox. Entrance 100 yds on left.

John & Camilla Playfair
Neighbrook Manor
Aston Magna, Moreton-in-Marsh
Gloucestershire GL56 9QP
Tel: 01386 593232
Fax: 01386 593500
E-mail: info@neighbrookmanor.com
Web: www.neighbrookmanor.com

C.J. Williams
Windy Ridge
Longborough, Moreton-in-Marsh
Gloucestershire GL56 0QY
Tel: 01451 832328/830465
Fax: 01451 831489
E-mail: cjw@windy-ridge.co.uk
Web: www.windy-ridge.co.uk

Entry No: 189   **Map no: 10**

Entry No: 190   **Map no: 10**

Allegedly Cardinal Wolsey owned Rectory Farmhouse, then Henry VIII took it from him and gave it to Christ Church College, Oxford. Since then it has had only two private owners, such is its immense charm. Passing a development of converted farm buildings to get to the warm Cotswold stones of this place makes the discovery doubly exciting. Sybil, an interior decorator, has created something immaculate, cool and beautiful. Bed linen is white, walls are cream; the huge enamel bath has a stunning pink exterior. Sybil used to own a restaurant - breakfast, next to the Aga, is a cosy affair.

Rooms: 2 doubles, 1 suite with sitting room, both en suite (shower).

Price: From £32.50 p.p. Single occ. £40.

Meals: Breakfast until 9.30am. Dinner available locally.

Closed: Christmas & New Year.

Masses of charm and style here - this 1789 farmhouse is clearly much loved: it lured Angela and Michael away from the city. Outbuildings, courtyards and cartsheds in the same warm stone, and a pool. Your hosts are friendly and fun and terrific cooks; Angela's a trained *Cordon Bleu*. Dinners are served in the lovely, low-ceilinged dining room where oil paintings offset the beams and flagged floors. Country bedrooms have generous curtains in Colefax florals and *toile de Jouy*. There are robes in the bathrooms and walking and riding country all around. Ask if you may swim in the pool.

Rooms: 1 twin, 1 double, 1 king-size with extra single, all en suite.

Price: £25-£35 p.p. Single supp. £10.

Meals: Breakfast until 9.30am; packed lunch £7; dinner inc. wine, £25, both by arrangement.

Closed: Christmas.

B4068 from Stow to Lower Swell, left just before Golden Ball Inn. Far end of gravel drive on right.

Sybil Gisby
Rectory Farmhouse
Lower Swell
Stow-on-the-Wold
Gloucestershire GL54 1LH
Tel: 01451 832351
E-mail: rectory.farmhouse@cw-warwick.co.uk

In middle of village, past the Plough Inn on left; look for gates on right.

Angela Storey
Grove Farm House
Cold Aston, Cheltenham
Gloucestershire GL54 3BJ
Tel: 01451 821801
Fax: 01451 821108
E-mail: angela@cotswoldbedandbreakfast.com
Web: www.cotswoldbedandbreakfast.com

Entry No: 191   **Map no: 10**   **Entry No: 192**   **Map no: 10**

Look over the garden wall as you breakfast on home-made jams and home-laid eggs and enjoy those wonderful, long views. The garden, too, is worth a long look - it has featured in magazines and James and Karin are passionate about it. The 16th- and 17th-century manor house has a flagstoned hall, huge fireplaces, sit-in inglenooks and Cotswold stone mullioned windows. One of the bedrooms has a secret door that leads to a surprising fuchsia-pink bathroom. The other, though smaller, has wonderful garden views. An easy-going and lovely house with owners to match.

Rooms: 1 double, en suite (bath/shower); 1 twin/double, en suite (bath).

Price: £35 p.p. Single supp. £15.

Meals: Breakfast usually 8-9.30am. Menus available for local pubs & restaurants.

Closed: Christmas.

From Cirencester, A429 towards Stow. Right at Apple Pie House Hotel, signed Clapton. Follow signs. In village, pass triangular green on left & house straight ahead on left on corner.

Karin & James Bolton
Clapton Manor
Clapton-on-the-Hill
Nr. Bourton-on-the-Water
Gloucestershire GL54 2LG
Tel: 01451 810202
Fax: 01451 821804
E-mail: bandb@claptonmanor.co.uk

Entry No: 193　　　　**Map no: 10**

Everything you could want from a glorious, truly English country home. The magnificent Georgian manor sits in 15 acres. The two-acre lake is alive with wildfowl and there's a little boat to paddle off in. You really should come with friends and make a house party of it; there are luxurious self-catering cottages in the old coaching yard. You can play tennis or croquet, swim, ride and clay pigeon shoot on the Bredon Hills. You can even get married here. Antique furniture, sumptuous beds and drapes and the super Herford family. Perfection. *Minimum two nights stay at weekends.*

Rooms: 4 four-posters, 1 twin, 1 twin/double, all en suite. Self-catering cottages and Coach House sleeps 2-11.

Price: From £42.50-£60 p.p. Single occ. up to £75.

Meals: Breakfast: flexible - served in bed at no extra cost! Dinner – Manor, from £32; cottages, £15 by arrangement.

Closed: Christmas. Self-catering available all year.

From Cheltenham, A435 north, then B4079. About 1 mile after A438 x-roads, right to Kemerton. Leave rd at War Memorial. House behind church.

Bill & Diana Herford
Upper Court
Kemerton
Tewkesbury
Gloucestershire GL20 7HY
Tel: 01386 725351
Fax: 01386 725472
E-mail: uppercourt@compuserve.com

Entry No: 194　　　　**Map no: 9**

The magnificent, softly undulating countryside has inspired musicians, writers and poets; you'll see why. Sit on the terrace - which is candlelit in the evenings - take in the views and Michael and Jo will bring you a glass of award-winning wine produced at the neighbouring vineyard. They are genuine, kind, fun and you will relax immediately. Michael loves old cars - the Puma racing car was made right here - and they often tour in France. The pretty and immaculate bedrooms are in a converted grain barn which has a soaring A-frame ceiling.

Rooms: 1 twin, en suite (bath); 1 double with private bath/shower. In cottage, 1 twin (with wheelchair access).

Price: £30-£32 p.p. No single supp.

Meals: Breakfast times flexible; dinner by arrangement.

Closed: Never.

From Gloucester A40 to Ross-on-Wye, right onto B4215 signed Newent. After approx. 7 miles, right (signed Dymock). After '3 Choirs Vineyard', next right (before M50). House 1 mile down lane, 3rd on right.

Jo & Michael Kingham
The Old Winery
Welsh House Lane
Dymock
Gloucestershire GL18 1LR
Tel: 01531 890824
Fax: 01531 890824

Entry No: 195   **Map no: 9**

Petrina is a natural and imaginative cook - a eulogy from a French chef in the visitors' book endorses this - and both she and James are natural hosts. They thrive on the bustle and conversation of having guests, so you'll feel immediately at ease. Very early risers can even help themselves to tea and coffee, having let the dogs out! There's plenty of space for everyone - bedrooms are large and airy and the beds are Emperor-size, no less. Large gardens and sweeping views - an attractive and elegant house to which the Pughs bring a real sense of fun. Petrina loves young children.

Rooms: 2 king-size twins/doubles, en suite; 1 double with private shower room.

Price: £30 p.p.

Meals: Breakfast times flexible; dinner £17.50; gourmet dinner £22.50.

Closed: Never.

A40 from Gloucester towards Ross-on-Wye, then B4215 towards Highnam. 2 miles on left is Whitehall Lane. House approx. 0.5 miles down lane, on right, behind laurel hedge.

James & Petrina Pugh
Whitelands
Whitehall Lane
Rudford
Gloucestershire GL2 8ED
Tel: 01452 790406
Fax: 01452 790676
E-mail: pughwhitelands@talk21.com

Entry No: 196   **Map no: 9**

Delectably old-fashioned, there's a feel of timelessness and authenticity in this magnificent house - Grade-I listed and in a fascinating village. The family has lived at Frampton since the 11th century - the dining and drawing rooms have exquisite examples of carved wood and the hall an impressive, bold Doric frieze. The house speaks the elegant language of Vanburgh and has a Strawberry Hill Gothic orangery (self-catering). One bedroom has a Flemish tapestry, a four-poster bed with hand-embroidered curtains and own dressing room; the other, equally large, is a twin with lovely views, antiques and panelling. Dutch ornamental canal, lake, old-master views... gorgeous!

Rooms: 1 twin, en suite; 1 four-poster with dressing room with a single bed and private bathroom.

Price: £45-£50 p.p.

Meals: Breakfast times flexible. Good restaurant opposite & 2 pubs on the village green.

Closed: Never.

From M5 junc. 13 west, then B4071. Left through village green, then just look to left! Entrance between 2 large chestnut trees 200 yds on left.

Mrs Henriette Clifford
Frampton Court
Frampton-on-Severn
Gloucestershire GL2 7EU
Tel: 01452 740267/740698
Fax: 01452 740698
E-mail: clifford.fce@farming.co.uk

Entry No: 197   **Map no: 9**

A perfect English scene... a late 18th-century house tucked down a lane off the country's longest village green. It's a wonderful home and Carol wants you to treat it as such. When we visited, the Aga was being nurtured back to optimum health, there was a jigsaw puzzle that invited a challenge, dogs and cats happily co-existed; the visitor's book was inscribed: "We'll be back" (and return they do). There are lovely gardens, hens (breakfast eggs) and orchards and Carol has decorated big bedrooms in muted yellows and rich velvety plums. *Children over 10 welcome.*

Rooms: 1 twin/double, 1 twin, both en suite (bath/shower).

Price: £26.50 p.p. No single supp.

Meals: Breakfast until 9am. Dinner available locally.

Closed: Christmas & New Year.

A38 towards Bristol, turn west onto B4071. 1st left & drive length of village green. 300 yds after it ends, right into Whittles Lane. House last on right.

Carol & William Alexander
The Old School House
Whittles Lane
Frampton-on-Severn
Gloucestershire GL2 7EB
Tel: 01452 740457
Fax: 01452 741721
E-mail: bedandbreakfast@f-o-s.freeserve.co.uk

Entry No: 198   **Map no: 9**

Gloucestershire

Boards creak and you duck - it is a farmhouse of the best kind, simple, small-roomed, stone-flagged, beamed and delightful. The walls are white, the furniture is good and there are pictures everywhere. In spite of great age (16th century) there are lots of windows and good light. They farm 400 acres organically (cows and sheep) and your horse can come, too. Your welcome will be as generous as your farmer's breakfast. The views across the Severn estuary to the Cotswolds are "devastating" and there is, simply, no noise - unless the guinea fowl are in good voice.

Rooms: 1 double, 1 twin with shared, private bathroom.

Price: £20-£25 p.p.

Meals: Breakfast times flexible; packed lunch £5-£10.

Closed: Occasionally.

Come in Spring and the nightingale's song is the only sound that could disturb your slumber, but this is a year-round, soothing retreat, a Victorian hunting lodge with views over the rolling Cotswold Hills. You enter into an enchanted wood - surrounded by a RSPB Sanctuary and a pine arboretum planted by Thomas Gambier Parry in 1844. Carol and David are friendly, unobtrusive and fascinated by organic gardening, as reflected in the 13-acre grounds. The bedrooms with new beds and bathrooms have the most wonderful valley views.

Rooms: 1 double/twin en suite (bath); 1 double, en suite (shower).

Price: £25-£30 p.p. Single supp. £5.

Meals: Breakfast times flexible; dinner £17.50, by arrangement.

Closed: Never.

2 miles south of Newnham on A48, opposite turning for Bullo Pill, there is large 'pull-in' with phone box on right. Turn here. Follow farm track to end.

From Gloucester A40/A48 r'bout follow A40 (Ross) for 0.7 miles. At brow of hill right up drive of black & white cottage; follow track for 0.75 miles into woods. House at top.

Penny & David Hill
Grove Farm
Bullo Pill
Newnham
Gloucestershire GL14 1DZ
Tel: 01594 516304
Fax: 01594 516304

David & Carol Wilkin
The Pinetum Lodge
Churcham
Gloucestershire GL2 8AD
Tel: 01452 750554
Fax: 01452 750402
E-mail: c.wilkin@amserve.net

Entry No: 199   Map no: 9

Entry No: 200   Map no: 9

Gloucestershire

Country roads swoop through soft countryside and into honey-coloured villages full of tempting shops and inns - neighbouring Nailsworth has stacks of good restaurants; at the Mill your surroundings are bucolic. The large lake at the side of the house is at windowsill level, giving you a strange feeling of being underwater! The lake, the mill race and Judy - genuinely friendly - make this place special. You have your own wing and entrance with sitting room. Bedrooms are fresh and simple with modern furniture. Bring the family, climb the hills, play in the garden.

Rooms: 1 twin/double (extra single if needed), 1 twin, both en suite (shower).

Price: £23-£27 p.p. Single supp. £5.

Meals: Breakfast times flexible. Good pubs for supper within walking distance.

Closed: Christmas.

From Stroud, A46 towards Bath. After 2 miles right to North Woodchester then 2nd left, down hill, sharp right up short drive.

Mrs Judy Sutch
Southfield Mill
Southfield Road
Woodchester, Nr. Stroud
Gloucestershire GL5 5PA
Tel: 01453 872896
Fax: 01452 872896

Entry No: 201   **Map no: 9**

Little has changed in 500 years: only birdsong fractures the peace of the old stone house in the appropriately named hamlet of Calmsden ('place of calm'). The alcoved stone fireplace in the living room is what sold the house to the delightful Baxters - that and the wonky floors, the beams that go the wrong way and the ceilings that need ducking. Unwind in the bedrooms among fat pillows and magazines. The smell of home-baked bread will lure you from your room for breakfast. You eat in the dining room; wood-panelled from top to toe, it's like a captain's study. *Children by arrangement.*

Rooms: 1 twin/double, en suite (bath/shower); 1 twin/double, en suite (shower); 1 single with private bathroom.

Price: £25-£35 p.p.

Meals: Breakfast until 9am. Excellent pub 1.5 miles away.

Closed: 1 December-28 February.

From Cirencester A429 north. After 5 miles, 2nd right signed Calmsden, just before Hare & Hounds pub. Continue for 1.5 miles. 3rd house on right.

Bridget Baxter
The Old House
Calmsden
Nr. Cirencester
Gloucestershire GL7 5ET
Tel: 01285 831240
Fax: 01285 831240
E-mail: baxter@calmsden.freeserve.co.uk

Entry No: 202   **Map no: 9**

Chickens strut on the lawn – and what a manicured lawn for a working farm! Your charming hosts built the honey-stone house 20 years ago and have kept it immaculately. Light pours into perfectly-proportioned rooms through windows hung with velvet and chintz; china sits in alcoves either side of the fireplace. Bedrooms, with lovely views, feel just right. After your expertly cooked breakfast - with eggs from those happy hens – you'll be ready for a swim or a game of tennis. Jeannie and James can organise fishing locally, and watersports, cycling and golf, too.

Rooms: 1 twin, 1 double/twin, 1 en suite (bath), 1 with private bathroom.

Price: £30 p.p. Single supp. £10.

Meals: Breakfast times flexible. Dinner available locally.

Closed: Christmas & New Year.

A417 Cirencester-Fairford road. Pass Meysey Hampton sign & entrance on right opposite sign for Waiten Hill & Cherry House.

Jeannie Keyser
Lady Lamb Farm
Meysey Hampton
Cirencester
Gloucestershire GL7 5LH
Tel: 01285 712206
Fax: 01285 712206
E-mail: jekeyser1@aol.com

Entry No: 203   **Map no: 4**

You get the feeling of a new start in old surroundings: here is a home created from a barn that just 10 years ago was derelict. The décor is fresh - so are the flowers - and the furniture and books old; all is bright and the conservatory looks over the garden that the Barrys have lovingly created. The charming owners are happy and proud to have you in their home. Beds are incredibly comfortable with excellent sheets and pillows; there's fine furniture and lovely paintings. This is unspoilt Cotswolds and this delightful house sits in splendid peaceful isolation.

Rooms: 1 double, en suite (bath); 1 twin, 1 double sharing bath & shower.

Price: £32-£35 p.p. Single supp. by arrangement.

Meals: Breakfast 8-9am. Excellent pubs nearby for dinner.

Closed: Christmas, New Year & Easter.

From Cirencester A417 towards Lechlade. At Meysey Hampton x-roads left to Sun Hill. After 1 mile left at cottage. House 400 yds down drive.

Richard & Jill Barry
Hampton Fields
Meysey Hampton
Cirencester
Gloucestershire GL7 5JL
Tel: 01285 850070
Fax: 01285 850993

Entry No: 204   **Map no: 4**

English to the core - and to the bottom of its lovely garden where there many delightful places to sit. Steep honey-coloured gables, mullioned windows and weathered stone tiles enclose this lovely 17th-century house that sits on a quiet village lane. Caroline is a calmly competent hostess with a talent for understated interior décor. You may sit in the very large dining room to read and the two ample, airy guest rooms are furnished with antiques and have either a *chaise longue* or easy chairs. Caroline can organise local bike hire and delivery.

Rooms: 1 twin, 1 double, both en suite (bath & shower).

Price: £32 p.p. Single supp. £10.

Meals: Breakfast times flexible. Excellent pub nearby for dinner.

Closed: December & January.

A fine new Georgian house, built in 1990 using reclaimed stone and tiles. The drawing room is elegant with magazines, dogs and Turkish needlepoint cushions strewn about; every downstairs room has an open fire. The bedrooms, in the old farmhouse wing, overlook the garden, tennis court and swimming pool. They are decorated with fine fabrics and have comfortable beds and good linen. Clare loves to paint and cook - she runs painting courses from her studio. The house is totally secluded and very quiet, yet you can walk across a few fields to visit other great gardens and the rather good village pub. *Riding, tennis and pool by arrangement.*

Rooms: 1 king-size double, en suite (bath).

Price: £40 p.p. Single supp. £15.

Meals: Breakfast times flexible. Excellent pub nearby for dinner.

Closed: Christmas, New Year & Easter.

From Malmesbury B4040 for Easton Grey. Right to Shipton Moyne, through village & at 1st x-roads take 'no through road' on right. Follow drive for 0.5 miles, bearing left where drive bends to left.

South through village from A417. Right after Masons Arms. House 200 yds on left.

Roger & Caroline Carne
The Old Rectory
Meysey Hampton
Nr. Cirencester
Gloucestershire GL7 5JX
Tel: 01285 851200
Fax: 01285 850452
E-mail: caroline.carne@lineone.net

The Inskip Family
Park Farm
Shipton Moyne
Tetbury
Gloucestershire GL8 8PR
Tel: 01666 880464
Fax: 01666 880488
E-mail: clareinskip@hotmail.com

Entry No: 205   Map no: 4

Entry No: 206   Map no: 4

The Kings have farmed here for 75 years and 40 of those have been shared with B&B guests; welcoming Sonja really knows her stuff and the whole family is involved in the arable and dairy enterprise. The famous Westonbirt Arboretum - breathtaking whatever the season - is a stroll away across the field; the Kings' fine cedar tree sadly succumbed to the elements but its grand trunk is being planked to make a summer house. Bed-heads have drapes that give the impression of a half-tester - and throughout the house are two generations' worth of fine needlework. An honest value B&B.

Rooms: 1 twin, 1 double, both en suite (shower); 1 twin with en suite (shower & basin) and separate wc.

Price: From £25 p.p.

Meals: Breakfast times flexible. Dinner available locally.

Closed: Never.

Mike and Carolyn are inspiring - they've opened a fully organic restaurant above which sits an absolutely charming B&B. "We do it for spirit, not money," says Carolyn and it's a place with heart that we are delighted to include. Please don't worry that your bedroom might not be en suite; they are all delightful - huge, like a studio, with oak or seagrass floors and lovely art on the walls. They've used local craftsmen to make the beds, light fittings, fire baskets, tables and crockery and you have your own entrance opposite the Herb Wheel.

Rooms: 1 twin, en suite (by end of '01); 2 doubles sharing bathroom.

Price: £25-£30 p.p. Single occ. £28-£35.

Meals: Breakfast times flexible. Fully organic restaurant.

Closed: End of January (2 weeks).

A433 from Tetbury for 5 miles. On entering Knockdown, farm on right before x-roads.

M5, junc. 13, A419 to Stroud, then A46 south to Nailsworth. Right at r'bout, immed. left & restaurant & house are opposite Britannia Pub.

Sonja King
Avenue Farm
Knockdown
Tetbury
Gloucestershire GL8 8QY
Tel: 01454 238207
Fax: 01454 238033
E-mail: sonjames@breathemail.net

Carolyn & Mike Findlay
Heaven's Above at The Mad Hatters
3 Cossack Square, Nailsworth
Gloucestershire GL6 0DB
Tel: 01453 832615
Fax: 01453 832615
E-mail: mafindlay@waitrose.com
Web: www.sawdays.co.uk

A treat: utterly delightful people with wide-ranging interests (ex-British Council and college lecturing; arts, travel, gardening...) in a manor-type house full of beautiful furniture. The house was born of the Arts and Crafts movement and remains fascinating: wood panels painted green and log-fired drawing-room for guests, quarry tiles on windowsills, handsome old furniture, comfortable proportions... elegant but human. The garden's massive clipped hedges and great lawn are impressive, as is the whole place. Refined but easy.

Rooms: 2 twins, 1 double, 1 with private bath/shower & 2 with shared bathroom.

Price: £31.50 p.p. Single supp. £5.

Meals: Breakfast until 9.15am; dinner £17.50, by arrangement. B.Y.O. wine.

Closed: December & January.

B4060 from Stinchcombe to Wotton-under-Edge. Up long hill, house at top on left; gateway marked.

Hugh & Crystal St John Mildmay
Drakestone House
Stinchcombe
Dursley
Gloucestershire GL11 6AS
Tel: 01453 542140
Fax: 01453 542140

Entry No: 209   **Map no:** 4

Boyts is ravishing, a 16th-century stone farmhouse in landscaped gardens. There is a huge fireplace in the sitting room, stone-flagged floors, window seats, wooden mullions, leaded windows around which climb a magnolia. The dining room has a fireplace, oil paintings, mahogany table. The bedrooms are just as lovely. The Italianate-style gardens have a canal and ornamental ponds, crested newts, ha-has and paddocks, and views to open farmland. Sally is lovely and John, ex-Army, has a keen, wry sense of humour.

Rooms: 1 double, 1 twin, both en suite (bath); 1 single with bath.

Price: From £35 p.p.

Meals: Breakfast until 9.30am. Pub with restaurant nearby.

Closed: 21 December-2 January.

From M5 junc. 16, A38 for Gloucester. After 6 miles, take Tytherington turn. From north, leave M5 at exit 14 & south on A38 towards Bristol. Tytherington turn after 3 miles.

Mr & Mrs Eyre
Boyts Farm
Tytherington
Wotton-under-Edge
Gloucestershire GL12 8UG
Tel: 01454 412220
Fax: 01454 412220

Entry No: 210   **Map no:** 3

An English idyll – a thatched and beamy cottage on the edge of a Hampshire village. Sarah, husband, children and dog are happy to have swapped city life for their rural retreat. They make you feel one of the family here, though guest rooms have their own entrance and feel very private. Both rooms are pine-furnished, clean and bright - the twin is on the ground floor and the cosy single sits at the top of its own little stairway. Enjoy breakfast or dinner in the dining room - a delightfully deep red room, and beamy. *Children over five welcome.*

Rooms: 1 twin room with sofa bed, 1 single, both en suite (bath/shower).

Price: £25 p.p. Single supp. £5.

Meals: Breakfast until 9am (Mon-Fri), flexible at weekends; packed lunch from £5; dinner, 3 courses, from £15.

Closed: Never.

Lindy and Tony have transformed their 200-year-old barn into a light and sunny home, kept simple with plain walls and seagrass flooring. Moroccan rugs, antiques and a woodburning stove add warmth and cheer to the drawing room. Lindy, who speaks French, organises garden tours and the bookshelves reflect her interest in garden design. Visitors can relax on the terrace overlooking mixed borders with cornfields beyond, admire the unusual waterfowl on the pond or saunter to the pub past the thatched cottages of this chocolate-box village. *Children over 10 welcome. Golf, fishing and antique shops nearby.*

Rooms: 1 double, en suite (shower); 1 twin with private bathroom.

Price: Double £30 p.p., twin £25 p.p. Single supp. £10.

Meals: Breakfast times flexible. Good food available locally.

Closed: Christmas & New Year.

Marlborough turn off A303 & through Monxton. After 2-3 miles, after golf driving range on left, 70 yds on, house signed right (thatched house at end).

From Salisbury, A354 towards Blandford, through Coombe Bissett. After 1.5 miles, left on bend to Rockbourne. Through village, 200 yds after 30 mph zone, house signed on left. After 50 yds, gravel drive on right.

The Hon Mrs Paul Chetwynd Talbot
Gunville House
Grately, Andover
Hampshire SP11 8JQ
Tel: 01264 889206
Fax: 01264 889060
E-mail: pct@onetel.net.uk

Lindy & Tony Ball
Marsh Barn
Rockbourne
Fordingbridge
Hampshire SP6 3NF
Tel: 01725 518768
Fax: 01725 518380

Entry No: 211   **Map no: 4**

Entry No: 212   **Map no: 4**

Outdoor types will be utterly at home at Sue's smallholding on the edge of the New Forest; there's plenty of space for wet clothes and muddy boots, and cattle graze within 10 feet of the window. You may hear the call of a nightjar in June; Dartford warblers nest nearby. Sue keeps a few sheep, free-range poultry, a horse and two cats; well-behaved dogs are welcome in the downstairs bedroom. Guests have their own little sitting room, warm, simple bedrooms, a friendly atmosphere and good home cooking.

Rooms: 1 double, en suite (bath/shower); 1 twin/double, en suite (bath).

Price: From £22 p.p. Single supp. £5. Reductions for longer stays.

Meals: Breakfast 7-9am; packed lunch £6; dinner, from £13, by prior arrangement.

Closed: Christmas & New Year.

On A338, 1 mile south of Fordingbridge, left at small x-roads for Hyde & Hungerford. Up hill & right at school on corner for Ogdens. Left at next x-roads for Ogdens North. House on right at bottom of hill.

Sue Browne
Sandy Corner
Ogdens North
Fordingbridge
Hampshire SP6 2QD
Tel: 01425 657295

Entry No: 213   **Map no: 4**

Enjoy a bracing early morning swim in the sea - it's a short sprint away; then back for a full English breakfast round the dining room's exotic glass-topped table, once owned by Gucci. Simon and actor Gary have decorated their 17th-century home - a poorhouse in a previous life - with theatrical flair. Beautiful bedrooms come with all sorts of unexpected extras like bath oils and sherry. Go for the one with the four-poster piled high with cushions to disguise the fact that the headboard was stolen a century ago.

Rooms: 1 four-poster, 1 double, both en suite; 1 twin/family room with private bathroom.

Price: £25-£40 p.p. Single occ. £50. Children £15.

Meals: Breakfast until 9.30am. Dinner available locally.

Closed: Never.

From Lymington, B3058 for Milford-on-Sea. House on left, just past village green.

Gary Payne & Simon Box
The Bay Trees
8 High Street
Milford-on-Sea
Hampshire SO41 0QD
Tel: 01590 642186
Fax: 01590 645461

Entry No: 214   **Map no: 4**

A town house - on the road but quiet, especially at night. The Jeffcocks are impeccably mannered and they care about their guests. Numerous cafés, restaurants and inns are a stroll away and Josephine and David will direct you to Lymington's myriad charms. Narrow and deep, the Edwardian house has some lovely pieces of furniture, a deep red dining room, lots of books and family portraits. Bedrooms are traditionally furnished with tallboys, dressing tables and displays of good china. *Children over eight welcome.*

Rooms: 1 twin, 1 double, sharing two private bathrooms.

Price: £25-£30 p.p. Single supp. £8.

Meals: Breakfast times flexible. Dinner available nearby.

Closed: Christmas & New Year.

A new house for Anthea, but the same enthusiastic welcome as in her previous Special Place. She adores her new acquisition - it dates from the 13th century when Richard de Ranville sailed here from Normandy and settled his family. Now Grade II*-listed, the herringbone brickwork is fascinating. There are five acres of garden and paddock, lovely prints and lots of books and large beds in big rooms that overlook a courtyard of old barns. The dining room – in the palest grey – has two large decorative carved wall lights. Anthea is a dynamo doing B&B for the fun of it.

Rooms: 3 twin/king-size, all en suite (bath/shower); 1 of these can be a family room.

Price: £25-£30 p.p. Single supp. £10.

Meals: Breakfast times flexible. Dinner available locally.

Closed: Christmas & New Year.

From Brockenhurst A337 to Lymington. Pass hospital to traffic lights on corner of Southampton Rd & Avenue Rd. Left into Avenue Rd. 20 yds on, a short driveway, 1st right, leads to back of house.

Exit M27 at junc. 2, A3090 for Romsey. Climb hill, then look for 'Gardener's Lane' on left. Drive 100 yds further on, on south side of dual carriageway & marked by a flagpole. Crossing marked with 2 white posts.

Josephine & David Jeffcock
West Lodge
40 Southampton Road
Lymington
Hampshire SO41 9GG
Tel: 01590 672237
Fax: 01590 673592
E-mail: jeffcock@amserve.net

Bill & Anthea Hughes
Ranvilles Farm House
Romsey
Hampshire SO51 6AA
Tel: 02380 814481
Fax: 02380 814481

Entry No: 215   **Map no: 4**

Entry No: 216   **Map no: 4**

Such attention to detail - beautiful china, white linen, stylish decoration. There's a warm and distinctive feel to this central but quiet 1860s mews house with pale oak floors, generous windows, an old oak beam and brick fireplaces. One bedroom has views to the east over Winchester and from the other you see Christ Church. Buffet breakfast is served with freshly-squeezed orange juice, fresh fruit salad, compote, organic yogurt, home-baked bread and there's the full English, too. "Perfection," said one guest. *Children over 11 welcome.*

Rooms: 1 twin, 1 double, both en suite (bath & shower).

Price: £32.50 p.p. Single occ. £55.

Meals: Breakfast until 9.30am. Dinner available locally.

Closed: Occasionally.

Susie is a natural, easy, courteous host in a house that sent our inspector into mild raptures. A galleried landing joins the newish addition to the old Victorian flint-and-brick schoolhouse (you can't see the join!). An instantly welcoming sense of family life greets you. And it gets better. The kitchen is a pure country-life retreat, all old oak and terracotta, the nerve centre of the vivacious Susie's cooking and entertaining - plainly a matter of great pride to her. You have your own delightful sitting room with open fire and piles of books. The garden is expansive.

Rooms: 1 double, 1 twin, both with private bathroom.

Price: £28 p.p. Single supp. £8-£10.

Meals: Breakfast until 9.30am; dinner, 3 courses, £22, by arrangement.

Closed: Mid-December-mid-January.

From M3, junc. 11, follow signs for Winchester. At 2nd r'bout, B3335 to St. Cross. 1.5 miles on, left after 1st pedestrian crossing into St. James Lane. Road 3rd on left. Parking available.

From M3 exit 9, A272 to Petersfield. After 2 miles, fork right to Warnford & Preshaw, over x-roads. House 2nd on left after 300 yds.

Gill Dowson
4 Alexandra Terrace
Winchester
Hampshire SO23 9SP
Tel: 01962 863356
Fax: 01962 868826
E-mail: gill.dowson@virgin.net

Susie Church
The Old School House
Lane End
Longwood, nr. Winchester
Hampshire SO21 1JZ
Tel: 01962 777248
Fax: 01962 777744

Entry No: 217   **Map no:** 4

Entry No: 218   **Map no:** 4

Lovely people and a charming house, Georgian in look - rather like an old rectory. It is in its own 15-acre grounds, yet just minutes from Winchester; elegantly decorated, full of antiques and ancestral portraits. The bedrooms have chintz, mahogany furniture and beautiful views. Sue modestly calls herself an 'amateur artist' - some of her watercolours decorate the bedrooms. An inspiration to the more energetic or divinely inspired, the house is on the Pilgrim's Way so the walking is ready-made. *Children over 10 welcome.*

Rooms: 1 twin, en suite (bath/shower); 1 twin with private bathroom.

Price: £25-£30 p.p. Single supp. £5.

Meals: Breakfast times flexible. Dinner available locally.

Closed: Christmas & New Year.

From M3, junc. 9, A272 to Winchester. At next r'bout, straight over. Left at small r'bout signed Morestead, then immed. left. 1 mile after Morestead, right to Owslebury. Through village, then left fork to Whadden Lane. 1st entrance 200 yds down lane on left.

Sue & Tim Torrington
Great Hunts Place
Owslebury, Nr. Winchester
Hampshire SO21 1JL
Tel: 01962 777234
Fax: 01962 777242
E-mail: tt@byngs.freeserve.co.uk
Web: www.byngs.freeserve.co.uk

Complete privacy in a B&B is rare. Here you have it, just 12 minutes' walk from the centre of town, Cathedral and water meadows. Relax in your own half of a Victorian townhouse beautifully furnished and decorated, and immensely welcoming. Fizzy serves sumptuous breakfasts and fresh flowers abound - guests have been delighted. You are also left with an 'honesty box' so you may help yourselves to drinks. The rooms are small and cosy with lovely big, antique mirrors, bedspreads and furniture; there is a log fire in the sitting room and a small garden, too. *Children over seven welcome*

Rooms: 1 twin, 1 double, both en suite (shower & bath).

Price: £25-£30 p.p. Single occ. £40.

Meals: Breakfast times flexible. Dinner available nearby.

Closed: Christmas.

Leave M3 at junc. 9 & take A272 Winchester exit, then signs for Winchester Park & Ride. Under m'way, straight on at r'bout signed to St. Cross. Left at T-junc. St. Faith's Rd about 100 yds ahead.

Guy & Fizzy Warren
Brymer House
29/30 St. Faith's Road
St. Cross, Winchester
Hampshire SO23 9QD
Tel: 01962 867428
Fax: 01962 868624
E-mail: brymerhouse@aol.com

Lord Nelson's cloak hung here - he was a friend of Admiral Thomson who created the house. Four generations of Hanbury-Batemans have lived here and beautiful furniture remains from each. Wooden and stone floors reflect the light that floods in; upstairs, all is carpeted. There are intriguing curios, statues and vases and Elisabeth, who is Austrian and an interior designer, brings it all together in elegant harmony. Bedrooms are immaculate; ornate mirrors and antique furniture. Lovely mature gardens, tennis court and croquet lawn. A good area for walking and fishing, too. *Babes in arms and children over 12 welcome.*

Rooms: 1 large twin, en suite; 1 large twin with basin and private bathroom.

Price: £35 p.p. Single supp. £10.

Meals: Breakfast times flexible; dinner, 3 courses, £25; 2 courses, £15, by arrangement.

Closed: Never.

From Andover, on A303, past petrol station, turn for Longparish. From B3048, 1st right for Forton, then 1st left onto private road.

Bill Hanbury-Bateman
Forton House
Long Parish
Andover
Hampshire SP11 6NN
Tel: 01264 720236
Fax: 01264 720885
E-mail: bandbbest@aol.com

Entry No: 221   **Map no: 4**

In the heart of a pretty thatch village with a working forge, the house is a beautiful, rambling, red-brick place, three 17th-century cottages knocked into one. The family adore it – it's been their home for years. Rachel is easy and happy for you to have full use of the family sitting room with comfy sofas during your stay. The garden is yours while you're here, too - long and green, with a stream and a croquet lawn at the end. Bedrooms are simple and cosy and can interconnect if you are a family.

Rooms: 1 twin with private bathroom (bath/shower); 1 single, en suite (bath).

Price: £25 p.p. No single supp.

Meals: Breakfast times flexible. Dinner available locally.

Closed: Ocassionally.

From Petersfield A272 towards Winchester. After about 3 miles left following signs to East Meon. There, left after church in to The Cross.

Rachel Mackinlay
Cross Keys
East Meon
Petersfield
Hampshire GU32 1NN
Tel: 01730 823251
Fax: 01730 823632

Entry No: 222   **Map no: 5**

Super hosts and one of the greatest gardens in the book... seven tended acres sit within 100 acres of woodland. There are Japanese and dahlia gardens, rare crocuses, fine specimen trees, formal terraces, a croquet lawn and exotica, all managed with flair and imagination. You breakfast in the chinoiserie dining room - the allegorical tableau is charming - and bedrooms are furnished in traditional style and have gorgeous garden views. The tennis court is hidden in the garden among some of the largest Wellingtonia in the country. The perfect English country house. *Children over 12 welcome.*

Rooms: 2 twins, 1 en suite (bath), 1 with private bathroom.

Price: From £30 p.p. Single supp. £10.

Meals: Breakfast times flexible; dinner, inc. wine, £20 by arrangement.

Closed: Christmas Day.

South on A3 to traffic lights at Hindhead. Straight across & after 400 yds, right onto B3002. Continue for 3 miles. Entrance to house (signed) on right in a wood.

Jeremy & Philippa Whitaker
Land of Nod
Headley
Bordon
Hampshire GU35 8SJ
Tel: 01428 713609
Fax: 01428 717698

Entry No: 223   **Map no: 5**

A lovely, beamy but roomy 16th-century farmhouse on a site with a medieval history. Harriet is planning a sculpture garden to add to the magic of the beautiful, two-acre landscaped gardens - already there is a lake, an upstairs conservatory, a heated covered pool, outdoor chess and a croquet lawn. Splendid breakfasts in the spectacular A-frame dining room, and the bedrooms are large, comfortable and even dramatic; one has a four-poster and a grand marble bathroom. Harriet and Julian are flexible and kind and will tell you about lovely walks in this designated AONB. *Children over eight welcome.*

Rooms: 1 twin, 1 double, 1 four-poster, all en suite (bath/shower).

Price: £30-£35 p.p. Single supp. by arrangement.

Meals: Breakfast 8-9am. Dinner available locally.

Closed: Christmas.

From A272 at Rogate, turn towards Harting/Nyewood. Cross humpback bridge; drive signed to right after 300 yds.

Harriet & Julian Francis
Mizzards Farm
Rogate
Petersfield
Hampshire GU31 5HS
Tel: 01730 821656
Fax: 01730 821655
E-mail: julian.francis@hemscott.net

Entry No: 224   **Map no: 5**

"Not a whisper of noise," says our inspector of this delightful house, part 17th century and part 19th, in one of the rare, undiscovered corners of rural England. If you enjoy the luxuries of space and tranquillity, this pristine house, full of antiques, old paintings and fine furniture, will bring joy to your heart. Large, airy and comfortable bedrooms with immaculate white linen and carpets that are soft underfoot. Guy not only makes bread but also grows fruit and vegetables which Amanda loves to cook and share, *en famille*, with guests at her elegant dining table. There's tennis, too. *Children over 12 welcome.*

Rooms: 1 twin, en suite (bath); 1 double, en suite (bath/shower).

Price: £34 p.p. Single supp. £10.

Meals: Breakfast times flexible; packed lunch, from £5, by arrangement; dinner, 3 courses, £22.

Closed: Occasionally.

From Tenbury Wells, to Leysters, on A4112, left at x-roads in village. Ignore sign to Leysters church. House on left, with wooden gate (after postbox in wall).

Guy & Amanda Griffiths
The Old Vicarage
Leysters, Leominster
Herefordshire HR6 0HS
Tel: 01568 750574
Fax: 01568 750208
E-mail: guy.griffiths@virgin.net
Web: www.oldvicar.co.uk

Entry No: 225   Map no: 9

An utterly fascinating place and with a butterfly house, too - Leslie is a keen lepidopterist. The 17th-century farmhouse, cider house, dairy, granary and 14-acre private nature reserve are perched at the top of a small valley; the views are tremendous. Excellent food is the hallmark of your stay - the Wiles are committed to using as many organic ingredients as possible, serve only organic wine and smoke their own fish and meat and make their own bread. One suite is across the courtyard, the other three in the granary annexe; they are all timber-framed, compact and have their own sitting rooms. You can be very private. *Children over eight welcome.*

Rooms: 4 suites, all with private bath/shower room & sitting room.

Price: £29.50 p.p. Single occ. £39.50.

Meals: Breakfast until 9.30am; dinner £15.50-£21.50.

Closed: Never.

From Leominster, A49 north but turning right onto A4122, signed Leysters. Lower Bache then signed after village of Kimbolton.

Rose & Leslie Wiles
Lower Bache House
Kimbolton
Nr. Leominster
Herefordshire HR6 0ER
Tel: 01568 750304
E-mail: leslie.wiles@care4free.net

Entry No: 226   Map no: 9

Herefordshire

A wonderful place that, after Herculean labours, has been brought back to life by James and Henrietta. It is set in parkland, high above the River Lugg, with views to the Black Mountains. There are comforting features such as a cast-iron bath in an attractive, modern bathroom, huge (and many) windows releasing light into rooms filled with some grand old furniture and interesting prints. It is snug, cosy, grand and without pretence - country house living at its most appealing. They cook a great breakfast, too. *Children over five welcome.*

Rooms: 2 doubles, 1 twin, all en suite.

Price: £25 p.p. Single supp. £10.

Meals: Breakfast times flexible; dinner £17.50.

Closed: Christmas & Easter.

Super hosts - a concert singer and a wine merchant - in whose company you can't fail to relax. You have all the advantages of being in a small town with a rural atmosphere thrown in; on one side the church, on the other a large garden which disappears into rolling hills. The dining room is magnificent, with full-height Georgian windows and shutters, oak burr sideboard and an ornate bookcase. The décor is charming with bare boards and paintwork effects and there are cotton sheets, lovely china, flowers, a roll-top, cast-iron bath and, for breakfast, home-made jams and marmalades. You can hire mountain bikes.

Rooms: 1 twin with basin, 1 double, both sharing bathroom.

Price: From £25 p.p.

Meals: Breakfast until 9.30am. Dinner available locally.

Closed: Christmas & New Year.

From Leominster B4361 north. 0.5 miles on, left for Eyton. 1.5 miles on, left for Kingsland. House 0.5 miles on right.

Coming into Kington, follow signs for town centre. Through middle of town & up long steady hill to St. Mary's church. House on left opposite.

James & Henrietta Varley
Eyton Old Hall
Eyton, Leominster
Herefordshire HR6 0AQ
Tel: 01568 612551
Fax: 01568 616100
E-mail: varleyeoh@hotmail.com
Web: www.eytonoldhall.fsnet.co.uk

Andrew & Lis Darwin
Church House
Church Road, Kington
Herefordshire HR5 3AG
Tel: 01544 230534
Fax: 01544 231100
E-mail: darwin@kc3.co.uk
Web: www.churchhousekington.co.uk

Entry No: 227   **Map no:** 9

Entry No: 228   **Map no:** 9

The picture belies the inviting warmth inside the house - the sitting room is snug with a woodburner and sofas and the kitchen is very much the gravitational centre of this home. Grace is chatty and informal and very settled in her unpretentious, modernised mill house. Rooms are small, with exposed beams and slate window sills, and only the old mill itself interrupts the view of the surrounding greenness. You drift off to sleep with the sound of the Arrow River burbling nearby - a real tonic for frazzled city-dwellers. *Children over four welcome.*

Rooms: 1 double, en suite (shower); 1 double sharing bathroom & wc with extra twin.

Price: £18-£22 p.p. No single supp.

Meals: Breakfast until 9am; dinner, from £12, by arrangement.

Closed: Christmas.

A438 from Hereford. After Winforton & Whitney-on-Wye & after toll bridge on left, sharp right for Brilley. Left fork to Huntington, over x-roads & next right to Huntington. Next right into 'No through' road, then 1st right.

Grace Watson
Hall's Mill House
Huntington
Kington
Herefordshire HR5 3QA
Tel: 01497 831409

Entry No: 229   **Map no: 9**

Pink fir apple potatoes and orchard fruit often end up on the dinner table: food is taken seriously here (they've won awards) and dinner is a four-course banquet. Steve and Jill decorate with panache, too: luxurious drapes and medieval-style high-backed chairs in the dining room and leather sofas and oak floorboards in the sitting room. Bedrooms are fresh and bright and bathrooms seductive (there's a *chaise longue* in one), candlelit and rather magical. The old farmhouse is perfectly quiet at night and Steve and Jill are warm and well-travelled. You'll feel at home. *Children over 10 welcome.*

Rooms: 1 double with private bathroom; 1 twin, en suite (shower); 1 twin with self-catering option (kitchen and shower).

Price: £35 p.p. Single supp. £10. Self catering £25 p.p., min. three nights.

Meals: Breakfast times flexible; dinner £25.

Closed: Never.

A4110 north to Wigmore. At 'Welcome' sign straight for 150 yds, then right. Drive 1st on left.

Steve Dawson & Jill Fieldhouse
Pear Tree Farm
Wigmore
Herefordshire HR6 9UR
Tel: 01568 770140
Fax: 01568 770141
E-mail: steveandjill@peartreefarmco.freeserve.co.uk
Web: www.peartreefarmco.freeserve.co.uk

Entry No: 230   **Map no: 9**

History comes alive in this gracious 16th-century manor house, visited by Wordsworth and King Charles II (who danced on the landing...); it is in a charming black and white village and surrounded by beautiful gardens and real countryside. The wrought-iron gates were admired by Pevsner and date from 1720. There are period furnishings throughout and you sleep in high brass beds with linen sheets; bathrooms are large and comfortable. Relax in front of the huge fire in the flagstoned hall or sit by the pool in summer.

Rooms: 1 twin, en suite (bath); 1 double with private bathroom.

Price: From £25 p.p.

Meals: Breakfast times flexible; dinner from £15, by arrangement.

Closed: Never.

Quite breathtaking. This Georgian gentleman's residence overlooks one of the finest views in England. Recline on the sofa in your divinely comfortable bedroom and gaze across the Wye Valley to the Malvern Hills and west to the Black Mountains. The rooms are gracious with fine family paintings and furniture. The magnificent four acres of garden include terracing, a walled garden with perfumed rose walk and parterres with rills of water and a 14th-century barn. An elegant country home - and Stephanie's cooking is worth a detour.

Rooms: 1 double, 1 twin, both with private bathrooms.

Price: From £28 p.p. Single supp. £5.

Meals: Breakfast times flexible; packed lunch from £3.50; dinner from £16.

Closed: Christmas.

From Leominster, A44 & follow signs for Brecon. After 6 miles, left into Dilwyn. Round 3 sharp bends. House set back on right behind stone gate piers & gates.

From A438 Hereford/Brecon road, towards Kington on A4111 through Eardisley village. House 2 miles up hill on left, behind a long line of conifers.

Tom & Jane Hawksley
The Great House
Dilwyn
Hereford
Herefordshire HR4 8HX
Tel: 01544 318007

Stephanie & John Grant
Bollingham House
Eardisley
Herefordshire HR5 3LE
Tel: 01544 327326
Fax: 01544 327880
E-mail: bollhouse@bigfoot.com

Entry No: 231   Map no: 9

Entry No: 232   Map no: 9

The floorboards squeak and creak in this renovated 17th-century grain barn, lovingly renovated by the Tong family with weatherboarding and stone tiling. It has a vast open threshing bay which frames the Welsh border woods and hills like an old-time idyll of rural England. The cattle byres house the conservatory; the bedrooms have simple modern furniture and share a shower room (a quick trot downstairs for those in the family room). Ann makes her own bread and preserves which she serves to guests. Honest value, rustic simplicity and superb views.

Rooms: 1 family (double & single), 1 twin, sharing shower & wc.

Price: £22 p.p. Children under 12, £16.

Meals: Breakfast about 8.30am; packed lunch, from £3; dinner £16. B.Y.O. wine.

Closed: Never.

An ecclesiastic entrance hall sweeps you into this imposing, red-brick Victorian vicarage; it was built for a wealthy friend of the diarist Francis Kilvert. Your attentive hostess Jill has recently decorated the light and well-proportioned rooms with period furniture, good fabrics and attractive, plain colours: we liked the duck-egg blue double with French bed (and it has a terrific bathroom, too). A sitting room for guests to relax in; plans for the garden and potager are well under way. Come for peace and elegance in a rural setting. Marvellous Wye Valley views too. *Children over 10 years welcome.*

Rooms: 1 double, en suite (bath & shower); 1 twin with private bathroom.

Price: £25 p.p.

Meals: Breakfast until 9.30am; dinner, £15, by arrangement.

Closed: Christmas & New Year.

From Hay, B4350 to Clifford. Pass Castle & right to Bredwardine. 3rd left at top of hill, signed Priory Wood. Pass between chapel & small playing field. Castleton Barn ahead on right.

A438 from Hereford, then A480 to Stretton Sugwas. After 8 miles, left to Norton Wood. House 1st on right.

Ann Tong
Castleton Barn
Priory Wood, Clifford
Nr. Hay-on-Wye
Herefordshire HR3 5HF
Tel: 01497 831690
Fax: 01497 831296

Jill Gallimore
The Old Vicarage
Norton Canon
Hereford
Herefordshire HR4 7BQ
Tel: 01544 318146

Entry No: 233   **Map no: 9**

Entry No: 234   **Map no: 9**

Herefordshire

Breathtaking in its ancient dignity - most of the house was built in 1500, and its undulating floors, great oak beams and two-foot thick walls are awe-inspiring. There are splashes of colour and candles everywhere and the timber-framed bedrooms are exceptional. The four-poster room has an Indian-style bathroom with ornate carved wood and a huge roll-top bath; the suite, a four poster-bed and a sitting area with two sofas. There's a guest sitting room, too. Jackie spoils you with decanters of sherry and wine or chocolates for special occasions. In summer the delightful garden is filled with the scent of herbs and flowers.

Rooms: 1 double, 1 king-size four-poster, 1 suite with king-size four-poster, all en suite (bath).

Price: Double £27 p.p. Four-poster £32 p.p. Suite £36 p.p. Single supp. £15.

Meals: Breakfast until 10am. Dinner available locally.

Closed: Christmas.

From Hereford, A438 into village. House on left with a green sign & iron gates.

Jackie Kingdon
Winforton Court
Winforton
Herefordshire HR3 6EA
Tel: 01544 328498
Fax: 01544 328498
E-mail: winfortoncourt@talk21.com

Entry No: 235   **Map no: 9**

A setting that reminds you of much that is special about this corner of Britain: the Monnow Valley, the Brecon Beacons, the Black Mountains; an ever-changing scene of lush tranquillity. The house is small, late Victorian and filled with warmth and charm - you eat Aga-cooked breakfasts and dinners at a long plank table and Caroline is an accomplished cook. The Knights Templar, then the Knights of St. John, once owned Garway church; it is a Norman gem. Somehow, the tranquillity and assurance of the church have communicated themselves to this house. *Children over eight welcome.*

Rooms: 1 four-poster, 1 twin, both with basin, sharing bathroom. Separate shower & wcs.

Price: £20-£25 p.p. Single supp. £5-£10.

Meals: Breakfast until 9.30am; dinner, £17.50, by arrangement.

Closed: Never.

From Hereford A49 towards Ross. After 5 miles A466 towards Monmouth. After 7 miles B4521 towards Abergavenny. At Broad Oak right towards Garway. 1st right past school signed Garway Hill. House 150 yds on right.

Caroline Ailesbury
The Old Rectory
Garway
Herefordshire HR2 8RH
Tel: 01600 750363
Fax: 01600 750364
E-mail: garwayoldrectory@yahoo.co.uk

Entry No: 236   **Map no: 9**

Herefordshire

The front is Georgian, the back Victorian. Inside, thick, thick walls and stone flags speak of a more ancient history. Valerie and Carol are clearly content in their uncontrived home. The pretty, traditional bedrooms have marvellous views of the richly-wooded countryside. Their grandchildren are regular visitors: your children may share toys in the house and garden, and you also have your own large piece of the two-and-a-half-acre garden and use of the tennis court. There's a small library; music appreciation is high on the agenda.

Rooms: 1 twin with private bathroom; 2 doubles sharing bathroom, shower & wc.

Price: £24.50 p.p. Children under 5, £5; 5-12, £15.

Meals: Breakfast times flexible. Restaurants a short drive away.

Closed: Never.

From Ross-on-Wye east on A40 towards Gloucester. Right to Hope Mansell. Take 3rd lane on left opposite Gallery. After 1 mile, house on left between lane sign-posted 'village hall' & church.

Mrs Carol Ouvry/Mrs Valerie Godson
The Old Rectory
Hope Mansell, Ross-on-Wye
Herefordshire HR9 5TL
Tel: 01989 750382
Fax: 01989 750382
E-mail: rectory@mansell.wyenet.co.uk

Entry No: 237   **Map no: 9**

You sleep in the ancient heart of the house, among 12th-century timbers and 18th-century additions. Grove House is wonderfully warm and cosseting - the dark wood gleams and large, luxurious rooms glow in firelight. In the elegant guests' drawing room there are books by the fire and plump armchairs and sofas to sink into and, in the bedrooms, window-seats, ornately-carved canopied beds and Jacobean panelling. Michael is an excellent cook and dinner is a special occasion, so do eat in. You can play tennis, swim in the neighbour's pool or walk the Malvern Hills. Perfect.

Rooms: 3 doubles, 2 four-posters, 1 twin/double, all en suite.

Price: £36.50 p.p. Single supp. £15. Small children free.

Meals: Breakfast times flexible; dinner £22.

Closed: Christmas & New Year.

Leave M50 at junc. 2, towards Ledbury. 1st left to Bromsberrow Heath. Right by post office & up hill. House on right.

Michael & Ellen Ross
The Grove House
Bromsberrow Heath
Ledbury
Herefordshire HR8 1PE
Tel: 01531 650584

Entry No: 238   **Map no: 9**

Forests must have fallen to build this house; the 1612 barn behind the Georgian façade is a soaring tangle of timbers, a paean to carpentry. The hall, open to the roof, is beautiful, with Chippendale panels in the staircase - oak beams and timber crucks are on bold display. Guests have a sitting room; breakfast is served in the beamed dining room. The bedrooms are comfortable; in some Judi provides towelling robes for the quick flit to the antique bath. A delightfully unexpected house with a charming hostess, and there is a lovely walled garden, too... all this in the centre of Ledbury.

Rooms: 1 double, en suite (shower); 1 double, 1 twin, both with basin, sharing bathroom.

Price: £29-£32.50 p.p. Single occ. from £48.

Meals: Breakfast until 9.30am; packed lunch sometimes available by request. Dinner available locally.

Closed: Christmas.

From Ledbury bypass, A449 signed Worcester/town centre. Barn House on left just past Somerfield but before central town x-roads.

Judi Holland
The Barn House
New Street
Ledbury
Herefordshire HR8 2DX
Tel: 01531 632825
E-mail: barnhouseledbury@lineone.net
Web: www.thebarnhouse.net

Entry No: 239   **Map no: 9**

An honest, authentic, farmhouse with hanging game, livestock, an assortment of farm buildings and a deep sense of rural peace. Elizabeth, a busy farmer's wife, manages it all efficiently with husband Peter - they were lambing when we were there. This is a traditional livestock and hop farm which still dries its own hops; in September you can watch their oast house at work. You will eat home-produced meat, preserves and vegetables - Elizabeth is a fine cook. The buildings, about 500 years old, ramble and enfold both gardens and guests. Bedrooms are timber-framed with bright fabrics.

Rooms: 1 twin, en suite (bath/shower); 1 twin, 1 double, en suite (bath).

Price: £20-£25 p.p. Single occ. £28.

Meals: Breakfast times flexible; dinner, 3 courses, £14.

Closed: Never.

From Hereford, east on A438. A417 into Stretton Grandison. 1st right past village sign, through Holmend Park. Veer left past phone box. House on left.

Elizabeth & Peter Godsall
Moor Court Farm
Stretton Grandison
Nr. Ledbury
Herefordshire HR8 2TP
Tel: 01531 670408

Entry No: 240   **Map no: 9**

Breakfast beside the great log fire in the Tudor dining room on chilly mornings, or under the spreading chestnut tree on warm days. The house and hosts are entirely natural and easy to be with. The rambling old manor with gardens and croquet lawn sits just beside the lovely 12th-century church. Rooms are big, family-style, with books, flowers and garden views; bedrooms are without a whiff of anything designery. You will be most comfortable. Relax after dinner in the cosy, little, oak-panelled sitting room. Two excellent pubs within walking distance, too.

Rooms: 2 twins/doubles, both en suite (bath).

Price: £25 p.p. Single supp. £5.

Meals: Breakfast times flexible; packed lunch on request; dinner £18.50 by arrangement.

Closed: Never.

Just walk into that barn and look up. Wow! The roof is breathtaking, a copse of beams and timbers. Few conversions are as successful as this one, but Judy is an artist, a painter, and impossibly resourceful - so no wonder. It is fresh, new, bright and clean; it is comfortable, too, and as they have moved from Prior's Court (in previous editions of our book) they will bring cohorts of loyal fans - so come soon. It is a generous place - they will ferry you to the pub in the evening. Lovely people.

Rooms: 1 double, en suite (bath & shower); 1 twin/double with private bathroom (bath & shower).

Price: £25 p.p. Single supp. £5.

Meals: Breakfast times flexible. Dinner available locally.

Closed: Never.

From A417 south, left to Ullingswick at x-roads. Through village, left then right at signs to Ullingswick church. Drive on right before church lychgate.

At Burley Gate r'bout on A417, A465 towards Bromyard. At Stoke Lacy church, on right, right then 2nd right to entrance.

Christopher & Susan Dalton
Upper Court
Ullingswick
Herefordshire HR1 3JQ
Tel: 01432 820295
Fax: 01432 820174
E-mail: ucbb@hotmail.com

Roger & Judy Young
Dovecote Barn
Stoke Lacy
Herefordshire HR7 4HJ
Tel: 01432 820968
Fax: 01432 820969
E-mail: dovecotebarn@mail.com

Entry No: 241   **Map no:** 9

Entry No: 242   **Map no:** 9

What a treat to stay in an attractive listed 17th-century farmhouse set high up on a sheep-strewn hill amid its own working farm. The views reach to the Cotswolds on a fine day and the garden is extensive, with a tennis court, croquet lawn and stables. Within, more character than luxury: big old fireplaces and beams, comfortable sofas and wonky floors that squeak. Bertie is a dab hand at breakfast, using free-range, home-produced eggs; Caroline cooks a delicious dinner. Bedrooms are engagingly timeworn, with good carpets, fine old family furniture and views. Utterly peaceful – and fun, too.

Rooms: 1 twin with private bathroom. Further twin/double let to members of same party.

Price: £25 p.p. No single supp.

Meals: Breakfast times flexible; dinner £18.

Closed: Occasionally.

From Bromyard, 3 miles on B4203 towards Great Witley. Pass Saltmarsh Castle on left. Next drive on right. (Tarmac drive & wooden gates.) 3 miles from Bromyard Post Office.

Bertie & Caroline Cotterell
Upper Norton
Tedstone Wafre
Bromyard
Herefordshire HR7 4PN
Tel: 01885 483141
Fax: 01885 488710
E-mail: woodenconcepts@btinternet.com

Entry No: 243   **Map no: 9**

The whole place is peppered with antiques and has an undeniable charm, but you don't have to tiptoe for fear of spoiling a contrived tidiness – Julia is easy-going and natural. Bedrooms are beamy and snug – the en-suite room is under the thatch with garden views, the other two look onto an avenue of horse chestnuts that were planted on the village green to commemorate the jubilee of George V. There's a duck pond and an excellent village pub. Hard to believe that this 15th-century cottage is only five minutes' drive from Stansted; no noise here, though - the flight path is in the opposite direction.

Rooms: 2 doubles, 1 twin, all en suite.

Price: From £27.50 p.p. Single occ. from £35.

Meals: Breakfast times flexible; packed lunch, from £3-£5, on request.

Closed: Never.

From Stansted Mountfitchet B1051 for approx. 5 miles, through Elseham. Left for Henham (signed). Right at War Memorial. Wood End Green on right with avenue of large trees. Cottage on far right corner.

George & Julia Griffiths
Pleasant Cottage
Wood End Green, Henham
Bishops Stortford
Hertfordshire CM22 6AZ
Tel: 01279 850792
Fax: 01279 850792

Entry No: 244   **Map no: 11**

Lutyens built this wonderful house in 1901 for his mother-in-law, Lady Lytton. Set down a long drive in six acres of beautiful gardens and fields, each elevation of the house is different. Architectural peculiarities - such as internal, octagonal windows - abound and Samantha has applied her considerable artistic skills to the interior; the downstairs rooms, particularly, are elegant and formal. Unusual colour schemes offset magnificent antiques, tapestries and chinoiserie. The family is happy to share its home and can converse in a clutch of languages.

Rooms: 1 double, en suite (shower); 1 family suite (1 double room/1 twin room) with bathroom; 1 double with private shower sometimes available.

Price: £35 p.p. Single occ. £45. Family suite £70 for two, £15 per extra person.

Meals: Breakfast times flexible. Dinner available locally.

Closed: 20 December-3 January.

Into Knebworth on B197, turn into Station Rd which becomes Park Lane. 300 yds after crossing m'way bridge, left into public footpath. After 300 yds, bear left through lodge gates. House at end.

Samantha Pollock-Hill
Homewood
Knebworth
Hertfordshire SG3 6PP
Tel: 01438 812105
Fax: 01438 812572
E-mail: sami@pollock-hill.fsnet.co.uk
Web: www.homewood-bb.co.uk

Entry No: 245   **Map no: 11**

A handsome Grade II-listed rectory in the village where George Bernard Shaw lived - his house is now owned by the National Trust. Relax on the sun-drenched terrace for breakfast or settle by the log fire in the 17th-century dining room. The bedrooms are reached through a flower-filled, cobbled courtyard and there's an ivy-clad squash court in the garden. Helen and Dick are kind and relaxed; they will tell you of wonderful walks and bike rides and introduce you to their enchanting local inn. All this only 35 minutes from London. *Children by arrangement.*

Rooms: 3 doubles/twins, both en suite.

Price: £37.50 p.p. Single supp. by arrangement.

Meals: Breakfast times flexible; light supper trays or dinner, from £8-£20, by arrangement.

Closed: Christmas.

Exit A1 at junc. 4. Follow signs to B653, towards Wheathamstead. At r'bout continue on B653 & take 1st right signed Codicote & The Ayots. Left up Bride Hall Lane, signed Shaws Corner. Right into drive before red phone box in village.

Helen & Dick Dunn
The Old Rectory
Ayot St. Lawrence
Welwyn
Hertfordshire AL6 9BT
Tel: 01438 820429
Fax: 01438 821844
E-mail: AyotBandB@aol.com

Entry No: 246   **Map no: 11**

An oasis only 30 minutes by train from central London and 10 minutes from Luton Airport; many guests choose Paddock Lodge for its convenience. You are surrounded by cornfields, woods and lovely views and the house is large and old, yet wonderfully cosy; a big, quiet garden, too. The kitchen is bright and informal and dinner is served in the pretty dining room. There are antiques, Limoges porcelain, lovely soft furnishings and unfussy bedrooms with comfortable beds. Claire, friendly and chatty, sweeps visitors of all ages into her easy-going welcome.

Rooms: 1 twin, en suite (bath); 1 twin with private bathroom & shower.

Price: £30 p.p. Single occ. £35.

Meals: Breakfast times flexible; dinner, £25, by arrangement.

Closed: Christmas & New Year.

From A1 junc. 4, B653 for Wheathampstead. After Brocket Hall, follow signs to Kimpton. After 2nd r'bout, follow signs to Kimpton & 2nd left to Porters End. 1st house on left after 0.5 miles.

Alex & Claire van Straubenzee
Paddock Lodge
Porters End
Kimpton
Hertfordshire SG4 8ER
Tel: 01438 832423
Fax: 01438 833527
E-mail: vanstraubenzee@btinternet.com

Entry No: 247   **Map no: 11**

Old-fashioned roses, pelargoniums, a willow tunnel and 40 thriving varieties of clematis – a horticultural haven in the heart of open fields. Sue, relaxed and friendly, will point you towards rare wild flower sites in this remote spot. Her green fingers extend into the pretty conservatory too, where you eat breakfast - local sausages and home-made muffins - surrounded by greenery and with perfect views. Bedrooms are cottagey – we liked the double with its white and brass bed. The peachy guest sitting room is elegant, too, with doors that open onto the garden. *Children over 12 welcome.*

Rooms: 1 twin, 1 single, both with private bathroom; 1 double, en suite (shower).

Price: From £25 p.p. Single occ. from £30.

Meals: Breakfast until 10am. Dinner available locally.

Closed: Christmas & New Year.

South on A413 from Wendover. Pass Jet station, left to Kings Ash. 2 miles on, left at x-roads to Old Swan Pub. Pass Pub. 0.5 miles on, ignore sharp right, but go sharp left onto bridlepath. 2nd gate along.

Mike & Sue Jepson
Field Cottage
St Leonards
Nr. Tring
Hertfordshire HP23 6NS
Tel: 01494 837602

Entry No: 248   **Map no: 10**

They are both garden photographers and their garden is testimony to their careers. Their home, neighbouring an 11th-century church, is in the loveliest part of the island, an AONB, with high ground and great walks on the Downs. Nearby is Newtown River and Nature Reserve - a favourite with walkers and bird-watchers; pretty Yarmouth is nearby. Guests have their own entrance into a super twin room with a private sitting room which has a mix of modern furniture and some old pieces. Nothing is too much trouble for your hosts. Sheila brings in your delicious breakfast: fresh fruit, free-range eggs, croissants, the full works. Peaceful and private.

Rooms: 1 twin with sitting room, bathroom and separate entrance.

Price: £35 p.p. Single supp. £5.

Meals: Breakfast times flexible. Dinner available locally.

Closed: Christmas Day.

From Yarmouth take road to Shalfleet through village. After 0.5 miles right for Calbourne. House by church across green.

Sheila & Oliver Mathews
The Old Rectory
Calbourne
Isle of Wight PO30 4JE
Tel: 01983 531247
Fax: 01983 531253
E-mail: oliver@mathews-photography.com

Entry No: 249   **Map no: 4**

The Harrisons bought this stunning Jacobean pile for its matchless gardens: 15 acres of pathed wilderness, exotic and subtropical flowers. A stroll is an adventure; you come across an old swimming pool cascading with plants, a bench on a lofty vantage point, a crystal clear stream banked with bamboo, a smooth lawn, a walled garden, a sunken rose garden and a grass tennis court. In a quiet village in lovely downland this massive house has inviting rooms and acres of space; it would take a lot more furniture to fill it. Come to the Isle of Wight if only to see the garden.

Rooms: 3 doubles, 3 twins, all en suite (bath/shower), in two separate wings.

Price: £22.50-£28 p.p. Single supp. £10.

Meals: Breakfast 8-9.15am; light meals available if ordered in advance. Pub 3 minutes' walk through gardens.

Closed: Christmas.

From Newport, drive into Shorwell, down a steep hill, under a rustic bridge & right opposite a thatched cottage. Signed.

John & Christine Harrison
North Court
Shorwell
Isle of Wight PO30 3JG
Tel: 01983 740415
Fax: 01983 740409
E-mail: christine@north-court.demon.co.uk

Entry No: 250   **Map no: 4**

You sleep on a French rosewood bed, and there's a huge cast iron bath IN your room - ideal for wallowing by candlelight with a glass of wine. There's a head-clearing simplicity in this unique 'first-floor' Saxon house with living space on top and the windowless ground floor reserved for defence purposes or storage. Limewashed walls, wooden floors and exposed A-frame beams in both bedrooms and a private garden. The cottage with huge sofa and Shaker-style dining furniture is equally stunning. *Children over 12 welcome.*

Rooms: 1 double, en suite (bath); 1 double, en suite (bath/shower). Self-catering cottage, sleeps 4+.

Price: £30-£40 p.p. Single occ. by arrangement. Cottage £300-£600 p.w.

Meals: Breakfast times flexible. Dinner available locally.

Closed: Never.

0.5 miles south of Chale Green on B3399; after village, left at Gotten Lane; house at end of lane.

Caroline Smith
Gotten Manor
Gotten Lane
Chale, Isle of Wight PO38 2HQ
Tel: 01983 551368
Fax: 0870 1369453
E-mail: b&b@gottenmanor.co.uk
Web: www.gottenmanor.co.uk

Entry No: 251   **Map no: 4**

Sue loves colour - all the rooms feel light and airy and furnishings are a mixture of faded traditional and family-crafted pieces. Bedrooms and bathrooms feel fresh. The garden room has lovely rural views and from the terrace, where you can breakfast on sunny mornings, you can admire Sue's ongoing restoration of the three-acre garden, consider a game of tennis or croquet, or a walk into historic Westerham. Only 22 miles from the bustle of London, yet the feel is bucolic and Sue will spoil you with home-made treats.

Rooms: 1 twin, 1 double, with basins, sharing large bathroom; 1 twin with private bathroom.

Price: £25 p.p. Single supp. £15.

Meals: Breakfast 7am-9am; can be flexible. Excellent selection of places for dinner in Westerham.

Closed: Christmas week.

M25, junction 6, follow signs to Westerham (A25). After Westerham town sign & 30mph sign, 1st left into Farley Lane. After approx. 200 yds, left at top, then left again.

Sue & Alastair Marr
Worples Field
Farley Common
Westerham
Kent TN16 1UB
Tel: 01959 562869
E-mail: marr@worplesfield.com
Web: www.worplesfield.com

Entry No: 252   **Map no: 5**

In May the scent from the azaleas and rhododendrons is intoxicating. But even the glories of the garden cannot diminish the impact of this part-Edwardian, part-Tudor house. The Streatfeilds have been in Chiddingstone for centuries - the castle was their seat - but carry their history lightly. They are well-mannered, intelligent, easy folk. Some furniture is well-worn and faded but everything feels authentic. Bedrooms are huge, with views over the gardens, grazing sheep and hills, and there are fireside chairs in the library. Everything for children, too. It's worth every penny. *Minimum 2 nights' stay at weekends.*

Rooms: Main house: 1 twin, 1 double, sharing bathroom; 1 double with private bathroom. Annexe: 1 double, en suite (bath).

Price: £27.50-£30 p.p.; single occ. £30-£40.

Meals: Breakfast until 9am; light suppers and dinners £12.50-£20.

Closed: Christmas & New Year.

From A21, Hildenborough exit. Follow signs to Penshurst Place, then to vineyard. Pass it. Right at T-junc. for Edenbridge. Through village, bear left, signed to Edenbridge. House 0.5 miles on left.

Mr & Mrs Mervyn Streatfeild
Hoath House
Chiddingstone Hoath
Nr. Edenbridge
Kent TN8 7DB
Tel: 01342 850362
Fax: 01342 841066
E-mail: jstreatfeild@hoath_house.freeserve.co.uk

Entry No: 253   **Map no: 5**

Nicholas is known to the family as Marco Pierre Morris - an enthusiastic cook, he loves to prepare breakfasts of home-made breads, jams, yogurt, eggs and, maybe, hash browns or kippers. On arrival, you may try his home-made cakes and drop scones. Guests have their own beamed sitting room in the old Bake House and bedrooms are simple, but fresh. The house dates from about 1750 and, curiously, manages to be in two places at once – the parish boundary runs straight through the middle with one half in Leigh, the other in Chiddingstone.

Rooms: 2 twins, both en suite (1 shower, 1 bath); 1 twin with private bathroom.

Price: £22.50-£25 p.p. Single occ. £35.

Meals: Breakfast times flexible. Dinner available locally.

Closed: Never.

B2027 0.5 miles north of Chiddingstone Causeway. Equidistant between Tonbridge, Sevenoaks & Edenbridge.

Nicholas & Ginny Morris
Charcott Farmhouse
Charcott
Leigh, Tonbridge
Kent TN11 8LG
Tel: 01892 870024
Fax: 01892 870158
E-mail: nicholasmorris@charcott.freeserve.co.uk

Entry No: 254   **Map no: 5**

The views from the doorstep are tremendous - you won't want to move! There's not a road or railway line within sight of this working farm which has been in the family since 900. Without it is handsome and imposing; within, comfort and elegance go hand-in-hand: large dining and drawing rooms, high ceilings and beautiful mahogany furniture. Rosemary, kindness itself, looks after guests well - they always comment on the peace and quiet. Bedroom, huge, light and never fussy, have very large bathrooms... and those views! *Children over 12 welcome.*

Rooms: 2 twins, 1 en suite, 1 with private bathroom; 1 double with private bathroom.

Price: £27.50-£32 p.p. Single occ. variable.

Meals: Breakfast until 9am; Sundays until 9.30am; dinner, from £12.50, by arrangement.

Closed: 1 December-31 January.

At lights in centre of Hawkhurst, A268 towards Rye. 1.5 miles after lights, at Four Throws post office, immed. right into Conghurst Lane. Driveway signed on left after 1.25 miles on left.

Rosemary Piper
Conghurst Farm
Hawkhurst
Kent TN18 4RW
Tel: 01580 753331
Fax: 01580 754579
E-mail: rosa@conghurst.co.uk

Entry No: 255   **Map no:** 6

Gabled windows look over open countryside, and roses and climbers decorate the pretty pink and blue brickwork. Such a handsome house. In the garden there are all sorts of things for your comfort - huge, cotton parasol and wooden tables and chairs. You are right on Romney Marsh which begs to be explored. In the stable twin you have complete privacy, your own sitting room and garden furniture; it's very quiet and pretty and you can come and go as you like. The Sherstons have an easy humour and know well how to look after guests. *Children over 10 welcome.*

Rooms: 1 twin in stable with sitting room and bathroom; 1 double, en suite (bath); 1 twin with private bathroom.

Price: From £22-£30 p.p. Single occ. from £25.

Meals: Breakfast times flexible. Excellent pub 1.5 miles away.

Closed: Never.

M20, exit 10 for Brenzett. A2070 for approx. 6 miles. Right for Hamstreet, & immed. left. In Hamstreet, right onto B2067, left for Warehorne church. Through Warehorne to level crossing. House 1 mile on, on right.

The Sherston Family
Terry House
Warehorne
Ashford
Kent TN26 2LS
Tel: 01233 732443
Fax: 01233 732466
E-mail: jsherston@ukonline.co.uk

Entry No: 256   **Map no:** 6

So robust is the wisteria-clad 15th-century timber framed Hall that it survived intact when it slid 50 feet down the hill in a dramatic subsidence in 1726. Noel Coward, who stayed here, would have admired its obduracy, as will you. A striking entrance leads straight to the huge sitting room, with massive fireplace and a panelled oak staircase. Everywhere 18th- and 19th-century paintings gaze down - some are for sale. Bedrooms are suitably simple and all have 40-gallon iron bathtubs and panoramic views. Fun people - it's hard to leave.

Rooms: 2 doubles, both en suite (bath/shower), 1 with adjoining twin for children.

Price: £30 p.p. Single supp. £5.

Meals: Breakfast until 9.30am. Dinner available locally.

Closed: Christmas & New Year.

From M20 at junc. 11, A20 south, then B2068 (Stone St), to Lympne. Approx. 0.25 miles on is County Members pub, & school sign on right. Left opposite convex mirror. House at end of lane.

Peter & Matty Gaston
The French House
Lympne, Nr. Hythe
Kent CT21 4PA
Tel: 01303 265974
Fax: 01303 262545
E-mail: gastons@frenchouse.freeserve.co.uk
Web: www.frenchouse.freeserve.co.uk

Entry No: 257   **Map no: 6**

The Lathams are well-travelled, friendly and active, yet firmly attached to their home and its surrounding 200 acres of land. The house is a curious mix of styles: Tudor, Georgian and modern coexist in harmony. High ceilings and a conservatory with terracotta-tiled floor, brimming with greenery, conjure up images of the decadent '20s. You'll find good furniture, yet the house is truly homely; bedrooms are comfortable with traditional bathrooms. Guests have their own log-fired drawing room with wonderful views of all that countryside. Only 10 minutes from the Chunnel. *Children over 10 welcome.*

Rooms: 3 twins, 2 en suite (bath), 1 let only to members of same party willing to share bathroom.

Price: £27.50-£30 p.p. Single occ. £35.

Meals: Breakfast until 9.30am; dinner, £20-£25, by arrangement.

Closed: Christmas & New Year.

From M20 junc. 11, B2068 north. After 4.6 miles, left opposite B.P. garage. House at bottom of hill on left, after 1.7 miles. Left into drive.

Richard & Virginia Latham
Stowting Hill House
Stowting
Nr. Ashford
Kent TN25 6BE
Tel: 01303 862881
Fax: 01303 863433

Entry No: 258   **Map no: 6**

Deep in the countryside and near the coast, but only 15 minutes from Canterbury, Woodmans was originally two 17th-century cottages and has been a pub and private hotel. Rendered, with a Kent peg-tiled roof, it's a comfortable warren of a place, full of books and flowers, relaxing and peaceful. There's a private entrance to the bedroom which has sloping beams, packed bookshelves, potted plants and a big bathroom. Breakfast will be brought on a tray to your room if you don't feel like emerging, or to the garden on sunny mornings. *Babies welcome.*

Rooms: 1 double, en suite.

Price: £30 p.p. No single supp.

Meals: Breakfast until 9.30am; packed lunch £5; dinner, 3 courses, £20.

Closed: Never.

If you enter by the back door you will miss the dazzling effect of the hall on first sight. It beckons you into the rest of the house. When house and garden are gorgeous, hosts enchanting and the area hums with history, what more can one ask? Fine bedrooms, good furniture, a big, cast-iron bath that will diminish you. Katie arranges flowers beautifully and is generous with them amid the Georgian elegance; both she and Neil, who runs an Audio Book Library from the converted stables, are very present to enjoy your company. *Children over eight welcome.*

Rooms: 2 doubles, en suite (bath).

Price: £37.50 p.p. Single supp. £10.

Meals: Breakfast until 9.30am (Mon-Fri); weekends by arrangement; dinner, £25, by arrangement; light suppers can be organised.

Closed: Christmas & New Year.

From A2, 2nd exit to Canterbury. Follow ring road & B2068 for Hythe. Over A2, on for 2 miles, through Lower Hardres, past Granville pub. Right for Petham & Waltham. 1.5 miles after Waltham, right into Hassell St. House 4th on left.

From Canterbury A257 towards Sandwich. On approach to Ash, stay on A257 (do not enter village), then left at sign to Weddington. House 200 yds down on left.

Sarah Rainbird
Woodmans
Hassell Street, Hastingleigh
Nr. Ashford
Kent TN25 5JE
Tel: 01233 750250

Katie & Neil Gunn
Great Weddington, Ash
Nr. Canterbury
Kent CT3 2AR
Tel: 01304 813407
Fax: 01304 812531
E-mail: traveltale@aol.com
Web: www.greatweddington.co.uk

Entry No: 259   **Map no: 6**   **Entry No: 260**   **Map no: 6**

Jac cheerfully deals with everyone's needs - she'll drive you into Canterbury, babysit and prepare family meals or special suppers. Chris cooks a great breakfast. You have the run of the house with its two inglenooks and complete privacy in your own wing, with a sitting room. Bedrooms are spotless and fresh, with ribbon-trimmed duvet covers and floral borders. Bathrooms are modern and the garden is great for children. The Brays' two grown-up boys are county cricket players; the county ground is a 10-minute walk away.

Rooms: 1 double, 1 double/twin, both en suite (shower); 1 double with adjoining twin, en suite (bath).

Price: From £20 p.p. Children £5-£15.

Meals: Breakfast times flexible; lunch £5; dinner £10; by arrangement.

Closed: Never.

From M20 exit 11, B2068 for Canterbury. After crossing A2, house, white with post box in wall, is about 100 yds on right. (Head for county cricket ground & phone if lost.)

Chris & Jac Bray
Sylvan Cottage
Nackington Road
Canterbury
Kent CT4 7AY
Tel: 01227 765307/769728
Fax: 01227 478411
E-mail: jac@sylvan5.fsnet.co.uk

Entry No: 261   **Map no: 6**

The six acres of gardens with a pond, obelisk and orchards are immaculate; the views in this AONB are magnificent. Susan and Markham clearly love meeting new people. This is a large, traditional country house - strong colours contrast well with dark, antique furniture and Liberty prints; the hall is hung with Chinese silk carpet, Thai pictures and Indian pictures. The music room has an organ that Markham plays, occasionally giving concerts for charity – guests are welcome to attend. There is a luxurious indoor swimming pool.

Rooms: 1 four-poster, 1 double, 1 twin, all en suite (shower).

Price: £29-£32 p.p. Single supp. £3.

Meals: Breakfast until 9.15am; dinner, 2 courses, £17 (incl. coffee).

Closed: Christmas.

From A2 at Faversham, Brogdale Road to Eastling. 1.5 miles past Carpenters Arms pub, right (by postbox). House 0.5 miles on right.

Susan & Markham Chesterfield
Frith Farm House
Otterden
Faversham
Kent ME13 0DD
Tel: 01795 890701
Fax: 01795 890009
E-mail: markham@frith.force9.co.uk

Entry No: 262   **Map no: 6**

There has been a house here since the Domesday Book. The old part, built of Kentish ragstone, has massive white-painted (medieval?) beams; the 19th-century extension continued the low ceilings. Two inviting bedrooms have white broderie duvet covers and fresh flowers. Meals are eaten in the elegant dining room while kingfishers and herons find their dinner in the spring-fed pond outside. Denise is quietly welcoming, generous and loves children, gardening, her ginger cat and Mabel, a West Highland terrier. Superb for ferry and tunnel.

Rooms: 2 twins, sharing bathroom.

Price: From £25 p.p. Single occ. from £30.

Meals: Breakfast times flexible; packed lunch £7.50; dinner, 3 courses, £17.50, by arrangement.

Closed: Christmas.

Exit at M20 junc. 9. At 2nd r'bout A20 to Lenham. After 1 mile, left at Godinton Lane. After 2 miles, house 2nd on right. Red postbox by gate.

Charles & Denise Wilkinson
Worten House
Great Chart
Ashford
Kent TN23 3BU
Tel: 01233 622944
Fax: 01233 662249
E-mail: charles.wilkinson@btinternet.co.uk

Entry No: 263   **Map no: 6**

This beautiful, porticoed, brick house has a gorgeous drawing room, fabulous antiques and family portraits. There's a secret garden within the grounds and an arbour and a pond. The large front bedroom is tremendous, more like a suite, with good furniture, fine views and an open fire in winter - a rare treat. Bathrooms have towelling robes, shower caps, etc. John is unflappable and a touch mischievous; Gillian welcomes you into their home with well-judged humour and easy charm - you'll like her. *Children over 12 welcome.*

Rooms: 3 doubles, 1 en suite (bath), 2 with private bathrooms.

Price: From £35 p.p. Single supp. £5.

Meals: Breakfast until noon; dinner £25.

Closed: Christmas & New Year.

From Dover, M2 to Medway Services. Into station, continue on road past pumps. Ignore exit signs. Left at T-junc., 1st left & continue for 200 yds. Left at next T-junc. House 3rd on left.

Gillian & John Yerburgh
Hartlip Place
Place Lane
Nr. Sittingbourne
Kent ME9 7TR
Tel: 01795 842583
Fax: 01795 842673
E-mail: jyerburgh@aol.com

Entry No: 264   **Map no: 6**

A small manor house built in the 1600s by a wealthy wool merchant to store and display his wares. Its ancient character and architectural details have survived intact. It's a delightfully artistic, beamed, home. Mr Wetton, charming and friendly, does most of the looking after; Anne is a picture framer. Bedrooms are charming and lack nothing. Grand piano in the drawing room, a conservatory for breakfast and an English country garden to explore. Basil and Bertie, the resident alpacas, are an enchanting improvement on mechanical mowers.

Rooms: 1 twin, en suite (bath), 1 twin, en suite (bath/shower), 1 double, en suite (shower).

Price: £28 p.p. No single supp.

Meals: Breakfast until 9am. Dinner available locally.

Closed: Christmas & New Year.

From Maidstone/Hastings A229. At lights at Linton x-roads, turn off for Coxheath & through village. 1st left down Hunton Hill. Pass church, park & school, then right into Grove Lane.

Gavin & Anne Wetton
The Woolhouse
Grove Lane
Hunton
Kent ME15 0SE
Tel: 01622 820778
Fax: 01622 820645

Entry No: 265   **Map no: 6**

The Parkers were so taken with the drawing room that they bought the house. Once the house library, the room is huge, with ribbon-and-wreath cornicing and a panelled ceiling. Breakfast is served here - maybe home-made yogurt with Kentish cherries? One of the bedrooms has French doors to the terrace, both are light and inviting with fluffy towels and treats on the tea tray. Your hosts are great garden lovers, as you will see from theirs, and very knowledgeable about the ones you can visit locally, too. *Children over five welcome.*

Rooms: 1 double with private bathroom; 1 twin, en suite.

Price: £25-£35 p.p. Single supp. £10.

Meals: Breakfast times flexible. Dinner available locally.

Closed: Christmas & New Year.

A262 to Goudhurst. There, B2079 to Marden. West Winchet is 2 miles from village, on left.

Annie Parker
West Winchet
Winchet Hill
Goudhurst, Cranbrook
Kent TN17 1JX
Tel: 01580 212024
Fax: 01580 212250
E-mail: jeremyparker@jpa-ltd.co.uk

Entry No: 266   **Map no: 6**

Carolyn is experienced and easy-going about looking after guests; you will settle in quickly. Her Grade II-listed, 16th-century and heavily beamed house was begun in 1545. A small flock of sheep and two horses peacefully graze the 20 acres; dogs, cats and chickens (own eggs for breakfast) roam freely. Both the Carrells' children were raised and married from here and happy family vibes remain. The bed heads in the twin were made from old Horsmonden church pews; all rooms are light and airy with pastel colours, floral curtains and green views. Guests can use the drawing room and there's a terrace for tea. *Children over 10 welcome.*

Rooms: 1 twin with private bathroom; 2 singles, both with basins, sharing bathroom and separate wc.

Price: £24-£27 p.p.

Meals: Breakfast times flexible. Dinner available locally.

Closed: 1 November-1 April.

4 miles south of Tunbridge Wells on A267. 1 mile south of Frant Village, on left. Name on fence at bottom of drive.

Mrs Carolyn Carrell
Rowden House Farm
Frant
Tunbridge Wells
Kent TN3 9HS
Tel: 01892 750259

Entry No: 267   Map no: 6

The dynamic Bradburys have taken over 500-year-old Little Hodgeham and stamped their distinctive style on it. Greens and golds in the dining room and you eat off white porcelain with silver cutlery. Mouthwatering meals come from a state-of-the-art kitchen: award-winning Bethersden sausages, green back bacon and hash browns for breakfast, and superb dinners too. Mark and Anne are discreet hosts - there if you need them, but happy to let you revel in privacy, too. There's a pool. *Self-catering suite in barn, ideal for families.*

Rooms: 1 twin, 1 four-poster, both en suite (bath). Barn: double, twin, shower, sitting room and kitchen.

Price: £30-£32.50 p.p. Single supp. £7.50. Barn, £80 per night, £250-£375 p.w.

Meals: Breakfast until 9am (week); flexible (weekends); dinner, 3 courses, £18; weekday supper £10, by arrangement.

Closed: Christmas & New Year.

From Tenterden, A28 in direction of Ashford. At Bull pub in Bethersden, turn off towards Smarden. Beamed yellow house on right after 2 miles.

Mark & Anne Bradbury
Little Hodgeham
Smarden Road
Bethersden
Kent TN26 3HE
Tel: 01233 850323
E-mail: little.hodgeham@virgin.net

Entry No: 268   Map no: 6

The stream meanders and the wild deer roam - the Ribble Valley, an AONB, feels like a time-locked land. The Queen is a frequent visitor to the local royal estate and she knows well the charm of the area. The Smiths are easy and comfortable to be with and here, in their former 18th-century tithe barn where church rafters hold up the guest sitting room, you settle among plump sofas, antiques, and some lace and flounces. You have the whole of the top floor and your own entrance. Breakfast is a feast - the jams and the muesli are home-made - and the garden is a peaceful retreat, full of interesting plants and wildlife.

Rooms: 1 twin/double, en suite (shower); 1 double, en suite (bath/shower); 1 double with private bath.

Price: From £24 p.p. Single supp. £5.

Meals: Breakfast 7.15-9.15am. Dinner available locally at good pubs.

Closed: Christmas & New Year.

M6 junc. 31, A59 to Skipton, left to Clitheroe. Through Clitheroe & Waddington, further 0.5 miles, left along Cross Lane. 0.75 miles on, having passed Colthurst Hall, house on left.

Jean & Gordon Smith
Peter Barn Country House
Cross Lane/Rabbit Lane
Waddington, Clitheroe
Lancashire BB7 3JH
Tel: 01200 428585
E-mail: jean@peterbarn.fsnet.co.uk

Entry No: 269   **Map no: 14**

Passing traffic is less frequent than passing horses - why not bring your own? The lasting impression of this cottage (17th century and added to) is of an uplifting lightness and brightness; the house is filled with laughter and the Cowdells are terrific hosts. There's a fine collection of paintings and furniture, which has been amassed over the years. Double oak doors lead from the dining room to the guest sitting room and there are fresh flowers everywhere. Bedrooms are restful and fresh - one has three-way views - and the garden was designed by Bunny Guinness from *Gardeners' Question Time. Children over 12 welcome.*

Rooms: 2 twins/doubles, 1 en suite (bath) with extra single bed, 1 en suite (shower).

Price: From £22.50 p.p. Single supp. £5.

Meals: Breakfast times flexible; packed lunch £3. Dinner available locally.

Closed: Occasionally.

From A46 Newark-Leicester rd, onto B676, signed Melton. At staggered x-road, straight over for Grimston. 1 mile on, right to Grimston. There, up hill, past church. House on left, just after right-hand bend at top.

Mr & Mrs R.L. & M.E. Cowdell
The Gorse House
Grimston, Melton Mowbray
Leicestershire LE14 3BZ
Tel: 01664 813537
Fax: 01664 813537
E-mail: cowdell@gorsehouse.co.uk
Web: www.gorsehouse.co.uk

Entry No: 270   **Map no: 10**

"More character than many period homes," says our inspector; it's hard to believe this single-storey house was built in the '60s. Bridget's an interior decorator and her talent is evident. There's a conservatory feel to the light-filled, stone-floored dining room with French doors onto the extremely pretty garden. Checked curtains, matching, padded headboards and a gilt-trimmed Edwardian copy of a Louis XIV chair in the bedroom - the beds are extremely comfortable. A full-height mirror in the bathroom with deep, cast-iron bath. Bridget has an easy humour and huge warmth.

Rooms: 1 twin with private bathroom across the hall.

Price: £19.50 p.p. Single supp. £5.

Meals: Breakfast times flexible; dinner, 2 courses, from £12.50, by arrangement.

Closed: Christmas & New Year.

Rabbits and squirrels may play for you on the croquet lawn while you breakfast - it is surprising that the house is near a main road and that Lincoln is so close... It's a fine, unusually asymmetrical, 18th-century manor enclosed in the most magnificent walled garden; do explore the gorgeous bothy. Jill looks after you well - home-made cake when you arrive and huge breakfasts to set you up for the day. The large bedrooms are plain and simple with garden views, pale paint and floral curtains. *Children over 10 welcome.*

Rooms: 2 twins, 1 en suite (bath/shower), 1 with private bath/shower; 1 double, en suite (shower).

Price: From £24 p.p. Single supp. £5.

Meals: Breakfast times flexible. Dinner available locally.

Closed: Christmas & New Year.

A607 Grantham to Lincoln road. On reaching Carlton Scroop take 1st left for Hough Lane. Last house on left.

From Lincoln, A15 south. In Bracebridge Heath, house last on left hidden among trees with walled garden.

Mrs Bridget Hankinson
Churchfield House
Carlton Scroop
Grantham
Lincolnshire NG32 3BA
Tel: 01400 250387
Fax: 01400 250241

Jill & Michael Scoley
The Manor House
Sleaford Road
Bracebridge Heath
Lincolnshire LN4 2HW
Tel: 01522 520825
Fax: 01522 542418

Entry No: 271   **Map no:** 10

Entry No: 272   **Map no:** 10

Anne and Chris have worked hard restoring their 18th-century Barnack stone farmhouse and it matters to them that you enjoy the old beams and shutters, the freshly-decorated bedrooms and the lovely country views. Anne is a good Aga cook and you'll savour the local bacon and sausages and home-made preserves. Chris is funny and something of a poet; he can be persuaded to recite some of his verses. There's B&B here for horses, too, and bridleways, cycle trails and George the potbellied pig.

Rooms: 1 double, en suite (half size bath); 1 twin with private bathroom.

Price: £25-£30 p.p. Single supp. £10.

Meals: Breakfast times flexible. Many local pubs and restaurants.

Closed: Christmas & New Year.

Drift off to sleep on a cloud of rose scent: Ozric makes the only genuine English rose oil and water, distilled here in an outbuilding. Outside your bedroom lies a bed of roses, three and a half acres of them: magical. The house is full of intriguing features: two boat-shaped windows that open onto the garden; a vast studio/sitting room built in the 1900s by Gardner of the R.A. and filled with paintings and African carvings. There are some fearsome fish on the Portuguese tiles around the claw-footed bath, but Ozric and Chantal are extremely warm and welcoming.

Rooms: 1 twin, 1 double, both with private shower room; 1 double, en suite (bath).

Price: £30 p.p.

Meals: Breakfast times flexible. Dinner available locally.

Closed: Christmas & New Year.

Leave A1 at Wansford, travelling towards Peterborough on A47 for 0.75 miles. Left to Southorpe; through village, house 100 yds after phone box on right.

Anne Harrison-Smith
Midstone House
Southorpe
Stamford
Lincolnshire PE9 3BX
Tel: 01780 740136
Fax: 01780 749294
E-mail: ahsmidstonehouse@amserve.net

From Bourne, A15 north towards Sleaford, 1st hamlet on left signed to Cawthorpe. House last on right before road becomes a track.

Ozric & Chantal Armstrong
Cawthorpe Hall
Bourne
Lincolnshire PE10 0AB
Tel: 01778 423830
Fax: 01778 426620
E-mail: bandb@rosewater.co.uk

Entry No: 273   **Map no: 11**

Entry No: 274   **Map no: 11**

Lincolnshire

Come in April, if you can; the surrounding fields are a sea of yellow with acre upon acres of daffodils. The peace, the marshes, the solitude, though, are here year-round. Follow the model steam train round the garden, ride the bikes, watch the birds. Pipwell is lovingly decorated in rich blues and greens, each room with its own character. An attractive country house scene of old pine tables, fresh flowers, the smell of home-made cakes (for you), things suspended and perched, makes the house feel human and warm; so does Lesley's friendly welcome.

Rooms: 1 double, en suite (bath/shower); 1 double with private shower room; 1 twin, en suite (shower).

Price: £22-£24 p.p. Single occ. £30-£35.

Meals: Breakfast 7-9am; packed lunch, £4.

Closed: Christmas & New Year.

Turn off A17, 1.5 miles north-east of Holbeach, into Washway Rd. Past phone box, pub & garage; house on left.

Lesley Honnor
Pipwell Manor
Washway Road
Saracen's Head, Holbeach
Lincolnshire PE12 8AL
Tel: 01406 423119
Fax: 01406 423119

Entry No: 275   **Map no:** 11

Just nine miles from Boston 'Stump' - Britain's largest parish church. Michael, ex-MP, ex-Navy, was active in the quest to illuminate the church's glories at night; now floodlit, you can see it from miles around. The Brothertons are smashing people, massively interesting and easy and they both enjoy cooking and tending their huge fruit and vegetable garden. The impressive Queen Anne vicarage was built in 1707 with local handmade bricks which have mellowed gloriously. The typical square Lincolnshire hall has stone flags leading to a red-pine-panelled staircase. The double room is large, light and charming; the twin is simpler.

Rooms: 1 twin, 1 double, both with private bathroom.

Price: £25 p.p. Single supp. £10.

Meals: Breakfast until 9am; packed lunch £4.50; dinner, including wine and pre-dinner drink, £24.50, by arrangement.

Closed: Christmas & Boxing Day.

Wrangle is 9 miles north of Boston on A52. In village follow signs to Angel Inn. House opposite church by War Memorial.

Michael & Julia Brotherton
The Old Vicarage
Wrangle
Boston
Lincolnshire PE22 9EP
Tel: 01205 870688
Fax: 01205 871857
E-mail: jb141@aol.com

Entry No: 276   **Map no:** 11

Lincolnshire

The rolling wolds and flat fens of unsung Lincolnshire go on for ever. The Grange sits beautifully among it all, artistically old-furnished, oak-doored and beamed and with floral curtains. Original tiles and shutters, claw-footed baths and fireplaces create an atmosphere that can only unwind you. The kitchen is the sort of place where you want to chat to Anthony while he cooks your Lincolnshire sausages. Frances is a furniture historian. *Children over seven welcome.*

Rooms: 1 double, en suite (bath & shower); 1 twin/double with private bath & shower; 1 extra single occasionally available.

Price: £25 p.p. for single night; £20 p.p. for longer stays. Single supp. by arrangement.

Meals: Breakfast times flexible. Dinner available locally.

Closed: Christmas & New Year.

Wide open Lincolnshire farmland on the edge of the Wolds - you'll love your bedroom views! This immaculately-kept farm has been in the family for five generations and an award-winning farm trail helps you explore, or maybe you just want to watch the sunset by the trout lake... Sarah is young, energetic and welcoming and brings you delicious home-made cake on arrival. Sink into squashy leather sofas after supper in front of the fire. Bedrooms have dark wooden beds; bathrooms are spick and span. Donkeys graze in the paddock in the winter and your horse is welcome.

Rooms: 2 doubles, both en suite (bath).

Price: £22.50 p.p. Single supp. £5.50.

Meals: Breakfast times flexible; packed lunch £5; supper £8-10; dinner, 3 courses, £14; B.Y.O. wine. No meals at harvest time.

Closed: Christmas & New Year.

From Spilsby A16 north for 1 mile. In Partney bear left at church, signed A16 Grimsby. Drive 60 yds on left, down grassy track.

Turn off A157 in East Barkwith at war memorial, into Torrington lane. House 0.75 miles on right after sharp right-hand bend.

Frances & Anthony Collard
The Grange
Partney
Spilsby
Lincolnshire PE23 4PQ
Tel: 01790 753151
Fax: 01790 753151

Sarah & Jonathan Stamp
The Grange
Torrington Lane
East Barkwith
Lincolnshire LN8 5RY
Tel: 01673 858670
E-mail: jonathanstamp@farmersweekly.net

Entry No: 277   **Map no: 16**

Entry No: 278   **Map no: 16**

Utter stillness here at the base of the Lincolnshire Wolds and the view of the lake from the bedrooms is dreamy. Ann is new to B&B and thoroughly spoils her guests. Lincolnshire sausages and her own jams and marmalades at breakfast, tea on arrival and home-made cake. Guests have the run of downstairs; the traditional, neat sitting room and the dining room have views of the lake and formal gardens. A lovely one-mile walk along the line of the old railway starts from the door. Ann will help you plan trips further afield, too. *Children over 12 welcome.*

Rooms: 1 twin, en suite (shower); 1 double, en suite (bath).

Price: £24 p.p. Single supp. by arrangement.

Meals: Breakfast times flexible; dinner £10-£15, by arrangement. B.Y.O wine.

Closed: Christmas.

From Wragby A157 for Louth. After approx. 2 miles, at triple road sign, right turn. Red postbox at drive entrance, past graveyard.

Ann Hobbins
The Manor House
West Barkwith
Lincolnshire LN8 5LF
Tel: 01673 858253
Fax: 01673 858253

Entry No: 279   **Map no: 16**

The farmhouse is 200 years old and John Wycliffe, who translated the Bible into English, was rector at the village church in the XIV century. Christine is one of the most welcoming and helpful people we have met - she also bakes a delicious cake; Bill, newly-retired from farming, is friendly, too. You have your own sitting room with open fire and a dining room with garden views. The bedrooms are light, airy and peaceful; one is as plain and simple as the other is floral. Guests keep coming back. *Children over five welcome.*

Rooms: 1 twin/double, en suite (shower); 1 double with private bathroom.

Price: £22.50 p.p. Single supp. by arrangement.

Meals: Breakfast times flexible; light suppers, from £8, by arrangement. Good local pubs.

Closed: Christmas & New Year.

From Lincoln, A15 north. 2nd left after Scampton RAF station signed Fillingham. 1st right onto B1398. 2nd left to Fillingham. 1st house at bottom of hill on right.

Christine & Bill Ramsay
Church Farm
Fillingham
Gainsborough
Lincolnshire DN21 5BS
Tel: 01427 668279
Fax: 01427 668025
E-mail: fillinghambandb@lineone.net

Entry No: 280   **Map no: 16**

The luxury of a good hotel - excellent beds, gorgeous bathrooms, even air conditioning - yet here you have the personal touch that we so like. You eat breakfast in the big, colourful, kitchen, complete with Aga, wooden floor and table and take Carole's advice on what's on in London. The bright, comfortable bedrooms are a mix of brass, sisal flooring, crisp linen, bathrobes, wood and contemporary décor. The open space of Primrose Hill, fringed with delightful shops, is nearby. So, too, are Regent's Park, Camden Lock and market.

Rooms: 1 twin, en suite (bath/shower); 1 double with private bathroom/shower.

Price: From £45 p.p. Single supp. from £30.

Meals: Extensive Continental breakfast 8-9am Mon-Fri, 8.30-9.30am Sat-Sun, times negotiable! Dinner available locally.

Closed: Rarely.

5 minutes walk from Chalk Farm tube: cross Adelaide Rd, right for 20 steps, then left into Bridge Approach. Cross bridge, turn right. Free parking weekends.

Andrew & Carole Ingram
30 King Henry's Road
Primrose Hill
London NW3 3RP
Tel: 020 7483 2871
Fax: 020 7483 4587
E-mail: mail@caroleingram.com
Web: www.30kinghenrysroad.co.uk

Entry No: 281   Map no: 5

There's a dramatic vibrancy to Valerie's home. Just off Upper Street, with its numerous restaurants, and right by the Almeida and Sadler's Wells, she has many artists and actors to stay and has a theatre background herself. The Victorian house is stuffed with oriental, French and Italian pieces. The basement bedroom is filled with light and character. Walls, doors and much of the furniture are ragged, sponged and stencilled in the colourful style of the Bloomsbury Set. The theatrical mood continues in the conservatory, crammed with tropical plants, ferns, seashells and candles. An inspiring place to stay.

Rooms: 1 double with private shower room.

Price: £42.50 p.p. Single occ. £65.

Meals: Breakfast 8-9am; extensive Continental only. Dinner available locally.

Closed: Rarely.

From Highbury & Islington tube, right out of station. Down Upper Street, past Town Hall. Left immed. before garage. Free overnight & weekend parking (Sat 1.30pm on); otherwise meters.

Valerie Rossmore
26 Florence Street
Islington
London N1 2FW
Tel: 020 7359 5293
Fax: 020 7359 5293
E-mail: valerie.rossmore@onmail.co.uk

Entry No: 282   Map no: 5

London

This is special indeed, and remarkable value for London, so close to Regent's Park. A very modern Japanese-style house built round a courtyard with a peaked glass roof so that it fills with light and air. Wood and glass take pride of place, colours and shapes are subtle and pure, bedrooms have low platform beds, the minimalist-decor living quarters are open-plan, green-planted and ethnic-ornamented with treasures from far-flung holidays. Rodger and Sue are a delightful, articulate couple; Peckham the parrot completes the picture. *Children by arrangement.*

Rooms: 1 double, 1 single, sharing bathroom (single only let to member of same party).

Price: £40 p.p.

Meals: Extensive Continental breakfast 7.30-10am. Dinner available locally.

Closed: Never.

From Camden Town tube station, take Camden Rd towards Holloway. Pass Camden Rd BR station & 4th right into Murray St. House on corner of Murray St & Camden Mews. Parking free at weekends; meters during week.

Sue & Rodger Davis
66 Camden Square
London NW1 9XD
Tel: 020 7485 4622
Fax: 020 4785 4622
E-mail: rodgerdavis@btinternet.com

Entry No: 283   **Map no: 5**

In the heart of vibrant Camden Town, well set back in a quiet, wide, tree-lined street, moments from Regent's Park - a superb central London base! The stunningly spacious kitchen was designed by Peter (an architect and lighting specialist) and every room in the modernist house has had the best brought out of it - small rooms are cleverly laid-out and there's a really super large double. All is distinctive and understated with cool colours and fresh flowers. The Bells run this established B&B with a cool professionalism. *Near to Camden Lock and market.*

Rooms: 1 twin with bunks, 1 twin/double sharing bathroom; 1 small double, en suite (shower & private wc).

Price: £45 p.p. Single night supp. £5 p.p. Single supp. £10.

Meals: Breakfast 7-10am. Dinner available locally.

Closed: Never.

From Camden Town tube station, up Parkway. Albert St 2nd on left. House on left. Parking free Sunday; otherwise meters. Public transport: Camden Town tube (Northern Line).

Joanna & Peter Bell
78 Albert Street
London NW1 7NR
Tel: 020 7387 6813
Fax: 020 7387 1704

Entry No: 284   **Map no: 5**

Take in the village atmosphere of Portobello Market, or cruise the tempting shops of Notting Hill. This grand mid-Victorian town house has tall sash windows and wrought iron balconies. The French flavour of the elegant drawing room, with pictures, gilt mirrors, ormolu and bronze candlesticks, fine china and Louis XIV furniture under crystal chandeliers, contrasts with the minimalist state-of-the-art kitchen. The Turnbulls are flexible, easy hosts and you can borrow the key to nearby Ladbroke Square Gardens. *Children over 12 welcome.*

Rooms: 1 dble, en suite (bath); 1 twin, private bathroom. Single also available.

Price: £40 p.p.

Meals: Breakfast times flexible. Dinner available locally.

Closed: Never.

From Notting Hill Gate tube on north side towards Portobello Market. At lights by Devonshire pub, right & cross road. Kensington Park Rd 50 yds on left. House 200 yds on left with black door. Weekend parking free 1.30pm Sat; otherwise meters.

Ben & Bev Turnbull
9 Kensington Park Road
London W11 3BY
Tel: 020 7229 0231
Fax: 020 7792 1266
E-mail: bevturnbull@hotmail.com

Entry No: 285   **Map no: 5**

Wonderful rooms in an 1860s Kensington Victorian town house. The newly-decorated bedrooms are in one of the lightest basements that we've ever seen and you have your own key and entrance. The rest of the house is still the family home. There's an easy formality: mahogany table and dresser, antique chairs and floral fabrics, and breakfast is served in the dining room overlooking the charming, secluded garden. Nanette really enjoys people. *Near to Kensington Gardens, Holland Park, High St Kensington. Children over 12 welcome.*

Rooms: 2 twins, en suite (bath & shower); 1 double, en suite (shower).

Price: £42.50-£47.50 p.p. Single supp. £25.

Meals: Cooked breakfast 8.30-9am (Mon-Fri), 9-9.30am (Sat-Sun). Dinner available locally.

Closed: Never.

Left out of Earls Court Rd station, over Cromwell Rd, then left into Pembroke Rd. Warwick Gardens 3rd on right. Parking £6 per day next door. Public transport: High St Kensington/Earl's Court tube (8 mins' walk).

Nanette Stylianou
47 Warwick Gardens
London W14 8PL
Tel: 020 7603 7614
Fax: 020 7602 5473
E-mail: nanette@stylianou.fsnet.co.uk

Entry No: 286   **Map no: 5**

Sunny's gorgeous family home is right opposite Holland Park and well-placed for High Street Kensington and Notting Hill. The whole top floor is generally given over to guests, complete with fridge. Both rooms have been beautifully decorated in gentle yellows and greens with pale green carpets, soft white duvets, pelmeted windows and a lovely, curved chest of drawers in the double. The bathroom is marble-tiled and sky-lit. Great comfort is guaranteed. Breakfast is taken Continental-style. This whole house is bright. *Near to Kensington Gardens, Albert Hall. Children over 10 welcome.*

Rooms: 1 double, 1 single, sharing bathroom.

Price: £40-£45 p.p. Single occ. £60.

Meals: Breakfast 8-10am. Dinner available locally.

Closed: Occasionally.

This is fun! A house-cum-gallery in a conservation area where each room exhibits original, modern art. The bedroom has all the useful things that you don't want to lug around town with you - radio, hairdryer and alarm clock. Bold colours, wooden floors, huge curtain-less windows and indoor trees give an exotic feel. Breakfasts are cooked on the Aga and eaten in the vast and stylish kitchen with deck views over the subtropical garden (full of intriguing spaces, wooden pathways and unusual plants). Biddy is kind and easy-going. *Near to Greenwich and Blackheath Village.*

Rooms: 1 twin, en suite (shower).

Price: From £30 p.p.

Meals: Breakfast times flexible; dinner from £18, by arrangement.

Closed: Never.

Public transport: Nearest tube Holland Park, 7 mins walk, or High St Kensington. Best buses, 9 & 10 to Knightsbridge. Off-street parking sometimes available.

From Brockley station, cross Brockley Rd & up Cranfield Rd. Cross at church & continue along rd. Pass church, Breakspears Rd is almost opp. Free parking. Trains: Brockley to London Bridge. Buses: 171 & 36 to centre.

Sunny & Al Murray
101 Abbotsbury Road
London W14 8EP
Tel: 020 7602 0179
Fax: 020 7602 1036
E-mail: al.sunny@101abb.freeserve.co.uk

Biddy Bunzl
57 Breakspears Road
London SE4 1XR
Tel: 020 8469 3162
Fax: 020 8469 3162
E-mail: bunzl@btinternet.com

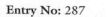

Entry No: 287   **Map no: 5**

Entry No: 288   **Map no: 5**

Just off the King's Road, this quiet, perfectly central house is Georgian and strewn with wisteria. It is set back from the road, with its own off-street parking. Inside, it's a real family home with no pretensions. Jane serves breakfast in the stunning kitchen-cum-conservatory that looks onto a lovely London garden. Top-floor bedrooms are cheerful and sunny and have unique views of one of London's most magnificent buildings - Sir Christopher Wren's Royal Hospital - and of an Avenue of Gardens. Jane loves cooking, so do eat in. *Near the Thames, Sloane Square and Harrods.*

Rooms: 1 twin and 1 family room with single and double futon, both sharing bathroom (bath & shower).

Price: £40-£50 p.p. Single supp. £10.

Meals: Continental breakfast only, 8-10am. Dinner £20, by arrangement; B.Y.O. wine.

Closed: Never.

Parallel with King's Road between Smith Street & Royal Avenue. Parking available.

All the personality, charm and individual attention of a private house - right in the heart of London, too. But also a huge canopied four-poster bed, private telephone, fax and laundry facilities, your own sitting room and a great bathroom. Continental breakfast with newspaper is equally inspired. Everything is prepared by Jenny the housekeeper. This means the orange is freshly squeezed and the jams are home-made. You will not find better comfort or facilities in Central London at these prices. A very special place. *Near to Westminster Abbey, Tate Gallery, Buckingham Palace.*

Rooms: 1 king-size four-poster with sitting room & bathroom.

Price: £55 p.p. Single occ. £100.

Meals: Breakfast 8-9am; Continental included; full English £8. Many excellent local restaurants nearby.

Closed: Christmas.

1-minute walk from Pimlico tube (Rampayne St exit), or 5-minute walk from Victoria. Best bus, 24 to Trafalgar Sq. Parking: NCP or 2-hour meters.

Jane Barran
17 St. Leonard's Terrace
London SW3 4QG
Tel: 020 7730 2801
Fax: 020 7730 2801

Mrs Helen Douglas
Number Ninety-Six
96 Tachbrook Street
London SW1V 2NB
Tel: 020 7932 0969
Fax: 020 7821 5454
E-mail: helen@numberninety-six.co.uk
Web: www.numberninety-six.co.uk

Entry No: 289   **Map no: 5**

Entry No: 290   **Map no: 5**

In a book full of country houses to make city dwellers envious, Richard and Caroline's home turns the tables. It's a charming 1857 house at the end of one of those colourful cul-de-sacs just off the Kings Road. The loveliest shops and restaurants are a step away, yet here birds sing and peace prevails. Perfect. Your bedroom is extremely light, bright and fun with checks and a wrought-iron bed; the shower room is compact and sparkling. You eat Continental breakfast in the wooden-floored conservatory which is bathed in morning sun.

Rooms: 1 double with private shower room.

Price: £40 p.p. Single supp. £10.

Meals: Continental breakfast until 9.30am. Dinner available locally.

Closed: Christmas.

From Sloane Square tube, head down Kings Road. Bywater Street is 500 yds along on right. House at end.

Caroline & Richard Heaton-Watson
20 Bywater Street
London SW3 4XD
Tel: 020 7581 2222
Fax: 020 7581 2222
E-mail: caheatonw@aol.com

Entry No: 291   **Map no: 5**

This part of London is full of sky, trees and wildlife; Pissarro captured on canvas the view up the hill in 1870 and the original painting can be seen in the National Gallery. There's good stuff everywhere - things hang off walls and peep over the tops of dressers; bedrooms are stunning, with antiques, textiles, paintings and big, firm beds. Sue, a graduate from Chelsea Art College, employs humour and intelligence to put guests at ease and has created a very special garden, too. Tim often helps with breakfasts.

Rooms: 1 twin/double, en suite; 1 twin, 1 single sharing shower room.

Price: From £40 p.p.

Meals: Breakfast until 10am; dinner, £25 p.p, by arrangement.

Closed: Never.

Main line trains from Victoria or London Bridge, 20 mins to Crystal Palace, then 7 mins walk. Sue will give you directions or collect you. Good buses to West End & Westminster.

Sue & Tim Haigh
24 Fox Hill
Crystal Palace
London SE19 2XE
Tel: 020 8768 0059
Fax: 020 8768 0063
E-mail: suehaigh@foxhill-bandb.co.uk
Web: www.foxhill-bandb.co.uk

Entry No: 292   **Map no: 5**

Privacy is the key element here - you have exclusive use of your own Coach House (only one party at a time), separated from your hosts' home by a stylish terracotta-potted courtyard. Enjoy breakfast in your sunny kitchen, or let the gracious Meena treat you to an all-organic full English (she's a whizz at porridge, too). The big but cosy main attic bedroom has *toile de Jouy* bedcovers, cream curtains, rugs on dark polished floors. The brick-walled ground floor twin is pleasant and light and airy, too. An exceptionally quiet south London B&B. *Minimum stay three nights. Children over seven welcome.*

Rooms: 1 triple (double & single), en suite (bath); 1 twin with private shower.

Price: £32-£50 p.p.

Meals: Breakfast times flexible; dinner, all organic, £35, by arrangement.

Closed: Never.

From r'bout on south side of Wandsworth Bridge, head south down Trinity Rd on A214. At 3rd set of traffic lights, 1.7 miles on, left into Upper Tooting Park. 4th left into Marius Rd, then 3rd left.

Meena & Harley Nott
The Coach House
2 Tunley Road
London SW17 7QJ
Tel: 020 8772 1939
Fax: 0870 133 4957
E-mail: thecoachhouse@cwc.net
Web: www.thecoachhouse.cwc.net

Entry No: 293   **Map no: 5**

It's a handsome house in a conservation area that manages to be both elegant and cosy. Nothing jars in the cream-coloured bedroom with its comfy furniture, fine fabrics and original features; the bathroom is light and airy. Newspapers are thoughtfully left out for you to read over breakfast in the restful dining room overlooking a secluded terrace and garden. Mary and David love to share what they know of the capital's delights and, on a quiet, tree-lined street, theirs is a relaxing London base. You are just a stride from Tooting Bec Common. Good value, too. Minimum two-day stay.

Rooms: 1 double, en suite (bath).

Price: £30 p.p. Single supp. £10.

Meals: Breakfast until 9.30am (Mon-Fri); flexible (Sat-Sun); dinner, 3 courses, £20, by arrangement.

Closed: Occasionally.

From Tooting Bec tube, along Balham High Rd towards Balham. 3rd road on right. 7 minutes' walk from Tube. Free parking weekends; otherwise meters.

Mary Hodges
108 Streathbourne Road
London SW17 8QY
Tel: 020 8767 6931
Fax: 020 8672 8839
E-mail: mary.hodges@virgin.net

Entry No: 294   **Map no: 5**

Come here for peace and undemanding luxury; this Victorian cottage with a delightful courtyard garden is a perfect antidote to the rigours of city life. Barbara is new to B&B and keen for you to feel relaxed and happy. The bedroom is bright, quiet and restful, with flowers and a fireplace and you sleep on a new mattress under a goose down duvet (worth the trip alone!). Barbara was an orchestral musician and is a keen traveller; she has amassed fascinating artefacts from far-off places.

Rooms: 1 double with private bathroom.

Price: £40 p.p. Single supp. £20.

Meals: Breakfast times flexible. Dinner available locally.

Closed: Occasionally.

From Queenstown Rd, (A326) turn into St. Philip Sq (look out for church) & into St. Philip St. 137 bus to Sloane Sq (10 mins) & to Knightsbridge. Free overnight parking (5.30pm-9.30am) & at weekends; otherwise Pay & Display.

Barbara Graham
20 St Philip Street
Battersea
London SW8 3SL
Tel: 020 7498 9967
Fax: 020 7498 9967
E-mail: barbaragraham@telco4u.net

Entry No: 295   **Map no: 5**

This is a sophisticated London base; your hostess is delightful and adept at putting guests at their ease. The yellow-walled drawing room has masses of interest and the dining/kitchen room is charming, with blue damask-patterned walls, pink napkins and pink flowers. Bedrooms are cool, cream and clutter-free, with glazed chintz curtains and gilt mirrors and picture frames; the en suite bathroom has yellow-painted woodwork and the other is crimson. Sally is well-travelled; she organises heritage tours of Britain, so is full of ideas for you.

Rooms: 1 double, en suite (bath); 1 small double with private bathroom downstairs.

Price: £30 p.p. Single occ. £40.

Meals: Continental breakfast, times flexible. Many restaurants nearby.

Closed: Never.

From Fulham Broadway tube, walk directly ahead down Harwood Road. At T-junc. right into New Kings Rd. 2nd left into Wandsworth Bridge Rd. No 34 is a few houses along on right. (5-minutes' walk.) Parking from 5pm-9am free.

Sally Usher
34 Wandsworth Bridge Road
London SW6 2TH
Tel: 020 7731 2805
Fax: 020 7731 2805

Entry No: 296   **Map no: 5**

This is a bright, cheerful Fulham home where life gravitates to the back of the house. The kitchen is home to dachshunds and cats who may need to be moved from the sofa. The walls are bright yellow, the tablecloth gingham, the carpets matting... and everything throughout the house feels freshly painted and cosy. The groovy colours continue upstairs with electric greens and cloudy sky blues. Rooms are very comfortable with thick duvets on beds, and the large bathrooms are white and immaculate. There's a plethora of great restaurants nearby. Be well looked after in central London. *Children over 10 welcome.*

Rooms: 1 double, en suite, 1 twin, 1 single, both with private bath.

Price: £35-£40 p.p. Single supp. £10-£15. p.p. Single £40.

Meals: Continental breakfast only until 9.30am. Dinner available locally.

Closed: Never.

Public transport: 2 minutes from Parson's Green tube (District Line, Wimbledon branch). No.14 bus to Knightsbridge. Parking in street all day.

Rachel Wilson
29 Winchenden Road
London SW6 5DH
Tel: 020 7731 3901
E-mail: rachel.k.wilson@talk21.com

Entry No: 297   **Map no: 5**

India's fine art and fabrics decorate Amanda's pretty Fulham house. You breakfast in the coral rag-rolled family kitchen; French windows open onto a small garden where you can eat in summer. The lower-ground bedroom and bathroom, in blue and white, are bright and breezy and the upstairs double has elephant wallpaper; in both you'll find mineral water biscuits and bathtime goodies. There's also Huggy the dog - a sometime star of the screen. New Kings Road are less than a minute by foot and across the road is Parsons Green and an excellent pub restaurant. *Children over 12 welcome.*

Rooms: 1 twin/double, en suite (bath); 1 twin/double, 1 single room, both with private bath.

Price: £37.50 p.p. Single supp. £10-£15.

Meals: Continental breakfast only, until 9.30am. Dinner available locally.

Closed: Rarely.

3 mins from Parsons Green tube (District Line, Wimbledon branch). Straight over green, keeping White Horse pub on left; Bradbourne St is over King's Road, ahead. House on left. Parking free 5pm-9am & Sunday; otherwise Pay & Display.

Mrs Amanda Turner
3 Bradbourne Street
Fulham
London SW6 3TF
Tel: 020 7736 7284
E-mail: info@luxuryinlondon.clara.co.uk
Web: www.luxuryinlondon.co.uk

Entry No: 298   **Map no: 5**

Caroline mixes the sophistication of the city with the human warmth of the countryside and her lovely big kitchen is clearly the engine-room of the house. It leads through to a light breakfast room on seagrass matting, with doors onto a pretty brick garden with its chairs and table - hope for fine days. The house is long and thin - Fulham style - and reaches up to the guest room in the eaves, which needs no more explanation than the picture above. A really warm place to stay in a very accessible part of the Metropolis. *Near to Kings Road antique shops.*

Rooms: 1 twin/double, en suite (shower) and private bathroom.

Price: £40-£45 p.p. Single supp. £25. Price negotiable for longer stays.

Meals: Continental breakfast only, 8.30-9.30am (Mon-Fri), 8.30-10am (Sat-Sun). Dinner available locally.

Closed: Never.

Public transport: 4 minutes' walk to Parsons Green tube. Parking: £4.80 per day in street.

Caroline Docker
8 Parthenia Road
Fulham
London SW6 3BD
Tel: 020 7384 1165
Fax: 020 7610 6015
E-mail: caldock@btinternet.com

Entry No: 299   **Map no: 5**

You enter Joan's homely kitchen conversion directly from a peaceful mews. Continental breakfasts on the central wooden table mean home-made marmalade, toast, croissants etc. Bedrooms upstairs are pretty with antique furniture and brand new beds - and your bath resides in a gleaming white room. This is a real home in a very central position and Joan herself is a keen traveller who enjoys meeting people from all over the world. She puts mineral water in the rooms and there's a quiet, sunny patio and lovely roses in the garden. *Children over 12 welcome.*

Rooms: 1 double, 1 single, sharing bathroom.

Price: Double £35 p.p. Single £45. Single occ. of double £50.

Meals: Breakfast 8.30-9.30am. Dinner available locally.

Closed: Occasionally.

Public transport: 4 minutes' walk to Fulham Broadway tube (District Line, Zone 2), & several buses. Parking: ticket parking, £4.80 per day, in street.

Joan Lee
5 Hartismere Road
London SW6 7TS
Tel: 020 7385 0337
Fax: 020 7385 0337

Entry No: 300   **Map no: 5**

A soothing, restful retreat from London's hustle and bustle - it's villagey here and you could happily while away an afternoon browsing in smart shops or walking along the Thames. Helen and Nigel have created 'Chelsea chic' in leafy Barnes - throughout their taste is impeccable. There's an Edwardian bergère sofa in the large cream double and a Victorian roll-top in the next door bathroom; the other guest room is at the top of the house with river views from its bathroom in the winter. The Smiths are an engaging, well-travelled couple, interested in art, gardening and fly-fishing - they have a lovely retriever, too. *Children over 12 welcome.*

Rooms: 1 king-size, en suite (bath); 1 queen-size with private bathroom.

Price: From £35 p.p. Single supp. £10.

Meals: Breakfast until 9.30am. Dinner available locally.

Closed: Christmas & New Year.

From Great West Rd, take Hammersmith Bridge to Barnes. At lights by Browns Restaurant, right along Lonsdale Rd for just over 1 mile. Left into Gerard Rd & 1st left into Charlotte Rd. House 1st on left. Free parking.

Helen & Nigel Smith
1 Charlotte Road
Barnes
London SW13 9QJ
Tel: 020 8741 5504
Fax: 020 8741 5504

This unusual, relaxed and very English set-up in a Norman Shaw listed house in a quiet, leafy, conservation area is a monument to Elisabeth's creative inspirations. She is a sculptor and caster, so classical busts and reliefs in stone, marble and plaster peer at you from surprising places. The bedroom is a lovely large space with table and armchairs. You have your own galley kitchen where a fridge is well stocked for your arrival, complete with home-made bread. Elisabeth is a warm hostess; she loves music in the house and also lets the charming music room, with Steinway A grand, to musicians. *Minimum stay two nights. Near to Kew Gardens.*

Rooms: 1 twin, en suite bath. Double-bedroomed flat for lets of 1-6 months.

Price: £30 p.p. Single supp. £15. Music room £30 extra. Ask re price for flat.

Meals: Breakfast times flexible - help yourself. Dinner available nearby.

Closed: Never.

Turnham Green tube, 4 minutes walk. Visitors' parking outside, plus 1 off-road space.

Elisabeth Whittaker
11 Queen Anne's Grove
Bedford Park
London W4 1HW
Tel: 020 8995 9255
E-mail: elisabeth.whittaker@virgin.net

It's amazing how many owners in this book have lived all over the world (the Andrews have returned from Brunei and the Middle East) and how many have experience in catering - Margaret is a professional cook. This is a large Richmond home (1930s leaded bay windows) with a big lawny garden at the back. The bedroom is big and decorated in pale blue; everything is new-feeling and fresh. There is a road passing the front door which should be mentioned, but double glazing sorts out most of the noise. There will be no half measures here and delicious dinners can be arranged in advance. *Near to Richmond Park, Kew, Hampton Court and the Thames.*

Rooms: 1 twin with private bathroom.

Price: £30 p.p. Single supp. £10.

Meals: Breakfast - Continental - until 10am; full English £5 extra; dinner, £30, by arrangement.

Closed: Christmas & New Year.

Public transport: Best bus, 33 to Hammersmith. 12-minute walk to Richmond station for trains & tube. Free parking.

Margaret Andrew
131 Queens Road
Richmond
London TW10 6HF
Tel: 020 8948 6893
Fax: 020 8948 6893

Entry No: 303　　　　**Map no: 5**

The two acres of formal rose beds, borders, lawns and orchards sweep down to the Thames - what a magical, secluded London base. For garden lovers, Hampton Court Palace (home to the International Flower Show) is next door and Windsor, Wisley and Kew a short drive away. This exceptionally elegant Palladian house has fine moulded ceilings, portraits, books and flowers. Bedrooms are sumptuous with fine fabrics, exquisite furniture and lovely views. Sonia serves delicious home-cooking including a fine repertoire of Jewish and Continental recipes and uses home-grown fruit and vegetables. French and Italian spoken.

Rooms: 1 double, en suite; 1 double with private bathroom.

Price: £44-£49 p.p.

Meals: Breakfast, a richly varied menu of cooked dishes, until 9am; dinner £25.

Closed: Occasionally.

From Hampton Court r'bout, A308, west, for 300 yds. Left through wrought iron gates to house at end of drive. 5 minutes from Hampton Court station & London Waterloo, 30 minutes.

Dr Louis & Sonia Marks
Paddock Lodge
The Green
Hampton Court
London KT8 9BW
Tel: 020 8979 5254
E-mail: 101723.1100@compuserve.com

Entry No: 304　　　　**Map no: 5**

A perfectly shaped 18th-century house - its setting is utterly rural and the large grounds deserve exploration. You can play tennis, swim in the heated outdoor pool, shelter under an arbour or cross the bridged pond to an enchanting island. This is a very traditional house with displays of china, an oak, oval dining table that seats 12 and antique furniture; bedrooms are coolly elegant and there are good views all around. This is a place of peace - close to Sandringham, good sailing, golf courses and walking and beaches.

Rooms: 1 twin/double, en suite (bath).

Price: £35 p.p.

Meals: Breakfast times flexible; dinner, 2/3 courses, £19.50-£22.50.

Closed: Christmas.

A bustling, easy-going, lived-in farmhouse with comfortable touches of elegance such as grand piano and gilt cornicing. Two of the bedrooms are huge and high-ceilinged, with chairs from which to admire the view through the long windows. Bedrooms are neither designery or lavish, but homely and generous with towels, bathrobes and other extras, such as a fridge and sofa. There are plenty of dogs and horses (stabling available) and delightful farming hosts - walls bear the proofs of their successes at point-to-pointing and showing. *Children over 12 by arrangement.*

Rooms: 2 doubles, 1 en suite (shower), 1 with bath/shower; 1 twin with private bathroom & wc.

Price: £20-£25 p.p. Single supp. £5.

Meals: Breakfast times flexible. Pub within walking distance for dinner.

Closed: Never.

From Kings Lynn A47 towards Swaffham. 4 miles on, left at Middleton by church & left again into Hill Road. Right into drive (opp. Paul Drive).

From Kings Lynn, A148 towards Cromer. 3 miles after Hillington, 2nd of 2 turnings right to Harpley (no signpost) opp. Houghton Hall sign. 200 yds on, over x-roads & white house 400 yds on left.

Mrs C. Knight
The Old Hall
Middleton
Kings Lynn
Norfolk PE32 1RW
Tel: 01553 840490
Fax: 01553 840708
E-mail: emidas@talk21.com

Amanda Case
Lower Farm
Harpley
Nr. Kings Lynn
Norfolk PE31 6TU
Tel: 01485 520240

Entry No: 305   **Map no: 11**

Entry No: 306   **Map no: 11**

An unusual study in *chiaro e oscuro*: light outside and dark inside. The vertical reach of the planking takes the eye up beyond the everyday to a place where realism and practicality are, thank Heavens, not needed. Yet the interplay of new and old wood, light and dark again, is exciting in an age of the bland exteriors of warehouse and supermarket architecture. The owners have a casual approach to hospitality, it must be admitted, leaving you the raw materials to construct your own bed and furniture. But you may come and go and indulge in whatever whimsical behaviour you wish - nobody will object.

Rooms: Board and loggings available. Palliasse provided.

Price: 1 germinated cutting.

Meals: A breakfast buffet of grubs, plant fertiliser and pot plants. Dinner in neighbour's vegetable patch 9pm-11pm while he's down the pub.

Closed: During harvest.

Follow a shed delivery van to an address in Norfolk. Wait several years while junk accumulates, then ask owner nicely.

Sean Timber
Shed Comforts, Lumberland Place
Stake-by-Nayland
Norfolk LOG 1NG
Tel: 030 2BY23BY2
Fax: 030 2BY42BUY6
E-mail: snore@shedybyes.zzz
Web: www.shedybyes.zzz

Entry No: 307   **Map no:** 11

You can have a real fire in one of the bedrooms - Mary will light it if you ask. She runs a bustling, welcoming household with good humour; "clean, but not always tidy", which is fine by us. There's a natural, family feel - a homely kitchen with old, cream Aga, jade woodwork and bright china - and a bold design sense, too; much that is wooden has been painted and everything draped in brightly-coloured coverings. Upstairs, faded carpets, fresh flowers, good sheets, a lovely bathroom and A-frame ceilings. In the sitting room: deep sofas, a log-burner, wooden floor and beams.

Rooms: 1 double, en suite (bath); 1 double with private shower. Cot and fold-up bed available.

Price: £25-£30 p.p. Single supp. £2.50. Discounts for longer stays by arrangement.

Meals: Breakfast times flexible. Dinner available locally.

Closed: Christmas.

From Burnham Market, follow signs to Fakenham for 2 miles; next village is North Creake. Over bridge, sharp left, house 0.25 miles on right.

Mary & Jeremy Brettingham
Glebe Farmhouse
Wells Road
North Creake, Fakenham
Norfolk NR21 9LG
Tel: 01328 730133
Fax: 01328 730444
E-mail: mm@eastnortheast.co.uk

Entry No: 308   **Map no:** 11

Extraordinarily kind and generous hosts - a guest wrote to tell us so - and they really enjoy having people in their 200-year-old converted barn/smithy. There are bees and free-range hens, and vegetables and fruit are home-grown organic; Jane is an imaginative, Aga-abetted, cook. There are farmland views and a wildflower garden where you can have fresh juice before breakfast in the large friendly kitchen with candles suspended above the table and dried flowers from the beams. One bedroom is softly carpeted and the other is more rustic with sea-grass matting. The coast and Walsingham are close-by.

Rooms: 1 twin/double with private bathroom; 1 twin/double with private shower room.

Price: £22 p.p. No single supp.

Meals: Breakfast until 9am, or by arrangement; dinner, 3 courses, £14; B.Y.O wine.

Closed: Christmas.

A148 from Fakenham towards Kings Lynn, then left for Dunton. Straight through Dunton. Keep on main country lane. Barn on left before phone box.

Michael & Jane Davidson-Houston
Manor Farm Barn
Tatterford
Nr. Fakenham
Norfolk NR21 7AZ
Tel: 01485 528393

A conservation award-winning farm tucked away in the heart of rural Norfolk; you are next door to a tiny 13th-century church and are surrounded by lovely gardens (the coast is only 20 minutes away). The two guest rooms, with large sitting room and small kitchen, are in the beautifully converted stables. Antiques, lovely rugs, cushions and artefacts add to the luxury. Breakfast is delicious, with home eggs, bacon and sausages and is served in the dining room of the main house. Libby and Robin have created something special. Kennel and stable available. *Children over 10 welcome.*

Rooms: 1 double, 1 twin in stable annexe, both en suite.

Price: From £25-£35 p.p. Single supp. £10.

Meals: Breakfast until 9.30am. Dinner available locally.

Closed: Never.

A1065 Swaffham/Fakenham road. 6 miles on, through Weasenham. After 1 mile, right for Wellingham. There, house on left, next to church.

Elisabeth Ellis
Manor House Farm
Wellingham
Nr. Fakenham, Kings Lynn
Norfolk PE32 2TH
Tel: 01328 838227
Fax: 01328 838348

Elizabeth is capable and funny - a winning combination. Recently she got the local church bells ringing again after years of silence (tractor grease did the trick...). This is an arable farm with dogs, geese and chicks in spring, yet the house is unusually elegant. You have your own sitting room and bedrooms have high ceilings and pretty details - hand-painted tiles above the basins, padded headboards, lovely prints... Organic farm eggs for breakfast and Elizabeth's excellent lemon cake for tea; city-dwellers will feel that they have escaped from it all. *Children over 12 welcome.*

Rooms: 1 twin, en suite (bath); 1 twin, 1 double sharing bathroom.

Price: £21-£25 p.p. Single supp. in season, £5.

Meals: Breakfast 8.30am-9am (Mon-Fri), 8.30-9.30am (Sat-Sun). Dinner in winter £15, by arrangement.

Closed: Christmas & New Year.

From Fakenham B1146 towards East Dereham. After 2 miles, left to Gt. Ryburgh. In village, 2nd left up Highfield Lane opposite pink cottage & on for 0.5 miles; house on right.

Elizabeth Savory
Highfield Farm
Great Ryburgh
Fakenham
Norfolk NR21 7AL
Tel: 01328 829249
Fax: 01328 829422

Entry No: 311   **Map no: 11**

For the whole of the 19th century this was Litcham's doctor's house and today, over 200 years after it was built, the red-brick Hall remains at the centre of the community, with church fêtes held in the three-acre garden. This is a thoroughly English home with elegant proportions. The hall, drawing room and dining room are gracious and beautifully furnished. There are good reading lights and books by the beds and the big-windowed guest rooms look onto the lovely formal garden with box edges and gravel paths. John and Hermione are friendly and most helpful. *Children by arrangement; dogs and use of pool similarly.*

Rooms: 2 twins, both with private bathroom. Sitting room available. Extra room available occasionally.

Price: £25-£30 p.p. Please book in advance.

Meals: Breakfast times flexible; dinner £15-£20, on request.

Closed: Christmas.

From Swaffham, A1065; right to Litcham after 5 miles. House on left as you come into village. Georgian red brick with stone balls on gatepost.

John & Hermione Birkbeck
Litcham Hall
Litcham
Nr. Kings Lynn
Norfolk PE32 2QQ
Tel: 01328 701389
Fax: 01328 701164

Entry No: 312   **Map no: 11**

Mrs Garnier has become a legend among B&B-ers - she has done it for so long and looks after her stupendous Grade II*-listed house single-handedly. She tells colourful stories of the house and her family's long local history: from 1349 until the Dissolution of the Monasteries, it was a college of priests; later, it was saved from ruin and brought back to life. It has a stunning panelled dining room, big bedrooms (the sky blue one is particularly pretty) and great views. Incredible value for such a special house. *Children over seven welcome.*

Rooms: 1 twin, 1 twin/double, both en suite (bath); 1 double with private bathroom. Also extra shower and wc.

Price: From £20 p.p.

Meals: Breakfast times flexible; afternoon tea included. Lunch & evening meal available in local pub.

Closed: Never.

Norfolk at its best - huge skies and views that go on forever from this fine Georgian vicarage. An elegant staircase springs from the flagstoned inner hall lit by the glass pyramid high above. Two lovely bedrooms - one facing west captures terrific sunsets - have good furniture, books, china and pictures. The dining room is sunlit, too, and Rosie produces local fare: Cley kippers, mussels, crab, home-produced eggs and preserves and game in season. Just five miles from the coast - swim, sail, walk, cycle, visit the seals... *Use of grass tennis court by arrangement.*

Rooms: 1 twin/double, en suite (bath); 1 double with private bathroom.

Price: From £23 p.p. Please ask about single supp. and children's rate.

Meals: Breakfast usually 9am or by arrangement; dinner, 3 courses, £18, by arrangement. B.Y.O. wine.

Closed: Christmas & New Year.

From Thetford A1075 north towards Watton. After 9 miles, left to Thompson. After 0.5 miles take 2nd left at red postbox on corner. Left again, house at dead end.

From Fakenham, to Cromer for 6 miles. Left at Crawfish pub into Hindringham, down hill & left, before church, into Blacksmith's Lane. Follow lane, bear right, house on left at top.

Mrs Garnier
College Farm
Thompson
Thetford
Norfolk IP24 1QG
Tel: 01953 483318
Fax: 01953 483318
E-mail: collegefarm@amserve.co.uk

Rosie & Robin Waters
The Old Vicarage
Blacksmith's Lane
Hindringham
Norfolk NR21 0QA
Tel: 01328 878223
E-mail: watersrobin@hotmail.com

Entry No: 313   **Map no: 11**

Entry No: 314   **Map no: 12**

Norfolk

A fairytale house - you almost expect Hansel and Gretel to come skipping out from the woods. Mary has brought deep luxury to this historic former gamekeeper's flint lodge. There are two private guest suites: you have your own entrance, sitting room, double room and bathroom. And considerable luxury, too - king-size brass beds, excellent mattresses and high spec. bathrooms. Mary, an art historian, is caring and wants you to feel cosseted; you will. Charcoal used to be burnt in the woodland and the surrounding countryside is enchanting. Under the huge Norfolk skies are bird-watching reserves, sandy beaches and salt marshes.

Rooms: 2 suites with king-size beds, both en suite (bath & shower).

Price: £40 p.p. Reduction for 3 nights or more. Single occ. £80.

Meals: Breakfast until 10am. Dinner available locally.

Closed: Christmas.

Everything is of hotel-like perfection - breakfast, coffee, beds, furnishings - yet the level of care is personal (a perfect combination for many). The river laps at the walls of the 18th-century windmill and a magnificent sitting room overlooks the marshes; some bedrooms take in the endless seascape and one has a walk-around balcony. Jeremy took over the Mill in '98 - a guest who fell in love with the place. He upped sticks from his Battersea restaurant and now does wonders with local ingredients: caught-that-day fish or the delicious seamarsh samphire. Bring your binoculars.

Rooms: 3 twins/doubles, 4 doubles, all en suite (bath).

Price: £34-54 p.p. Singles usually pay double occ. rate.

Meals: Breakfast 8.30-9am; dinner £17.50.

Closed: Never.

Off A148 onto B1156 signed Blakeney. At x'roads, straight over (pass sign to Saxlingham). Approx. 0.5 miles on, house on right with gravel drive & lamp post.

From Holt take Cley Road, through narrow, & only, street in Cley. Mill signed on left. Over bridge to car park.

Mary Alexander
The Map House
Smokers Hole
Saxlingham, Nr Holt
Norfolk NR25 7JU
Tel: 01263 741304
E-mail: enquiries@maphouse.net
Web: www.maphouse.net

Jeremy Bolam
Cley Mill
Cley-next-the-Sea
Holt
Norfolk NR25 7RP
Tel: 01263 740209
Fax: 01263 740209

Entry No: 315   **Map no: 12**

Entry No: 316   **Map no: 12**

The garden was alive with spring bulbs when we visited and a squadron of white ducks joined in the welcome; they give lovely breakfast eggs, says Jo, but they do trample the tulips! This 17th-century rectory is a big, easy-going family home with a large, jolly drawing/dining room, a double guest room with a canopied brass bedstead and a croquet lawn. Your children are more than welcome and the grown-up family is fun. Jo is an enthusiastic local and architectural historian; she and Giles are keen sailors. Swim, sail or seal-watch on the nearby coast. *All-weather tennis court available by arrangement.*

Rooms: 1 twin with private bath, shower & wc; 1 double, en suite (bath).

Price: £22.50 p.p. Discount for children.

Meals: Breakfast times flexible; dinner £12.50 by arrangement. B.Y.O. wine.

Closed: Christmas & New Year.

From Fakenham A1067 towards Norwich. At Guist clock tower, left; 2nd of 2 turnings to Wood Norton. House on right after 100 yds, through overgrown entrance, over 2 cattle grids.

Jo & Giles Winter
The Old Rectory
Wood Norton
Norfolk NR20 5AZ
Tel: 01362 683785

Entry No: 317   Map no: 12

A gorgeous place! Sarah has opened up the Georgian Old Laundry beside Heydon Hall, one of Norfolk's finest Grade I Elizabethan houses. The white walls, scrubbed tables and stone flags are still in place, but immense luxury has been added. You have your own sunny dining/sitting room where you eat breakfast with cream furniture on mellow stone floors. Bedrooms have pretty fabrics at the windows and on the headboards; one has a bathroom with a fireplace and a free-standing bath. You have a private courtyard and there's a swimming pool that you can use if you ask beforehand.

Rooms: 2 twins/doubles, 1 en suite (bath), 1 with private bathroom.

Price: £30 p.p. Single supp. in high season, £5.

Meals: Breakfast times flexible; dinner by arrangement. Good pub nearby.

Closed: Self-catering only at Christmas.

From Norwich, B1149 for 10 miles. 2nd left after bridge, signed Heydon. After 1.5 miles, right into village, straight into park, over cattle grid, past Hall to left & follow signs.

Sarah Bulwer-Long
The Old Laundry
Heydon Hall
Heydon
Norfolk NR11 6RE
Tel: 01263 587343
Fax: 01263 587805

Entry No: 318   Map no: 12

Norfolk

The best of both worlds - a lovely family buzz in the neighbouring Manor Farmhouse where you take breakfast and privacy in the converted barn where you stay. You can come and go as you like and curl up with a book in front of the fire if it's raining... Perfect. The thatched, late 16th-century barn has three bedrooms - two lofty - and everything is fresh, new and luxurious; one has views to Happisburgh's red and white striped lighthouse. There's a vaulted sitting room, a courtyard garden and a billiard table in the flint stable, too. Your hosts are charming. *Children over six welcome.*

Rooms: 2 doubles, 1 double/twin, both en suite (2 baths, 1 shower).

Price: From £22 p.p. Single supp. by arrangement.

Meals: Breakfast times flexible; dinner, 3 courses, from £12.50, by arrangement.

Closed: Christmas & New Year (then available as a holiday let).

From Norwich, A1151/A149 almost to Stalham. Left, signed Walcott. At T-junc. left again. 1 mile on, right for H'burgh. Next T-junc., right. Next T-junc. left. Past houses on left & fields. Rd bends to right, look for house sign by fence.

David & Rosie Eldridge
Manor Farmhouse
Happisburgh
Norfolk NR12 0SA
Tel: 01692 651262
Fax: 01692 650220
Web: www.northnorfolk.co.uk/manorbarn

Entry No: 319   **Map no:** 12

There's an elegance and a prettiness - in perfect measure. Light, airy rooms with long Georgian windows have been dressed in beautiful fabrics - checks, *toile du Juoy* and elegant ochre stripes. Each of the bedrooms is enticing - one has a deep cerise backdrop, the other, two lovely woven wicker chairs. Bibby cooks using local produce and butchers' sausages. Worstead, the birthplace of the worsted cloth, is a charming village and only a short stroll away. A pretty garden and a large, heated pool, too. Come at the end of July and you can join in the fun of the village festival.

Rooms: 1 twin, with basin and private shower; 1 double, en suite (bath).

Price: £23-£25. Single supp. £10

Meals: Breakfast times flexible; packed lunch available at various prices. Dinner available locally.

Closed: Christmas & New Year

From Norwich, B1150 (N. Walsham Road). At Westwick, right towards Worstead. Under railway bridge. On entering village, left at Manor House on to School on left. House on right.

Michael & Bibby Horwood
Holly Grove
Worstead
North Walsham
Norfolk NR28 9RQ
Tel: 01692 535546
E-mail: michaelhorwood@freenetname.co.uk
Web: www.broadland.com/hollygrove

Entry No: 320   **Map no:** 12

Old, and beautiful, a large tapestry hangs in the stairwell and foot-square stone slabs make up the ground floor. The rugs are old, too, from Persia and the East. There's a grand piano in the smaller sitting room. This is the sort of house we love to include, for we value the well-worn dignity, furniture and style of such unassuming good taste. The bedrooms have colourful bedcovers and overlook the mature garden, a place for croquet and badminton. The twins can be a self-contained flat. Marvellous value and Elizabeth will kindly drive the car-less to local NT properties, Sandringham or Cambridge.

Rooms: 1 double, en suite and 2 twins with private bathrooms. All can be let as private flat with sitting room & kitchen.

Price: £25 p.p. Single supp. £5.

Meals: Breakfast times flexible; dinner, 2 courses, £12, by arrangement.

Closed: Occasionally.

From Norwich 10-15 minute drive. Bramerton is signposted from A146 (Norwich-Lowestoft road). House opposite church, with white 5-bar gate.

Elizabeth Perowne
The White House
Bramerton
Norwich
Norfolk NR14 7DW
Tel: 01508 538673

Entry No: 321   **Map no: 12**

The house is immaculate, with many antiques and fine paintings, yet not at all intimidating; its style and elegance is carried with ease. The Puseys are a thoroughly human and friendly couple who keep horses (stable room for yours, too), a cat and two very large, much-loved lurchers. They open their arms to their guests, feed them finely and sleep them in extreme comfort. In the rich, red dining room is an interesting collection of glasses, plates and paintings, and there's a beautiful drawing room for guests, too. *Children over five welcome.*

Rooms: 1 double, en suite (shower); 1 twin with private shower & bath.

Price: £30 p.p. Single supp. £8.

Meals: Breakfast times flexible; packed lunch, from £5; dinner, £18; both by arrangement.

Closed: Occasionally.

1 mile S of Norwich on r'bout at junction of A47 & A140 to Ipswich, take exit for Caistor St. Edmund. After a mile, left at x-roads & house on immediate right.

Kassy & Jonathan Pusey
The Old Rectory
Caistor St. Edmund
Norwich
Norfolk NR14 8QS
Tel: 01508 492490
Fax: 01508 495172
E-mail: pusey@paston.co.uk

Entry No: 322   **Map no: 12**

So many interesting objects it takes time to absorb the splendour: in the drawing room, gorgeous prints and paintings, unusual furniture, decorative lamps... Caroline has a fine eye for detail. The guest room has a Regency-style canopied king-size bed and decoration to suit the era of the house (1850). The large garden is just as fascinating, with rooms and a very large, jungly pond that slinks between the trees. You can eat in the courtyard or the conservatory; Caroline prepares lovely dinners using much local produce. *Children over nine welcome.*

Rooms: 1 double (kingsize), 1 single, both with private bathrooms.

Price: Single £20, double £25 p.p.

Meals: Breakfast until 10am, but quite flexible; packed lunch £5; lunch £10; dinner £15.

Closed: Christmas & New Year.

A11 Attleborough-Wymondham. Take Spooner Row sign. Over x-roads by Three Boars Pub. At T-junc. left to Wymondham. 1 mile on, look for rusty barrel on left. Turn into farm track.

Light pours into this 17th-century timber threshing barn - a jewel of a conversion tucked away in the heart of Norfolk. Fine antique Chinese furniture (Julie lived in Hong Kong for years) looks just right inside the lofty, open-plan, A-frame interior. Music systems are disguised by exotic oriental cabinets; little fat Buddhas - like the one in the delightful, colour-washed twin - rest in quiet corners. The twin opens directly onto its own patio (the double has garden access, too) and there's a courtyard and a grass tennis court. It's all so friendly and fascinating that you may not want to leave.

Rooms: 1 twin, en suite (bath); 1 double with private bathroom.

Price: £25 p.p. Single supp. £10.

Meals: Breakfast times flexible; packed lunch by arrangement; dinner £15. B.Y.O. wine.

Closed: Christmas & New Year.

From A140 at Long Stratton, take Flowerpot Lane (opposite Shell garage) to Wacton. At x-roads, left & 500 yds on, left again at tall hedge. Follow signs.

Caroline Musker
Sallowfield Cottage
Wattlefield
Wymondham
Norfolk NR18 9PA
Tel: 01953 605086
E-mail: caroline.musker@tesco.net

Mrs Julie Franklin
Le Grys Barn
Wacton Common
Long Stratton
Norfolk NR15 2UR
Tel: 01508 531576
Fax: 01508 532124
Web: www.norfolkbroads.com/legrysbarn

Entry No: 323   **Map no: 12**   **Entry No: 324**   **Map no: 12**

Flemish flax weavers used to wash the flax in the moat and dry it in the magnificent barn. Grade II*, red-brick and mellow, the house has a grand scale; soaring ceilings, handsome fireplaces, huge sash windows, cast-iron baths, parquet floors, good, large, beds. It's full of light, and chandelier, balustrade and frescos add grandeur. Guests have their own sitting room. Evenings here are heavenly - a drink on the terrace, dinner, then a wander through the rose walk and the ancient trees. The garden is two and a half acres, with a tennis court. Richard and Teena are super.

Rooms: 1 large double with private bathroom; 1 large twin, en suite (bath).

Price: £35 p.p. Single supp. £15.

Meals: Breakfast until 10am; dinner from £20, by arrangement.

Closed: Occasionally.

A house on a hill - unusual for East Anglia; the lawns fall away and views stretch out over farmland. Richard and Patricia are utterly charming and so easy to talk to; their respective passions are fishing and gardening - the garden is superb. There are fresh flowers, family photographs, agricultural prints and a feeling of light and space. The guest sitting room is generously furnished and Patricia will light a fire for you. The double, predominantly green, bedroom is the biggest; all have thick carpets and a quiet Victorian elegance.

Rooms: 1 twin/double, en suite (bath); 1 twin with private bathroom plus 1 double let to same party willing to share bathroom. Extra wc and basin available.

Price: From £25 p.p. Single supp. £5, one-off payment.

Meals: Breakfast times flexible. Good pubs and restaurants nearby.

Closed: Never.

A143 Yarmouth/Beccles road. In Toft Monks take Post Office Rd (opposite Toft Lion pub) for 0.4 miles to T-junc. Right down Aldeby Rd for 0.1 mile, fork right. House on right, 0.2 miles on.

A143 Diss/Yarmouth rd for 9 miles. At r'bout left for Harleston, then immed. left to Starston. Over x-roads, into village, over bridge, immed. right. After 0.5 miles, drive on left by white railing.

Richard & Teena Freeland
The Elms
Toft Monks
Beccles
Norfolk NR34 0EJ
Tel: 01502 677380
Fax: 01502 677362
E-mail: richardfreeland@btconnect.com

Mrs Patricia Lombe Taylor
Conifer Hill
Low Road
Starston, Harleston
Norfolk IP20 9NT
Tel: 01379 852393
Fax: 01379 852393

Entry No: 325   **Map no:** 12

Entry No: 326   **Map no:** 12

"God made the country and man made the town," said William Cowper. In this God-given corner of England you're immersed in a restorative peace. The church and the ironstone, listed vicarage have sat side by side since the 18th century. Birdsong and the sound of tennis being played on the grass court add to the Englishness of it all; you will effortlessly sink into the country house pace. The cream twin and the pale green double are extremely comfortable. Lots of choice for breakfast and your favourite newspaper can be waiting on the table. *Children by arrangement.*

Rooms: 1 double, en suite (shower); 1 twin with private bathroom.

Price: From £30 p.p. Single supp. £5.

Meals: Breakfast times flexible; packed lunch, £3-£5 and dinner, £12-£15, by arrangement.

Closed: Christmas.

The house is a 300-year-old thatched cottage. The gardens and the beautiful things in it are a treat. And then there's Liz – a charming and gracious hostess. There's something special at every turn: a Bechstein piano in the cottage sitting room, a Jacobean trunk in the single room, Gothic headboards in the twin, a beautiful bureau in the bathroom. Guests have said that "staying here is like staying with a good friend". *Cordon Bleu* dinners and the lovely conservation village of Staverton complete the idyll. *Children over eight and babes in arms welcome.*

Rooms: 2 doubles, 1 twin, all en suite (bath/shower); 1 single, en suite (bath).

Price: £37.50 p.p. Single supp. £10.

Meals: Breakfast times flexible; dinner, 3 courses, £25.

Closed: Christmas & New Year.

From M40 junc. 11, dual carriageway for Northampton. 0.75 miles on, left at r'bout for Northampton, & left again 2 miles on. Follow signs for Canons Ashby to Moreton Pinkney. There, fork right across green on track. Beside church.

From Daventry, A425 to Leamington Spa. 100 yds past Staverton Park Conference Centre, right into village, then 1st right. Keep left, & at 'Give Way' sign, sharp left. House immed. on right.

Colonel & Mrs T.J.S. Eastwood
The Old Vicarage
Moreton Pinkney, Daventry
Northamptonshire NN11 3SQ
Tel: 01295 760057
Fax: 01295 760057
E-mail: tim@tandjeastwood.fsnet.co.uk
Web: www.tandjeastwood.fsnet.co.uk

Mrs Elizabeth Jarrett
Colledges House
Oakham Lane
Staverton, Daventry
Northamptonshire NN11 6JQ
Tel: 01327 702737
Fax: 01327 300851

Entry No: 327   **Map no: 10**

Entry No: 328   **Map no: 10**

Northamptonshire & Northumberland

Part of the Althorp estate, this former 1840s farmhouse is a family home at the end of a grand avenue of lime trees; in the garden you'll see traces of medieval ridge and furrow farming methods. Valerie and Ian, who collect and sell blue and white Staffordshire pottery, are great company; they are very knowledgeable and enthusiastic about the area and pull off the trick of giving you both comfort and privacy. Their daughter runs a livery from the stable yard and extensive paddocks - the riding is superb and your horse is welcome, too. The large, simple bedrooms have sofas and armchairs and great views.

Rooms: 1 twin with private bathroom; 1 double, en suite (bath), plus extra twin, let only to members of same party.

Price: £25 p.p. Single supp. £5.

Meals: Breakfast times flexible; dinner £15. B.Y.O wine.

Closed: Never.

From Northampton, A45 towards Daventry. After approx 1.5 miles, 3rd exit at r'bout (signed Althorp). After 1 mile, 1st exit at r'bout (signed Nobottle). In 2 miles, house just beyond Nobottle on left, on brow of hill.

Valerie Cocks
Nobottle Grange
Nobottle
Northampton
Northamptonshire NN7 4HJ
Tel: 01604 759494
Fax: 01604 590799
E-mail: nobottlegrange@hotmail.com

Entry No: 329   **Map no:** 10

The Clydes have striven for perfection: every picture, ornament, piece of china, fabric and colour has been chosen to perfectly complement each artfully-designed room. Bedrooms have bold William Morris wallpapers, excellent beds and windows that are elaborately dressed. Your hosts are generous, too - with their breakfasts, enticing tea trays, fluffy robes, toiletries displayed among shells and glassware and bowls of fruit... They also ran a restaurant for 22 years, are down-to-earth and keen walkers. *Children by arrangement.*

Rooms: 1 twin, en suite (shower); 2 doubles, en suite (bath).

Price: £32.50-£35 p.p. Single supp. £7.50-£10.

Meals: Breakfast times flexible; packed lunch £4; dinner £21.

Closed: Never.

From Haydon Bridge, left onto B6319. After 300 yds cross railway. 1st right (B6319). After 2 miles, stone farmhouse on left with dark blue door.

Angela Clyde
Allerwash Farmhouse
Newborough
Nr. Hexham
Northumberland NE47 5AB
Tel: 01434 674574
Fax: 01434 674574
Web: www.allerwash.ntb.org.uk

Entry No: 330   **Map no:** 19

The topiary is magnificent! And the old dovecote fascinates foreigners. This is a solid, Victorian house set in expansive, breathtaking Northumbrian scenery – a magnet for walkers and nature-lovers. Your gently hospitable hostess welcomes families now that her children have fled the nest, though their Beatrix Potter books and little knick-knacks remain. Lots of photographs, too, mostly of the family on horseback! Twin bedrooms are straightforward but large and perfectly adequate. All have wonderful views.

Rooms: 3 twins (2 with basin, 1 without), sharing 2 guest bathrooms.

Price: £20 p.p.

Meals: Breakfast until 9am. Dinner, from £20, by arrangement.

Closed: Occasionally.

We know this house and Lynne is the new owner; she has great plans for the 1800s gentlemen's residence. Oak dressers, Zoffany wallpapers, Georgian shutters, waxed floorboards, Indian rugs, lilac paint, oak antique beds... you get the picture. The setting is lovely and the wonders of Northumberland beckon the walker, the naturalist, the stressed city soul. There's an organic vegetable garden within five acres of land and there will be stables for your horse, too. Lynne makes her own jams and breakfasts are generous. She's kind, efficient and capable.

Rooms: 2 doubles, en suite (shower), 1 twin, en suite (bath).

Price: £45 per room. £25 single.

Meals: Breakfast times flexible. Restaurants within a short drive.

Closed: Christmas & New Year.

From A68, south of Tyne at r'bout, east towards Stocksfield. Take B6309 right signed Hindley. 1st left, then biggest house at end.

A69 signed Ovington, on left if travelling to Hexham. Through Ovington village, passing 2 pubs. House signposted on left, after sharp corner.

Mrs J. Aldridge
Old Ridley Hall
Stocksfield
Northumberland NE43 7RU
Tel: 01661 842816
E-mail: oldridleyhall@talk21.com

Lynne Moffitt
Ovington House
Ovington
Prudhoe
Northumberland NE42 6DH
Tel: 01661 832442

Entry No: 331   **Map no: 20**

Entry No: 332   **Map no: 20**

Readers have written to tell us how happy they have been here. Just three miles from Hadrian's Wall, the house is at the end of a long drive, over the burn and an old stone bridge and surrounded by ancient woodland and birdsong. The house is well lived-in, elegant and comfortable. The large bedrooms are pretty and thoughtfully furnished with antiques and lovely prints. There is a walled garden and breakfast can be taken on the terrace. Katie grew up in this lovely house and can tell you all about the area. *Children over 10 welcome.*

Rooms: 1 double, 1 twin, both en suite (bath); 1 twin with private bathroom.

Price: £30 p.p. Single supp. £10.

Meals: Breakfast until 9am. Dinner available locally.

Closed: October-February.

Guests co-exist around a pretty courtyard - your rooms are in self-contained suites, each named after the wood used within, and each with its own entrance. The bedrooms are small, but you have use of a sitting room and library within the courtyard and eat in the 18th-century house - once the home of Capability Brown - in an oak-beamed, inglenooked dining room. Walk in the hills or play croquet on the lawn before dinner. Celia is a friendly and attentive hostess who loves cooking; Stephen makes and restores furniture and there is much evidence of his artistry.

Rooms: 1 family suite, 1 double, 1 four-poster, all en suite (shower); 1 family suite, en suite (bath).

Price: £23.50-£25 p.p. Single supp. £10.

Meals: Breakfast 8.30-9.30am; dinner £18, by arrangement.

Closed: 1 November-1 March.

7 miles north of Corbridge on A68. Left on A6079 & after 1 mile, right through Lodge gates with arch. House 0.5 miles down drive.

From Newcastle A696 (signed Jedburgh). 5 miles north of Belsay, right onto B6342. House on left after 300 yds.

Simon & Katie Stewart
The Hermitage
Swinburne
Nr. Hexham
Northumberland NE48 4DG
Tel: 01434 681248
Fax: 01434 681110
E-mail: stewart@thehermitagenow.freeserve.co.uk

Celia & Stephen Robinson-Gay
Shieldhall
Wallington
Morpeth
Northumberland NE61 4AQ
Tel: 01830 540387
Fax: 01830 540490
E-mail: robinson.gay@btinternet.com

Entry No: 333   **Map no: 20**

Entry No: 334   **Map no: 20**

Dorothy takes pride in creating an easy, sociable atmosphere - three couples who met here one weekend came back for a reunion. This is a pretty spot and the Jacksons know every inch of the countryside and coastline that surrounds their 1715 home. They farm 400 acres of mixed arable land that sweeps down to the coast yet still find time to greet and get to know their guests. The bedrooms are large, bright and well-furnished; there is a conservatory at the back (where you can have tea on arrival), an airy guests' sitting room and splendid views to the sea.

Rooms: 2 doubles, 1 twin, all en suite (shower). Bathroom also available.

Price: £26 p.p. Ask about single supp.

Meals: Breakfast until 9am; packed lunches from £3.50; dinner, £14, by arrangement.

Closed: Christmas & New Year.

Sophisticated, gracious living in an immaculately elegant Georgian villa perched on a rocky promontory - the sea views are magnificent. The Athertons are avid antique collectors, charming and friendly, amusing and energetic perfectionists. Weekday breakfasts are feasts of fresh fruit, organic yogurt, croissants, scone and fruit compotes; weekend breakfasts are either the full English or locally-smoked Craster kippers or smoked salmon. Superb bedrooms have beautiful curtains, huge French mahogany beds and luxurious linen and towels. There is a sumptuous drawing room with grand piano and well-stocked library, too. Perfect.

Rooms: 3 doubles, 2 en suite (bath), 1 with private bathroom.

Price: £37.50 p.p. Single occ. £60.

Meals: Breakfast until 9am. Dinner available locally.

Closed: Christmas & New Year.

From Alnwick, A1068 to Alnmouth. At Hipsburn r'bout follow signs to station & cross bridge. 1st lane to left, house approx. 0.5 miles from road.

A1068 Warkworth/Alnmouth. On entering High Buston, Hall is 1st building on right.

Brian & Dorothy Jackson
Bilton Barns
Alnmouth, Alnwick
Northumberland NE66 2TB
Tel: 01665 830427
Fax: 01665 830063
E-mail: dorothy@biltonbarns.co.uk
Web: www.biltonbarns.co.uk

Ian & Therese Atherton
High Buston Hall
High Buston, Alnmouth
Northumberland NE66 3QH
Tel: 01665 830606
Fax: 01665 830707
E-mail: highbuston@aol.com
Web: www.members.aol.com/highbuston

Entry No: 335   **Map no: 20**

Entry No: 336   **Map no: 20**

Sylvia is a doyenne of farmhouse B&B, with 25 years' experience under her belt. She recently received an MBE for her 'Household and Farming Museum' and is justly proud of her gong. She has a wonderful sense of community and Charlie, even if he's been up since dawn with his sheep, will come and have a chat as you have breakfast. Large bedrooms, long views, handmade quilts, family furniture, generous breakfasts. True farmhouse B&B. *Children over 10 welcome.*

Rooms: 2 doubles, en suite (shower); 1 twin with private bathroom.

Price: £30 p.p. Single supp. £10.

Meals: Breakfast times flexible. Dinner available locally.

Closed: Christmas & New Year.

A totally surprising one-storey house, full of beautiful things. It is an Aladdin's cave, larger than you could imagine. The garden/breakfast room is the hub of the house and has a country cottage feel to it; here you'll eat locally smoked kippers and award-winning 'Bamburgh Bangers' and home-cured bacon from the village butcher. There's a sun-trapping courtyard for summer breakfasts. Guests have a cheerful sitting/dining room and bedrooms have fresh flowers and very good books. Mary is welcoming, amusing and has stacks of local knowledge.

Rooms: 1 twin, 1 double, sharing private bathroom.

Price: £25-£27.50 p.p. Single supp. £7.50.

Meals: Breakfast 8.30-9am; dinner, £18.50, by arrangement.

Closed: Christmas & occasionally in winter.

6 miles north of Alnwick on A1, left when you hit dual carriageway, signed North Charlton. House 300 yds up on left through trees.

From Newcastle north on A1, then right signed Bamburgh on B1341. Continue to village, pass 30mph sign & hotel, then 1st right. House 400 yds on right.

Charles & Sylvia Armstrong
North Charlton Farm
Chathill
Alnwick
Northumberland NE67 5HP
Tel: 01665 579443
Fax: 01665 579407
E-mail: ncharlton1@agriplus.net

Mary Dixon
Broome
22 Ingram Road
Bamburgh
Northumberland NE69 7BT
Tel: 01668 214287
E-mail: mdixon4394@aol.com

Entry No: 337   **Map no: 20**

Entry No: 338   **Map no: 20**

Barbara has created a homely haven out of this local stone, Grade II-listed manse that adjoins the southernmost Church of Scotland - you glimpse its stained glass windows from the garden. Much is home-made: traditional Scottish griddle-scones on arrival with, perhaps, home-made marmalade (pineapple and orange), bread, fruit cake and shortbread. There are log fires, comfy sofas and two newly decorated, elegant guest rooms with good period furniture. Barbara has a great sense of humour.

Rooms: 1 double, 1 twin, both en suite (bath).

Price: £25 p.p. Single supp. £7.50.

Meals: Breakfast until 9am; packed lunch from £4; dinner, £17.50, by arrangement.

Closed: 20 December-5 January.

From Newcastle A1 north, then B6353 left to Lowick. In town, left at Post Office, then 1st right, signed.

Barbara Huddart
The Old Manse
Lowick
Berwick-upon-Tweed
Northumberland TD15 2TY
Tel: 01289 388264
E-mail: glenc99@aol.com

Entry No: 339   **Map no: 20**

Few houses can match the majesty of this Northumberland landscape - Pallinsburn challenges it. The architecture spans several centuries; the heart of the house is Jacobean and there are interior columns and ornate plasterwork. The bedrooms are on the expected grand scale and are generously furnished with antiques, chairs, chaise longue. From the window seats you can gaze at the Cheviot Hills. The finest linen and fresh flowers complete the luxury. A fire can be lit for you in the panelled dining room and Mrs Westwood, the housekeeper, will expertly settle you in. *Children over five welcome.*

Rooms: 2 four-posters, both en suite (bath).

Price: £40-£48 p.p. Single supp. £15.

Meals: Breakfast times flexible; dinner occasionally available by arrangement. Also available locally.

Closed: Occasionally.

North from Newcastle on A1. Left on A697 north of Morpeth turn. Continue 5 miles south of Coldstream. Pass Bluebell Inn on left. Drive on right 0.5 miles on. Lodge at gate.

Mr & Mrs Lyell
Pallinsburn
Coldstream
Berwick-upon-Tweed
Northumberland TD12 4SG
Tel: 01890 820202

Entry No: 340   **Map no: 20**

Built in 1920 for the manager of the local coal mine, here's a well-proportioned house with a big, open hall filled with flowers and with numerous rooms off it. Guests have two sitting rooms with sofas and log fires. Colin and Erica are amusing and have lots for you to do: golf (six holes), snooker, darts, croquet, tennis and swimming. If the weather's dreary, there are lots of games to play by the fire. Bedrooms have ample lounging-around space and fireplaces. Bathrooms are big and one has black and cream Edwardian tiles; it is now decorated as a 'print room'.

Rooms: 2 doubles, 1 with private bathroom, 1 en suite (shower); 1 twin, en suite (bath).

Price: £24-£28 p.p. For 3 nights or more, £24 p.p. Single supp. £5.

Meals: Breakfast times flexible; dinner, for 4 people or more, £22; light supper from £12, by arrangement. Meals also available locally.

Closed: Christmas.

From A617 Newark-on-Trent to Mansfield, 0.25 miles west of Kirklington, right at 2 small white bollards, just before turn to Eakring.

Erica McGarrigle
Archway House
Kirklington
Newark
Nottinghamshire NG22 8NX
Tel: 01636 812070
Fax: 01636 812200
E-mail: mcgarrigle@archway-house.co.uk

Entry No: 341   **Map no: 10**

Hilary is chatty and fun and never happier than when her home is full of guests; her breakfasts are generous and are taken at separate tables in two connecting rooms. Pink and pretty, the house has a cottagey feel, though it is bigger than it looks. Filled with interesting things, pastel bedrooms are small and very homely and Southwell's Minster, 'the most rural Cathedral in England', can be seen from some of them. Hilary has lived in the town for 38 years; you can walk to the shops and pubs.

Rooms: 1 twin, 1 double, both en suite (bath/shower); 1 double en suite (shower); 1 twin with private bathroom.

Price: From £32 p.p. Single occ. from £35.

Meals: Breakfast 8-9am; earlier by arrangement. Plenty of pubs & restaurants within walking distance.

Closed: Never.

From Nottingham, A612 to Southwell. Right into Westgate & pass Minster. Approx. 100 yds on, fork right at the library & almost immed. right down alley beside Old Forge.

Hilary Marston
The Old Forge
Burgage Lane
Southwell
Nottinghamshire NG25 0ER
Tel: 01636 812809
Fax: 01636 816302

Entry No: 342   **Map no: 10**

You'll be bowled over by the view. From the generous windows of the majestic red drawing room, beyond the manicured gardens, the Vale of Belvoir is at your feet. The house has been in the family for generations and has an eclectic feel. Gilt-framed portraits, a grandfather clock and a majestic dining room recall a grander age. Plastic chairs on the terrace and fake flowers speak of a no-nonsense approach to contemporary life. Definitely ask for one of the front bedrooms. Beyond the lawns and cherished roses you are blessed with that view.

Rooms: 2 doubles, 1 twin, all with private bathrooms; 1 twin, en suite (shower).

Price: £22.50-£25 p.p. Single supp. £2.50-£5.

Meals: Breakfast times flexible. Good pubs nearby.

Closed: Christmas.

From Nottingham, A606 to Upper Broughton. Drive to top of hill, then sharp left into Colonel's Lane. Signed.

Hilary Dowson
Sulney Fields
Colonel's Lane
Upper Broughton, Melton Mowbray
Nottinghamshire LE14 3BD
Tel: 01664 822204
Fax: 01664 823976
E-mail: acollinson@compuserve.com

Entry No: 343   **Map no:** 10

Ten acres in which to dream – this 18th-century stone house sits behind a Norman church in a perfect Cotswold hamlet. "England at its most idyllic," says our inspector. The beautifully renovated farmhouse combines character and elegance: a comfy sitting room, sweet bedrooms (one with its own sitting room) and flowers from a garden that is Clare's delight. She and Robin are friendly, vibrant, easy with children – there are children's arts and crafts workshops in the holidays and ponies in the yard (children can ride). Ponies in the fields too, sheep and glorious views. *Self-catering possible.*

Rooms: 1 double, 1 twin, both with private bathroom; 1 double/twin, en suite (bath), with own sitting room.

Price: £29-£40 p.p. Single supp. £15.

Meals: Breakfast until 9.30am. Dinner from £20, by arrangement. Good pubs and restaurants in town.

Closed: Never.

From Burford, A40 towards Cheltenham. 1st left, signed Westwell. 2 miles to T-junc., then right, through village. Right to Aldsworth then 1st right onto concrete drive. Continue to end.

Clare & Robin Dunipace
The Glebe House
Westwell, Burford
Oxfordshire OX18 4JT
Tel: 01993 822171
Fax: 01993 824125
E-mail: robin.dunipace@dial.pipex.com
Web: www.oxford-cotswolds-holidays.com

Entry No: 344   **Map no:** 10

Climb the hill from Burford and escape the tourist crush to sink into the seclusion of this 14th-century house. It was the Star Inn until the 18th century, then a Georgian front was added by Christopher Kempstler, a colleague of Christopher Wren's. There's barely an even floor to be found - the large double dips giddily to the bed. Old pieces include an antique butler's cradle, Edwardian corner chairs and French bedside tables. The amiable cats are banned from guest rooms but are companionable on a summer's evening in the garden.

Rooms: 1 double, 1 twin, both en suite (bath/shower); 1 double (plus small single off) with private shower.

Price: £25-£30 p.p. Single occ. £40. Single let with twin, £25.

Meals: Breakfast until 9am. Dinner available locally.

Closed: Never.

From London, M40 to A40, round Oxford ring road, right at Burford r'bout. House 800 yds on left. Private parking.

Judith Hicks
Glenthorne House
174 The Hill
Burford
Oxfordshire OX18 4QY
Tel: 01993 822418

Entry No: 345   Map no: 10

A charming Cotswold stone house - originally the village pub - with a 14th-century core; there's a special elegance and atmosphere. Breakfasts are served in a the wooden-framed conservatory with spectacular views – on a clear day you can see for over 30 miles. The airy bedroom that looks out onto the village green has extremely comfortable beds with a delightful bathroom. The professionally landscaped one-acre garden has a series of rooms and lovely vistas and contains many unusual plants, including the perfectly-named Teapot Tree. A delightful, homely place.

Rooms: 1 twin, en suite (bath).

Price: £35 p.p. Single supp. £10.

Meals: Breakfast until 9.30am. Dinner available locally.

Closed: Christmas.

From Witney, 4 miles towards Charlbury on B4022, then left to Leafield. There, pass church, ignoring left turn, but fork left by flagpole & school sign. 100 yds on, house on left, with circular lawn in front. Turn into gravel drive.

Mrs Tania Llewellyn
Old George House
Leafield
Oxfordshire OX29 9NP
Tel: 01993 878632
Fax: 01993 878700

Entry No: 346   Map no: 10

Our inspector calls it "a Sawday idyll". Bridget is gracious and elegant, the house and setting intoxicating. This is country elegance with few concessions to modernity: rugs and furniture fit beautifully, the kitchen is stone-flagged and wood-boarded. The Garden House is a wonderful B&B or self-catering hideaway - hunker down with books, play the piano, stroll out into the garden; you have your own bedroom, kitchen, sitting room, log fire and large bathroom with a stand-alone, cast-iron bath. The River Windrush trickles through the garden, the church and the ruins of Minster Lovell Hall sit beside it.

Rooms: 1 double in Garden House with bath & shower.

Price: £37.50 p.p. Single supp. £10.

Meals: Breakfast until 9.30am. Dinner available locally.

Closed: Never.

Helen has a real interest in birds - you'll see evidence of it in the house and the garden. This is a charming, easy-going 1720 farmhouse home where the two well-furnished bedrooms share a bright, big shower room - perfect for families or friends travelling together. Separate access to the twin room overlooking the cobbled courtyard is up a daunting iron spiral staircase. The double bedroom featured in a Laura Ashley catalogue. The affectionate sheepdog Chloe is so beloved by children that one American girl sends her a Valentine annually.

Rooms: 1 double, 1 twin, sharing shower room.

Price: From £24 p.p. Single occ. from £35.

Meals: Breakfast times flexible. Dinner available locally.

Closed: Christmas.

From Burford, A40 towards Oxford. At next r'bout, left for Minster Lovell, across bridge. Through village, house on right before church, in cul-de-sac marked 'Unsuitable for motor vehicles'.

A44 north from Oxford's ring road. At r'bout, 1 mile before Woodstock, left onto A4095 into Bladon. Take last left in village. House on 2nd bend in road, with iron railings.

Ms Bridget Geddes
The Old Vicarage
Minster Lovell
Oxfordshire OX8 5RR
Tel: 01993 775630
Fax: 01993 772534
E-mail: ageddes@lix.compulink.co.uk

Helen Stevenson
Manor Farmhouse
Manor Road
Bladon, Nr. Woodstock
Oxfordshire OX20 1RU
Tel: 01993 812168
Fax: 01993 812168
E-mail: helstevenson@hotmail.com

All the nooks, crannies and beams you would expect in such an ancient thatched cottage in a Cotswold village, but much more than that: lots of music, fun and laughter, too, not to mention a wealth of inside information about gardens to visit. Judith is a keen gardener who writes books on the subject; her passion for plants is palpable in her own wonderful cottage garden. Her style and intelligence are reflected in the lived-in, elegant house. Charming, bright pastel bedrooms, thoroughly relaxed atmosphere - and fresh everything...

Rooms: 1 double, 1 twin, both en suite (bath).

Price: £35 p.p. Single occ. £45.

Meals: Breakfast until 9.30am; dinner, 4 courses, £25, by arrangement.

Closed: Christmas & New Year.

Sibford Gower is 0.5 miles south off B4035 which runs between Banbury & Chipping Campden. House on main street, same side as church & school.

Judith Hitching
Gower's Close
Sibford Gower
Nr. Banbury
Oxfordshire OX15 5RW
Tel: 01295 780348
E-mail: j.hitching@virgin.net.co.uk

Entry No: 349   Map no: 10

There's a marvellous glow to this lovingly restored house. A rare, original and fine example of a large 1650s Yeoman farmhouse, it has more than its fair share of oak beams, stone-mullioned windows, big fireplaces and bread ovens. What's more, there are fine antiques, paintings and, in the attic, a games room with a full-size billiards table. Beamed bedrooms are large, light and airy, with views to the valley or to the church; this is an exceptionally pretty village with a proper green. The Hainsworths' two dogs are lovely - "weird-haired" pointers, apparently!

Rooms: 1 double, 1 twin, both en suite (bath).

Price: From £32.50 p.p. Single supp. £12.50.

Meals: Breakfast times flexible. Dinner available in excellent village pub & restaurant.

Closed: Never.

From A422, 7 miles north-west of Banbury, left down hill through Alkerton, then up hill. 1st left by church. Mill House on right.

Keith & Maggie Hainsworth
Mill House
Shenington
Banbury
Oxfordshire OX15 6NH
Tel: 01295 670642

Entry No: 350   Map no: 10

'A 10-out-of-10-house,' says our inspector. The Grove-Whites are super and they run their B&B as a real team. The house is charming: low ceilings, exposed beams and stone fireplaces and the bedrooms, perched above their own staircases like crows' nests, are decorated with rich, floral fabrics. All rooms are unusual and full of character, old and luxurious; the family's history and travels are evident all over. They have two delightful dogs - Ulysses and Goliath - and it's all so easy that you may not want to leave. There's a barn room, too, with its own entrance.

Rooms: 1 double, en suite (bath); 1 twin/double, en suite (bath/shower); 1 twin/double with private bathroom.

Price: £32 p.p. Single supp. £10.

Meals: Breakfast 8-9am; dinner £22.

Closed: Christmas.

From M40, junc. 10, A43 towards Northampton. After 5 miles, left to Charlton. There, left & house on left, 100 yds past the Rose & Crown.

Col & Mrs Grove-White
Home Farmhouse
Charlton, Nr. Banbury
Oxfordshire OX17 3DR
Tel: 01295 811683
Fax: 01295 811683
E-mail: grovewhite@lineone.net
Web: www.homefarmhouse.co.uk

Entry No: 351   **Map no: 10**

Parish records suggest that on the site of the 1760 house there was once a monastic farm where teachers at Oxford would come for enlightenment and inspiration; today you reap the same benefits, and in considerable comfort. Stephen and Sara happily share their books, piano, tennis court, gardens, lake and local knowledge. Sara is an interior designer - cushions, curtains and sofas are adorned with beautiful fabrics and the colours throughout are excellent. The beds are memorably comfortable with goosedown pillows and duvets. Breakfast is an easy affair and you have your own drawing room with log fire.

Rooms: 3 twins/doubles, all en suite (1 shower, 1 bath, 1 bath & shower).

Price: £30 p.p. Single occ. £38.

Meals: Breakfast times flexible; dinner £18, by arrangement.

Closed: Never.

In Kings Sutton follow signs to Charlton but, before leaving Kings Sutton, take last turning right, off Astrop Road, opp. a tree with a seat around it. Farmhouse at end of lane.

Sara & Stephen Allday
College Farmhouse
Kings Sutton
Banbury
Oxfordshire OX17 3PS
Tel: 01295 811473
Fax: 01295 812505
E-mail: seallday@cs.com

Entry No: 352   **Map no: 10**

This beautiful farmhouse was once owned by St. John's College, Oxford - the date stone above the entrance reads 1629, but parts of the house are even older. There's the happy buzz of family life here - it's relaxed and informal - and you settle in easily, welcomed by Mary Anne and Robert with tea and home-made shortbread and by the equally friendly Robert. Bedrooms are light and airy with small stone-arched and mullioned windows; there are Tudor fireplaces, timbered and exposed walls. The huge, twin bedroom has ornate plasterwork and garden and church views; the green and peach double is cosier, again with views.

Rooms: 1 double, 1 twin, both en suite (shower).

Price: £25 p.p. Single supp. £10.

Meals: Breakfast until 9am. Good restaurants nearby.

Closed: Mid-December-mid-January.

They are as laid back as they are efficient... the perfect owners for a house as ravishing as this. The décor is oak floors, white walls, wood, antiques, fine prints and a minimalist feel, with the odd dash of exotica from extensive long-haul travel. The drawing room has a vast, magnificent fireplace for winter. Anthea and Stephen are fun - clocks are their main business and the drawing room has a large, projected clock on the wall. Everywhere, there is head-clearing simplicity that allows the original features the space to impress.

Rooms: 1 twin/double, en suite (shower); 1 double, en suite (bath); 1 double with private bathroom.

Price: £ 40 p.p. Single supp. by arrangement.

Meals: Breakfast 9am (Mon-Fri), 10am (Sat-Sun). Dinner available locally.

Closed: Christmas & New Year.

From Oxford, A420 towards Swindon for 8 miles & right at r'bout, signed Witney (A415). Over 2 bridges, immed. right by pub car park. Right at T-junc.; drive on right, past church.

From M40, A329 towards Wallingford. In Stadhampton take lane immed. after mini-r'bout, left across village green. House straight ahead.

Mary Anne & Robert Florey
Rectory Farm
Northmoor
Nr. Witney
Oxfordshire OX8 1SX
Tel: 01865 300207
Fax: 01865 300559
E-mail: pj.florey@farmline.com

Anthea & Stephen Savage
The Manor
Stadhampton
Oxfordshire OX44 7UL
Tel: 01865 891999
Fax: 01865 891640
E-mail: action@timebeam.com

Entry No: 353   **Map no: 4**

Entry No: 354   **Map no: 4**

Horse-loving Joanna will teach you to ride, by arrangement, and even offers B&B to itinerant horses and their riders. Her husband, who is passionate about roses, may be able to organise rough shooting for field sports enthusiasts, complete with gun dog. Simple comfort in peaceful surroundings is the watchword at this extended, semi-detached old workers' cottage with its clean, functional, no-frills, lemon-yellow rooms in a separate garden flat overlooking a courtyard. If roses, wine, shooting, hunting and stud farms are your thing, you could do no better. Probably not for *Guardian* readers.

Rooms: 2 twins in garden flat, both en suite with garden access.

Price: £20 p.p. More than 3 nights, £15 p.p. Single occ. £25.

Meals: Breakfast 7.15-9.30am; flexible by arrangement. Dinner available locally.

Closed: Never.

Junc. 8/9 M4 to Henley. A4130 to Oxford. Crowmarsh Gifford r'bout, left onto Wallingford bypass. Right at next r'bout, over river, left at 1st of double r'bouts to Moulsford. A mile on, right into Caps Lane. Cottage 1st on left.

Mrs Joanna Alexander
The Well Cottage
Caps Lane, Cholsey
Oxfordshire OX10 9HQ
Tel: 01491 651959
Fax: 01491 651675
E-mail: thewellcottage@talk21.com
Web: www.thewellcottage.com

A baby grand that beckons those who can play and fires are lit on cold evenings. It's all utterly soothing and easy and reinforces the wonders of English country life. Persian rugs in the sitting room and ethnic touches here and there that tell of Sue's passion for real travel. More rugs in pretty bedrooms that are unmistakably 'country' and light; low ceilings and uneven floors reveal their 18th-century roots. There are eight acres of grounds with all-round views and gorgeous walks through Beech Woods strewn with bluebells in May.

Rooms: 2 twins/doubles, both en suite (bath & shower).

Price: £29 p.p. Single occ. £40.

Meals: Breakfast 7.30-9am. Good choice of places locally for dinner.

Closed: September-April.

From Henley NW on Peppard Rd for 3 miles, then right for Shepherds Green. House on right after 0.3 miles. Phone to advise time of arrival, & no bookings after noon on day of stay, please.

Sue Fulford-Dobson
Shepherds
Shepherds Green
Rotherfield Greys, Henley-on-Thames
Oxfordshire RG9 4QL
Tel: 01491 628413
Fax: 01491 628413

The architecture and the grounds are immediately captivating and the late Georgian interior is impressive in scale, with the light, height and space you expect from this period. The hall is galleried and the staircase, elegantly delicate, sweeps you regally up to the guest rooms. All rooms are large - bathroom suites hark back to the '70s - and all except one look onto the garden and far beyond. You have a large drawing room, woodland to explore, tennis and croquet to play; French doors open onto the grounds. Brian and Wendy are super. *Children over 12 welcome.*

Rooms: 2 twins, 2 doubles, 1 single, all en suite (bath).

Price: Twins/doubles £30 p.p. Single £40. Single occ. of double £50.

Meals: Breakfast 7.45-9.45am. Dinner available locally.

Closed: Christmas.

From Henley-on-Thames, A4155 towards Reading. After 2.5 miles, College on left & pub on right. Before pub turn into Plough Lane. House up hill on left.

Brian & Wendy Talfourd-Cook
Holmwood
Shiplake Row
Binfield Heath, Henley
Oxfordshire RG9 4DP
Tel: 0118 947 8747
Fax: 0118 947 8637

Entry No: 357   **Map no: 5**

Go for the room with the view across Rutland Water. The village provides boats for sailing or fishing, or horses or bikes - for the less active there are super antique shops and many ancient buildings to explore. This solid stone building was a Victorian coach house and the old stable yard at the back has alcoves of hanging roses with garden furniture for lazy summer afternoons; croquet on the lawn, too. Inside, high ceilings, stone archways, antique furniture and lots of space. The beds are spread with lacy linen and Cecilie is a delightful hostess and a brilliant cook.

Rooms: 1 twin, 1 double, both with private bathroom.

Price: £35 p.p. Single supp. £10.

Meals: Breakfast times flexible by arrangement; dinner £20, on request.

Closed: Occasionally.

From A1 Stamford by-pass A606 towards Oakham for 3 miles. Fork left for Edith Weston. Past village sign take 1st right, Church Lane. Past church right again down hill. House on right on left bend.

Cecilie Ingoldby
Old Hall Coach House
Edith Weston
Oakham
Rutland LE15 8HQ
Tel: 01780 721504
Fax: 01780 721311
E-mail: cecilieingoldby@aol.com

Entry No: 358   **Map no: 10**

Pam - theatrical, laughing, genuine is just lovely. The house is ancient, magpie-gabled and the church and pound are 800 years old. Beams criss-cross the rooms and vertical framing has been exposed to great effect. There's a grand piano in the drawing room and, on the rambling first floor, bedrooms are pretty and double-glazed. Pam's breakfasts are as generous as her spirit. There's an atmosphere of life, warmth, elegance and good taste and guests return time after time. *Children over 11 welcome.*

Rooms: 1 twin, 1 double, both en suite (shower); 1 family (double & 2 singles), en suite (bath/shower).

Price: £23-£25 p.p. Single occ. from £27.50.

Meals: Breakfast 7.30-9.30am. Packed lunch, by arrangement. Good pub within walking distance for dinner.

Closed: Never.

From Shrewsbury, A5 north. Through Nesscliffe & after 2 miles, left to Knockin. Through Knockin, past Bradford Arms. House 150 yds on left.

Pam Morrissey
Top Farmhouse
Knockin, Nr. Oswestry
Shropshire SY10 8HN
Tel: 01691 682582
Fax: 01691 682070
E-mail: p.a@knockin.co.uk
Web: www.topfarmknockin.co.uk

Entry No: 359   **Map no: 9**

David's family has farmed here for four generations - he tends a 200-head Friesian herd. In season you may have venison sausages from a locally-managed deer herd with your farm eggs for breakfast. The Breidden hills and views of the Severn dominate the setting and the simple garden, sensibly, does not try to compete with the views. There are three bedrooms in this 1740s border farmhouse - one with Sanderson curtains and borders and a half-tester bed with rope twist columns, a twin with Victorian wrought-iron bedsteads and a double with brass bed. A smashing place - simple and excellent value.

Rooms: 1 double, 1 twin, both with small en suite shower; 1 double, en suite (bath).

Price: From £22.50 p.p.

Meals: Breakfast times flexible; packed lunch £3, by arrangement. Dinner available locally.

Closed: Never.

From Shrewsbury A458 Welshpool road. After Ford, right onto B4393. At Crew Green, left for Criggion. House 1st on left after Admiral Rodney pub.

Liz Dawson
Brimford House
Criggion
Nr. Shrewsbury
Shropshire SY5 9AU
Tel: 01938 570235
E-mail: info@brimford.co.uk
Web: www.brimford.co.uk

Entry No: 360   **Map no: 9**

A heavenly Grade II-listed Georgian house in manicured gardens - just a 10-minute stroll from Abbey and town. Joan is a terrific cook - 1998 Aga Cook of the Year, no less - who radiates courtesy and charm; Charles cheerfully assumes the role of 'mine host'. Theirs is an atmospheric home, rich with antiques, polished mahogany and eye-catching wallpapers and fabrics. Home-made biscuits and flowers in every room: we loved the large, sunny double with Victorian half tester and *chaise longue*. Summer breakfasts and tea are taken in the conservatory.

Rooms: 1 double, en suite (bath/shower); 1 double with private bathroom; 1 twin, en suite (shower).

Price: £24.50-£28.50 p.p. Single supp. £10.50.

Meals: Breakfast times flexible; dinner, from £25 by arrangement.

Closed: Occasionally.

A5/A49 junc. (south of Shrewsbury bypass) follow signs to centre. Over 1st mini r'bout, 2nd exit at next, past Brooklands Hotel. 2nd left into Upper Rd. 150 yds on at large white house on bend, left & immed. right into Church Lane. Drive at bottom on left.

Joan Hathaway
Meole Brace Hall
Shrewsbury
Shropshire SY3 9HF
Tel: 01743 235566
Fax: 01743 236886
E-mail: enquiries@meolebracehall.co.uk
Web: www.meolebracehall.co.uk

Entry No: 361   **Map no: 9**

The handsome Georgian farmhouse - which has a lovely courtyard with period outbuildings - is splendidly decorated. Rooms are English to the core: florals and chintz, soft carpets and (deliciously comfortable) four-posters. Vivacious Christine cannot do enough to spoil her guests - bedrooms are beautified with extras like fresh carnations, fluffy bathrobes and cafetières, while Gareth their chef creates 'food adventures'... George runs the 350-acre farm with equal enthusiasm. A bountiful place.

Rooms: 3 doubles, 1 king-size, 1 family/twin, all en suite.

Price: £35-£50 p.p. Single supp. by arrangement.

Meals: Breakfast times flexible; packed lunch £5; dinner, £25; gourmet dinner, 5-course, £35.

Closed: Christmas & New Year.

4 miles south of Shrewsbury on A458. In Cross Houses, left after petrol station, signed Atcham. Down lane & right to Brompton; follow to farm.

George Roberts
Upper Brompton Farm
Cross Houses, Shrewsbury
Shropshire SY5 6LE
Tel: 01743 761629
Fax: 01743 761679
E-mail: upper.brompton.farm@dial.pipex.com
Web: www.upperbromptonfarm.com

Entry No: 362   **Map no: 9**

From the double room, with hand-printed wallpaper and oak chests, you look to Acton Burnell hill - England's first parliament was held here. The yellow room has lovely views of a lake, the garden and the Welsh Hills; sunsets can be spectacular. Wooden doors, floors, carved settle and chests sit well with elegant furniture and lovely prints and photographs. A two-acre garden hugs the house, there's a pool for summertime and a croquet lawn. Parts of the house were built in 1660; the site is mentioned in the Domesday book. Very special. *Children by arrangement.*

Rooms: 1 double, 1 double/twin, both en suite (bath); 1 family with double/twin & 2 singles, en suite (shower).

Price: £27.50-£32.50 p.p. Single occ. £32.50.

Meals: Breakfast times flexible; dinner, from £15, by arrangement. Also available locally.

Closed: Christmas & New Year.

From A5 & Shrewsbury, onto A458 towards Bridgnorth. Approx. 200 yds on, right to Acton Burnell. Entering Acton Burnell, left to Kenley. 0.5 miles on, left to Acton Pigot. House 1st on left.

Mrs Hildegard Owen
Acton Pigot
Acton Burnell, Shrewsbury
Shropshire SY5 7PH
Tel: 01694 731209
Fax: 01694 731399
E-mail: acton@farmline.com
Web: www.actonpigot.co.uk

Entry No: 363   **Map no: 9**

Uninterrupted views of the Stretton Hills and a large, Victorian house with a stunning conservatory to enjoy them from. Jackie and Jim are particularly welcoming and there's a traditional feel here with books, William Morris fabrics and big furniture. Lie in bed in the morning with sun streaming in and soak up the rural peace before eating a generous breakfast followed by a walk, a bike ride or a trawl through the local antique shops and a visit to Ludlow (25 mins.) and its famous restaurants. The garden is super... croquet buffs welcome. *Children over 12 welcome.*

Rooms: 1 double with private bath; 1 twin/double, en suite (bath).

Price: £25-£30 p.p. Single supp. £10.

Meals: Breakfast times flexible; packed lunch from £2.50. Good pubs and restaurants nearby.

Closed: Christmas & New Year.

From Shrewsbury, south on A49. 0.5 miles before Leebotwood, right to Smethcott. Follow signs uphill & drive on left just before Smethcott.

Jackie & Jim Scarratt
Lawley House
Smethcott, Church Stretton
Shropshire SY6 6NX
Tel: 01694 751236
Fax: 01694 751396
E-mail: lawleyhouse@easicom.com
Web: www.lawleyhouse.co.uk

Entry No: 364   **Map no: 9**

Since 1869 this Methodist chapel has stood among a tumble of rock, gorse, twisting streams, woodland and pasture, all crowned by the mysterious Devil's Chair ridge. The dining and sitting room, with its choir gallery, is open right to the roof. There is old pine furniture and patterned rugs on an original wooden floor and a woodburning stove on local stone flags. The twin has views over the streamed valley and the single (with an extra pull-out bed) looks up the steep Stiperstone Range. This is a walker's paradise and Jean will transport luggage to your next stop. Simple and good value.

Rooms: 1 twin, 1 single, sharing private shower, wc and basin.

Price: From £20 p.p.

Meals: Breakfast times flexible; packed lunch by arrangement. Dinner available locally.

Closed: Occasionally.

From Shrewsbury A488 for Bishop's Castle. Left on edge of Plox Green for Stiperstones. There, left before pub up Perkinsbeach Dingle. Chapel on right.

Jean Lees
The Old Chapel
Perkinsbeach Dingle
Stiperstones, Shrewsbury
Shropshire SY5 0PE
Tel: 01743 791449
E-mail: jean@a-lees.freeserve.co.uk

Entry No: 365   Map no: 9

Best of all must be the beds - 17th-century French wedding, Gothic brass, 1940s Italian boudoir, and more - but the whole converted crofter's cottage has lovely fabrics, beams, antiques and attention to detail. Run by mother and daughter, Jinlye sits, old, luxurious and sheltered, at 1,400 ft surrounded by ancient hills, rare birds, wild ponies and windswept ridges. The skies are infinite; humanity was here 12,000 years ago and you can walk deep in ancient wilderness before returning to superb home comforts. *Children over 12 welcome.*

Rooms: 3 doubles, 2 twins/doubles, 2 twins, all en suite; 1 double with private bath. Self-catering also available.

Price: £27-£40 p.p. Single occ. £42-£57.

Meals: Breakfast 8-9am; packed lunch by arrangement. Excellent pubs and restaurants nearby.

Closed: Never.

From Shrewsbury, A49 to Church Stretton, past Little Chef & right towards All Stretton. Right immed. past phone box & up hill to Jinlye.

Mrs Janet Tory
Jinlye
Castle Hill, All Stretton
Church Stretton, Shropshire SY6 6JP
Tel: 01694 723243
Fax: 01694 723243
E-mail: info@jinlye.co.uk
Web: www.jinlye.co.uk

Entry No: 366   Map no: 9

You get absolute privacy and peace in the converted dairy across the flower-filled yard. The twin beds are plumply made up and you can make yourself herbal and fruit teas and fresh coffee. From the large window you can watch the light changing over the rolling hills and beyond. A mile away from the hurly burly of the main road, it is delightfully peaceful and tranquil. Fiona, charming and utterly natural, serves you breakfast in the main house in a room with a woodburner and French windows leading to the garden.

Rooms: 1 twin, en suite (bath).

Price: £22.50 p.p. Single occ. £45.

Meals: Breakfast times flexible. Dinner available locally.

Closed: Never.

In a land of fat sheep and ancient hill forts, this 17th-century mill ended Gill and Andrew's search for a refuge from the city. With an absence of fussiness in the house, seclusion and natural beauty, this feels like a retreat, just what your hosts (a designer and an illustrator) want. Rooms are comfortable, freshly-decorated and spotless: the double has a Victorian brass bed and newly restored original roll-top bath. The stone and oak extension blends beautifully and has become a large twin room. The River Unk flows through the mill's three acres of meadowland and gardens. *Children over eight welcome.*

Rooms: 2 doubles, 1 en suite (bath), 1 with private bathroom; 1 twin, en suite (bath/shower).

Price: £25-£32 p.p. Single supp. £10.

Meals: Breakfast until 9.30am; dinner, £19, by arrangement.

Closed: Occasionally.

From Bridgnorth, A458 to Shrewsbury. 0.5 miles after Morville, right into a stone road & follow signs to farm.

From Clun A488 towards Bishops Castle. 1st left, signed Bicton. There, 2nd left signed Mainstone. House 1st right after Llananhedric Farm.

Mrs Fiona Thompson
Hannigans Farm
Morville
Bridgnorth
Shropshire WV16 4RN
Tel: 01746 714332
Fax: 01746 714332

Gill Della Casa & Andrew Farmer
The Birches Mill
Clun, Nr. Craven Arms
Shropshire SY7 8NL
Tel: 01588 640409
Fax: 01588 640409
E-mail: gill@birchesmill.fsnet.co.uk
Web: www.virtual-shropshire.co.uk/birchesmill

Entry No: 367   Map no: 9

Entry No: 368   Map no: 9

Come for the sophisticated comfort and elegance: stone-flagged floors, woodburning stoves, polished tables, antiques, vast and luxurious bathrooms, pure cotton sheets and amazing electronics in each bedroom to delight musicians and baffle the over-50s. There's a fascinating art collection, too, and the most perfect setting - in the hillside behind, Roger has created paths with seating areas and cabins from which to take in the superb views. An unstinting welcome from the ineffably charming Roger, and unequalled value. There's a huge, luxury cottage, too - a real retreat.

Rooms: 1 twin/double, with sitting room, 1 double, both en suite (bath). Self-catering cottage for 2.

Price: Twin/double £44 p.p.; double £35 p.p. Single supp. £12. Cottage from £160-£200 for 3 nights.

Meals: Breakfast until 9.30am; dinner by arrangement.

Closed: Never.

B4368 W to Clun. Left at fork towards Knighton on A488. Over bridge. Cockford is 1 mile from bridge, signed on left. House on right up drive.

Roger Wren
Cockford Hall
Clun
Shropshire SY7 8LR
Tel: 01588 640327
Fax: 01588 640881
E-mail: cockfordhall@virgin.net

Entry No: 369   Map no: 9

Good-sized bedrooms with fine furniture, luxurious beds, excellent linen, bathrobes and bathroom treats - there is no stinting on generosity. Standing in lush gardens that slope down to a millstream and across meadows to the River Teme, this is a gracious Georgian house with lovely views. It has a millstream and a weir, a motte and bailey castle site, a heronry, a point-to-point course and a ha-ha. Yvonne's reputation for imaginative cooking using local produce is a great attraction for walkers returning from a day in the glorious Welsh Border country - there's an interesting wine list, too. *Children by arrangement.*

Rooms: 1 double, en suite (shower); 2 twins/doubles with private bathroom.

Price: £25-£30 p.p. Single supp. £10.

Meals: Breakfast until 9am; dinner £20, by arrangement.

Closed: Never.

From Ludlow, A49 to Shrewsbury. At Bromfield take A4113. Right in Walford for Buckton, continue to 2nd farm on left. Look for large sign on building.

Hayden & Yvonne Lloyd
Upper Buckton
Leintwardine, Craven Arms
Ludlow
Shropshire SY7 0JU
Tel: 01547 540634
Fax: 01547 540634

Entry No: 370   Map no: 9

Shropshire

A tiny lane leads you to Cleeton Court, a part 14th-century attractively renovated farmhouse. With views over sheep meadows and heathland, you feel immersed in countryside. Ros greets you with fresh coffee and home-made cake - she is genuinely enthusiastic about B&B and likes to allow you to settle into your own pace. You have your own entrance and use of the drawing room - prettily striped in yellow and cream, with comfortable sofas and log fire. Bedrooms are full of character with beams, a four-poster with chintzy drapes and good pieces of furniture. An easy place to relax. *Children over five welcome.*

Rooms: 1 four-poster, 1 twin, both en suite (bath).

Price: £25-£35 p.p. Single occ. £35.

Meals: Breakfast times flexible. Many excellent restaurants in Ludlow & good local pubs.

Closed: Christmas & New Year.

From Ludlow, A4117 for Kidderminster for 1 mile. Left on B4364, signed Cleobury North. On for 5 miles. In Wheathill, right for Cleeton St. Mary & on for 1.5 miles. House on left.

Rosamund Woodward
Cleeton Court
Cleeton St. Mary
Ludlow, Shropshire DY14 0QZ
Tel: 01584 823379
Fax: 01584 823379
E-mail: jk.straughan@talk21.com
Web: www.cleetoncourt.co.uk

Entry No: 371 **Map no: 9**

The Rosses have built up a little empire of Special Places to Stay; just outside Ludlow's city wall and only 100 yards from the river (the ducks take their morning stroll past the house). In this beautiful street of listed buildings, there are two rooms at the main house, three suites in Bromley Court, two doubles in Westview House and two doubles in Mews Cottage. Staying in the latter two, you breakfast at Number Twenty Eight. Wherever you stay, your needs will be met with stacks of information, good beds, books, fresh flowery linen and bathrooms with all the extras. Michelin-starred restaurants nearby.

Rooms: In house: 1 twin, en suite (bath/shower); 1 double, en suite (shower). Cottage: 1 double/twin, 1 double, both en suite (bath/shower). Westview House: 2 doubles, both en suite (bath/shower). Bromley Court: 3 suites, en suite.

Price: From £38 p.p. Single supp. from £10.

Meals: Breakfast times flexible. Dinner available locally.

Closed: Never.

House at bottom of Lower Broad Street, between Broadgate & Ludford Bridge.

Patricia & Philip Ross
Number Twenty Eight
28 Lower Broad Street
Ludlow, Shropshire SY8 1PQ
Tel: 01584 876996 or freephone 0800 081 5000
Fax: 01584 876860
E-mail: ross.no28@btinternet.com

Entry No: 372 **Map no: 9**

Very much the sense of being invited into someone's home - albeit it a grand one. The stupendous site and size of this early Georgian house reflect the status of the ancestor who built it in 1740. The present-day Salweys are farmers and Hermione's scrumptious food is based on home-reared beef and lamb and garden vegetables. The large softly-furnished bedrooms have antique chairs and modern bedding; one has a Louis XV bed, another much chinoiserie. The Salweys are interesting people and the estate even has a Georgian bath house near the trout lake.

Rooms: 1 twin, 1 double, en suite (bath); 1 double with private bathroom.

Price: £40 p.p. Single supp. £10.

Meals: Breakfast times flexible; dinner £20.

Closed: 31 October-1 April.

Log fires and beams, a sparkling communal dining table, a large garden bursting with colour, welcoming hosts, modern comforts plus a certain elegance... all this amid a rare plethora of castles and historic towns. The house is part 17th century, off a country lane so quiet that buzzards and deer are often seen close by. The house is immaculate inside and out and the Cutlers, who lived in Zambia for 18 years, are very sociable. Leintwardine was once a Roman garrison; it is still in one of England's last unspoilt areas. *Children over 10 welcome.*

Rooms: 1 double, 2 twins, all en suite (shower); 1 double with private bathroom.

Price: £28-£31 p.p. Children 10-12, £13-£15. No single supp.

Meals: Breakfast times flexible. Dinner £18.

Closed: Christmas.

From Ludlow, over River Teme by traffic lights, 2nd right to Presteigne & Richard's Castle on B4361. After about 100 yds, drive is 1st right.

From Leintwardine, cross river & 1st right for Knighton. 1st left for Hereford & 1st right up narrow unmarked lane. House 300 yds on left.

Humphrey & Hermione Salwey
The Lodge
Ludlow
Shropshire SY8 4DU
Tel: 01584 872103
Fax: 01584 876126

Hildegard & Graham Cutler
Lower House
Adforton, Leintwardine
Craven Arms, Shropshire SY7 0NF
Tel: 01568 770223
Fax: 01568 770592
E-mail: lowerhouse@sy7.com
Web: www.sy7.com/lowerhouse

Entry No: 373   Map no: 9

Entry No: 374   Map no: 9

Shropshire & Somerset

A unique place – a late 15th-century, Grade-II listed house with a converted cider mill at one end. Your hosts bought Shortgrove seven years ago and enjoy nothing better than sharing it with guests. It's gloriously homely inside with beams everywhere; bedrooms cottagey, not grand, and two sitting rooms with plump chairs and an inglenook fire for chilly nights. The two-acre garden and marvellous Shropshire views are framed by exquisitely leaded windows; you are on a gated common, away from all roads. All this and Beryl, a great cook, producing magic (and marmalade) from her Aga.

Rooms: 1 twin, en suite (bath); 1 double with private bathroom.

Price: From £28 p.p. Single supp. £10.

Meals: Breakfast times flexible; dinner £20.

Closed: End October-Easter.

Off A49, 1 mile south of Woofferton into School Lane. Immed. left at 2nd School Lane sign. Through lane at end onto common. Fork left where track divides. House at far end.

Beryl Maxwell
Shortgrove
Brimfield Common
Ludlow
Shropshire SY8 4NZ
Tel: 01584 711418

Entry No: 375   **Map no: 9**

In the 16th century the house was a row of weavers' cottages; today it is one thoroughly English home. Savour the interesting furniture, comfortable sofas, beautiful bits and pieces and paintings with stories to tell. The 14th-century French-style castle casts its spells over the house - you can see it from one of the guest bedrooms and the house's huge stone fireplace may have come from there. From the drawing room you walk into a garden where birdsong fills the scented air. Jane, charming and flexible, will look after you well. *Cot and highchair available for babies.*

Rooms: 1 family, 1 twin, sharing connecting bathroom (separate entrances). Possible extra double with shared bathroom.

Price: £20 p.p. No single supp.

Meals: Breakfast times flexible. Good pub food a few yards away.

Closed: Christmas.

On A361 out of Frome, right to Nunney. Down hill to market square, left over humpback bridge & immed. left. House 1st on right (2 Horn St).

Jane Stagg
The Bell House
Nunney
Nr. Frome
Somerset BA11 4NP
Tel: 01373 836309
Fax: 01373 836309
E-mail: janenunney@aol.com

Entry No: 376   **Map no: 4**

An exquisite house. Phoebe, a shepherd, sought the perfect home for her flock and she found it. Terracotta walls, rugs, flagstones and brick - stunning. The antique beds have handmade mattresses, good linen and fat pillows; in the barn you have luxurious, privacy. The indoor swimming pool has a breathtaking view through a Gothic, arched window. The house is a treasure box of decorative arts from the carved Dutch fireplaces to the Turkmen rugs. It's magnificent. So, too, is the cottage, right.

Rooms: Barn: huge double suite with dressing room and kitchen/living area. House: Cider Cellar double, en suite. Main double suite with drawing room. 3 single rooms, usually let to one party.

Price: £150 per suite. Cider Cellar £90-£120 per room. Singles by arrangement.

Meals: Breakfast times flexible; dinner from £25, by arrangement.

Closed: Never.

Phoebe returned this Victorian cottage to the estate last year. With wonderful views of Pennard Hill and the Mendips beyond, the cottage has been stunningly redesigned. Newly opened out, the ground floor is an airy, luxurious living space with a superb vast kitchen (double Aga, dishwasher, etc.) leading into a sunroom, study and large drawing room. The cottage is available on B&B basis and on full/part occupancy; Phoebe is flexible about arrangements. If you take the cottage in conjunction with Pennard Hill Farm, left, it would be ideal for a house party.

Rooms: 2 doubles, 1 twin with two bathrooms.

Price: From £90-£160 per room.

Meals: Breakfast times flexible; dinner from £25, by arrangement.

Closed: Never.

From Wells, A39 to Glastonbury. 0.5 miles on, left at North Wootton sign, following signs for West Pennard. At T-junc., right onto A361. 500 yds on, 1st left. 1 mile up hill. 1st drive to left at top.

Directions as for Pennard Hill Farm. Do not go to hamlet of East Pennard.

Phoebe Judah
Pennard Hill Farm
Stickleball Hill
East Pennard, Shepton Mallet
Somerset BA4 6UG
Tel: 01749 890221
Fax: 01749 890665
E-mail: phebejudah@aol.com

Phoebe Judah
Golden Fleece Cottage
at Pennard Hill Farm
Stickleball Hill, East Pennard
Shepton Mallet, Somerset BA4 6UG
Tel: 01749 890221
Fax: 01749 890665
E-mail: phebejudah@aol.com

Entry No: 377   **Map no:** 3

Entry No: 378   **Map no:** 3

Wandering among the medieval outbuildings, you might almost imagine that you'd stumbled upon a museum: there's an ancient forge, bellows, a cider press, a pony trap and a threshing floor - not to mention Tony's collection of classic cars. The 18th-century farmhouse, with flagstone floors, old beams, pine panelling, country antique furniture and examples of Wendy's embroidery, is sunny and delightful. On the southern slopes of the Mendips, it is the perfect base for walks - if, that is, you're not lying in the garden, dozing under the old apple tree. *Children over 10 welcome.*

Rooms: 1 double, en suite (shower); 1 twin/double, en suite (bath); 1 double with private bathroom.

Price: £26-£30 p.p. Single supp. £10.

Meals: Breakfast 8-9am. Dinner available nearby.

Closed: Christmas.

From Wells towards Cheddar on A371. At Westbury-sub-Mendip pass Westbury Inn & Post Office Stores on right. House 200 yds on, after lay-by on left.

Tony & Wendy Thompson
Stoneleigh House
Westbury-sub-Mendip
Nr. Wells
Somerset BA5 1HF
Tel: 01749 870668
Fax: 01749 870668
E-mail: stoneleigh@dial.pipex.com

Entry No: 379   **Map no:** 3

One of our favourites - the cosiest hillside cottage filled with the prettiest things. French-inspired bedheads and wardrobes made by a local craftsman, antique patchwork quilts and jolly china on the old Welsh dresser in the kitchen. And there's Catherine - warm, spirited, cultured; she'll make you fresh coffee, chat about the area, even give you a guided tour of Wells Cathedral, if you wish. Set in eight acres, there are fields and superb walking country all around. You can play tennis or croquet too, and have your own pretty sitting room with books and magazines. Excellent value.

Rooms: 1 twin/double, en suite (bath/shower). Further twin available for members of same party.

Price: £22.50 p.p. Single supp. £5.

Meals: Breakfast times flexible. Dinner available locally.

Closed: Christmas & New Year.

A371 to middle of Croscombe. Right at red phone box & then immed. right into lane. House up on left after 0.25 miles. Drive straight ahead into signed field.

Michael & Catherine Hay
Hillview Cottage
Paradise Lane
Croscombe, nr. Wells
Somerset BA5 3RL
Tel: 01749 343526
Fax: 01749 676134
E-mail: cathyhay@yahoo.co.uk

Entry No: 380   **Map no:** 3

Rosalind's enthusiasm for welcoming guests is unstinting; she is cheerful and chatty and as a geologist and walking enthusiast, is knowledgeable about the area too (there are lots of books and maps for you). There are sheep, goats, chickens, ducks and friendly cats. The large Garden Suite has been adapted for wheelchair users; accessible from its pretty secluded walled garden and with an inglenook fireplace, it retains its 17th-century charm. The other rooms are homely with new pine and white units. Lovely views and you can walk to Wells Cathedral to hear evensong.

Rooms: Garden Suite: 1 twin/double & extra single, en suite (shower). 2 doubles, both en suite (1 with bath, 1 with shower); 1 single, 1 twin/double sharing bathroom & separate wc.

Price: From £22 p.p.

Meals: Breakfast until 9am; packed lunches & light snacks by arrangement. Dinner available locally.

Closed: Occasionally.

From Wells, A371 towards Shepton Mallet for 1 mile, then left onto B3139. In Dulcote, left at stone fountain. Farmhouse clearly marked, 4th on right after Manor Barn.

Rosalind Bufton
Manor Farm
Dulcote
Wells, Somerset BA5 3PZ
Tel: 01749 672125
Fax: 01749 672125
E-mail: rosalind.bufton@ntlworld.com
Web: www.wells-accommodation.co.uk

Entry No: 381   **Map no:** 3

One of the grandest houses in this book, Pennard has been in Susie's family since the 17th century - the cellars date from then, the superstructure is stately, lofty Georgian - but the Deardens are delightfully unstuffy and welcoming. Guests have the run of the library, formal drawing room, billiards room and six acres of garden with a spring-fed pool to swim in. Or walk in 300 acres of cider orchards, meadows and woods. Susie was born and brought up here, and knows a lot about the area; multilingual Martin deals in antiques from the house. It is warm and civilised with plain, properly unhotelly bedrooms.

Rooms: 1 double, 1 twin, both en suite (bath/shower); 1 twin/double with private bathroom.

Price: From £30 p.p. Single supp. by arrangement.

Meals: Breakfast times flexible. Good pubs and restaurants nearby.

Closed: Christmas.

From Shepton Mallet south on A37, through Pylle, over hill & next right to East Pennard. Pass church to T-junction at very top. House on left.

Martin & Susie Dearden
Pennard House
East Pennard
Shepton Mallet
Somerset BA4 6TP
Tel: 01749 860266
Fax: 01749 860266
E-mail: m.dearden@ukonline.co.uk

Entry No: 382   **Map no:** 3

Somerset

The Good Life in the depths of Somerset: organic vegetables, home-made marmalade and own milk and eggs. The Dowdings have returned from France - they had a Special Place there - and have converted the old stone barn into a super self-contained apartment. There's a continental feel to this organic farm - you can do your own thing or have Susie cook breakfast and dinner for you (Charles grinds their own wheat for daily bread-making). Central to the oak-floored sitting room is a woodburner and bedrooms have oak floors, exposed beams, lime-washed walls and *toile de Jouy* curtains.

Rooms: 1 double, en suite (bath); 1 twin with private bathroom.

Price: £25 p.p. 3 nights or more £20 p.p. Children £15.

Meals: Breakfast in the barn until 9.30am, or you can cook your own; dinner £5-£15, served in farmhouse.

Closed: Never.

From A303 at Wincanton A371 for Castle Cary. Before Cary, right on A359 for Bruton. 2nd right for Shepton Montague. At x-roads by Montague Inn straight across. Continue ignoring sign to Redlynch. Round a sharp bend with church on left. Farm is next on right. Past house and right into yard behind.

Charles & Susie Dowding
Lower Farm
Shepton Montague
Wincanton
Somerset BA9 8JG
Tel: 01749 812253
E-mail: susiedowding@netscapeonline.co.uk
Web: www.lowerfarm.org.uk

Entry No: 383   **Map no: 3**

English to the core, this listed and charming Regency house has the feel of a small country hotel with flagged hall, high ceilings and long windows. The five bedrooms are decorated with good period furniture, fine bedspreads and elaborate drapes. First floor rooms feel grand, the second floor rooms, cosier. Roy is chatty and excellent company; ask him to show you the views from the Observatory at the top of the house. He's a jazz musician (clarinet), too, and a wildlife enthusiast: the grounds have recently been planted with thousands of trees and the lake stocked with exotic ducks and black swans.

Rooms: 1 four-poster, 1 twin, 1 double, 1 family, all en suite (bath); 1 family with private bath. Also two self-catering cottages - phone for prices.

Price: £24.50-£42.50 p.p. Single occ. £45-£53.

Meals: Breakfast until 9am. Dinner available locally.

Closed: Christmas.

From London, M3 junc. 8, A303. At Podimore r'bout A372 to Somerton. Lynch at junction of North Street & Behind Berry.

Mr Roy Copeland
The Lynch Country House
Somerton
Somerset TA11 7PD
Tel: 01458 272316
Fax: 01458 272590
E-mail: the_lynch@talk21.com
Web: www.thelynchcountryhouse.co.uk

Entry No: 384   **Map no: 3**

With huge flair the Burnhams have married old with new and sumptuousness with simplicity. Coir matting sits happily with dark, antique furniture; wrought-iron real candle chandelier and high-backed chairs give the dining room a sense of warm, pre-Raphaelite Gothic. Bedrooms are not flowery or fussy but uncluttered; linen is crisp, cotton robes soft. Jane is a keen cook; the garden yields herbs and vegetables, and breakfast includes Heal Farm sausages and bacon. You may not want to leave the deep comfort of the 300-year-old thatched cottage. *Children by arrangement.*

Rooms: 1 twin with private bath; 1 double, en suite (shower).

Price: £25 p.p. Single occ. £35.

Meals: Breakfast until 9am; dinner from £19.

Closed: Christmas.

From Somerton Lake B3153 for Langport. Right 2 miles on for Pitney just before Halfway Inn. Through Pitney. House last but one on right, with dark green railings.

Peter & Jane Burnham
Estate Farmhouse
Pitney
Langport
Somerset TA10 9AL
Tel: 01458 250210
Fax: 01458 253227

Entry No: 385   **Map no: 3**

Espaliered fruit trees and high walls surround the outdoor pool - you may see badgers and kingfishers, and, certainly, ducks waddling to and from the pond. Clanville is a cosy, manageable mini Manor and Sally is the kindest host who has created an atmosphere in which guests and family co-exist with ease. Bedrooms have solid, traditional furniture; downstairs there are Persian rugs on wooden floors and an old rocking horse in the dining room where local produce is served for breakfast. The Snooks, who have lived here since 1898, have 200 acres and a dairy herd. You'll like them.

Rooms: 1 family/twin, en suite (bath/showe); 1 king-size, 1 single, both en suite (shower).

Price: £25-£27.50 p.p.

Meals: Breakfast until 9am. Dinner available locally.

Closed: Christmas & New Year.

From Wincanton, A371 towards Shepton Mallet. After Castle Cary, left on B3153 towards Somerton. Under railway bridge & white gate & cattle grid is immed. on right.

Sally Snook
Clanville Manor
Castle Cary
Somerset BA7 7PJ
Tel: 01963 350124
Fax: 01963 350719
E-mail: info@clanville.co.uk
Web: www.clanvillemanor.co.uk

Entry No: 386   **Map no: 3**

Somerset

The dining room with its crystal decanters, fine china and wooden window seat overlooks the flower-adorned stable. This is deeply rural, yet elegant. Philip and Susan are palpably happy here on the Somerset Levels, a rare natural wetlands habitat of unique tranquillity. One bedroom has pale yellow striped wallpaper and fine mahogany pieces and another is cream and rose with armchairs; both have garden views. The drawing room with a fine, stone hearth and grand piano has French windows to the gorgeous garden. *Babies and children over 12 welcome.*

Rooms: 1 twin, 1 double, both with private bathroom.

Price: £30 p.p. Single supp. £5.

Meals: Breakfast until 9am; dinner, £17.50, by arrangement.

Closed: Christmas & New Year.

Having lived in many parts of the world, Jane and Iain are now firmly planted here. Brook House, built in 1690 of local hamstone, was one of four farms in this conservation hamlet and it is now surrounded by two acres of garden and paddock. Mullioned windows, National Trust paints and mahogany antiques; it's traditional with every comfort. French country feel bedrooms with carved headboards and handsome furniture; from the twin under the eaves you can glimpse the stream which marks the boundary. Your friendly hosts are keen gardeners. *Children over 10 welcome.*

Rooms: 1 double, en suite (shower); 1 twin with private bathroom.

Price: £29 p.p. Single supp. £10.

Meals: Breakfast times flexible; dinner £16-£19, by arrangement.

Closed: Christmas & New Year.

From Langport, A372 through Aller & right at left-hand bend signed Beer. Pass Bere Farm on right & take 1st lane on left at stone barn.

From A303 A37 to Yeovil, up hill to big r'bout & follow signs to Thorne. Right at r'bout & straight across at next 2 x-roads. 1st right to village, house 1st on right.

Philip & Susan Morlock
Beer Farm
Bere Aller
Langport
Somerset TA10 0QX
Tel: 01458 250285
Fax: 01458 250285

Jane & Iain Galloway
Brooke House
Thorne Coffin
Yeovil
Somerset BA21 3PZ
Tel: 01935 433396
Fax: 01935 475556
E-mail: jane@logspt.demon.co.uk

Entry No: 387   Map no: 3

Entry No: 388   Map no: 3

Soft hamstone and thatched roofs - the village is a delight. Courtfield, Grade II-listed, hidden in a fine, walled, two-acre garden, is a family home so you'll relax easily. Richard, a keen lepidopterist, is a professional painter and you can see his and his daughter's work all around. There is a tennis court and a stunning conservatory; perfect for breakfast or for a candlelit dinner with views of the floodlit church. Valerie has a real flair for entertaining inherited from her Russian father who was an hotelier in Cairo. The bedrooms are large, unfussy and delightful. *Children over eight welcome.*

Rooms: 1 twin, 1 double, both with private bathroom.

Price: £28 p.p. Single supp. £10.

Meals: Breakfast times flexible; dinner £18, by arrangement. B.Y.O. wine.

Closed: Christmas & New Year.

From A303, A356 south towards Crewkerne. 2nd left to Norton-sub-Hamdon. House in centre of village at foot of Church Lane.

Richard & Valerie Constable
Courtfield
Norton-sub-Hamdon
Stoke-sub-Hamdon
Somerset TA14 6SG
Tel: 01935 881246
E-mail: courtfield@hotmail.com

Entry No: 389   **Map no: 3**

Extremely pretty with its thatched roof and Strawberry Hill Gothic windows, this house is instantly captivating. You won't find family bustle, but there is immense comfort. Soft, large sofas in the guest sitting room, thick carpeting, easy chairs in the bedrooms and excellent meals at house-party dinners. Carved Tudor oak beams in the sitting room and panelled passages speak of the house's history, and there are French doors from the dining room onto the sweeping lawns. In a tiny conservation hamlet surrounded by farmland, the peace is deep.

Rooms: 5 twins/doubles, all en suite (bath/shower).

Price: From £37.50 p.p. Single supp. £10.50.

Meals: Breakfast times flexible; dinner, 4 courses, £19.50, by arrangement.

Closed: Never.

At Horton Cross r'bout (junc. A303/A358) A358 towards Chard. After Donyatt, left signed Ilminster. After 1 mile, right signed Cricket Malherbie. House on left after a mile, 200 yds past church.

Michael & Patricia Fry-Foley
The Old Rectory
Cricket Malherbie
Ilminster, Somerset TA19 OPW
Tel: 01460 54364
Fax: 01460 57374
E-mail: theoldrectory@malherbie.freeserve.co.uk
Web: www.malherbie.freeserve.co.uk

Entry No: 390   **Map no: 3**

Robert, an ex-restaurateur, is a South African and as easy as they so often are; Lesley's cooking gets heaps of praise from guests and she runs cookery courses too. It's a perfect Somerset cottage with an apple orchard and views across fields to the lofty church. The interior is utterly in keeping: pine, coir carpets, wooden beams and a warm sense of fun. Bedrooms are light, restful and simple, with white walls and old pine. All this, and with such easy access to the M5. *Children over 10 welcome.*

Rooms: 1 twin, en suite (bath); 1 double, en suite (shower).

Price: £25-£28 p.p. Single supp. by arrangement.

Meals: Breakfast until 9am; supper from £15; dinner from £18, both available on request.

Closed: Christmas.

The Ritchies devote a huge amount of energy to their B&B and have done a fine job of renovating this exquisite 17th-century farmhouse in Somerset's lovely Quantock Hills. There's a homely feel with splashes of style where they matter - well-framed prints, good fabrics, comfortable sofas - and they've done everything to ensure your comfort. Rooms are very pretty, fresh and large and look over the cobbled courtyard or open fields; many are dual aspect. Breakfast will include home-baked bread and home-made jams. Charles and Jane prepare meals using fresh local ingredients, so do eat in.

Rooms: 1 twin with private bathroom; 1 double with private shower; 1 double, en suite (shower).

Price: £22.50-£25 p.p. Single supp. £5.

Meals: Breakfast until 9am. Dinner £20.

Closed: Never.

Exit M5 at junc. 26 & take West Buckland road for 0.75 miles. 1st left just before Stone garage. Bear right; 3rd house at end of lane, below church.

Leave M5 at junc. 25. A358 towards Minehead. Leave A358 at West Bagborough turning. Follow through village for 1.5 miles. Farmhouse 3rd on left past pub.

Lesley & Robert Orr
Causeway Cottage
West Buckland, Wellington
Somerset TA21 9JZ
Tel: 01823 663458
Fax: 01823 663458
E-mail: orrs@westbuckland.freeserve.co.uk
Web: www.welcome.to/causeway-cottage.co.uk

Charles & Jane Ritchie
Bashfords Farmhouse
West Bagborough
Taunton, Somerset TA4 3EF
Tel: 01823 432015
Fax: 0870 1671587
E-mail: charlieritchie@netscapeonline.co.uk
Web: www.bashfordsfarmhouse.co.uk

Entry No: 391   **Map no:** 3

Entry No: 392   **Map no:** 3

A restrained, elegant style sets off the natural beauty of the 300-year-old farmhouse: handsome furniture and soft colours sit easily with stone flags, beams and wooden panelling. It's a beautiful house, with its own spring, kept meticulously by friendly Pamela who also makes all her own jams, marmalade and bread. Bedrooms and bathrooms are generous in size and very attractive. You are 1,000 feet up on the Quantocks where the views are long and the scenery stunning; the Smiths' 20 acres of fields and woodland are alive with songbirds. *Children over 10 welcome.*

Rooms: 2 doubles, 1 twin, en suite (1 bath, 2 showers).

Price: £23-£25 p.p. Single occ. £30.

Meals: Breakfast until 9.30am. Pubs nearby.

Closed: Never.

So much to delight the eye... elegant Georgian lines, beautiful art, a 19th-century French mirror, French Empire chairs, a mixture of checked, striped and *toile de Jouy* fabrics - all existing in absolute harmony. This is one of the most stylish retreats that you'll find. There's comfort, too... thick bathrobes, warm towels, the fattest pillows. The house, 18th century, Grade II-listed, has been renovated by the dedicated Deacons. Elizabeth's cooking is sublime and imaginative. You are in the heart of the Somerset Levels, surrounded by mystical views and countryside of huge environmental significance.

Rooms: 2 doubles, both with private bathroom; 1 twin, en suite (shower).

Price: From £40 p.p. No single supp.

Meals: Breakfast times flexible; Dinner, 3-4 courses, £20-£25. B.Y.O. wine.

Closed: Occasionally.

From Taunton, A358 north towards Williton. Approx. 7 miles on, right for West Bagborough. Through village, up hill for 0.5 miles. Farm on left.

From M5, junc. 24. 5 miles away via Huntworth & Moorland. After about 2 miles, house on right after sharp right-hand bend.

Mrs Pamela Smith
Tilbury Farm
Cothelstone
Taunton
Somerset TA4 3DY
Tel: 01823 432391

Crispin & Elizabeth Deacon
Saltmoor House
Saltmoor
Burrowbridge
Somerset TA7 0RL
Tel: 01823 698092
E-mail: saltmoorhouse@amserve.net

Entry No: 393   **Map no: 3**

Entry No: 394   **Map no: 3**

Somerset

Massive stone walls, heavy timbers, flagged floors and lack of fussiness give this Grade I-listed 15th-century farmhouse a real solidity. Explore the West Bedroom with timbered walls, a ceiling open to the beamed roof and a four-poster bed, and don't miss the oak-panelled Gallery Bedroom with recently uncovered secret stairway. Feel baronial while seated for breakfast beside the Great Hall's massive fireplace at the 16-ft oak table. Minimum disturbance to fabric and flavour and maximum atmosphere. There's a new stable room, too - although less architecturally stunning, it's perfect for wheelchair users. Anne is kind and smiley.

Rooms: 1 family, 3 doubles, all en suite (shower &/or bath).

Price: £22-£28 p.p. Single occ. £32.

Meals: Breakfast until 9.30am. Dinner available locally.

Closed: Never.

From Bridgwater, A39 west around Cannington. After 2nd r'bout, follow signs to Minehead. 1st left after Yeo Valley creamery. Farm 1st house on right.

Ann Dyer
Blackmore Farm
Cannington
Bridgwater
Somerset TA5 2NE
Tel: 01278 653442
Fax: 01278 653427
E-mail: dyerfarm@aol.com

Entry No: 395   **Map no:** 3

An unusual-looking house... so no surprise to discover that it was the romantic fantasy of a love-struck local man, George Carew; he built it for his mistress in 1830. The interior is as striking as the Italianate terracotta, triple-gabled exterior. 'Heritage' colours are much in evidence and have been matched with lovely pieces of furniture, polished wood floors and rugs. There's a drawing room for you and the bedrooms are well proportioned with garden views through leaded windows. Breakfast is a feast of fresh fruit, local sausages and bacon, cheerfully served in front of the log fire in winter.

Rooms: 2 doubles; 1 twin with basins, all sharing bathroom and separate wc.

Price: £22.50 p.p. Single supp. £2.50.

Meals: Breakfast until 9am. Excellent pubs nearby for dinner.

Closed: Christmas & New Year.

A358 from Taunton for Minehead, for 9.5 miles (passing Flaxpool garage on left). Next right at brow of hill for Crowcombe & past church. House (with 5-bar gate) 500 yds past pub on right.

Rosie & Luke Macdonald
Hooks House
Crowcombe
Taunton
Somerset
Tel: 01984 618691
E-mail: lukemacdd@hookhouse.fsbusiness.co.uk

Entry No: 396   **Map no:** 3

At the neck of the Brendons and at the foot of the Quantocks, Richard and Kate have set their cap at doing a professional job. At their 300-year-old corn mill, they like guests to gather for a drink before dinner at a formally-set table - breakfasts and suppers are ambitiously varied and all home-made. There are two bedrooms in the house – one pink and floral and a cooler, cream twin - and a three-bedroomed apartment. Our favourite is the Garden Suite, with a double bed and a wooden-floored sitting room with cream damask sofa bed. A steam railway and darting wildlife complete the idyll.

Rooms: 1 double, 1 twin in house, both en suite (bath); 3-bed apartment and a Garden Suite for 2/4.

Price: £25.50-£37.50 p.p. Single supp. £10.

Meals: Breakfast times flexible; dinner, 5 courses, £22.50.

Closed: Never.

You eat beside an open fire - vegetables from the walled garden, fruit from the orchard, home-baked bread, jams and eggs from the hens. This is an organic smallholding and your enthusiastic hosts have added an easy comfort to the 17th-century rectory farmhouse. Quarry tiled floors, log fires, books and a piano in the cosy sitting room, and American folk art and Susan's pastels add charm. Bedrooms are big with fresh flowers and great views (even from the Victorian bath in the en suite). The natural beauty of the Quantock Hills surrounds you and walks start from the front door.

Rooms: 1 double, en suite (shower) with extra sofa bed; 1 double/twin, en suite (bath) with extra pull-out bed; 1 double with shared bathroom.

Price: From £20 p.p. Single supp. £7/£8.

Meals: Breakfast times flexible; dinner 3 courses, £16; light supper £7, both by arrangement.

Closed: Christmas.

A358 Taunton to Minehead, left at sign to Stogumber. 2nd left, then 1st right, down hill & over ford. House on left.

Richard Spicer & Kate Butler
Northam Mill
Water Lane, Stogumber
Taunton, Somerset TA4 3TT
Tel: 01984 656916
Fax: 01984 656144
E-mail: bmsspicer@aol.com
Web: www.northam-mill.co.uk

From Bridgwater, A39 for Minehead. 7 miles on, left at Cottage Inn for Over Stowey. Village 1.8 miles on. House on right after church.

Susan & Richard Lilienthal
Parsonage Farm
Over Stowey
Bridgwater
Somerset TA5 1HA
Tel: 01278 733237
Fax: 01278 733511

Entry No: 397   **Map no: 3**

Entry No: 398   **Map no: 3**

Somerset

The Quantocks are a treat and from here you have at least 38 square miles of great walking. Wildlife bounds, flits and creeps through the garden, woods and heathland: wild deer, hill ponies, badgers and over 50 species of birds. Laze on the terrace or by the ornamental pond in the rambling garden and soak in the views to the Mendips and Glastonbury Tor. You have your own self-contained wing with sitting room, old and antique furniture, china and flowers. Breakfast *al fresco*, dine by candlelight or eat at the local pub - the Taylor-Youngs will drive you to and from.

Rooms: 1 twin/double, en suite (bath).

Price: £26.50-£28.50 p.p.

Meals: Breakfast times flexible; packed lunch £4; supper from £8. All by arrangement.

Closed: Never.

From Bridgwater, A39 through Cannington. Main road forks right (at Cottage Inn); straight on & over x-roads to Over Stowey. Left signed Ramscombe Forestry Trail. Keep to tarmac by turning right up hill. Cottage in front. Left through gates.

Michael & Penny Taylor-Young
Friarn Cottage
Over Stowey
Bridgwater
Somerset TA5 1HW
Tel: 01278 732870
Fax: 01278 732870

Entry No: 399   Map no: 3

The Vincents have made the house 'smile' again; handsome and Georgian - it overlooks Watchet harbour and marina. Both bedrooms are pleasing - the double has duck-egg blue walls and pretty floral curtains and looks down onto a Mediterranean courtyard; the twin, with blue chintz valances and matching curtains, has a sea view. Expect home-made cakes and biscuits and generous breakfasts; Susan holds cookery demonstrations. Within sight and sound of sea and steam railway, the garden is a lovely place to relax - among palm trees, ponds and burgeoning borders and a revolving summerhouse. *Children by arrangement.*

Rooms: 1 double with private bathroom; 1 twin, en suite (shower).

Price: From £25 p.p.

Meals: Breakfast times flexible. Dinner available locally.

Closed: Christmas.

From railway station & footbridge in Watchet, follow up South Road (towards Doniford). After 50 yds, left into Beverly Drive. House 50 yds on left.

Susan & Roger Vincent
Wyndham House
4 Sea View Terrace
Watchet
Somerset TA23 0DF
Tel: 01984 631881
Fax: 01984 631881
E-mail: rhv@dialstart.net

Entry No: 400   Map no: 3

A little lane tumbles down to the centre of Dunster - the fascinating village is just two minutes' walk away - yet up here you have wide open views of fields, sheep and sea, and Exmoor footpaths start behind the house. Janet, helpful and kind, loves people to explore by bike or foot and can help with luggage and transport. The 1860s house retains its Victorian features and bedrooms are quiet and simple – the double has a view to Blue Anchor Bay, the castle and church. Stripped pine, cream curtains, fresh flowers – it's homely. Garden fruit for breakfast and home-laid eggs, too. *Children by arrangement.*

Rooms: 1 double, 1 twin/double, both en suite (shower); 1 twin, en suite (bath).

Price: £20-£25 p.p. 10% discount for 3 nights or more. Single occ. £25.

Meals: Breakfast times flexible; packed lunch from £3.50. Dinner available locally.

Closed: Christmas.

From Williton, A39 for Minehead for 8 miles. Left to Dunster. There, right fork into 'The Ball'. At T-junc. at end of road, right. House 75 yds on right.

Mrs Janet Lamacraft
Higher Orchard
30 St. George's Street
Dunster
Somerset TA24 6RS
Tel: 01643 821915

House and hostess are at once elegant, unpretentious and friendly. The picture-book Priory - 'Old' it is, 12th century old - leans against its church, has a rustic gate, a walled garden, a tumble of flowers. Indoors, the old oak tables, flagstones, panelled doors, books and higgledy-piggledy corridors sing "there'll always be an England". But a perfect English house in a sweet Somerset village needs a touch of pepper. Cosmopolitan Jane has a red sitting room and some Italian-style hand-painted wardrobes. There's a roomy self-catering cottage with colour-washed walls and a log fire, too.

Rooms: 1 ground-floor twin, 1 double, both with private shower; 1 twin, 1 four-poster, both en suite (bath).

Price: From £25-£35 p.p. Single supp. by arrangement. Cottage, from £150 p.w.

Meals: Breakfast flexible. Dinner available locally.

Closed: Christmas.

Turn off A39 into Dunster, right at blue sign 'unsuitable for goods vehicles'. Follow until church. House adjoined.

Jane Forshaw
The Old Priory
Dunster
Somerset TA24 6RY
Tel: 01643 821540

Hugo owns The Crown Hotel in Exford and wife Pam's new venture must be the most luxurious B&B on Exmoor. Dark wood Heals beds have embroidered linen, fat pillows and sumptuous cushions; beside them are big bedside lamps and a tray with bottles of mineral water. Deep luxury. Downstairs - part 14th, part 18th-century - there are real fires everywhere and fine prints and oils. Breakfast is a feast of freshly-squeezed orange juice, fresh fruit salad, butcher's sausages and bacon. The Jeunes have stables and a dressage arena – you can bring your horse – and a lovely garden.

Rooms: 1 twin, 1 double, both en suite (shower).

Price: £25-£30 p.p. No single supp.

Meals: Breakfast times flexible. Dinner available locally.

Closed: Never.

From Dulverton, passing post office on left, take B3223 (signed Exford). Follow wooded road up hill for 2.5 miles. After sharp left bend, house signed on right.

Pam & Hugo Jeune
Highercombe
Nr. Dulverton
Somerset TA22 9PT
Tel: 01398 323451
Fax: 01398 323451
E-mail: 21pjuk@yahoo.com
Web: www.highercombe.co.uk

Entry No: 403   **Map no: 3**

Views of farmland from this characterful, old, pink, tree-protected house. Edgcott is a haven on the edge of rambling heathland. You'll find few nods to anything 'designery' - two bedrooms are on the small side and furniture tends towards basic style, but this doesn't detract from the place and its quirkiness. The price is fair, too. Mrs Lamble is a gentle hostess and enjoys cooking using her own garden vegetables. She's also an Exmoor enthusiast and her knowledge of the area is invaluable; rides, walks, village visits galore will be suggested. You may also play the family piano.

Rooms: 1 twin, 1 double, both with private bathroom; 1 twin/double, en suite (bath/shower).

Price: £21-£24 p.p. No single supp.

Meals: Breakfast times flexible; dinner, 4 courses, £15, by arrangement. B.Y.O. Excellent pubs in village.

Closed: Never.

From Taunton take A358, then left on B3224 to Exford. There, take Porlock Lane. House 0.25 miles from village.

Gillian Lamble
Edgcott House
Exford
Somerset TA24 7QG
Tel: 01643 831495
Fax: 01643 831495

Entry No: 404   **Map no: 3**

You can breakfast on the Walkerdine's narrow boat if it's fine and in the evening they will serve you dinner on board and take you for a gentle chug up the canal. The cottage takes its name from the nearby bridge on the Shropshire Union Canal (one of England's prettiest). Diana, who has just received an MBE for her work with deaf children, makes her own soup, bread and jam, while David grows the vegetables. Bedrooms have floral curtains and covers - all is spotless and cosy with open fire, oak furniture and fresh flower.

Rooms: 2 doubles, both with private bathrooms (1 bath & 1 shower).

Price: £28-£32 p.p. Single supp. £8.

Meals: Breakfast times flexible; packed lunch £5; dinner £17.50.

Closed: Christmas & New Year.

Mary Queen of Scots was imprisoned in Chartley Castle opposite this half-timbered Tudor manor house. Push open the Elizabethan black, studded oak door to discover panelled walls, a terracotta dining room and a wealth of oak beams. A warm, higgledy-piggledy feeling in the hall with umbrellas, walking sticks, wellies, riding boots; in the Sudbury yellow drawing room, family portraits and exquisite furniture. The bedrooms are large, airy and flower-filled, the four-poster bedroom is oak-panelled and has a secret door to the bathroom. Uneven floors, hearty breakfasts, delightful, engaging hosts. *Children over 12 welcome.*

Rooms: 1 four-poster; 1 twin, both en suite (shower).

Price: From £25 p.p. Single supp. £5.

Meals: Breakfast until 9.30am. Good food available locally.

Closed: Christmas & New Year.

From Stafford, A518 signed Newport, 4 miles on, left at Haughton opp. church signed Church Eaton. There, right along main street. At end of village, left along Little Onn road. Over canal bridge & left after 300 yds. Cottage on left.

Halfway between Stafford & Uttoxeter on A518, just past Chartley Castle ruin on left & at top of hill, on right.

Diana Walkerdine
Slab Bridge Cottage
Little Onn
Church Eaton
Staffordshire ST20 0AY
Tel: 01785 840220
Fax: 01785 840220
E-mail: dwalkerdine@allcomm.co.uk

Jeremy & Sarah Allen
Chartley Manor Farm
Chartley
Nr. Stafford
Staffordshire ST18 0LN
Tel: 01889 270891

Entry No: 405   Map no: 9

Entry No: 406   Map no: 9

Inigo Jones was commissioned to transform the ancient, crumbling castle into a baronial mansion. The 1270 pink-stone crenellated pile retains its guardhouse, moat and turrets; the stunning interior is Jacobean with vast, oak-panelled drawing and dining rooms with massive carved fireplaces. Upstairs, billiards and pool in an immense room; *everything* is on a superlative scale. Bedrooms are panelled and regal, bathrooms excellent. Yvonne travelled much in China and has generously furnished her new oriental room with eastern antiques and hand-built Chinese furniture. Splendid. You can self-cater in the lovely stone turrets.

Rooms: 3 four-posters, all en suite (baths/showers); 2 self-catering turrets, both for 2/4 with living room, dining area, bathroom and kitchenette.

Price: £38-£44 p.p. Singles charged at room rate. Turrets from £60 per night.

Meals: Breakfast until 9.30am. Dinner available locally.

Closed: 1 November-February. Self-catering always available.

Caverswall is signed, nr Blythe Bridge, just off A50. Take M1 junc. 23A, or M6 junc. 14/15. Entrance between 2 churches in village.

Yvonne Sargent
Caverswall Castle
Caverswall
Staffordshire ST11 9EA
Tel: 01782 393239
Fax: 01782 394590
E-mail: yasargent@hotmail.com

As Stewards of the Countryside, the Balls are restoring wildlife habitats, ponds, hedgerows, wetlands and footpaths and 105 acres of pasture where they graze Texel sheep and various rare breeds. The cosy bedrooms are in cottages next to the main farmhouse; Diana pops round every morning to serve breakfast at separate tables in the communal dining room and she'll cook dinner for larger parties - just let her know when you book. Set out to discover Croxden Abbey for some 12th-century Cistercian history... or spend the day at Alton Towers. *Children over five welcome.*

Rooms: Farrier's Cottage: 2 doubles, 1 family, all en suite (shower). Mews: 1 double, 1 bunk room, both en suite (shower).

Price: From £20 p.p. Single supp. £10.

Meals: Breakfast until 9am; packed lunch £5; dinner from £10 for parties only (min 6), by arrangement.

Closed: Never.

From A50 B5030 at Uttoxeter towards Rocester. There, left into Hollington Rd. Nabb Lane 1.5 miles on right.

Diana Ball
Woodhouse Farm
Nabb Lane, Croxden
Uttoxeter, Staffordshire ST14 5JB
Tel: 01889 507507
Fax: 01889 507282
E-mail: ddeb@lineone.net
Web: www.alton-towers.glo.cc

An oak-panelled, four-postered Tudor retreat only two miles from Alton Towers. This is an enchanting, rambling, farmhouse, the kind of time capsule you can't simulate: oak timbers, stone, tapestry drapes, curios, pewter and books galore. There are gorgeous, almost grand, lawned grounds, full of birdsong, and a summerhouse, tennis and croquet. Rare breed cattle graze peacefully. Rooms have majestic four-poster beds (with good mattresses) and great views. Chris and Margaret are busy, informal people and the attitude here is very much 'stay as friends'.

Rooms: 3 doubles, all en suite (1 with shower, 2 with baths).

Price: £23-£26 p.p. Single supp. £3-£5.

Meals: Breakfast until 9.30am. Dinner available locally.

Closed: Christmas Eve & Day.

Lovers of the outdoors are blissfully happy in this pocket of countryside; the place is full of wildlife, birds, dogs, cats, horses. "Utterly charming people, too," wrote our inspector. Phyl and Aubrey are devoted to all things horsey and love dressage. It is gorgeous riding country, with vast views. The feel is very much a 'working' home - Phyl makes bread and oat cakes for breakfast and collects fruit from the orchard for home-made jams. In the dining room, a Welsh dresser and grandfather clock; in the lovely kitchen, an Aga and pine table. Just being around your hosts induces a special relaxation.

Rooms: 1 twin, en suite (bath); 2 doubles sharing private bathroom.

Price: £25 p.p.

Meals: Breakfast until 9am. Dinner available locally.

Closed: Christmas.

From Uttoxeter, B5030 for Rocester & Alton Towers. By JCB factory, left onto B5031. At T-junc. after church, right onto B5032 & over bridge. 1st left signed Prestwood. Farm 0.75 miles on right.

In village, follow signs to Denstone College & enter grounds. Left in front of College buildings. On for 300 yds to stud.

Chris & Margaret Ball
Manor House
Prestwood
Nr. Denstone, Uttoxeter
Staffordshire ST14 5DD
Tel: 01889 590415
Fax: 01335 342198
E-mail: cm_ball@yahoo.co.uk

Phyl & Aubrey Price
Denstone Stud and Riding Centre
Hall Riddings
Denstone
Staffordshire ST14 5HW
Tel: 01889 591472
Fax: 01889 591472

Entry No: 409   **Map no: 9**

Entry No: 410   **Map no: 9**

A classic of its kind, just what you expect from an old vicarage in Suffolk, run by Jane, who adores her house and garden. There's a fine Pembroke table in the flagstoned hall, a large open log fire in the sitting/dining room, a long refectory table covered in magazines like *County Life* and *The Field*, a comfortable sofa, a piano and family photos and hunting scenes. Bedrooms are large, chintzy and handsomely furnished. It is an elegant, pretty, traditional English country house. Jane grows her vegetables and keeps hens and house with equal talent. *Children over seven welcome.*

Rooms: 2 twins, both with private bathroom; 1 single room off one of the twins.

Price: From £28 p.p. Single occ. £32.

Meals: Breakfast times flexible; packed lunch £6; dinner £18, BYO wine.

Closed: Christmas Day.

A Queen Anne exterior and a surprising, sumptuous 1617 oak-panelled Tudor hall. The splendid dining room has massive moulded beams and a fireplace with carved stone pillars and faces. It is a richly interesting, beautiful house, delicate yet lived-in, and with lots of family photos. The double bedroom has an ornate Tudor four-poster, more ancient beams, stunning American fabrics at the windows and on the bed and good views. The twin room is in the attic, with uneven oak floors, views and an enchanting garret mood. Diana and her garden are charming.

Rooms: 1 four-poster, 1 twin, both with private bathrooms.

Price: Four-poster, £32 p.p., twin £28 p.p.

Meals: Breakfast until 9.30am. Dinner available locally.

Closed: Christmas.

From Cambridge, A1307 towards Haverhill. Left to Withersfield. At T-junction, left. Almost 3 miles on, high yew hedge & at 'Concealed Entrance' sign on left, sharp turn into drive.

Leave Long Melford on A1092, Clare road. Right to Stanstead on B1066 & right again in village, signed Shimpling. House set back on right 0.5 miles on.

Ms Jane Sheppard
The Old Vicarage
Great Thurlow
Newmarket
Suffolk CB9 7LE
Tel: 01440 783209
Fax: 01638 667270

Diana Banks
Bretteston Hall
Stanstead
Sudbury
Suffolk CO10 9AT
Tel: 01787 280504
Fax: 01787 280504

Entry No: 411   **Map no: 11**   **Entry No: 412**   **Map no: 11**

An immaculate place - gleaming, dark wood antique furniture, fresh flowers and sherry on the oak dresser (17th century, no less). The house is 15th century, timber-framed and thatched and you have your own sitting room with books and an open fire. Home-laid eggs for breakfast, local bacon and home-made bread. A measure of the Oatens' generosity, the bedrooms have goose-down duvets, a decanter of Madeira, fresh fruit, sweets and Penhaligons toiletries, along with co ordinated furnishings, comfortable beds and good furniture. Bridget and Robin are delightful people who really enjoy having guests.

Rooms: 1 twin/double, en suite (bath & shower); 1 double, en suite (bath) with small sitting room.

Price: £30-£32.50 p.p. Single occ. £35-£45.

Meals: Breakfast times flexible. Excellent local pubs & restaurants nearby.

Closed: Occasionally.

From Bury St. Edmunds, A413 towards Haverhill, then B1066 towards Glemsford for 6 miles to Hartest. After 30mph signs, continue for approx. 0.25 miles; lane on left (signed Cross Green) on sharp double bend.

Bridget & Robin Oaten
The Hatch
Pilgrims Lane
Cross Green, Hartest
Suffolk IP29 4ED
Tel: 01284 830226
Fax: 01284 830226

Entry No: 413   Map no: 11

A paean to architecture - Tudor, Queen Anne, Georgian and Edwardian - this is a perfectly preserved and recently restored Grade I-listed house. Ionic and Corinthian columns on fireplaces, Jacobean and Georgian panelling, shuttered windows. All of the large bedrooms have bathrooms with original fittings. The delicious breakfasts are as splendid as the beautiful walled garden and two majestic plane trees - possibly the oldest and tallest in East Anglia. The house was previously owned by the novelist Norah Lofts who was inspired to write many of her books from here. The feel of a country house in a town.

Rooms: 1 double, 1 four-poster, 1 twin/double, all en suite.

Price: £45-£55 p.p. Single occ. £55-£65.

Meals: Breakfast times flexible; dinner available locally.

Closed: Never.

From A14, take Bury Central exit & follow brown signs towards Historic City Centre. At r'bout, 1st left into Northgate St. House on right, shortly after lights. Courtyard parking at far end of house.

Joy Fiennes
Northgate House
Northgate Street
Bury St. Edmunds, Suffolk IP33 1HQ
Tel: 01284 760469
Fax: 01284 724008
E-mail: northgate_hse@hotmail.com
Web: www.northgatehouse.com

Entry No: 414   Map no: 11

Diana was once a stage manager in the London theatre and it shows; she is outgoing, fun, brilliant with people and has a marvellous sense of taste. The bedrooms are perfect, with attractive duvets and curtains, pale walls and garden flowers by the beds. On the tea tray are biscuits, proper coffee and a cafétiere. The sitting room is a stunning terracotta and a lovely place to be. The garden is surprisingly large, with a terrace, fishpond, lawn and herbaceous borders - very pretty; sit and enjoy it. To cap all this Diana will also cook you mouth-watering dinners.

Rooms: 1 twin, 2 doubles, all en suite (shower or bath).

Price: From £25 p.p. Single occ. from £40.

Meals: Breakfast times flexible; dinner from £16.50. B.Y.O. wine.

Closed: Christmas & January, but open New Year.

An impressive, beautifully decorated and furnished Grade I-listed house dating from the 13th century. The hub of this beamed, oak-floored, high-ceilinged family home is the huge stone-flagged Great Hall where you relax among huge sofas and cushions to gaze into the enormous inglenook fireplace. The bright, many-windowed, beam-vaulted bedrooms have handmade mattresses and beds, pure cotton sheets and flowers everywhere; each has its own character. Wonderful details including intriguing Elizabethan wall paintings. *Children over 10 welcome.*

Rooms: 1 double, 1 twin/double, both en suite (bath/shower); 3 four-posters, all en suite (bath & showers).

Price: £39-£54 p.p. Single occ. £59-£69.

Meals: Breakfast until 9am (Mon-Fri), 9.30am (Sat-Sun); packed lunch £5; dinner £25, by arrangement.

Closed: Christmas & New Year.

From Sudbury, B1115 to Lavenham. Pass Swan Hotel on right, next right into Market Lane, cross Market Place, turn right, then left. Red House on right next to school.

Turn at The Swan onto Water St then right after 50 yds into private drive.

Diana Schofield
The Red House
29 Bolton Street
Lavenham
Suffolk CO10 9RG
Tel: 01787 248074
Web: www.lavenham.co.uk/redhouse

Tim & Gilli Pitt
Lavenham Priory
Water Street, Lavenham
Sudbury, Suffolk CO10 9RW
Tel: 01787 247404
Fax: 01787 248472
E-mail: mail@lavenhampriory.co.uk
Web: www.lavenhampriory.co.uk

Entry No: 415   Map no: 11

Entry No: 416   Map no: 11

This little pink cottage was once a pub, but has been tenderly restored to create a pretty, family house; your room, in the converted barn, will appeal to the romantic in you. Sue welcomes you with a glass of Madeira by the enormous inglenook fire, then takes you through the neat little garden full of honeysuckle, aqualegia and Canterbury bells to the barn. A stable door opens into the primrose yellow bedroom with exposed beams and soaring rafters. The chintz-headed king size bed is covered in cushions, there are fresh flowers on the table and watercolours of Mauritius on the walls. Stunning!

Rooms: 1 double, en suite (shower).

Price: £30 p.p. Single supp. £7.50.

Meals: Breakfast times flexible; packed lunch £3. Dinner available in Lavenham.

Closed: Never.

From Sudbury, B1115 to Lavenham. Pass Swan Hotel on right, next right into Market Lane. Straight across Market Place into Prentice Street. House last on right at bottom of hill.

Mrs Sue Wade
Anchor House
Prentice Street
Lavenham
Suffolk CO10 9RD
Tel: 01787 249018
Fax: 01787 249018
E-mail: suewade@tinyworld.co.uk

Entry No: 417   **Map no:** 11

The atmosphere is relaxed and laid-back, yet Juliet has masses of imaginative ideas for making the most of the wonderful countryside: nature trails, local walks, bike rides (you can borrow a bike), tennis and ideas for car-free days out. The house is a glorious unspoiled 16th-century hall farmhouse, lived in and loved by the family for 300 years. Period furniture and lovely bedrooms overlooking a wild flower meadow and the walled garden. Home-grown bacon and sausages and bantam eggs for breakfast and equally delicious dinners. Juliet is fun, energetic and a keen conservationist.

Rooms: 1 double/family room with basin, 1 twin, 1 single/twin, all sharing private bathroom.

Price: £27.50-£32.50 p.p. Reduction for children and longer stays.

Meals: Breakfast until 9.30am; packed lunches and children's high tea available; supper from £15, by arrangement; B.Y.O. wine.

Closed: Occasionally.

From Lavenham, A1141 towards Monks Eleigh. After 2 miles, right to Milden. At x-roads, right to Sudbury on B1115. The Hall's long drive is 0.25 miles on left.

Juliet & Christopher Hawkins
The Hall
Milden
Nr. Lavenham
Suffolk CO10 9NY
Tel: 01787 247235
Fax: 01787 247235
E-mail: gjb53@dial.pipex.com

Entry No: 418   **Map no:** 11

Breakfast on summer mornings on the terrace in the walled garden with home-made marmalade, jams and fruit compotes; in winter, settle beside an arched Tudor brick fireplace in the dining hall. Janus-like, the house looks both ways, Georgian to the front and richly-beamed, 1485 Tudor behind; Alfred Munnings R.A. was a frequent visitor. The bedrooms - one has flower-patterned paper and the other pink-sponged walls - are elegant and very English: padded bedheads, thick curtains, armchairs, writing desks, candles, standard lamp, lots of books... pretty and full of thoughtful touches.

Rooms: 1 twin, en suite (bath), separate wc; 1 double, en suite (shower).

Price: £30 p.p. No single supp.

Meals: Breakfast until 9.30am; dinner £15, by arrangement (if staying more than one night); B.Y.O. wine.

Closed: Christmas.

In the heart of Constable country and reached through a web of winding lanes, Sparrows is an idyllic retreat. It is peaceful, tranquil and homely. You have the run of this gorgeous 15th-century house: a warm, light drawing room with a grand piano, oak beams, open fireplace; a sun room to catch the evening light, a cosy dining room with Suffolk tiles and inglenook fireplace. You have your own staircase, a king-size bed and a delightful room with many thoughtful touches. Low, leaded windows overlook the peaceful gardens which include a grass tennis court. Rachel is a delight - and a great cook.

Rooms: 1 king-size with private bathroom.

Price: From £25-£27 p.p. Single occ. £30.

Meals: Breakfast until 9.30am; dinner, £15, by arrangement; B.Y.O. wine. Also excellent local pubs.

Closed: Christmas & New Year.

Take B1115 from Sunbury towards Lavenham for 3.5 miles. Turn right to Lt. Waldingfield. House is on left, 200 yds beyond The Swan.

Approx. 4 miles between Hadleigh & A12 on country road, 2 miles from Shelley & 1 mile from Polstead. Ring for details as many approaches possible!

Mrs Susan T. del C. Nisbett
Wood Hall
Little Waldingfield
Nr. Lavenham, Suffolk CO10 0SY
Tel: 01787 247362
Fax: 01787 248326
E-mail: nisbett@nisbett.enta.net
Web: www.sawdays.co.uk

Rachel Thomas
Sparrows
Shelley
Ipswich
Suffolk IP7 5RQ
Tel: 01206 337381
E-mail: thomas@sparrows.freeserve.co.uk

Entry No: 419   **Map no: 11**

Entry No: 420   **Map no: 12**

A lovely early 16th-century house in the River Stour valley made famous by John Constable, now an Area of Outstanding Natural Beauty. The River Box meanders through the delightful garden and numerous old English climbing roses wind through the trees and over the 17th-century barn and stables. Each of the romantically decorated bedrooms is different - some are beamed and all look over the garden, river and fields beyond and there's a charming sitting room with inglenook fireplace. Your hosts are attentive and friendly and your privacy is respected. Hard tennis court available.

Rooms: 1 ground-floor twin/double (with outside access), 1 double, both en suite (bath); 1 single with private bathroom.

Price: £30 p.p.

Meals: Breakfast until 9.30am. Dinner available at excellent local pubs.

Closed: Christmas & New Year.

3 miles from the A12, on B1068 between Higham & Stoke-by-Nayland. House on south side of road, 300 yds east of Thorington Street.

Patrick & Jennie Jackson
Nether Hall
Thorington Street
Stoke-by-Nayland
Suffolk CO6 4ST
Tel: 01206 337373
Fax: 01206 337496
E-mail: patrick.jackson@talk21.com

Entry No: 421   **Map no: 12**

Meg really enjoys guests of all ages; you can row, canoe or punt to Stratford St. Mary for a pub lunch. Or you may fish, play tennis or swim in the pool. This Elizabethan jewel is snug beside the equally lovely church. The beautiful drawing room with carved pine mantelpiece and marble hearth faces south over the water meadow. There, cattle graze contentedly; beyond, the Rivers Brett and Stour lazily flow. Blue and white Spode china, silver cutlery, embroidered sheets and fresh fruit and flowers add to the architectural elegance, yet this is a welcoming house.

Rooms: 1 double, en suite (bath); 1 family (twin/double plus single), 1 large twin, both with private bathroom.

Price: £26-£30 p.p. Single occ. £28-£35.

Meals: Breakfast times flexible. Excellent places for dinner nearby.

Closed: Never.

West off A12 at Stratford St. Mary. House on left, opposite church sign, 1 mile down Higham road. House has pink timbers & a sign on wall.

Meg Parker
The Old Vicarage
Higham
Nr. Colchester
Suffolk CO7 6JY
Tel: 01206 337248
E-mail: oldvic.higham@bushinternet.com

Entry No: 422   **Map no: 12**

Bathe by candlelight in excellent bathrooms. There is more than a touch of theatre about this beautifully proportioned house. The dining room is an opulent, dramatic red, the drawing and sitting rooms are peppered with intriguing touches of exotica, and large fireplaces and fresh flowers. The bedrooms have maps, books, radio, fresh flowers and garden views; one has a four-poster with beautiful embroidered linen. Over seven acres of gardens and woodland and, also, a meadow with orchids and a carpet of wild flowers which has been designated a County Wildlife Site. Cindy and her young family are delightful.

Rooms: 1 double, 1 single (with basin), sharing private bathroom; 1 double, en suite (bath).

Price: From £22-£34 p.p. Fri. & Sat. £2 p.p. extra.

Meals: Breakfast times flexible; dinner, 2/3 courses, £14-£21, by arrangement. B.Y.O. wine.

Closed: Never.

From A12 Woodbridge bypass, exit at r'bout signed Melton. Follow for 1 mile to lights; there, right. House immed. on right.

Mrs Lucinda de la Rue
Melton Hall
Woodbridge
Suffolk IP12 1PF
Tel: 01394 388138
Fax: 01394 388982
E-mail: delarue@meltonh.fsnet.co.uk

Entry No: 423   Map no: 12

This is deeply special, the remains of an Augustinian monastery often visited by Mary Tudor, breathtaking, a tour-de-force by a gifted designer who loves the old stones of the place. Decorative stonework clasps the windows, the dining room soars with vaulting and is filled with light. A stripped oak floor, stone pillars and fireplace for the dining room - cloister-like, and fabulous. 47 steps lead up to cascades of damask, huge stone-arched windows, sea-grass matting... the highest standards but fun, too. Frances, artist and musician, is delightful; the area is silent but for the call of the birds. Come.

Rooms: 1 very large double with private bathroom (down small staircase); 1 large double, en suite (shower); 1 small double, en suite (bath & shower).

Price: £37.50-£55 p.p. Single supp. £15.

Meals: Breakfast times flexible; dinner, for 10 or more, by arrangement. Several restaurants nearby.

Closed: Occasionally.

From A12 at Woodbridge, B1084 towards Orford. In Butley village at the Oyster Inn, take Hollesley road for 1 mile to x-roads. Private entrance to Priory on immediate right after x-roads.

Frances Cavendish
Butley Priory
Butley, Nr. Woodbridge
Suffolk IP12 3NR
Tel: 01394 450046
Fax: 01394 450482
E-mail: cavendish@butleypriory.co.uk
Web: www.butleypriory.com

Entry No: 424   Map no: 12

An estuarine corner of rare loveliness; the views are wide and clean, you can stroll to the river to be among the gulls, avocets and duck. The remote and ancient farmhouse is an aesthetic treat, charmingly scruffy, flagstoned, filled with things that we found beautiful and interesting, surprising, uplifting, fun, exquisitely unmodernised... yet comfortable. The library is crammed with books, the kitchen is a beachcomber's haven. Solitary, winter-bleak splendour with an engagingly relaxed, interesting, artistic and cultured architect. Come if you are easy and open, and do what you want.

Rooms: 1 double with private bathroom.

Price: £30 p.p. Single supp. £10.

Meals: Breakfast times flexible. Good pubs & restaurants nearby.

Closed: Occasionally.

From Orford Market Square, take lane towards castle, & 1st right past castle, marked 'Gedgrave Only, No Through Road'. House on left after 0.5 miles by a lone pine.

Mr Hugh Pilkington
Richmond House
Gedgrave
Nr. Orford
Suffolk IP12 2BU
Tel: 01394 450102
Fax: 01394 450313

Entry No: 425   **Map no:** 12

Wrap-around sea-views – you are almost on the beach. Phil (from Zimbabwe) and Juliet are easy-going hosts, and enjoy sharing this very special place. The furniture is Victorian, some mahogany, some walnut, the colours soft, the bedlinen the sort you always meant to buy at home. The white cotton crocheted bedspreads come from the market at Victoria Falls. There are old things, good taste, books and magazines galore, fresh milk on the morning tea tray, home-made biscuits, rugs on wooden floors and a special light from every window. You can borrow bikes, play table tennis in the cellar, sail. Perfect.

Rooms: 1 double, 1 twin, both en suite.

Price: £30-£32.50 p.p. Single occ. £50-£55.

Meals: Breakfast until 9.30am; packed lunch £5; dinner from £10-£15 by arrangment.

Closed: Never.

From Ipswich A12 north. Right onto A1094 after 20 miles. House in centre of Aldeburgh seafront with parking outside.

Juliet & Phil Brereton
Ocean House
25 Crag Path
Aldeburgh
Suffolk IP15 5BS
Tel: 01728 452094
Fax: 01728 453909
E-mail: jbreroh@aol.com

Entry No: 426   **Map no:** 12

With enthusiasm and good taste, Jane is restoring her 16th-century Tudor farmhouse in deepest, softest Suffolk. Partly moated, and with a thatched summerhouse, it has 17th-century additions, an abundance of beams, fleur de lys mouldings and, on the bressaumer beam above the fireplace, intriguing 'witch' markings. Fresh flowers everywhere and the decoration is restrained and stylish. The house has mostly seagrass flooring and splashes of chintzy colour. Rooms are let only to one party. Jane was a professional cook and can conjure up an inspiring dinner.

Rooms: 1 double, 1 twin, sharing private bathroom & shower.

Price: £25 p.p. Single supp. £10.

Meals: Breakfast times flexible; dinner £15-£20, by arrangement.

Closed: Christmas & New Year.

From A1120 at Earl Soham, take Kenton road & follow signs to Monk Soham for approx. 2 miles. Right fork at top of hill. House 2nd entrance on right.

Jane & Peter Cazalet
Monk Soham Hall
Monk Soham
Nr. Woodbridge
Suffolk IP13 7EN
Tel: 01728 685178
Fax: 01728 685944
E-mail: janecaz860@aol.com

Entry No: 427   **Map no:** 12

The undeniable charms of this mellow red-brick Georgian town house lured the Haddons away from London life. Catherine, an interior designer, has poured her considerable energy and talent into its restoration and with a young family *in situ* the whole place feels alive and loved, elegant yet informal. There are lovely fabrics and beautiful colours. Breakfast is served in the panelled dining room and upstairs there is a delightful double bedroom, a cottagey twin and a charming family suite in the attic. Magnificent gardens, too, with a parterre and rose garden.

Rooms: 1 double, 1 twin sharing bathroom. 1 twin, en suite (shower).

Price: From £30 p.p.

Meals: Breakfast times flexible; dinner, from £15, by arrangement.

Closed: Christmas & New Year, unless by arrangement.

Turn off A12 to Saxmundham. Through town & under railway bridge; house 1st on right.

Catherine & Christopher Haddon
Beech House
North Entrance
Saxmundham
Suffolk IP17 1AP
Tel: 01728 605700
Fax: 01728 605909

Entry No: 428   **Map no:** 12

A sunken garden and covered terrace lead you to a glorious sunroom which is just for you, to read, relax or eat in. Large bedrooms are in the roof of this 1860s converted granary, with high, beamed ceilings and arched windows - they feel very private. Potions for the bath, robes, candlesticks and bottled water are there for you, too. All around are impressive medieval churches - why not take off on the bikes with a packed lunch? The beach is only three miles away. Carole, gentle and flexible, is involved in the June Aldeburgh Festival and the year-round Snape Maltings concerts.

Rooms: 1 double with private bathroom next door; 1 twin, en suite (shower). Granary stable, self-catering for 2-4, £165-£315 p.w.

Price: £25 p.p. No single supp.

Meals: Breakfast times flexible; packed lunch available; dinner, 3 courses, from £12, by arrangement.

Closed: Never.

From A12, B1119. From Saxmundham to Leiston, left onto B1122 towards Yoxford. 2 miles on, left just before Theberton (30 mph sign). 1st left, then right up 1st driveway.

Mrs Carole Bidder
The Granary
Theberton
Nr. Leiston
Suffolk IP16 4RR
Tel: 01728 831633
Fax: 01728 831633
E-mail: granaryyhrntyon@aol.com

Entry No: 429   **Map no: 12**

Surrounded by gardens and apple orchards Robin and Patricia are dedicated to the delights of producing their own fruit, veg, free-range eggs, poultry and lamb. Guests wax lyrical about the food. Robin has an artistic streak – a mural is on display over the dining room mantelpiece - and Patricia, a landscape architect, enjoys sharing her garden. The 15th-century, Grade II-listed farmhouse - all beams and open fires - is a haven of peace. Rooms are simply but comfortably furnished and delightfully scattered with books, flowers and the odd patchwork quilt.

Rooms: 1 double/twin, en suite; 1 double, 1 twin, sharing private bathroom.

Price: £30 p.p. No single supp.

Meals: Breakfast times flexible; dinner, 3 courses, £20, by arrangement.

Closed: Occasionally.

A12 to Yoxford, B1122 to Leiston. After r'way crossing right by pond down unmarked road. House at end of lane on right.

Robin Hare
Fordley Hall
Middleton
Saxmundham, Suffolk IP17 3LT
Tel: 01728 668236
Fax: 01728 668458
E-mail: robin@fordleyhall.co.uk
Web: www.fordleyhall.co.uk

Entry No: 430   **Map no: 12**

Atmosphere and architecture - it's easy to see what seduced Jackum and David into converting this Grade-II Victorian chapel into their home. Your bedrooms are charming - the Stable Room has cream walls, oak floors and wooden beams; the flag-floored Retreat Room is cosy with bright rugs and bedcovers from far-flung places. An air of tranquillity pervades, from the wind chimes in the peaceful courtyard garden to breakfast served by the lovely rose window in the chapel or in the colourful conservatory. Potions and lotions by your bath, books and flowers in every corner, bacon from the Queen Mother's suppliers.

Rooms: 1 double with private bathroom & garden access; 1 twin, en suite (shower).

Price: £27.50-£32.50.p.p. Single occ. £32.50-£40.

Meals: Breakfast times flexible. Good restaurants locally.

Closed: December-February.

From A12 in Yoxford A1120 towards Peasenhall & Stowmarket. Chapel 200 yds on right.

Jackum & David Brown
The Old Methodist Chapel
High Street
Yoxford
Suffolk IP17 3EU
Tel: 01728 668333
E-mail: browns@chapelsuffolk.co.uk
Web: www.chapelsuffolk.co.uk

Entry No: 431   **Map no: 12**

The tennis court and large garden are surrounded by the 12th-century listed moat - this is a gorgeous old place with stacks of interest. Ancient stairs rise and fall all over the 13th-century house and there are sloping floors and unstained beams. The dining room, for the candlelit dinners at the large table, was once the dairy. The family room has a billiard table and toy cupboard, and the sitting room a baby grand, open fire, fresh flowers and lots of books. Elizabeth is delightful and generous: home-made cake on arrival, local honey, home-made bread and marmalade for breakfast.

Rooms: 2 twins, 1 double, sharing bathroom. Extra wc available.

Price: £22 p.p. No single supp. Children 10-15, £10-£15.

Meals: Breakfast times flexible; dinner and supper, from £12.50-£14, available on request (24 hrs notice preferred). B.Y.O. wine.

Closed: December-February.

A1120 (Yoxford to Stowmarket) to Dennington. B1116 north for approx. 3 miles. Farm on right 0.9 miles north of Bell pub.

Elizabeth Hickson
Grange Farm
Dennington
Woodbridge
Suffolk IP13 8BT
Tel: 01986 798388

Entry No: 432   **Map no: 12**

Walberswick is enchanting, and so is Ferry House, too. It was built in the 1930s for a playwright, using a butterfly design to catch the light - it has Art Deco touches, hand-painted fireplace tiles, simple but pretty rooms, fresh flowers everywhere, lots of books and co-ordinated, cotton linens. Cathryn and John love sharing their home with guests. There's a warm cloakroom for wet birdwatchers' clothes and a welcoming glass of sherry. You are only 200m from the River Blyth and the sea and there is a self-catering studio for two. *Children over 10 welcome.*

Rooms: 1 double with en suite wc & basin; 2 singles sharing wc & basin. Guest bathroom, too. Self-catering Coach House studio also available.

Price: From £20 p.p.

Meals: Breakfast until 9.30am; packed lunch £3.50 by arrangement. Dinner available locally.

Closed: Christmas week.

From A12 B1387 to Walberswick. Ferry House on left at far end of village, near river.

Cathryn Simpson
Ferry House
Walberswick
Southwold
Suffolk IP18 6TH
Tel: 01502 723384
Fax: 01502 723384
E-mail: ferryhouse.walberswick@virgin.net

Entry No: 433   **Map no: 12**

The elegance within is hinted at by the enchanting Suffolk brick façade. Here is a Georgian vicarage in its own tranquil corner with easy access to the heritage coast. Well-proportioned rooms are grand but not too grand – fine old furniture, family portraits in gilded frames, photographs, books. The bedrooms are a treat: four-poster beds, towelling robes and garden views; you have your own delightful sitting room, too. Paula is good company, loves cooking and keeps the flowers fresh. For breakfast expect the best - local sausages and bacon, home-made toast and marmalade, linen napkins in silver rings.

Rooms: 1 double with private bathroom; 1 double and 1 twin sharing private bathroom.

Price: £25 p.p. Single occ. £30.

Meals: Breakfast times flexible; packed lunch £4, by arrangement. Good pubs nearby.

Closed: Never.

From A12, 4 miles north of Yoxford, left towards Wenhaston. Pass Star Inn & village school on left. After 200 yds, on left is red brick wall around churchyard. Drive at far end of wall.

Mrs P. Heycock
The Old Vicarage
Church Corner, Wenhaston
Southwold, Suffolk IP19 9EG
Tel: 01502 478339
Fax: 01502 478068
E-mail: theycock@aol.com
Web: www.southwold.blythweb.co.uk/oldvicarage

Entry No: 434   **Map no: 12**

Pat, kind and immensely caring, is an experienced B&B-er - she has been with Sawdays since the beginning - and we have no hesitation in recommending her new home, even though she was in the process of moving in when we visited. The modern house has secluded gardens and is close to a large heath - the perfect place for early-morning walks, Pat has brought with her lovely family furniture, pictures and many books. The natural charms of Suffolk are the icing on the cake: Heritage Coast, medieval churches, Southwold. Nearby is Woottens Nursery, popular among serious plant collectors.

Rooms: 1 twin, en suite (shower); 1 double/twin with private bathroom.

Price: £18-£25 p.p. Single supp. £4.

Meals: Breakfast 8-9am; dinner, £12, by arrangement.

Closed: Occasionally.

From A12, 3.3 miles north of Darsham level crossing, left at x-roads towards Wenhaston. Left at Star Inn & immed. right into lane. House 2nd on left.

Patricia Kemsley
Rowan House
Hall Road, Wenhaston
Southwold
Suffolk IP19 9HF
Tel: 01502 478407

Entry No: 435   **Map no: 12**

Irresistible: a listed Jacobean farmhouse with Georgian additions, meticulously restored, oozing with character, both ancient and modern, and in a very quiet hamlet with a 12th-century thatched church. Sarah, well-travelled and entertaining, has created a relaxed atmosphere in which you feel entirely at home. Let her cook for you - she does this excellently from her Aga-warm kitchen - using local ingredients. The bedrooms have gorgeous fabrics, fresh flowers and linen sheets; one has a medieval bedstead with carved head- and footboards, two have super new bathrooms and all are peaceful.

Rooms: 1 double, 1 twin, both en suite (bath); 1 single with private bathroom.

Price: From £30 p.p.

Meals: Breakfast times flexible; dinner, from £18.50, by arrangement.

Closed: Christmas.

A12 towards Wangford. Left signed Uggeshall. Farmhouse 1st on left before church.

Sarah Jupp
Church Farmhouse
Uggeshall
Southwold
Suffolk NR34 8BD
Tel: 01502 578532
Fax: 01953 888306
E-mail: sarahjupp@compuserve.com

Entry No: 436   **Map no: 12**

An enchanting, soft, 16th-century Suffolk combination of bricks and beams; the Willises generously allow you to stay and enjoy it all day if you wish. It is friendly and cottagey, with antique furniture and William Morris-type floral sofas and chairs. The dining room was once a cheese-room where 'Suffolk Bang' was made and from here you can wander into the kitchen to chat with Rosemary. You have your own wing; one of the bedrooms is a delightful half-timbered room with sloping ceiling. Four miles away is Wingfield Old College, home of the summer arts festival.

Rooms: 2 doubles, 1 twin, both with private bathroom.

Price: From £23.50 p.p. Single occ. from £26.

Meals: Breakfast times flexible. Dinner available locally.

Closed: Christmas week.

From Scole/A140, right onto A143 towards Great Yarmouth. After 7 miles, right at Harleston. B1116 to Fressingfield. Pass church & Fox & Goose on left. At top of hill, right, then left into Priory Road.

Stephen & Rosemary Willis
Priory House
Priory Road
Fressingfield, Eye
Suffolk IP21 5PH
Tel: 01379 586254
Fax: 01379 586254

Entry No: 437   **Map no:** 12

To be friendly and flexible but not intrusive - that was the aim of Joan and David when they started B&B five years ago. They have succeeded. Theirs is a converted stables and squash court originally belonging to the adjacent manor house, and it has a mature charm. There are many trees in the garden, a paddock and a pool. Surprisingly, amid a hushed tranquillity, you are close to the M25 and airports. Bedrooms are not large but one opens onto the garden, one has a balcony and the Applestore is self-contained. There's a self-catering annexe, too. *Children over eight welcome.*

Rooms: 1 twin with private shower room; 1 double, en suite (bath) with sitting room; Applestore twin, en suite (shower).

Price: £35 p.p. (£37.50 from May 2002). Single supp. £7.50. Self-catering annexe, from £400 p.w.

Meals: Breakfast 7-9am. Dinner available locally.

Closed: Never.

From M25, exit 11, A319 into Chobham. Left at T-junc., left at mini-r'bout by Total garage onto A3046. After 0.7 miles, right between street light & postbox. House 2nd on left.

Joan & David Carey
Swallow Barn
Milford Green
Chobham, Nr. Woking
Surrey GU24 8AU
Tel: 01276 856030
Fax: 01276 856030
E-mail: swallowbarn@compuserve.com

Entry No: 438   **Map no:** 5

This late-Georgian parsonage, in a pretty village setting, has all the warmth and cosy comfort of a traditional English home plus warm colours, light streaming in through French windows, the wrap-around snugness of plump sofas, and those deft touches that make all the difference - like the dark green bathrobes in your room (the en suite shower rooms are small). There is sherry by the log fire, home-cooked food using free-range meats and local produce, and chats over dinner with your well-travelled, articulate and relaxed hosts.

Rooms: 2 twins/doubles, 1 double, both with small en suite shower; 1 double with private bathroom. All available as singles.

Price: £25-£55 p.p.

Meals: Breakfast 7-8.30am Mon-Fri, 8-9am Sat-Sun; dinner, 4 courses, from £18; light supper £10.

Closed: Christmas.

At M25 junc. 13, A30 towards Egham. At next r'bout, A30 to Basingstoke. Uphill to lights. Right, then 3rd right, at T-junc., left. House immed. on right. Parking is tight, but the Clarks will help.

Sandi & Peter Clark
The Old Parsonage
Parsonage Road
Englefield Green
Surrey TW20 0JW
Tel: 01784 436706
Fax: 01784 436706
E-mail: the.old.parsonage@talk21.com

Entry No: 439   **Map no: 5**

It is a surprise to bump along a farm track and find 400 acres of farmland so close to London, but this is Surrey, the most densely wooded and rural home county. The lovely manor has all the impressive features you'd expect; an easy-going John enjoys the higgle and piggle of the 1550s house - wooden floors, big fires, worn carpets and rugs, window seats and church panel doors. Bedrooms and bathrooms are big with timbered walls and views to a walled rose garden, two acres of lawn, a tree-lined pond and a hillock on which horses graze.

Rooms: 1 twin with private bathroom; 2 doubles, both en suite (bath).

Price: £30 p.p. Single supp. £10.

Meals: Breakfast until 9.30am; supper with wine, £25, by arrangement.

Closed: Never.

From A3 at Guildford, A323 for Aldershot. Continue to black & white r'bout. 400 yds beyond, house signed left.

John & Pooh Tangye
Littlefield Manor
Littlefield Common
Guildford
Surrey GU3 3HJ
Tel: 01483 233068
Fax: 01483 233686

Entry No: 440   **Map no: 5**

This feels as rural as Devon, yet you are (almost) within walking distance of Guildford. It's a gorgeous 16th-century Grade-II listed farmhouse on a country lane beneath the Pilgrim's Way. Beyond the pretty terraced garden - Michael's passion - views of the North Downs and wooded hills stretch out, with hardly a house in sight. Bedrooms have been beautifully furnished by Alison, an interior designer, with good fabrics and antique French beds. Log fires are lit in winter when the wind whistles around and there are two lovely dogs to greet you - Herbert and Ha'penny. Perfectly placed for airports and Ascot.

Rooms: 2 doubles, both with private bathroom.

Price: £30 p.p. Single occ. £45.

Meals: Breakfast times flexible. Dinner available locally.

Closed: Christmas & New Year.

From top of Guildford High St, along Epsom Rd & right into Tangier Rd. At top, bear left into Warren Rd. At sharp right-hand bend at top (One Tree Hill Rd), on for 0.3 miles, then bear right into Halfpenny Lane. House 0.7 miles on left.

Michael Bennett
Old Great Halfpenny
Halfpenny Lane, St Martha
Guildford
Surrey GU4 8PY
Tel: 01483 567835
Fax: 01483 303037
E-mail: alisonbird1@btinternet.com

A homely place with a lovely walled garden and super hosts. Gillian welcomes guests from all over the world (she speaks French, German and Spanish), yet she and David will make you feel like their first ever; their conversation is lively and informed. The house, 16th-19th century, has exposed timber frames and bold colours - like the dining room's red. The guest sitting room, with its log fireplace and piano, is hung with a collection of hats and ethnic treasures. In the walled garden the distant rumble of the A3 reminds you how well placed you are for Gatwick and Heathrow.

Rooms: 1 twin/double, en suite (bath/shower); 1 twin/double with private bathroom; 2 singles (1 with basin) sharing shower room.

Price: £27.50-£35 p.p.

Meals: Breakfast until 9am. Dinner available locally.

Closed: Christmas & New Year.

A3 south. 5 miles after Guildford, Eashing signed left before service station. House 150 yds on left behind white fence.

David & Gillian Swinburn
Lower Eashing Farmhouse
Eashing
Nr. Godalming
Surrey GU7 2QF
Tel: 01483 421436
Fax: 01483 421436
E-mail: davidswinburn@hotmail.com

People return time and again - the house, the garden, the countryside and the hosts are exceptional. In a vast sitting room, low-slung beams and striking colours jostle for your attention. A sturdy, turning oak staircase leads you to the bedrooms; a peek at them all will only confuse you - they are all gorgeous. There's an ornate bedstead in the Chinese room and, in another, an oak bedstead and beams. A further room has a hint of French decadence: golds, magentas and silks. Sheila knows much about antiques and the local antique shops - and day trips to nearby London.

Rooms: 1 twin, 1 single sharing bathroom; 1 double, en suite (bath).

Price: £35-£40 p.p. Single supp. from £10.

Meals: Breakfast until 9am. Dinner available locally.

Closed: Never.

A3 to Milford, then A283 for Petworth. At Chiddingfold, Pickhurst Road is off green. House 3rd on left, with large black dovecote.

Sheila & John Marsh
Greenaway
Pickhurst Road
Chiddingfold
Surrey GU8 4TS
Tel: 01428 682920
Fax: 01428 685078
E-mail: jfvmarsh@nildram.co.uk.

Entry No: 443   **Map no: 5**

High it is, looking across two and a half acres of smooth lawns to the village and the Surrey hills. The 1532 rambling farmhouse has the sort of family clutter that makes you feel immediately at home. You have the big, log-fired living room, stone-flagged dining room and snug study for yourselves, while the three prettily furnished bedrooms share a bathroom upstairs. Unlike many houses with masses of beams, low ceilings and dark furniture, this is light and inviting. Patrick is quiet and gently courteous; Carol is kind and loves children. There are cots and Z-beds aplenty.

Rooms: 1 double, en suite; 1 double, 1 twin, sharing bathroom.

Price: £25-£30 p.p. Single occ. £25-£30.

Meals: Breakfast 6.30-9.30am; dinner available locally.

Closed: Christmas.

From A3, 1st exit after M25 (signed Ripley). Through Ripley & West Clandon, over dual carriageway (A246) onto A25. 3rd right to Shere. There, right to Cranleigh. House 5 miles on left, 1 mile past Windmill pub.

Patrick & Carol Franklin Adams
High Edser
Shere Road
Ewhurst/Cranleigh
Surrey GU6 7PQ
Tel: 01483 278214
Fax: 01483 278200
E-mail: franklinadams@highedser.demon.co.uk

Entry No: 444   **Map no: 5**

Originally a 16th-century inn, the farmhouse is now a peaceful haven set in five acres with a small lake that used to form part of a moat. A bridge takes you to a small island. Inside, low beams, wattle-and-daub walls, Jacobean-style furniture, antiques, rugs and log fires. One bedroom has a brass bedstead, another a four-poster; the attic bathroom has a whirlpool. At breakfast you can sit in the conservatory overlooking the lake and watch the entertaining ducks. Ann and David are relaxed, unpretentious, easy hosts who are pleased to help airport travellers.

Rooms: 1 double, 1 four-poster, both en suite (bath); 1 twin, en suite (shower).

Price: £30-£35 p.p. Single occ. £45-£55.

Meals: Breakfast until 9.30am. Dinner available locally.

Closed: Christmas.

At x-roads in Leigh, follow signs to Charwood. After 1 mile, 1st right (Herons Head Farm sign) after sign to Mynthurst. Continue up drive for 0.5 miles.

Ms Ann Dale
Herons Head Farm
Mynthurst
Leigh, Surrey RH2 8QD
Tel: 01293 862475
Fax: 01293 863350
E-mail: heronshead@clara.net
Web: www.heronshead.co.uk

Entry No: 445　　　**Map no: 5**

A wooded track leads to this beautiful mellow 17th-century farmhouse with tall chimneys and a cluster of overgrown outbuildings. Wood panelled walls and ancient oak beams, a vast open fireplace, mullioned windows and welcoming sofas create an atmosphere of relaxed, country-house charm. You breakfast in the Aga-warm kitchen and in spring the scent of bluebells reaches you through the open doors. The large, and comfortable, timbered bedrooms (one canopied bed incorporates original oak panelling) overlook fields, rolling lawns and woodland where you can stroll in peace. *Children by arrangement.*

Rooms: 1 double with private bathroom; 1 twin/double/family, en suite (bath) and an extra small single.

Price: £25-£35 p.p. No single supp. Advance booking only.

Meals: Breakfast times flexible; evening meals by arrangement. Also available locally.

Closed: Never.

Directions given on booking.

Maggie Paterson
Fitzlea Farmhouse
Selham
Nr. Petworth
Sussex GU28 0PS
Tel: 01798 861429

Entry No: 446　　　**Map no: 5**

A secret hideaway in the woods, Amberfold isn't just a B&B but a tranquil retreat, perfect for a pair of independent nature-lovers. You have your own lavishly-stocked fridge (replenished daily) - there's enough for a copious breakfast with plenty to spare for a picnic lunch as well. The rooms are pristine and decorated in a simple country style, you have your own front door and terrace, and there are miles of beautiful, unspoilt woodlands to explore right on the doorstep. Don't jump out of your skin if a deer comes to your window to investigate!

Rooms: 2 double studios, both with shower rooms.

Price: From £26 p.p. Single supp. from £10.

Meals: Breakfast self-service, so any time! Local pubs within walking distance.

Closed: Never.

*From Midhurst, A286 towards Chichester. After Royal Oak pub on left, Greyhound on right, go 0.5 miles, left to Heyshott. On for 2 miles, do **not** turn off, look for white posts & house sign on left.*

Alex & Annabelle Costaras
Amberfold
Heyshott
Midhurst
Sussex GU29 0DA
Tel: 01730 812385
Fax: 01730 812842

Entry No: 447   **Map no: 5**

Absolute attention to detail and luxury to revel in; Jeanette has done everything to ensure your comfort. This is Olde Worlde charm at its most authentic. The Lodge was built in pure Neo-Gothic style as the gatehouse to the local manor - its church windows are delicious. There are ornate mirrors, gold candles, generous, silky curtains, wall sconces and silver and crystal. The conservatory has a woodburner for chilly days and mini indoor garden with a small fish pond. The garden rambles around the house and is secluded and peaceful. The beds and the linen are sumptuous and Jeanette a delight.

Rooms: 3 doubles, en suite (2 with baths, 1 with shower).

Price: From £25 p.p. Single occ. £35.

Meals: Breakfast times flexible. Dinner available locally.

Closed: Never.

Village is 3 miles west of Chichester on B2178. Lodge 170 yds on left after Salthill Road. Look for sign for Oakwood School.

Jeanette Dridge
Chichester Lodge
Oakwood School Drive
East Ashling, Chichester
Sussex PO18 9AL
Tel: 01243 786560

Entry No: 448   **Map no: 5**

A house has been here since the Bronze Age and the history of Lordington could fill this book. Jacobean, with numerous modifications, it's vast and impressive, with majestic views past clipped yew and box, ha-ha and walled garden to the Ems Valley. The Hamiltons have brought warmth to the house, yet it remains engagingly old-fashioned. There's a floral double room and the twin, with Windsor bedheads, has toile wallpaper up and over wardrobe doors; both rooms are large with magnificent views. There's a lovely panelled drawing room, too, and the Hamiltons are extremely nice. *Children over five welcome.*

Rooms: 1 double, 1 twin, both with private bath.

Price: £25 p.p. Single supp. £10.

Meals: Breakfast times times flexible; packed lunch and supper, by arrangement.

Closed: Christmas & New Year.

From A3, B2070, towards Petersfield. After dual carriageway, left signed Royate. Fork right on B2146 signed Emsworth. Through Walderton. House gate on right 0.5 miles on, by letter box. Fork right through pillars.

Audrey Hamilton
Lordington House
Lordington
Chichester
Sussex PO18 9DX
Tel: 01243 375862
E-mail: audreyhamilton@onetel.net.uk

Entry No: 449   **Map no: 5**

Lots of beams, charming bedrooms, a cosily cluttered drawing room full of a Bechstein piano and comfortable armchairs: this is a haven for musicians - and cat-lovers. It has the feel of a well-loved and lived-in family home, and indeed Mary has lived here for 30 years. The house looks out over Chidham harbour "five minutes walk from the water's edge" and is surrounded by great walking and bird-watching country. A lovely setting for a delightful house.

Rooms: 1 twin, 1 double with shared bathroom; 1 double with private bathroom.

Price: From £21 p.p.

Meals: Breakfast times flexible. Excellent pub in village.

Closed: Christmas.

From Chichester, head for Portsmouth. Pass Tesco on right. 3rd exit off r'bout, to Bosham/Fishbourne. Follow A259 for 4 miles, pass Saab garage on right. Next left into Chidham Lane. House last on left, 1 mile down.

Mary Hartley
Easton House
Chidham Lane
Chidham, Chichester
Sussex PO18 8TF
Tel: 01243 572514
Fax: 01243 573084
E-mail: eastonhouse@chidham.fsnet.co.uk

Entry No: 450   **Map no: 5**

Masts of boats of all sizes moored in the popular Birdham Pool peep over the hedge of the sweet-scented, informal walled garden at this antiques-filled Grade II-listed Georgian house. The double bedroom, flouncy and feminine, overlooks this lively maritime scene. The 'Boat House' twin, which has its own key, has yellow and blue paintwork with fine paintings. Take a drink on the terrace, plan a night at the Chichester Festival Theatre or wander around the marina that has been used by many film crews. Coastal walks nearby, too. *Children over 12 welcome.*

Rooms: 1 double and 1 twin, both en suite (bath/shower).

Price: £30-£35 p.p. Single supp. £10.

Meals: Breakfast until 9.30am; packed lunch available; dinner, 4 courses with wine, £20, by arrangement.

Closed: Never.

A286 from Chichester to Witterings. Right to Birdham opposite Richardson's Nursery. Fork right into Martins Lane which becomes Lock Lane. House just before marina by big bay tree.

Susie Groom
The Red House
Lock Lane
Birdham Pool, Nr. Chichester
Sussex PO20 7BB
Tel: 01243 512488
Fax: 01243 514563
E-mail: susie.redhouse@ukonline.co.uk

Entry No: 451 **Map no: 5**

Bees buzz contentedly, water bubbles in the fountain and you may swim in the pool. The Sedgwicks – Nigel is studying History of Art and Juliet has a framing business - have created a much-loved haven. The bedrooms are large with generous tea trays; there's a Waring & Gillows bed from which you can gaze across the coastal plain to the South Downs. This is a sunny spot, hence the many local market gardeners. Juliet frequently travels to London for exhibitions via the excellent rail connection but the three-acre garden and double-glazing shield you from train noise.

Rooms: 1 king-size, en suite (bath); 1 double, 1 twin, sharing bathroom.

Price: £30-£35 p.p. Single supp. £5.

Meals: Breakfast times flexible; packed lunch and dinner, from £15-£25, by arrangement.

Closed: Christmas.

From Chichester A27 east (or west from Arundel). South on B2132 for Yapton. Right on Lake Lane just before level crossing. House 0.5 miles on right.

Nigel & Juliet Sedgwick
Todhurst Farm
Lake Lane, Barnham
Arundel
Sussex PO22 0AL
Tel: 01243 551959
E-mail: nigelsedg@aol.com

Entry No: 452 **Map no: 5**

Vivien is happy for breakfast to turn into an early-morning house-party in her lovely yellow kitchen; she spoils you with kippers and porridge and, later, home-made cakes for tea. You are close to Goodwood - husband Tim manages a local stud - and the house, built by Napoleonic prisoners of war, was once part of the Goodwood estate. Bedrooms are in the old cattle byres that were originally converted for the Reads' growing family. They are good-sized, attractively furnished and decorated and always have fresh flowers. Lovely views from the garden and there's a tennis court.

Rooms: 2 twins/doubles, both en suite (bath & shower).

Price: £27.50-£35 p.p. Single occ. £30-£35.

Meals: Breakfast times flexible. Dinner available locally.

Closed: Christmas.

A272 to Midhurst, then A286 to Singleton. Left signed Goodwood: up over Downs, pass racecourse, next right signed Lavant. House 1st on right 0.5 miles on.

Tim & Vivien Read
The Flint House
East Lavant
Chichester
Sussex PO18 0AS
Tel: 01243 773482
E-mail: www.theflinthouse@ukonline.co.uk

Entry No: 453   **Map no: 5**

Built for the miller in 1767, Duncton Mill, with its walled gardens and charming ensemble of farm buildings, is now the domain of Tom and Sheila, who put heart and soul into their home and B&B. The 70-acre estate is a dream for country-lovers and anglers are in their element here, too, with several spring-fed trout lakes in which to dangle their lines. The rolling South Downs spread out before you, there is an outdoor heated pool and good, local pubs. Breakfasts might include home-grown figs in late Summer. *Children over eight welcome. Self-catering available.*

Rooms: 1 twin/double (with single room attached), 1 double, both en suite (bath/shower).

Price: £25-£35 p.p. Single occ. £40.

Meals: Breakfast until 9.30am. Dinner available locally.

Closed: Christmas.

300 yds off A285 Petworth to Chichester road. Look for brown & white tourist signs just south of Duncton village.

Sheila & Tom Bishop
Duncton Mill House
Duncton, Nr. Petworth
Sussex GU28 0LF
Tel: 01798 342294
Fax: 01798 344122
E-mail: sheila@dunctonmill.com
Web: www.dunctonmill.com

Entry No: 454   **Map no: 5**

First a farm, then an ale house; what seems small from the outside opens into a rambling, higgledy-piggledy 16th-century period interior, with quirky angles and exposed timbers. Frances, with skill and dedication, did the renovation herself. And she landscaped the gardens - complete with a 1,000-year-old box hedge - where nightingales and owls enjoy the woodland. Bedrooms are beamed and neat with the best linen. Living and dining rooms are oak-beamed, uncluttered and cheerful. Your hostess is an independent character but always happy to share a drink and a chat in front of the inglenook fire.

Rooms: 1 double, 1 twin, both en suite (shower); 1 single, en suite (bath).

Price: From £27.50 p.p. Single from £35.

Meals: Breakfast times flexible. Restaurants available locally.

Closed: Never.

From Gatwick, M23 south & follow signs to Cuckfield. There, right at 1st mini-r'bout, left at 2nd, right at 3rd. Left at T-junc. Copyhold Lane 1st on right, after entrance to Borde Hill Gardens.

Frances Druce
Copyhold Hollow
Copyhold Lane
Borde Hill, Haywards Heath
Sussex RH16 1XU
Tel: 01444 413265
E-mail: 10@copyholdhollow.freeserve.co.uk
Web: www.copyholdhollow.freeserve.co.uk

Entry No: 455   **Map no: 5**

Just one ground-floor guest room and a good deal of homely comfort. You are at the opposite end of the house from the owners, so feel very private and your bathroom is just a couple of steps from the bedroom door. Modern pine dressing tables, rattan chairs, co-ordinating curtains and duvet covers and views of the lovely three-acre garden. The Sussex Archeological Society say the house has Elizabethan origins and some of the smaller, mullioned windows bear this out. Old, old timbers in the snug dining room and Jeannie and Nick, charming and easy to talk to.

Rooms: 1 double with private bathroom.

Price: £25 p.p. Single supp. £5.

Meals: Breakfast until 9am. Dinner available locally.

Closed: Never.

From Haywards Heath, B2028 to Lindfield. Carry on in direction of Ardingly. 1.5 miles after passing church at north end of Lindfield, house on left.

Jeannie & Nick Leadsom
Little Lywood
Ardingly Road
Ardingly, Lindfield
Sussex RH16 2QX
Tel: 01444 892571
E-mail: nick@littlelywood.freeserve.co.uk

Entry No: 456   **Map no: 5**

All doors lead to the garden, it seems. Masses of wisteria and roses scent the air and you can play croquet amid the beauty; the guest sitting room and the dining room have their own patio, too. You'll feel nurtured in this large, late-Victorian country house; Norma fills the bedrooms with flowers, the bathrooms with soaps and shampoos and is happy to make restaurant bookings for you. The pretty twin has matching chintz dressing-table and curtains, the king-size double comes with dressing-gown and slippers. Fine views to Ashdown Forest, too. *Children over 11 welcome.*

Rooms: 1 twin, en suite (shower), 1 king-size double with basin, and private bathroom (shower).

Price: £25 p.p. Single supp. £5.

Meals: Breakfast times flexible. Dinner available locally.

Closed: Occasionally

A. A. Milne lived in the village and the bridge where Christopher Robin played Pooh Sticks is close by. The nostalgia remains. There's a dreamlike quality to this Queen Anne house, a former rectory, with its lovely garden and seductive, 13th century church-side setting. It is time-worn inside and beautifully old-fashioned with the oak stairs, a display of antique swords and an ancient tapestry in the hall. Your carpeted bedroom with iron bedstead is plain but comfortable and has a single room off it. Bunny is happy in her new role of host and keen to please.

Rooms: 1 double, en suite (bath); single room also available.

Price: £25 p.p. Single supp. £5.

Meals: Breakfast until 9am. Dinner available locally.

Closed: Occasionally.

A26 from Tunbridge Wells in direction of Uckfield. At Crowborough Cross, take Beacon Rd. 4th right into Warren Rd. Bottom of hill to Rannoch Rd. Right. House on left after 200 yds.

In the middle of Hartfield, take road between The Haywagon & The Anchor. Past church, down bumpy road & continue round & down to the Grange.

Norma Backhouse
Hope Court
Rannoch Road
Crowborough
Sussex TN6 1RA
Tel: 01892 654017

Bunny Murray Willis
The Grange
Hartfield
Sussex TN7 4AG
Tel: 01892 770259
Fax: 01892 771110

Entry No: 457   Map no: 5

Entry No: 458   Map no: 5

Rarely have we met such dedicated hosts, Jennifer organising behind the scenes, Graham proving that nothing is too much trouble. He makes preserves, too, and will book a table at the village pub for you. Visitors from 54 nations have enjoyed the comforts of this unspoilt, wisteria-clad 1930s bastion of old-Englishness set to the gentle music of fantails. It is surrounded by peaceful views over lovely gardens of three and a half acres, has a huge fruit and veg plot that could feed an army, and log fires in winter. *Children over 10 welcome.*

Rooms: 1 double with private bath & wc; 2 twins sharing 1 bathroom & 2 wcs.

Price: From £30 p.p. Single supp. £10.

Meals: Breakfast times flexible. Dinner available locally.

Closed: Never.

Celia's enthusiasm for this beamy house is delightful. She used to sell antiques, but probably not very profitably as she admits to keeping "the ones I liked and didn't want to sell" – and it is easy to see why. This is a typical 15th-century beamed Sussex farmhouse with bags of character. The beautiful garden has been lovingly restored to its original layout and there are two bridged wildlife ponds. The two single rooms are full of charm and style with some interesting pieces of furniture (of course). The double is equally lovely and light and airy and overlooks the garden.

Rooms: 1 double with private bathroom; 2 singles with shared bathroom.

Price: £28 p.p.

Meals: Breakfast times flexible. Dinner available locally.

Closed: Christmas & New Year.

From M25, A22 to Maresfield. At mini-r'bout in centre of village, under stone arch opposite church & pub, & over 5 speed bumps. House 1st on left.

From Uckfield, A26 Lewes road. Right for Isfield & on for 1 mile. Right over level crossing & house on steep left bend with high fence & gate, approx. 0.5 miles on.

Major Graham & Jennifer Allt
South Paddock
Maresfield Park
Nr. Uckfield
Sussex TN22 2HA
Tel: 01825 762335

Celia Rigby
The Faulkners
Isfield
Sussex TN22 5XG
Tel: 01825 750344
Fax: 01825 750577

Entry No: 459   Map no: 5

Entry No: 460   Map no: 5

There's been a house here since the 12th century, though the present building dates from the 17th. The house is decorated in beautiful, traditional English style. The food is wonderful. Paris-trained Sarah conjures up an adventurous, but always beautifully-judged menu; sea bass or Sussex lamb, for example. She will also prepare you a hamper for Glyndebourne (10 minutes away) and the orange juice for breakfast is freshly squeezed. A perfect escape for cultured sybarites and there's a heated pool and a tennis court. The garden is spectacular.

Rooms: 3 twins, 2 en suite (1 bath, 1 shower); 1 with private bathroom.

Price: £45 p.p. Single supp. by arrangement.

Meals: Breakfast until 9.30am; lunch from £16, hampers £25, both available on request. Dinner, 3 courses, £22.

Closed: Never.

A listed 17th-century house beside the church in the heart of a tiny village, just 10 minutes from Glyndebourne. Alison was chef to the Beatles and will not only give you a delicious hamper, but tables and chairs, too. Willie is a former world rackets champion who gives tennis coaching, and, in the large, pretty garden, there is a tennis court and a swimming pool. You can relax by the inglenook fire in the drawing room after a walk on the Cuckoo Trail or the South Downs walk, then settle down for a great supper - maybe home-grown vegetables with local fish. This is an easy-going, fun and informal household.

Rooms: 1 double, 1 single sharing bathroom; single room let only to member of same party.

Price: £25 p.p. Single £30.

Meals: Breakfast times flexible; dinner £20. B.Y.O. wine.

Closed: Christmas & Easter.

0.5 miles past Halland on A22, south from Uckfield, 1st left off Shaw r'bout towards East Hoathly, on for 0.5 miles. Drive on left with post box. Where drive divides into 3, take central gravel drive.

From Boship r'bout on A22, A267. 1st right to Horsebridge & immed. left to Hellingly. House next to church, in Mill Lane.

Sarah Burgoyne
Old Whyly
East Hoathly
Sussex BN8 6EL
Tel: 01825 840216
Fax: 01825 840738

Alison & Willie Boone
Globe Place
Hellingly
Sussex BN27 4EY
Tel: 01323 844276
Fax: 01323 844276
E-mail: aliboone@talk21.com

Entry No: 461   Map no: 5

Entry No: 462   Map no: 6

A rural haven with chickens and geese and 40 acres of grazing surrounded by 1,000 of woodland; this is just the place for walkers and bird-watchers (woodpeckers and hobbys, for example). From the garden room you can see "the spot where Harold camped before he got it in the eye in 1066". The Collins are good, knowledgeable company and their home is peaceful and relaxing. With exposed beams, a woodburning stove in the sitting room and an inglenook fireplace in the dining room, there's stacks of woody character and cosy bedrooms with unspoilt views through lead-latticed windows. *Children over 10 welcome.*

Rooms: 3 doubles, all en suite (bath).

Price: From £24.50 p.p. Single occ. from £29.

Meals: Breakfast 8-10am; supper around £10, by arrangement.

Closed: January.

Julia lived in Paris for 12 years, loves to cook and is an effervescent presence in this gorgeous 15th-century farmhouse with its hipped roof and asymmetric beams. It was renovated in the '30s and of the three bedrooms the double is the most striking, decorated in pale colours and with a beautiful view down the Tillingham valley. The twin rooms are more simply furnished; one is predominantly rose floral, the other muted green and white. It's peaceful here - there are three acres of mature gardens - and only five miles from Rye. *Children over five welcome.*

Rooms: 1 double, en suite (shower); 2 twins/doubles with basins & private bathrooms.

Price: £35-£40 p.p. Single supp. £5.

Meals: Breakfast times flexible; dinner, 3 courses, £18, by arrangement.

Closed: Christmas.

From Battle on A271, 1st right to Heathfield. After 0.75 miles, right into drive.

From A21, left onto B2089 for Rye. 0.5 miles after Broad Oak, left, signed Peasmarsh. Downhill, 1st right, house signed 0.5 miles on left.

Paul & Pauline Collins
Fox Hole Farm
Kane Hythe Road
Battle
Sussex TN33 9QU
Tel: 01424 772053
Fax: 01424 773771

Julia & Thierry Sebline
Hayes Farm House
Hayes Lane, Peasmarsh
Rye, Sussex TN31 6XR
Tel: 01424 882345
Fax: 01424 882876
E-mail: julia.sebline@virgin.net
Web: freespace.virgin.net/hayes.farmhouse

Entry No: 463   **Map no: 6**

Entry No: 464   **Map no: 6**

A grand house where both Wellington and Nelson are said to have stayed. The 'best' and biggest four-poster bedroom is full of Victorian and Georgian furniture; there's another four-poster and a simpler, though comfortable, twin room with monogrammed counterpanes. The Princess is a dog-lover - she has five - and an engaging host (she will regale you with her family's history). The dining room and guest drawing room are classically smart. All this just a few minutes walk from the centre of Rye.

Rooms: 1 half-tester, 2 four-posters, all en suite (shower).

Price: £38-£55 p.p. No single supp.

Meals: Breakfast times flexible. Dinner available locally.

Closed: Christmas & Easter.

House and owner have a vibrancy that is unique. Sara has created a special atmosphere in her truly welcoming, rule-free townhouse in lovely history-laden Rye. You'll be enchanted by original art, fine antiques and masses of books; attention to detail and many personal touches herald the fact that this is a real home. Super, luxurious bedrooms have views of either a quiet cobbled street or the large, quiet garden (complete with a Smugglers' Watchtower). There is a bookroom for rainy days and a sitting room with open fire, too. Breakfasts are generous and organic/free-range.

Rooms: 2 four-posters, both en suite (1 bath & 1 shower).

Price: £35-£45 p.p. Single occ. £45-£65.

Meals: Breakfast 8-9.30am Mon-Sat; 8-10am Sun; dinner available nearby.

Closed: Never.

From A21, left after Robert Bridge r'bout for Rye (B2089). On reaching 1-way system, 1st left & over mini-r'bout. Next left onto A268, & house on immediate left after small bridge.

In Rye, follow signs to town centre & enter Old Town through Landgate Arch into High Street. West Street 3rd on left. House halfway up on left.

Princess Tia Romanoff
Mountsfield
Rye Hill
Rye
Sussex TN31 7NH
Tel: 01797 227105
Fax: 01797 227106

Sara Brinkhurst
Little Orchard House
West Street
Rye
Sussex TN31 7ES
Tel: 01797 223831
Fax: 01797 223831
Web: www.littleorchardhouse.com

Entry No: 465   **Map no:** 6

Entry No: 466   **Map no:** 6

The gorgeous house has been many things - wool store, school and former home of poet Conrad Potter Aiken: the dining room, now painted deep red and full of plants' books and busts, was an old Baptist chapel. Jenny is engagingly easy-going and has created a lovely atmosphere. The rooms are pretty, not fussy, with good furniture. There are old four-posters and a big attic room with beams, timber frames and views over roof tops to open country. There's a library for rainy days and a fire in winter. A perfect retreat among Rye's cobbled streets.

Rooms: 10 doubles, all en suite; 1 double, 1 single sharing bathroom, 1 honeymoon suite.

Price: £31.50-£52.50 p.p.

Meals: Breakfast 8-9.30am (Mon-Fri); 8.30-10am (Sat-Sun). Dinner available locally.

Closed: Never.

From London, into centre of Rye on A268, left off High St onto West St, then 1st right into Mermaid St. House on left. Private car park, £3 a day for guests.

Jenny Hadfield
Jeake's House
Mermaid Street
Rye
Sussex
Tel: 01797 222828
Fax: 01797 222623

Undeniably beautiful within, and solidly handsome without. Jane is a gifted interior decorator; the colours are splendid and nothing seems to be out of place. However, Jane and Richard are easy and open; Jane was a ballet dancer and is refreshingly new to this B&B thing. Richard has green fingers and grows the fruit that will appear in pretty bowls on your breakfast table. The kitchen is engagingly beamed and straight out of a smart magazine. There are some fine pieces of furniture, sofas to sink into and enough comfort to satisfy a pharaoh.

Rooms: 1 double/twin, en suite (shower/bath); 1 double/twin, en suite (shower).

Price: £35-£38 p.p. Single occ. by arrangement.

Meals: Breakfast times flexible; dinner £20.

Closed: Christmas & New Year.

A46 from Evesham or Stratford-upon-Avon, then exit signed Salford Priors. On entering village, turn right opp. church, signed Dunnington. House on right, approx. 1 mile on, after 2nd sign on right for Dunnington.

Jane Gibson & Richard Beach
Salford Farm House
Salford Priors, Nr. Evesham
Warwickshire WR11 5SG
Tel: 01386 870000
Fax: 01386 870300
E-mail: salfordfarmhouse@aol.com

A theatrical home: dark wood, reds and pinks dominate and, in one bedroom - more theatre - plush velvet curtains opening to the bathroom. The conversion of the 1737 barn is immaculate: the kitchen, with Aga and stone floors, gives onto a stunning patio and conservatory and drawing room; bedrooms and bathrooms are plush, big and comfortable. Denise, cheerful and kind, runs her B&B with careful attention to detail. Much rural charm, a large garden, excellent value and yet so close to Birmingham and the NEC. *Prior booking essential. Children over 12 welcome.*

Rooms: 1 double, 2 twins, all en suite (bath).

Price: £32.50 p.p. Single occ. £40.

Meals: Breakfast until 8.30am. Dinner available locally.

Closed: Never.

At M6 junc. 4, A446 for Lichfield. At sign to Coleshill South, get in right lane & turn off. From High St, turn into Maxstoke Lane. After 4 miles, 4th right. House 1st on left.

Mrs Denise Owen
Hardingwood House
Hardingwood Lane
Fillongley, Nr. Coventry
Warwickshire CV7 8EL
Tel: 01676 542579
Fax: 01676 541336

Cathy's sense of humour carries her through each gloriously eventful day. This is a paradise for families - there's so much room to play and so much to see: sheep, turkeys, geese and Saddleback pigs. The 1640 farmhouse was extended 25 years ago using old bricks and beams and the bathrooms have recently been upgraded. Tiny timbered corridors lead to large bedrooms with wooden floors and leaded windows (the family room has everything needed for a baby). Next door is the magnificent Big Pool where you can fish with a day ticket.

Rooms: 1 king-size with single & cot; 1 twin, both en suite (bath).

Price: From £25 p.p. Single supp. £7.50.

Meals: Breakfast times flexible; packed lunch £3 & children's high tea £3, dinner with home-reared meat, from £15 all by arrangement.

Closed: Christmas & New Year.

From M40, junc. 15, A46 for Coventry. Left onto A4177. 4.5 miles to Five Ways r'bout. 1st left, follow for 0.75 miles; signed down track on left.

Cathy Dodd
Shrewley Pools Farm
Haseley
Warwick
Warwickshire CV35 7HB
Tel: 01926 484315
E-mail: cathydodd@hotmail.com

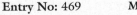

Wow! Hot bedroom colours make a change from the usual creams and chintzes - one's vibrant blue with a red ceiling, another yellow with blue and a further one is a super burnt orange, all with contemporary paintings. It's bold and vibrant, 'green' and fun - just like the lovely Prue. She's passionate about good food, too - organic and mostly vegetarian. Expect home-made bread, velvety egg puddings, succulent and stuffed mushrooms and a fresh fruit platter drizzled with lime and honey dressing. This substantial blue stone 1850s town house is right opposite Warwick's park and under a mile's riverside walk to the castle.

Rooms: 1 twin, en suite (bath & shower); 1 double, en suite (shower).

Price: From £27.50-£32.50. Single supp. £7.50.

Meals: Breakfast times flexible. Supper, by arrangement.

Closed: Occasionally.

On main Warwick to Leamington rd, directly opp. entrance to St Nicholas' Park.

Prue Hardwick
The Hare on the Park
3 Emscote Road
Warwick
Warwickshire CV34 4PH
Tel: 01926 491366
E-mail: pruespost@tesco.net
Web: www.thehareonthepark.co.uk

Entry No: 471   **Map no:** 10

Kim has the sort of kitchen city dwellers dream of: big and welcoming and it really is the hub of the house. She and John fizz with good humour and energy and take pride in those times when family and guests feel easy together. You will be offered tea on arrival, home-made jams for breakfast and perhaps even a guided walk round the fascinating, historic village. The house is large with a lovely garden, tennis court, terrace and croquet lawn. The rooms are big, soft and supremely comfortable with lovely pieces of furniture. A special place and genuine people.

Rooms: 1 twin/double; 1 double, with private bathrooms.

Price: From £25 p.p. Single supp. £8.

Meals: Breakfast times flexible; dinner, for four only, £20, by arrangement.

Closed: Never.

From Banbury, A361 north. At Byfield village sign, left into Twistle Lane, straight on to Priors Marston. 5th on left with cattle grid, after s-bend.

Kim & John Mahon
Marston House
Priors Marston
Southam, Warwickshire CV47 7RP
Tel: 01327 260297
Fax: 01327 262846
E-mail: john.mahon@coltel.co.uk
Web: www.ivabestbandb.co.uk

Entry No: 472   **Map no:** 10

"The quietest sleep I've had in years," said a guest. The peace, the views and the greenness will revive flagging spirits and soothe the frazzled. David and Julia are a generous, well-travelled and unassuming couple devoted to their ancient house and garden. Mallards glide over the pond and a stream runs by the 400-year-old yew. Inside, Cotswold stone walls, comfortable sofas, beamed dining and drawing room and huge inglenooks complement the bucolic scene, while uneven floors celebrate the character of this 300-year-old house.

Rooms: 1 twin, 1 double, sharing bath/shower room.

Price: £27 p.p. No single supp.

Meals: Breakfast times flexible. Excellent local pubs & restaurants nearby.

Closed: Christmas & New Year.

From A423, turn to Priors Hardwick. 1.8 miles on, left for Priors Hardwick. 1st hard left on S-bend ('No Through Rd' sign). Down bumpy farm lane, then right onto concrete road. House on right.

Julia & David Gaunt
Hollow Meadow House
Priors Hardwick
Southam
Warwickshire CV47 7SP
Tel: 01327 261540
Fax: 01327 261540

Entry No: 473   **Map no:** 10

Here's a big house in the country, minus the expected creaks and draughts and plus every mod con. Carpets are thick, beds four-poster and sumptuous; there's a new 'Oriental' room. This feels like a small hotel and there's even a helipad. Plush green sofas sit by the stone inglenook and you can have drinks here before eating an organic dinner in the candlelit conservatory. The garden is lush and landscaped and there are fields all around - look out for the fat Hebridean sheep. This is a fully organic, Soil Association registered farm. *Children over 12 welcome.*

Rooms: 3 four-posters, all en suite, 1 with dressing room.

Price: From £44 p.p. Single supp. £25.50.

Meals: Breakfast times flexible; dinner, 3 courses, £25.

Closed: Never.

From Stratford, A4200, over Clopton bridge & immed. left onto Tiddington Rd. 1st right onto Loxley Rd. Last house on left with white gates.

Ms Kate McGovern
Glebe Farm House
Loxley, Stratford-upon-Avon
Warwickshire CV35 9JW
Tel: 01789 842501
Fax: 01789 842501
E-mail: scorpiolimited@msn.com
Web: www.glebefarmhouse.com

Entry No: 474   **Map no:** 10

You can get from your bath to your seat in the Stratford theatre in 10 minutes, if you hurry. Perfect! This is a Grade II-listed thatched house, of 1501, a house of great and many beams. Even the barn where you sleep is 17th century, also thatched and listed Grade II. Each suite is magnificently accoutred, with its own sitting room and kitchenette, so you can peacefully enjoy a glass of wine post-performance. Breakfast - taken in the main house - is the time to be sociable here. Luxurious, beautiful, authentic and slap in the middle of a huge chunk of the best of England.

Rooms: 2 doubles, en suite (bath/shower).

Price: £30-£33 p.p. Single supp. £10.

Meals: Breakfast until 9am. Pub within 3 minutes' walk for dinner.

Closed: 1 December-7 January.

From Stratford, A422 Banbury road for 4 miles & turn off for Loxley. Through village & left at bottom of hill. 3rd house on right.

Mrs Anne Horton
Loxley Farm
Loxley
Warwick
Warwickshire CV35 9JN
Tel: 01789 840265
Fax: 01789 840645

Entry No: 475   **Map no:** 10

It's smart, stylish and full of personal touches. Angie decorates with strong colours. Chris, an interiors photographer, has an eye for arranging things; he also bakes bread most mornings. Flagstones and wooden floors downstairs; upstairs, one Art Deco-ish bedroom and the other decorated in warm shades of terracotta and cream, with cream sofa and dramatic canopied bed. The garden reaches out to the River Stour with its waterside willows and you can sit on the terrace watching the sun set over the North Cotswolds, or set off to explore the ancient ridge and furrow meadow.

Rooms: 1 double, 1 triple (double & single), both en suite (bath & shower).

Price: £30 p.p. Single supp. £15.

Meals: Breakfast 8.30am. Dinner available locally.

Closed: Christmas.

From Stratford, south on A3400 towards Shipston. After 3 miles, signed on right.

Angela & Chris Wright
Alderminster Farm, Alderminster
Nr. Stratford-upon-Avon
Warwickshire CV37 8BP
Tel: 01789 450774
Fax: 01789 450924
E-mail: chriswright72@hotmail.com
Web: www.tpointmc.demon.co.uk/alderminster/

Entry No: 476   **Map no:** 10

Spiky plants and driftwood in the garden - a refreshing change from the more familiar herbaceous borders and it would be hard to find a more secluded, peaceful retreat. Carolyn and John could not be nicer and every room feels right; seashell stencils and star-painted ceilings go perfectly with colour-washed walls. Bedrooms have wooden-latched doors to sunny, skylit bathrooms. The annexe room has its own entrance and a four-poster iron bedstead. They keep sheep, horses and poultry, so there are plenty of fresh eggs for breakfast. *Children over eight welcome.*

Rooms: 1 double/twin/family, en suite (bath/shower); 2 doubles, en suite (1 shower, 1 bath/shower).

Price: £20-£25 p.p. Single occ. from £28.

Meals: Breakfast times flexible. Dinner available locally.

Closed: Christmas.

From Stratford-upon-Avon, A422 to Pillerton Priors, then follow sign to Pillerton Hersey. There, turn down Oxhill Bridle Rd, opp. phone box. House at end. Or M40 junc. 12, 6 miles on B4451.

Carolyn & John Howard
Dockers Barn Farm
Oxhill Bridle Road
Pillerton Hersey, Warwick
Warwickshire CV35 0QB
Tel: 01926 640475
Fax: 01926 641747

Entry No: 477   **Map no: 10**

You'll be in your element if you fish or play tennis, for you can do both from the beautiful, landscaped gardens that slope gently down to the River Stour. Jane, a *Cordon Bleu* cook, runs her 16th- and 17th-century house with huge energy and friendliness. A pretty, blue twin bedroom and a single room are in a self-contained wing with its own large, elegant drawing and dining room; it's seductively easy to relax here. The A-shaped double, with ancient beams and oak furniture, is in the main part of the house; it has a lovely bathroom and shares the drawing and dining rooms.

Rooms: 1 twin, 1 single sharing private bathroom (single let only to members of the same party); 1 double with private bathroom.

Price: From £35 p.p. Single supp. by arrangement.

Meals: Breakfast until 9am (Mon-Sat); 10am (Sun); dinner, from £20, by arrangement.

Closed: Never.

From Stratford, follow A422 for 4 miles towards Banbury. After 4 miles, right at r'bout onto A429 for Halford. There, take 1st right. House with black & white timbers straight ahead.

Jane & William Pusey
The Old Manor House
Halford
Shipston on Stour
Warwickshire CV36 5BT
Tel: 01789 740264
Fax: 01789 740609
E-mail: wpusey@st-philips.co.uk

Entry No: 478   **Map no: 10**

An 1856 Victorian farmhouse, with log fires to warm your enthusiasm for a good walk on the Heart of England Way, or maybe a bike ride (cycles available). The views stretch on to folklore-sodden Meon Hill and if the stories of local witchcraft and other spookery fail to spark your imagination, there is every chance your bed will inspire you. The Angel Room has a pine box bed and a medieval frieze of flying angels. The two other rooms have four-posters with handmade quilts. Healthy and delicious breakfast menus change daily and make imaginative use of organic fruit from the orchard.

Rooms: 2 four-posters, en suite (shower); 1 twin/family room with private bath.

Price: From £30 p.p. No single supp.

Meals: Breakfast until 9am. Excellent local pubs.

Closed: Christmas Day.

Flagstoned floors, beamed ceilings, deep fireplaces, deep-set mullioned windows - pure Cotswold charm. Your sitting room has old books and polished furniture and the bedrooms, with low ceilings, are uncluttered. Zip-and-link beds in all the rooms; one ground-floor en suite room is suitable for guests with disabilities. There are broad paths and billowing plants and flowers that spill out between the courtyard paving stones; your hostess is a keen gardener and has some spectacular hostas, too. *Children over 12 welcome.*

Rooms: 3 twins/doubles, en suite (bath & shower); 1 single, en suite (shower).

Price: From £30 p.p. Single supp. £5.

Meals: Breakfast until 9.30am; supper, 2 courses, £15.50, by arrangement; B.Y.O. wine.

Closed: Never.

From Stratford, A3400 south, then B4632 (signposted Broadway & Mickleton) for 6 miles. Left for Upper Quinton. House 400 yds on left.

From Stratford-upon-Avon, A3400 towards Oxford. After 5 miles, right by church in Newbold-on-Stour & follow signs to Blackwell. Fork right on entering Blackwell. Entrance beyond thatched barn.

Mrs Gail Lyon
Winton House
The Green
Upper Quinton, Stratford-upon-Avon
Warwickshire CV37 8SX
Tel: 01789 720500
E-mail: gail@wintonhouse.com
Web: www.wintonhouse.com

Liz Vernon Miller
Blackwell Grange
Blackwell, Shipston-on-Stour
Warwickshire CV36 4PF
Tel: 01608 682357
Fax: 01608 682856
E-mail: sawdays@blackwellgrange.co.uk
Web: www.blackwellgrange.co.uk

Valerie was a student of fashion history and dotted around the Threlfalls' half of the 16th-century manor house are fashion prints, photographs, hatboxes, dressmakers' dummies... There are William Morris fabrics and paper in the dining room, a cosy guest sitting room in the gabled attic and a grand piano in the ballroom (concerts are held here). The Chinese guest room has many curios brought back from travels; the twin room is smaller. A conservatory looks onto a huge lawn - do look at the small Victorian vegetable garden with gravel walkways and the thatched Wendy House beneath giant copper beeches.

Rooms: 1 double, en suite (bath); 1 twin with private shower.

Price: £27-£32 p.p. Single supp. £7.

Meals: Breakfast until 9.50am. Dinner available locally.

Closed: Christmas & New Year.

In one hundred acres of farmland (mixed arable, suckler Jerseys and hay) the house is solid and traditional in a style familiar to farmhouse B&B habitués. There is an open fire in the dining room, a white cloth on the table, a baby chandelier and patterned curtains. The sitting room (yours) has two vast floral sofas and matching armchairs, pelmeted curtains, a piano, fire, and a grandfather clock. The comfort upstairs is of the same kind: big, soft beds with white covers, fitted carpets, walls with dados and prints, and floral curtains. It is quiet, friendly and authentic.

Rooms: 1 double, en suite (shower); 1 double/twin, en suite (bath/shower).

Price: £30 p.p. Single supp. £5.

Meals: Breakfast times flexible. Dinner available locally.

Closed: Occasionally.

From Cirencester, A419 south for 4 miles, leaving dual carriageway on left, signed Ashton Keynes. Left immed. after White Hart pub, 100 yds on, through stone pillars, house on right.

From Swindon or Cirencester, A419 to Cricklade, then B4040 for Malmesbury. 3 miles on, sign on left. Go to end of drive (0.5 miles).

Valerie & Roger Threlfall
1 Cove House
Ashton Keynes
Wiltshire SN6 6NS
Tel: 01285 861226
Fax: 01285 861226
E-mail: roger@covehouse.co.uk

Claire Read
Leighfield Lodge Farm
Malmesbury Road, Leigh
Swindon
Wiltshire SN6 6RH
Tel: 01666 860241
Fax: 01666 860241
E-mail: claireread@leighfieldlodge.fsnet.co.uk

Entry No: 481   **Map no:** 4

Entry No: 482   **Map no:** 4

Lots of thoughtful touches - carefully chosen books in the bedrooms, newspapers at breakfast if you wish, cosy chairs in the guest sitting room and a fire, too. Helen makes her own bread and jams and sets you up for breakfast in the dining room where you have views of the vast lawned garden, magnolias, chestnuts and lovely high stone walls that abut All Saints church. There's a tennis court out there, too. Fine flagstoned floors, little window seats and a carved lintel that dates the house as 1703... it is delightful and comfortable.

Rooms: 2 doubles, 1 en suite, 1 with private bathroom.

Price: £30 p.p. Single supp. £5.

Meals: Breakfast until 10am; dinner, 3 courses, £17.50, by arrangement.

Closed: Christmas & New Year.

Delightful quiet seclusion whatever the season; on colder days, large comfy sofas envelop you and fires warm you; in summer, you eat in the cool shade of the arbour, draped in wisteria and climbing roses. The garden is exceptional. The bright conservatory with its huge oak table is filled with a profusion of flowers and colour. Garden vegetables and herbs (mostly organic) are used to magnificent effect. Bedrooms are quiet with lovely country views and Liz and Colin are so easy and flexible that you quickly feel like a visiting friend.

Rooms: 1 twin, en suite (bath); 1 twin with private bathroom.

Price: £27.50-£30 p.p. Single supp. £7.50 by arrangement.

Meals: Breakfast times flexible; dinner, 2-3 courses, £14-£18.

Closed: Christmas & Easter.

A429 Malmesbury to Cirencester road. In Crudwell, at Plough, right signed Minety/Oaksey. Straight on, then left between church & tithe barn pillars.

From A429, B4040 through Charlton, past Horse & Groom pub. 0.5 miles on, left signed 'Bullocks Horn - No Through Road'. Continue to end of lane. Turn right. House 1st on left.

Helen & Philip Carter
Manor Farmhouse
Crudwell
Malmesbury
Wiltshire SN16 9ER
Tel: 01666 577375
Fax: 01666 823523
E-mail: user785566@aol.com

Colin & Liz Legge
Bullocks Horn Cottage
Charlton
Malmesbury
Wiltshire SN16 9DZ
Tel: 01666 577600
Fax: 01666 577905
E-mail: legge@bullockshorn.clara.co.uk

Entry No: 483 **Map no: 4**

Entry No: 484 **Map no: 4**

A delightfully natural yet stylish home - it's a charming 17th-century Cotswold Manor farmhouse where you'll receive super hospitality. Beautiful bedrooms look to the church and paddocks with horses grazing, or to the stable yard with its tumbling blooms and dozing dogs. Breakfasts are delicious and guests can enjoy either traditional farmhouse fare, smoked salmon with scrambled eggs or a typically Continental breakfast with fresh fruits and hot, home made breads. The delightful villages of Castle Combe and Lacock are just a stone's throw away. *Children over 12 welcome.*

Rooms: 2 doubles, both en suite (bath); 1 twin with private bathroom.

Price: £30 p.p. Single supp. £5.

Meals: Breakfast until 9.30am. Dinner available locally.

Closed: Christmas.

Wellington the parrot will sing you the Archers' signature tune if he's in the mood. This 16th-century farmhouse, with its charming melee of comfy sofas, books, pets and pretty china, breathes an air of warmth and easy fun. The heart and soul of it all is Julia – painter, gilder, fine-flapjack-maker and all round excellent cook - and Edward, who cycles to work each day (they have a picture-framing business) whatever the weather. Your bedroom, reached via the studio-cum-library – once a grainstore – gives you field views and perfect peace. A home-from-home that arty types, especially, will love. *Children over 10 welcome.*

Rooms: 1 double with private bathroom.

Price: £30 p.p. Single supp. £10.

Meals: Breakfast until 9.30am; packed lunch £4; supper £12, by arrangement.

Closed: Occasionally.

From M4 A429 to Cirencester (junc. 17). After 200 yds 1st left, signposted Grittleton; at Grittleton follow signs to Alderton. Farmhouse near church.

A4 from Bath to Chippenham. Right towards Bradford-on-Avon & left through Bathford to Kingsdown. Right to South Wraxall & follow road for about a mile. Left at stone cottage. Farm on right.

Victoria Lippiatt
Manor Farm
Alderton
Malmesbury
Wiltshire SN14 6NL
Tel: 01666 840271
Web: www.themanorfarm.co.uk

Julia Rooth
Mount Pleasant Farm
South Wraxall
Bradford-on-Avon
Wiltshire BA15 2SD
Tel: 01225 864580
Fax: 01225 868440
E-mail: juliarooth@rooths.co.uk

Entry No: 485　　　**Map no: 4**　　　**Entry No: 486**　　　**Map no: 4**

The sunken vine-hung, thyme-carpeted arbour and gazebo are magical in summer and there is much in the deliciously walled garden to hold your attention. Doi is relaxed and friendly: she does B&B because she loves it - breakfast is cooked just as you want it, when you want it. Gently-decorated bedrooms have space, views, flowers and old photographs; one has a half-tester bed. The dark blue dining room has wooden floors and a solid oak table with tapestry chairs and the drawing room, French windows overlooking the garden and an open fire.

Rooms: 1 triple with private bathroom; 2 doubles, 1 en suite (bath), 1 with private bath & shower.

Price: £25 p.p. Single supp. £5.

Meals: Breakfast times flexible. Dinner available locally.

Closed: Christmas.

In an ancient hamlet only a few miles from Bath, this impeccable house was, until 15 years ago, 'just' an early 19th-century barn. Few traces of its workday roots remain - it is a large, light house, carpeted and decorated in pale colours. The huge drawing room, with big dried flower arrangements, ornate frames and chintzy sofa has sliding doors giving onto eight acres of gardens, with tennis and, in the summer, croquet. Bedrooms are smaller, with skylights and sloping beamed ceilings, yet beds are big. Helga and David look after their visitors with great care.

Rooms: 1 twin/double, 1 double with private or shared bathroom.

Price: £30 p.p. Single supp. £5.

Meals: Breakfast times flexible; dinner, £15, by arrangement. Also excellent local pubs.

Closed: Never.

From Malmesbury B4042 towards Wootton Bassett. Left to Lea & Charlton. In Lea, right opposite school. House along drive through fields.

From M4 junction 17, west along A420. Right to Upper Wraxall. 1st left in village opposite village green. House at end of private drive.

Tony & Doi Newman
Winkworth Farm
Lea
Nr. Malmesbury
Wiltshire SN16 9NH
Tel: 01666 823267
E-mail: doinewman@winkworth89.freeserve.co.uk

Helga & David Venables
The Coach House
Upper Wraxall
Nr. Bath
Wiltshire SN14 7AG
Tel: 01225 891026
Fax: 01225 892355
E-mail: venables@compuserve.com

Entry No: 487   Map no: 4

Entry No: 488   Map no: 4

It is a rare treat to have your milk fresh from the cow - the Helyers have a fine pedigree herd of Holstein Friesians. This rather grand Victorian Gothic farmhouse is a working, tenanted arable and dairy farm. There are very large, pretty bedrooms with crisp linen, period furniture, impressive countryside views, a baby grand and a billiard room. Everything is grand but cosy and the Helyers are very friendly. Terrace doors are thrown open for an *al fresco* summer breakfast. The estate is 1,400 acres and an SSSI, treasured for its wild flowers and butterflies. *Children by arrangement.*

Rooms: 1 twin/double, en suite (shower); 1 twin, 1 double/family, both with private bathroom or shower room.

Price: £25-£27 p.p. Single occ. £35-£42.

Meals: Breakfast times flexible. Dinner available locally.

Closed: Christmas & New Year.

Leave A303 at junc. with A36 & follow signs for Salisbury. 2 miles on, right for The Langfords. In Steeple Langford, right for Hanging Langford. At T-junc. opposite village hall, left for Little Langford. House 0.25 miles on left.

Patricia Helyer
Little Langford Farmhouse
Little Langford
Salisbury, Wiltshire SP3 4NR
Tel: 01722 790205
Fax: 01722 790086
E-mail: bandb@littlelangford.co.uk
Web: www.dmac.co.uk/llf

Entry No: 489   Map no: 4

Evidence of artistic flair everywhere - patchwork, tapestries, rush and cane work; Sue, easy-going and articulate, teaches country crafts in her workshop. The fine George I farmhouse is in a quiet spot on the edge of the New Forest and has a lovely walled garden with fruit cages, a Wendy House and three Labradors snuffling about. Provençal paintings and fabrics in the breakfast room and orange trees in the beautiful conservatory. Bedrooms are ample and charming with patchwork quilts, brass beds, stencils. Sue, a Blue Badge Guide, can tell you about the area.

Rooms: 1 twin/family, 2 doubles, all en suite (shower); 1 single with private bathroom.

Price: £21-£25 p.p. Single supp. £10.

Meals: Breakfast until 9am. Dinner available locally.

Closed: Christmas & New Year.

From Salisbury, A36 towards Southampton. Approx. 5 miles on, look for Brickworth Lane on left, 200 yds before lights at junction A36/A27. Farmhouse at top of lane on right.

Sue Barry
Brickworth Farmhouse
Brickworth Lane
Whiteparish, Salisbury
Wiltshire SP5 2QE
Tel: 01794 884663
Fax: 01794 884186

Entry No: 490   Map no: 4

Wiltshire

A magical garden embraces this enchanting Queen Anne farmhouse. Watercolours, rich oils, polished antiques and the charm of your hosts fill the family home. You could wallow for hours in the roll-topped bath in the splendid oak-panelled bathroom. All the bedrooms are filled with light; one has three glorious views, another has a delightful intimacy, as does the sitting room just down the book-lined hall. Meander down to the swans on the river, stride out across the meadows or fish on the farm's lakes. Glorious. *Children over 12 welcome.*

Rooms: 2 twins/doubles, 1 en suite (bath and shower), 1 with private bathroom; 1 double, en suite (shower).

Price: £25-£30 p.p. Single supp. £10 in high season.

Meals: Breakfast times flexible. Good pub/restaurant nearby.

Closed: Christmas.

From Salisbury on A36 towards Southampton, right immed. at dual carriageway (no signs). Right at signs to Downton. Farm on right after 2 miles.

Ian & Annette Fergie-Woods
Witherington Farm
Nr. Downton
Salisbury
Wiltshire SP5 3QT
Tel: 01722 710222
Fax: 01722 710405

Entry No: 491   **Map no: 4**

Toast your toes on a warm stone floor in this quadrangle conversion. What were once Victorian agricultural outbuildings are now a harpsichord workshop and B&B. The geothermal underfloor heating system is just one of the initiatives that has won this environmentally-friendly set-up an award. Bedrooms, which feed off a long corridor, are functionally furnished and perfectly lit. Walls are white or bare brick, ceilings high and beamy: all is simplicity and calm. You'll want for nothing with Gail in charge (her blueberry pancakes are wonderful). Peter, her harpsichord-maker husband, is charming, too.

Rooms: 1 double, 1 double/twin, 2 singles, all en suite (shower).

Price: From £27.50-£30 p.p.

Meals: Breakfast times flexible. Restaurants locally.

Closed: December & January.

A354 from Salisbury to Blandford. In Coombe Bissett, right to Broadchalke. Ebblesway is signed 1 mile after White Hart on right behind Stoke Manor.

Gail & Peter Smalley
Ebblesway Courtyard
High Road, Broadchalke, Salisbury
Wiltshire SP5 5EF
Tel: 01722 780182
Fax: 01722 780482
E-mail: enquiries@ebbleswaycourtyard.co.uk
Web: www.ebbleswaycourtyard.co.uk

Entry No: 492   **Map no: 4**

Its origins lie way back in 1189, other bits were added in the 16th century. If you cherish a yearning to be close to the land and its ancient rhythms, this dynamic, hardworking farmhouse, full of character, people and pets, is for you. You come not to be feted, but to join in with it all. Meals are taken around a 400-year-old monastery refectory table; the food oozes country freshness and its nutritional values are satisfyingly 'old-world'. Downstairs is homely - slightly chaotic, even - but bedrooms are ordered and two have been freshly-decorated. Janet - robust and hardworking - is devoted to hunting and dressage.

Rooms: 1 king-size, en suite (shower); 1 twin, en suite (bath); 2 singles with either private bath or shower.

Price: £23-£28 p.p.

Meals: Breakfast 7.30-9am; dinner, 4 courses inc. wine, £20 by arrangement; reduction for 2 courses.

Closed: 23-31 December.

From Devizes, A360 to Salisbury or A342 to Andover. After 4 miles right on B3098. Manor 1 mile west of Urchfont.

Mrs Janet Firth
Eastcott Manor
Easterton
Devizes
Wiltshire SN10 4PL
Tel: 01380 813313

Entry No: 493   Map no: 4

Folded into the most stunning countryside, this Grade II-listed, one-time butcher's shop has been in Darea's family for years. Stylishly cluttered and sparkingly clean, there are beautiful objects and lovely pieces at every turn. Darea's enthusiasm for life, books and travel is infectious and she can identify every rich and rare specimen in her garden, keeps detailed diaries and albums of her many travels and (fortunately) hasn't thrown anything away. Your chintzy bedrooms are seductively cosy. Stonehenge, Longleat and Stourhead beckon; hostess, home and countryside are a treat.

Rooms: 1 twin, en suite (bath); 1 twin/double with washbasin and private bath.

Price: £30 p.p. Single supp. £5.

Meals: Breakfast until 9.30am. Dinner available locally.

Closed: Occasionally.

Leave A303 at junc. with A36 & follow signs for Wylye. In village, cross river & round sharp left-hand bend. House 25 yds on right.

Mrs Darea Browne
Perrior House
Wylye
Warminster
Wiltshire BA12 0QU
Tel: 01985 248228
E-mail: darea.browne@amserve.net

Entry No: 494   Map no: 4

The vibes are good - and not just because this is crop circle and Stonehenge country. Val and David moved out of London in search of peace; and here they've found it. Val is an enthusiastic gardener and specialist decorator. Her style isn't to over-design anything but there are subtle touches everywhere. Each room has lovely fabrics and bed linen, and bathrooms are bright and fun; the twin has hand-painted wallpaper. You have a cosy sitting room, too, with an open fireplace, and a more formal dining room for Aga-cooked breakfasts.

Rooms: 1 double, en suite; 1 twin, 1 single, sharing private bathroom.

Price: From £30 p.p.

Meals: Breakfast times flexible; dinner by arrangement. Dinner available locally.

Closed: Occasionally.

"'Splendid, sunny and sumptuous' are perfect words to sum up this house," said our inspector. Richard, a wine enthusiast and Pippa, a skilled cook, cosset you in huge style; the whole early Georgian house is elegantly furnished and decorated. Bedrooms are large and luxurious and from the triple-aspect drawing room you look out through French windows onto manicured lawns bordered by mature trees. There's a superb grass tennis court, magnificent walking and two first-class riding stables nearby. In 1643 the Battle of Roundway was fought on the Down behind the house.

Rooms: 2 large twins/doubles, both en suite (bath); 1 double with private bathroom.

Price: £35-£40 p.p. Single supp. £20.

Meals: Breakfast times flexible; dinner, for 4 or more, £22, by arrangement.

Closed: Christmas & Easter.

From Marlborough, A345 through Pewsey. 3 miles on, at Woodbridge Inn r'bout, right to Hilcott. House 2nd on left over cattle grid.

West along A4. Left just before Calne for Heddington. 2 miles to Ivy Inn & left at T-junc. House on left opp. church, 50 yds on.

Val & David Maclay
Hilcott Farm House
Hilcott
Marlborough
Wiltshire SN9 6LE
Tel: 01672 851372
Fax: 01672 851192

Richard & Pippa Novis
Heddington Manor
Heddington
Nr. Calne
Wiltshire SN11 0PN
Tel: 01380 850240
Fax: 01380 859176
E-mail: richardnovis@compuserve.com

Entry No: 495   Map no: 4

Entry No: 496   Map no: 4

Flagstone floors lead you into book-lined rooms scattered with family photographs and fresh flowers - stylishly cluttered, it's a seductively easy place to settle into. Clarissa is a professional cook and looks after you with bundles of energy and enthusiasm. Bedrooms with sprigged papers are bright and fresh: walls and 'throws' are cream, beds are wooden. The sunny yellow ground floor bedroom has garden views and there's a guest sitting room, too. Five acres of gardens include an orchard, vegetable garden, tennis court, pool, and strutting chickens that provide breakfast eggs - you have fresh raspberries in season, too.

Rooms: 1 twin, en suite (shower); 1 twin/double, en suite (bath); 1 double with private bathroom.

Price: From £28 p.p. Single occ. from £35.

Meals: Breakfast times flexible; dinner, 4 courses, £25.

Closed: Never.

From Marlborough, A346 Salisbury road for 3 miles. Right to Wootton Rivers. In village, right (opp. Royal Oak pub) & drive for 0.7 miles. Drive on right after sign for Clench Common.

Clarissa Roe
Clench Farmhouse
Clench, Nr. Marlborough
Wiltshire SN8 4NT
Tel: 01672 810264
Fax: 01672 811458
E-mail: clarissaroe@clenchfarmhouse.co.uk
Web: www.clenchfarmhouse.co.uk

Entry No: 497   **Map no: 4**

Bill has applied his considerable artistic flair – he paints in oils and watercolours – to the renovation of this 17th-century thatched cottage. The A-frame sitting room has bold Chinese yellow walls, three plump sofas, light wooden floor and books – it is unintimidatingly stylish. The bedrooms are in similar vein and Bill and Felicity are easy, cultured hosts. There's a heated swimming pool, which you can use, and a sunken Italianate garden whose borders are edged with clouds of lavender. On sunny days or summer evenings you can shelter, colonial style, under a tiled loggia with rattan furniture. Perfect. *Children by arrangement.*

Rooms: 1 double, en suite; 1 double, 1 twin, sharing private bathroom.

Price: £22-£26 p.p. Single supp. £5.

Meals: Breakfast times flexible; dinner £15, by arrangement.

Closed: Rarely.

From Marlborough, A346 Salisbury Rd south. At r'bout ending Burbage bypass, take B3087 Pewsey Rd. Right at x-roads 0.3 miles on. 1st house on right.

Felicity & Bill Mather
Westcourt Bottom
165 Westcourt
Burbage
Wiltshire SN8 3BW
Tel: 01672 810924
Fax: 01672 810924
E-mail: westcourt.b-and-b@virgin.net

Entry No: 498   **Map no: 4**

You could be a hundred miles from Marlborough, not two. Here is a lovely Queen Anne farmhouse tucked under chalk hills in the middle of the most extensive bluebell woods in the country. Elizabeth and Christopher, who have lived here for years, love sharing their home. Bedrooms are fresh, white and cosy, with painted pine furniture and modern patchwork quilts and guests have their own sitting room. The sun-trap garden is full of roses and lavender and views of the surrounding 25 rolling acres – marvellous walking country. Your horse is welcome, too.

Rooms: 2 doubles, 1 en suite (bath), 1 with private bathroom.

Price: £22.50-£26 p.p. Single supp. £5.

Meals: Breakfast times flexible; packed lunch £3.50. Good restaurants locally.

Closed: Christmas & New Year.

In the valley of the Kennet River - which flows briskly past the foot of an immaculate lawn - is this exquisitely decorated home. The house looks every inch a dolls' house, but Jeremy and Heather, friendly and relaxed, add a deft human touch. The elegance of excellent breakfasts taken in the conservatory is balanced by the comforting hubbub emanating from the family kitchen. There's a sitting room for you with an open fire and, upstairs, the cleverly converted bedrooms are ingeniously clustered around the chimney breast. Time here slips by effortlessly; many people come to visit the crop circles.

Rooms: 1 double, en suite (bath); 1 twin, 1 single sharing bathroom.

Price: £30 p.p. Single £35.

Meals: Breakfast times flexible; lunch/packed lunch from £3, available on request. Dinner available locally.

Closed: Christmas.

From Marlborough, A4 west for 2 miles. 1st left after end of 40mph limit, signed Clatford. Over x-roads, farm 1.5 miles on right through 5-bar gate.

From Hungerford, A4 towards Marlborough. After 7 miles, right towards Stitchcombe, down hill (bear left at barn) & left at T-junc. On entering village, house 2nd on left.

Elizabeth & Christopher Morgan-Smith
Clatford Park Farm
Marlborough
Wiltshire SN8 4DZ
Tel: 01672 861646

Jeremy & Heather Coulter
Fisherman's House
Mildenhall
Nr. Marlborough
Wiltshire SN8 2LZ
Tel: 01672 515390
Fax: 01672 519009

Entry No: 499   Map no: 4

Entry No: 500   Map no: 4

Good food, good wines (80 on the list) and a warm welcome await your arrival. Your hosts are accommodating - capable, friendly Ann, who does the cooking, and Tony, who imports wines - and their combined knowledge and palpable enjoyment are on show at meal times. When they held occasional 'Wine Weekends' they discovered that they loved entertaining so much that they threw open the doors of their home full-time. Bedrooms are spic-and-span, large, too, and overlook the long garden with views of the Malvern Hills.

Rooms: 1 twin/double; 1 double, both en suite (bath); 1 double with private bathroom.

Price: £25.50-£28.50 p.p. Single occ. £32. Discounts for longer stays; winter breaks available.

Meals: Breakfast 8-9am; dinner, 4 courses, £16.90.

Closed: Christmas & New Year.

From M50 junc. 1, onto A38 for Worcester. After 1.5 miles, left for Upton-on-Severn & cross River Severn. At T-junc., right onto B4211. Left onto B4209 for Malvern Wells. Farm 3rd on right.

Ann & Tony Addison
Old Parsonage Farm
Hanley Castle
Worcester
Worcestershire WR8 0BU
Tel: 01684 310124
Fax: 01684 310124
E-mail: OPWines@aol.com

Entry No: 501   **Map no: 9**

Here is a 12th-century timber frame house that has been dressed up in smart Georgian attire - it wears it well and surprises you with its beamy interior. The house sits at the foot of the majestic Malvern Hills, so there are fine views; all around the house the Archers have 26 acres and a two-acre trout-stocked lake (you may fly-fish). The dazzling black-and-white floored hall leads to antique-filled dining and drawing rooms. Bedrooms are large and the house Scotch awaits you. Elizabeth breeds and shows miniature horses.

Rooms: 1 twin, en suite (shower); 1 twin, 1 twin/double, en suite (bath/shower).

Price: £35 p.p. Single supp. £10.

Meals: Breakfast until 9.30am. Dinner available locally.

Closed: Never.

West on A4104 to Upton-upon-Severn. Once there, cross river, left up main street, continue for 3 miles until red phone box on left. Left at sign & take left fork.

Philip & Elizabeth Archer
Welland Court
Upton-upon-Severn
Worcestershire WR8 0ST
Tel: 01684 594426
Fax: 01684 594426
E-mail: archer@wellandcourt.demon.co.uk

Entry No: 502   **Map no: 9**

There has been a watermill on this site since the 14th century. Today the spectacular, beamed Granary is a 40-foot long kitchen-cum-dining-cum-sitting area; it's such a sociable space and Ann can chat to guests while preparing an all-organic breakfast with fruit from the garden. The huge curved beams in the bedrooms are ancient ship's timbers from Gloucester Docks. You are just 10-minutes' walk from Broadway, yet mercifully feel miles from the masses. Large bedrooms, two grand pianos which guests can use and kind hosts - Ann, a professional musician, and Hugh a disabled war veteran.

Rooms: 2 doubles, both with extra single, both en suite (shower).

Price: £37.50 p.p. Single occ. £45.50.

Meals: Breakfast until 9am. Dinner available locally.

Closed: Never.

"Guests staying here have everything my friends would have - biscuits by the bed, magazines, books, bath essences," says Christina. Here, in her listed limestone farmhouse that dates from 1820, she pampers guests without being overly solicitous. The house is deceptively big, with a cottagey drawing room and a modern open kitchen with sofa. The bedroom is a suite separated from the house by a latch door. There are panoramic views over rolling countryside. Newsham is in an AONB so do explore the waterfalls, moorland, castles and exquisite villages. A handy stopover en route to Scotland.

Rooms: 1 twin, en suite (bath & shower). Extra twin available for member of same family.

Price: £25 p.p.

Meals: Breakfast times flexible; dinner, 2-3 courses, from £12-£15, by arrangement.

Closed: Christmas & New Year.

From Oxford, A44 to Broadway. Take Snowshill Road out of Broadway & after 0.75 miles, Mill signed on right. Continue to end of drive.

From Scotch Corner west on A66. Approx. 7 miles on, down hill. Left to Newsham. Through village. 2nd left for Helwith. House on right at top, name on gate.

Hugh & Ann Verney
The Mill
Snowshill Road
Broadway
Worcestershire WR12 7JS
Tel: 01386 858298

Christina Farmer
Hill Top
Newsham
Richmond
Yorkshire DL11 7QX
Tel: 01833 621513
E-mail: cdfarmer@lineone.net

Entry No: 503   Map no: 9

Entry No: 504   Map no: 15

What an entrance! A Virginia creeper covers the outside, lilies fill the hall with a lingering fragrance and Richard's ancestors look down from the stone stairs. The house was once bigger and what remains is the Victorian section of a Georgian mansion. Now a manageable size, the house is in tiptop condition and very comfortable. A sense of space remains, with high, plaster-worked ceilings and pale bedrooms. Fireplaces everywhere, big baths, high beds, large windows onto the beautiful grounds and a terraced lawn that runs down to the Tees. You can fish, play tennis or croquet.

Rooms: 2 twins, both with private bathrooms.

Price: £30 p.p. No single supp.

Meals: Breakfast times flexible; dinner, 2-3 courses, from £20, by arrangement.

Closed: 10 December-1 February.

From A1, exit onto B6275. North for 4.2 miles. Turn into drive (on left before Piercebridge) & take 1st right fork.

One of our favourites - the whole place continues to amaze and captivate guests. In every room and in every corner of the *breathtaking* garden, the marriage of natural beauty and sophistication exists in a state of bliss. The four Doric columns at the entrance draw you through the hall into the dining room and to views of the Swale Valley. Beds from Heals, period furniture, cast-iron baths, myriad prints and paintings, dashes of exotica and one double bed so high you wonder how to get onto it. Tim and Austin, both ex-English teachers are excellent, engaging hosts.

Rooms: 1 double, 1 twin, both en suite (bath & shower); 1 double with private bathroom and sitting room.

Price: £35 p.p. Single supp. £10.

Meals: Breakfast until 10am. Dinner available in Richmond.

Closed: Never.

Next door to Halifax Building Society, opposite side of Barclays at bottom of Market Place. Green front door with small brass plaque.

Caroline & Richard Wilson
Cliffe Hall
Piercebridge
Darlington
Yorkshire DL2 3SR
Tel: 01325 374322
Fax: 01325 374947
E-mail: petal@cliffehall.freeserve.co.uk

Austin Lynch & Tim Culkin
Millgate House
Richmond
Yorkshire DL10 4JN
Tel: 01748 823571
Fax: 01748 850701
E-mail: oztim@millgatehouse.demon.co.uk
Web: www.millgatehouse.com

Entry No: 505   Map no: 15   **Entry No: 506   Map no: 15**

Trompe-l'œil, Persian rugs and period colours sit beautifully in this elegant Georgian town house. It is a short stroll from the centre of this pretty, old market town with its castle ramparts, theatre, pubs and Saturday market; step off the cobbled street and you find yourself in a country garden with stunning views of the Swale Valley. Guest rooms are on the ground floor - comfortable beds and pure cotton sheets. And there's a wonderful view of Easby Abbey.

Rooms: 1 twin with private bathroom; 1 double, en suite (shower).

Price: From £25 p.p. Single supp. £6.

Meals: Breakfast times flexible. Dinner available locally.

Closed: Christmas.

If feels as if you are caught in a tranquil time-warp; there is no TV, just utter calm and windows that frame beautiful views of Wensleydale. In the heart of the Yorkshire Dales National Park, this is a superb base for walkers. Gail and Ann bake their own bread and make jams and marmalade. Their delicious dinners are prepared with fresh, local produce. Two bedrooms have four-posters and all have those views. If you're arriving by car, take the 'over-the-top' road from Buckden to Hawes for the stunning countryside. Expect a real welcome from their two Labradors.

Rooms: 2 four-posters, 1 twin, 1 double, all sharing bathroom or shower room.

Price: £20-£21 p.p. Single supp. £5-£8.

Meals: Breakfast 8.30am; dinner, 4 courses, £14.50 (not Thurs); good value wine list.

Closed: 31 October-mid-February.

From Scotch Corner (A1 30 miles north of Wetherby), follow signs to Richmond. In Richmond, left at library & left into Frenchgate. House at top on right with black railings.

Approx. 320 yds off A684, on road north out of Hawes, signposted Muker & Hardraw.

Elizabeth & Ken Parham
58 Frenchgate
Richmond
Yorkshire DL10 7AG
Tel: 01748 823227
E-mail: liz@parham.f9.co.uk

Gail Ainley & Ann Macdonald
Brandymires
Muker Road
Hawes
Yorkshire DL8 3PR
Tel: 01969 667482

Entry No: 507   **Map no: 15**

Entry No: 508   **Map no: 15**

Rebuilt in 1810 after the ravages of plague and fire, a perfect Wensleydale village remains forgotten by time. Four 17th-century almshouses have become Rookery Cottage. It faces the village green and its fine, wood-panelled dining room was once the village post office. Spotless bedrooms, with cottage garden views, are decorated with refreshing simplicity; each has a painted basin, lovely linen and dried flowers. There's a conservatory for guests, too. Home-made jams and marmalades for breakfast and, perhaps, a kedgeree made from Ronnie's catch of the day. Dine at the pub opposite - one of the North Country's finest.

Rooms: 1 twin, 1 double, both with basin, sharing bathroom.

Price: £24-£29 p.p. Single supp. £10.

Meals: Breakfast 8.30-9am. Packed lunch £4.50 p.p. Excellent country inn opposite for dinner.

Closed: Never.

From Masham, A6108. Leyburn is 8 miles on. House on left, opposite Blue Lion Country Inn.

Mrs Ursula Bussey
Rookery Cottage
East Witton, Leyburn
Yorkshire DL8 4SN
Tel: 01969 622918
Fax: 01969 622918
E-mail: ursulabussey@aol.com
Web: www.rookerycottage.co.uk

Entry No: 509   **Map no: 15**

Gerry is the only person to have won the Grand National (1960 on Merryman II), and started it (in 1996). A portrait of the winning pair hangs in the dining/living room. He's a happy man. The bedrooms differ - one, a twin, sports an exciting cherry-red wall, the second, cream and peppermint colours. A double has a drawn threadwork bedspread. Views are of paddock and moorland. A mecca for real ale enthusiasts, Masham is the home of both Theakston and Black Sheep breweries. It is also boisterous field sports country, so possibly Pasture House is not for the objectors.

Rooms: 2 doubles, 1 twin with basins, all sharing bathroom & wc.

Price: £18 p.p. No single supp.

Meals: Breakfast times flexible; dinner, 3 courses, £10. B.Y.O. wine.

Closed: Christmas Day.

From A6108 (Ripon to Richmond road), turn off 0.35 miles north of Masham, towards Healey. Continue through Healey to junction signed Colsterdale. Take right fork. House 1st on left.

Avril & Gerry Scott
Pasture House
Healey
Masham
Yorkshire HG4 4LJ
Tel: 01765 689149
Fax: 01765 689990

Entry No: 510   **Map no: 15**

Oriella goes the extra mile for you and her flamboyancy and style make light of the practicalities of having guests. She is arty, fun-loving and kind and gives you a place to unwind, read, listen to music - you can wander into the totally secluded garden, too, and sit beneath aged copper beeches. There are tapestries, mirrors, thick oak tables and oriental pieces, something to catch the eye at every turn. The bedrooms are big, chintzy/paisley and the suite has a seven-foot square bed with the down of 226 ducks to snuggle under! A Georgian jewel.

Rooms: 1 suite, 1 double, 1 twin, all en suite (2 with bath/shower, 1 with bath).

Price: £45-£50 p.p. No single supp.

Meals: Breakfast times flexible; dinner, 4 courses, £25.

Closed: Never.

From A1 at Leeming Bar, A684 to Bedale. 0.5 miles out of town, turn off A684 to Newton-Le-Willows. Right at T-junc., left at Wheatsheaf pub, then immediate right through gates.

Oriella Featherstone
The Hall
Newton-Le-Willows
Bedale
Yorkshire DL8 1SW
Tel: 01677 450210
Fax: 01677 450014

Entry No: 511   **Map no: 15**

A perfectly proper house run with faultless precision by John and Harriet - former wine importer and interior decorator respectively. The walk to Fountains Abbey and Studley Royal is a real treat (the latter are the most complete remains of a Cistercian abbey in Britain); you are spoiled for things to do and see and can consider your options in the manicured garden. Magnificent countryside, views and deer are all around. Just two beautifully decorated bedrooms and bathrooms with thoughtful touches such as bathrobes and toiletries. *Golf, riding and clay pigeon shooting can be arranged.*

Rooms: 2 twins, both en suite (bath).

Price: £45 p.p. Single supp. £15.

Meals: Breakfast times flexible; dinner, £25, by arrangement.

Closed: Christmas & New Year.

A1 to Ripon. B6265/Pateley Bridge road for 2 miles. Left into Studley Roger. House last on right.

John & Harriet Highley
Lawrence House
Studley Roger
Ripon
Yorkshire HG4 3AY
Tel: 01765 600947
Fax: 01765 609297

Entry No: 512   **Map no: 15**

Peter and Marion are quiet hosts and their concern is for your rest and well-being. The mill cottage is over 200 years old, a stream runs through the garden and there's wildlife all around; just one mile from Harrogate, it's a good base for sight-seeing. There are oak beams and the breakfast corner has a rounded, stone 'cellar' roof; bedrooms and bathrooms are not large, but cosy and sparkling and you have your own sitting room. Peter was a professional golfer for 20 years and can arrange for you to play. *Children over 12 welcome.*

Rooms: 1 twin, 1 double, both en suite (shower); 1 twin with private bathroom.

Price: £22.50 p.p. Single supp. by arrangement.

Meals: Breakfast until 9am. Dinner available locally.

Closed: Occasionally.

Chris Knowles-Fitton's father was a devotee of Canada and built this timber-framed house in 1938 in the style of a log cabin. The solitude is restorative; the sitting room gives onto the wooden terrace whence views of the River Wharfe and the Dales Way - stupendous. There are books, rugs and oak furniture in the sitting room. Bedrooms have pastel colours with splashes of cheerful floral chintz cushions; curtains and bathrooms continue the theme. A relaxed atmosphere prevails, and there are great walks all around; you can fish for trout, too.

Rooms: 2 doubles, 1 twin, all en suite (bath & shower).

Price: £28 p.p. Single supp. £5.

Meals: Breakfast times flexible; packed lunch £4; dinner, £18, by arrangement.

Closed: Christmas & New Year.

From Ilkley for Skipton. Right at Addingham for Bolton Abbey, & straight on at r'bout. After 4 miles, pass old castle & bear right. Down steep hill, over bridge, up hill & on for 0.5 miles. At bottom of hill, cross bridge & immed. left.

Off A61 north of Harrogate, signed on road.

Peter & Marion Thomson
Knox Mill House
Knox Mill Lane
Harrogate
Yorkshire HG3 2AE
Tel: 01423 560650
Fax: 01423 560650

Pam & Chris Knowles-Fitton
Knowles Lodge
Appletreewick
Nr Skipton, Yorkshire BD23 6DQ
Tel: 01756 720228
Fax: 01756 720381
E-mail: chris.knowlesfitton@totalise.co.uk
Web: www.thedalesway.co.uk

Entry No: 513   **Map no: 15**   **Entry No: 514**   **Map no: 15**

You are in Brontë country and if you're keen to walk, you'll love it here. Step out of the front door, past the walled garden, through the field (horses, Jacob sheep) and into open countryside. Good big bedrooms in the solid, very old listed farmhouse and large bathrooms too, with bright, seventies' suites full of sudsy things, robes and fluffy towels. Geoff's breakfasts are generous in the finest Yorkshire manner. All is comfortable and homely with open fires and Pat and Geoff love to share their knowledge of walks, golf courses and local history.

Rooms: 1 king-size, en suite (bath & shower); 1 twin, en suite (shower); 1 twin with private bath.

Price: £20-£27.50 p.p. Single supp. £5-£7.50.

Meals: Breakfast times flexible; packed lunch by arrangement; dinner from £8.

Closed: Christmas & New Year.

It's English to the core - a solid former farmhouse standing on Pennine scenery, its stone mullion windows denoting 17th-century origins. Your gentle, gracious hosts offer guests their own, good-sized sitting room - carpeted and cosy, with flowery curtains, good antiques and, on chilly evenings, an open fire. Bedrooms are generous, too, and cottagey, with old brass beds and fresh flowers. Home-made muffins for breakfast, good, traditional English dinners, too – just the thing for walkers who've trekked the Calderdale or the Pennine Way. *Children over eight welcome.*

Rooms: 1 family suite, 1 double, both en suite (shower).

Price: £28 p.p. Single supp. by arrangement.

Meals: Breakfast times flexible; packed lunch £4; dinner £18.50.

Closed: Christmas & New Year.

A58 off M62. Straight until Stump Cross Inn. Immed. right down Staups Lane.

Ripponden is on A58. Right up Royd Lane 100 yds before lights. Right at T-junc. opposite Beehive Inn. On for 1 mile. House is on right. Gateway is on blind bend: reverse in.

Pat & Geoff Horrocks-Taylor
Field House
Staups Lane
Stump Cross, Halifax
Yorkshire HX3 6XW
Tel: 01422 355457
E-mail: stayatfieldhouse@yahoo.co.uk
Web: www.fieldhouse-bb.co.uk

Judith Marriott
Thurst House Farm
Soyland
Ripponden, Halifax
Yorkshire HX6 4NN
Tel: 01422 822820
E-mail: thursthousefarm@bushinternet.com

Entry No: 515   **Map no: 15**

Entry No: 516   **Map no: 15**

Dulce is a liveryman of the Worshipful Company of Gardeners and the two-acre walled garden, which includes a nursery and 'potager', are a gardener's dream. The lawns are sweeping and there is a grass tennis court, too. The Hall was once a children's home and Dulce and Ian took seven years to restore it to its former beauty - a labour of love. The house now feels very much like a family home; big, comfortable bedrooms with armchairs, fresh flowers and excellent bathrooms.

Rooms: 2 twins/doubles, both en suite (bath & shower); 1 twin with private shower. Family suite on request.

Price: £30-35 p.p. Single supp. £10.

Meals: Breakfast until 9.30am; dinner, 4 courses, £25; supper £17.50.

Closed: Never.

Each window frames an outstanding view - this spot, on the edge of the North York Moors National Park, was chosen for its views and the house arranged to soak up the scenery, from the Pennines to the Wolds. This is a stylish, elegant and large modern house with a huge mature hillside garden. Much thought has gone into the large bedrooms and bathrooms which are uncluttered and comfortable. Phillip and Anton love what they are doing, so you will be treated like angels and served freshly-cooked dinners of outstanding quality. *Children over 12 welcome.*

Rooms: 2 kings/twins, en suite (bath); 1 double with private bathroom.

Price: King-size £40 p.p.; double £32.50 p.p. (less for 3 nights or more). Single occ. £44-£55.

Meals: Breakfast 8-9.30am; dinner, 4 courses, £22.50.

Closed: Christmas & New Year.

From Bawtry, east on A631. Approaching Gringley, 1st left after school sign. Continue for 150 yds. House on left with iron gates.

From Thirsk, A19 south, then 'caravan route' via Coxwold & Byland Abbey. 1st house on left, just before Ampleforth.

Ian & Dulce Threlfall
Gringley Hall
Gringley on the Hill
Yorkshire DN10 4QT
Tel: 01777 817262
Fax: 01777 816824
E-mail: dulce@gringleyhall.fsnet.co.uk

Anton van der Horst & Phillip Gill
Shallowdale House
West End, Ampleforth
Yorkshire YO62 4DY
Tel: 01439 788325
Fax: 01439 788885
E-mail: stay@shallowdalehouse.demon.co.uk
Web: www.shallowdalehouse.demon.co.uk

Entry No: 517   **Map no: 15**

Entry No: 518   **Map no: 15**

"I'd have great difficulty believing that anyone could fail to have fun here," said our inspector. These are super folk who invite you to share their home - this is no stifling, set-piece B&B; dining and drawing rooms are nonetheless smart and bedrooms are traditional with quirky touches. You look out over the Vale of York, yet are only three minutes walk from the heart of the village and close to York and its Minster. Set in 28 acres that run down to the River Swale (fishing available), it has black sheep, ducks, horses and ponies, a croquet lawn and a tennis court. Only four miles from the A1.

Rooms: 1 twin/double, en suite (shower); 2 doubles, 1 en suite (bath), 1 with private bathroom.

Price: £30 p.p.

Meals: Breakfast until 9.30am; dinner, £25, by arrangement. Good food also available at pubs a walk away.

Closed: Occasionally in winter.

From A1(M), Boroughbridge exit. At North side of Boroughbridge follow Easingwold/Helperby sign. In Helperby, right at T-junction, right up Hall Lane. Left in front of school.

Sam & Annie Atcherley-Key
Laurel Manor Farm
Brafferton-Helperby
York, Yorkshire YO61 2NZ
Tel: 01423 360436
Fax: 01423 360437
E-mail: laurelmf@aol.com
Web: www.laurelmf.co.uk

Entry No: 519 **Map no: 15**

Drive through a stone archway into an old courtyard. A grandfather clock, whose mythological figure blows a furious wind, then greets you. This is a 17th-century, beamed, working farmhouse, once attached to Ampleforth Abbey. The three uncluttered, flowery bedrooms are frilled and co-ordinated and have lovely views. There is a half-tester brass and iron bedstead with a soaring, awning-like canopy in the double. A true, bluff Yorkshire farming welcome from Andrew and graceful efficiency from Margaret. *Children over 10 welcome.*

Rooms: 1 twin, 1 double, both en suite (shower); 1 twin with private bath & shower.

Price: £24-£28 p.p. Single occ. £30.

Meals: Breakfast 8.30-9.30, flexible by arrangement. Dinner available locally.

Closed: Christmas & New Year.

A170 from Thirsk for 12 miles. Right onto B1257 1 mile before Helmsley. 50 yds on, left by church. House at end of No Through Road.

Margaret & Andrew Wainwright
Sproxton Hall
Sproxton
Helmsley
Yorkshire YO62 5EQ
Tel: 01439 770225
Fax: 01439 771373
E-mail: info@sproxtonhall.demon.co.uk

Entry No: 520 **Map no: 15**

The Moors lie behind this solid, stone farmhouse, five yards from the National Park, in farmland and woodland with fine views... marvellous walking country. The house is full of light and flowers; bedrooms are pretty and not overly grand. The sitting room has deeply comfortable old sofas, armchairs and fine furniture. Rich colours and hunting prints give the dining room a warm and cosy feel. The Orr family has poured affection into this house and the result is a home that's happy and remarkably easy to relax in... wonderful.

Rooms: 2 twins/doubles, 1 en suite (shower), 1 with private bathroom.

Price: £35 p.p. For 3 or more nights, £30 p.p. Single supp. £10.

Meals: Breakfast until 9am; dinner, 3 courses including wine, £24.50.

Closed: Never.

From A170 Kirkbymoorside/Pickering road, turn into Sinnington. On village green, keep river on your left & fork right between cottages. Turn up lane, bearing right up hill. Farmhouse past church.

The Orr Family
Hunters Hill
Sinnington
York
Yorkshire YO62 6SF
Tel: 01751 431196
Fax: 01751 432976
E-mail: jorr@btclick.com

Entry No: 521   **Map no:** 15

Breakfast on home-baked soda bread, farm eggs and proper bacon; for dinner, savour the Kelly's own lamb and beef. You are in a remote valley near the North Yorkshire Moors where the 1800s courtyard is such a rare survivor of local rural architecture that the BBC filmed it for posterity. The rooms, with views to the craggy moor, were being refurbished during our visit but Jill and the unflappable Andrew gave the warmest welcome. A perfect place to feel in touch with the seasons. "Idyllic," wrote our inspector.

Rooms: 1 double, 1 family, 1 twin, all with private bathroom.

Price: £20 p.p. Single supp. £25.

Meals: Breakfast times flexible; packed lunch available; dinner, 3 courses, £15, by arrangement.

Closed: Never.

From Malton, A170 Pickering road to Cropton. Through Rosedale Abbey & up onto moor, following signs for Castleton. At 1st cattle grid after 2 miles, right. House on right, 2.5 miles on.

Jill Kelly
Stonebeck Gate Farm
Little Fryup, Danby
Whitby
Yorkshire YO21 2NS
Tel: 01287 660363
Fax: 01287 660363

Entry No: 522   **Map no:** 15

For 250 years this has been the family farm. The Kynges, who have sheep and cattle, have converted the farm to a fully organic enterprise and everything they produce and grow is chemical-free. It is a splendid, traditional country house, at the end of a long, tree-lined drive and in very English parkland. A stone-flagged hall leads to an exquisite dining room that holds much family history. The bedrooms have oak chests, deep basins and magnificent wardrobes. Everywhere there is the nobility of wood and fine furniture. Mrs Kynge's cooking has won many accolades. *Croquet and tennis available.*

Rooms: 1 king-size, 1 double, en suite (bath); 1 twin with private bathroom and separate shower. Self-catering for 4 also available.

Price: £28 p.p. Single supp. £5.

Meals: Breakfast times flexible; dinner £18.

Closed: 1 December-1 April.

From A19, A172 towards Stokesley for 3 miles. Left & straight over x-roads. Drive to house 0.25 miles on, on right.

Major & Mrs Julian Kynge
Potto Grange
Potto
Nr. Northallerton
Yorkshire DL6 3HH
Tel: 01642 700212
Fax: 01642 700978

Entry No: 523   **Map no: 15**

The entrance is dramatic - the Cleveland Hills rise up behind and, all around, there are 164 acres of parkland. The views go on forever, the wildlife comes to you. Footpaths lead you from the farm to the moors and take you past wild geese on the flight pond and cantering Soay sheep from St. Kilda in the Outer Hebrides. Martin and Margaret are interested, involved people: you feel your presence counts. Inside, china knick-knacks and florals contrast with the bright whiteness of the rooms. Guests must take dinner. You won't mind in the slightest. *Children over 12 welcome.*

Rooms: 2 doubles, 1 twin, 1 en suite (bath), 2 with private bath/shower.

Price: Dinner and B&B from £42.50 p.p.

Meals: Breakfast until 9.30am; dinner, 5 courses, included.

Closed: Christmas.

B1257 south from Stokesley to Great Broughton. Left at village hall onto Ingleby Road for 2 miles to church at Ingleby Greenhow. Entrance right after church, through stone pillars.

Margaret & Martin Bloom
Manor House Farm
Ingleby Greenhow
Great Ayton
Yorkshire TS9 6RB
Tel: 01642 722384
E-mail: mbloom@globalnet.co.uk

Entry No: 524   **Map no: 15**

Yorkshire

A peaceful spirit, warmth and friendliness pervade this elegant, bay-windowed farmhouse. Anne goes to great lengths to make you comfortable and her cooking is delicious. The house, which harmoniously incorporates the former cottage and dairy buildings, has pale, fresh colour schemes, an interesting collection of books and superb views. The pretty guest rooms face south and you will be drawn to explore the gentle, rolling dales, the moors and the coastline. York and Durham and other fascinating historic places are nearby. *Children over 12 welcome.*

Rooms: 1 twin, 1 twin/double, both with private bathrooms.

Price: £35 p.p. Single supp. £10.

Meals: Breakfast times flexible; dinner, from £22, by arrangement.

Closed: December & January.

Going north on A19 take A172 towards Stokesley. Pass sign on right to Carlton & Busby. House 0.5 miles further on left, with 2 red triangular deflectors at entrance to tree-lined drive.

Anne Gloag
Busby House
Stokesley
Yorkshire TS9 5LB
Tel: 01642 710425
Fax: 01642 713838

Entry No: 525   **Map no: 15**

Even in the mayhem of the lambing season they will greet you with a smile, tea and home-made biscuits - the Pearsons are the nicest, most genuine, straightforward farming folk imaginable. Their farmhouse is as unpretentious as they are: there's one bedroom here and three away from the homely hub in converted outbuildings. Rooms have a mixture of antique and modern furniture and views of the garden and of the Hambledon Hills. The road that runs past the house is quiet, yet you are well placed for the Dales and the Moors. Local sausages, home-made marmalade and own eggs for breakfast.

Rooms: 1 family, 1 twin, 1 double, 1 single, all en suite (shower). Gate Cottage: 1 double, en suite (bath).

Price: £22-£25 p.p. Single supp. £5. Gate Cottage: £25-£30 p.p.

Meals: Breakfast until 10am; dinner £15.

Closed: 1 December-28 February.

From Northallerton, A167 north for Darlington for 4 miles. House on right, signed.

John & Mary Pearson
Lovesome Hill Farm
Lovesome Hill
Northallerton
Yorkshire DL6 2PB
Tel: 01609 772311
Fax: 01609 774715
E-mail: pearsonlhf@care4free.net

Entry No: 526   **Map no: 15**

An Aga-cooked breakfast and fresh seasonal fruit await you - breakfasts are generous. The Cravens are equally generous of spirit and we *guarantee* you'll love their Labrador, Barney. The house is of mellow Yorkshire stone, built in 1767 and there is an air of quiet repose – traditional furniture, china in panelled alcoves, lovely prints and watercolours and a drawing room with Delph fire surround. Bedrooms are comfortable and snug and have proper tea trays and fresh flowers; in wintertime there are views to Pickering Vale. A very pretty village and garden enhance the enjoyment.

Rooms: 2 twins, both with private bathroom. One bathroom on 1st floor, one on 2nd.

Price: £30 p.p. Single supp. £5.

Meals: Breakfast 7.30-9am; packed lunch, £5, by arrangement.

Closed: Occasionally.

Through Thornton le Dale on A170 towards Scarborough. Road rises after village centre. Pass church on left. Hurrell Lane nr top of hill on right. House immed. on right.

Richard & Tuppie Craven
The High Hall
Hurrell Lane
Thornton le Dale
Yorkshire YO18 7QR
Tel: 01751 474371
Fax: 01751 477701
E-mail: CravenGriffin@aol.com

Entry No: 527   **Map no: 16**

A 20-minute stride down the fields to Levisham Station and the start of some wonderful jaunts on the North Yorkshire Moors Steam Railway. Warmth and comfort are the key notes of this family home – log fires on chilly nights, flowers in the rooms, home-made scones for tea. Cheery bedrooms are painted fresh yellow; all are carpeted and cosy. Have a drink at the local pub – a 50-yard stroll – or dine at home on Michael's beef and Yorkshire pudding (Heather does the puds). Superb walks from the doorstep – excellent riding, too. Bring your horse.

Rooms: 1 double/twin, 1 double, both en suite (shower); 1 double/twin, en suite (bath and shower).

Price: £20-£24 p.p. Weekly rate: £260-£280. No single supp.

Meals: Breakfast times flexible; packed lunch £3-£5; dinner £10-£12.

Closed: Never.

From A169 take Lockton/Levisham road. Once through Lockton, look for house sign after 0.75 miles on right, in Levisham.

Mrs Heather Holt
Rectory Farmhouse
Levisham, Pickering
Yorkshire YO18 7NL
Tel: 01751 460491
Fax: 08707 059863
E-mail: stay@levisham.com
Web: www.levisham.com

Entry No: 528   **Map no: 16**

The Cleveland Way runs along the cliffs a mile away and Christine is keen to help you plan your stay, including, maybe, a trip to the Alan Ayckbourn theatre? Comfort is the thing here. Christine loves interior design and bedrooms are carefully co-ordinated: one has a pink, green and floral theme and an original Victorian fireplace, the double has bolder blue, gold and deep rose matching headboard and drapes. There are bathrobes in fitted wardrobes and big showers. Breakfast either in the south-facing conservatory - there's a huge choice, including kippers - or at the polished mahogany table in the dining room. Billiards too.

Rooms: 1 twin, en suite (shower); 1 double, with private bath & shower.

Price: From £22.50 p.p. Single supp. £5.

Meals: Breakfast times flexible. Pubs in village.

Closed: Christmas.

A171 from Scarborough to Whitby, at Scalby x-roads, by tennis courts, take Station Rd on the right. House signed 500 yds on right.

John & Christine Goodall
Holly Croft
28 Station Road, Scalby
Scarborough
Yorkshire YO13 0QA
Tel: 01723 375376
Fax: 01723 360563

Entry No: 529   **Map no: 16**

Flamborough Head juts out into the storm-tossed North Sea and you can feel the force of nature. Just inland, the Manor House is a lovingly restored refuge: maple flooring, dark green walls and old oak table in the dining room; book-filled sitting room with brocade sofas, oak furniture, shuttered windows. Perhaps a coal fire in your room, or an elaborately carved Portuguese bed. The bathrooms have marble and Victorian fittings (cast-iron baths). Geoffrey is a naval historian and the house is stuffed with his books. The coastal walks are out of this world. Unquestionably special. *Children over eight welcome.*

Rooms: 1 double with private bathroom; 1 twin/double, en suite (bath).

Price: £33-£38 p.p. Single supp. £8.

Meals: Breakfast times flexible; dinner £22.

Closed: Christmas.

From Bridlington, B1255 to Flamborough. Follow signs to lighthouse, past church on right. House on next corner (Lighthouse Rd/Tower St).

Lesley Berry & Geoffrey Miller
The Manor House
Flamborough
Yorkshire YO15 1PD
Tel: 01262 850943
Fax: 01262 850943
E-mail: gm@flamboroughmanor.co.uk
Web: www.flamboroughmanor.co.uk

Entry No: 530   **Map no: 16**

A delightful find - this modern cottage is an excellent city alternative to corporate hotels. Both Stephanie's daughters are designers and a sense of style runs in the family. We loved the strong colours - the tiled hall with Chelsea Green walls, the bold yellow drawing room, the 'Madder Red' room that overlooks the garden, the intense blue single room which has a patchwork throw made from the daughters' childhood dresses. The Hornbys are easy-going and love good food. From here you can catch daily ferries to the continent. You'll want to return. *Children over eight welcome.*

Rooms: 1 double with private bathroom; 1 single also available to members of same party.

Price: £28 p.p.

Meals: Breakfast times flexible; supper/dinner £12/£18 including wine.

Closed: Never.

Where M62 becomes A63, follow Humber Bridge signs. At large r'bout north of bridge, left, A164 to Beverley. 3 miles on, right to Kirk Ella. Pass golf course & immed. after Post Office drive 1st on right after Hogg Lane.

Stephanie & Martin Hornby
Box Cottage
2 Hogg Lane
Kirk Ella, Hull
Yorkshire HU10 7NU
Tel: 01482 658852

Entry No: 531   **Map no: 16**

Scotland

National Trust Photographic Library/Mike Williams

Beautiful, glorious Scotland,
has spoilt me for every other country.

Mary Todd Lincoln

"One of the loveliest houses I've seen," said our inspector. The owners have real warmth and interest to match the vibrant, multi-hued brightness of their generous William Adam house. They also have ancestors to oversee the dining table, a club fender before the drawing-room fireplace, a garden room with masses of books and one bedroom described as a "green-combed retreat with a Rajahstani bedhead". All the bedrooms feel private (around corners, in other wings), beautiful and different with superb décor. And adjective-defying Galloway is all around.

Rooms: 1 double/twin, en suite (bath/shower); 1 double, en suite (bath).

Price: £27 p.p. Single occ. £33.

Meals: Breakfast 7.30-8.30am; dinner, 3 courses, £19, by arrangement.

Closed: Occasionally.

From Stranraer, A77 towards Portpatrick for 1.5 miles. Straight on at A716 towards Drummore. Drive on left after approx. 1 mile, at junction with B7077 signed Newton Stewart.

Peter & Liz Whitworth
Kildrochet House
By Stranraer
Wigtownshire DG9 9BB
Tel: 01776 820216
Fax: 01776 820216
E-mail: kldrochet@compuserve.com

Entry No: 532   **Map no: 17**

Guests have loved it here. There's polished oak furniture, high-backed chairs, silver, fresh flowers; it's traditional and smart, but not grand. David and Ginny really enjoy having guests. Beds are comfortable, the rooms bright and airy with fresh fruit, flowers, magazines and mineral water. Bathrooms have huge baths and everything you may have left behind. Walking sticks and fishing nets stand by the door and you can hear the stream that cuts through the private glen. For walkers, the Southern Upland Way goes past the door.

Rooms: 1 twin, 1 double, both with private bathroom.

Price: £28.50 p.p. Single occ. £34.

Meals: Breakfast 7.30-9am; packed lunch £5; dinner, 4 courses, £24.50; supper, 2 courses, £12.50; by arrangement.

Closed: Christmas & New Year.

A75 towards Stranraer. In Castle Kennedy, right opposite Esso station. Approx. 1.25 miles on, after right bend, right signed Chlenry. Continue down hill, farmhouse on left after 300 yds.

David & Ginny Wolseley Brinton
Chlenry Farmhouse
Castle Kennedy
Stranraer
Wigtownshire DG9 8SL
Tel: 01776 705316
Fax: 01776 889488
E-mail: WolseleyBrinton@aol.com

Entry No: 533   **Map no: 18**

A Regency castle, magnificent and unchanged. Bring your friends and have the whole place to yourselves. The rooms are huge, the furniture is original, with Victorian wallpaper in the drawing room; the billiard room is on the expected scale; there's a library, a family museum, an art gallery full of Scottish colourists and 2,000 acres, too. A castle, yet still, exquisitely, a home. In June, when the laburnum avenue is in full flower in the beautiful walled garden, James throws a 'yellow' party to complement the magnificence of the blooms.

Rooms: 4 four-posters, 2 doubles, 5 twins, 6 singles, all en suite bathrooms or sharing bathroom with 1 single.

Price: £115 p.p. Bookings made only for one party at a time. Minimum 4 people.

Meals: Breakfast times flexible; lunch from £20; dinner £75, includes all drinks.

Closed: Christmas.

From Maybole, south on B7023 through Crosshill, then left onto B741 towards Straiton. After 2 miles, estate wall. Lodge & gates on left & signed.

James Hunter Blair
Blairquhan Castle
Straiton, Maybole
Ayrshire KA19 7LZ
Tel: 01655 770239
Fax: 01655 770278
E-mail: enquiries@blairquhan.co.uk
Web: www.blairquhan.co.uk

Entry No: 534   **Map no: 18**

Within and without it is delightful and John and Moira are kind, relaxed and interesting; they have an unfussy manner that makes it easy to relax here. The atmospheric drawing room is stately and half-panelled. There are bay windows, oak and oils and bedrooms are done in fresh colours - blues and whites - with good linen and towels, fine furniture, decorative wash bowls, shutters rather than curtains. It is a fine house, with views to the River Doon flowing past the garden. The sea is only a mile away and Glasgow an hour. *Children over 10 welcome.*

Rooms: 1 double with private bath; 1 twin, en suite (shower).

Price: £35 p.p.

Meals: Breakfast until 9.30am. Dinner available locally.

Closed: Christmas & New Year.

B7024 into Alloway on south side of Ayr. Follow Burns Heritage Centre signs. House on left, opposite Burns Monument by church.

John & Moira Pollok-Morris
Doonbrae
40 Alloway
Ayr
Ayrshire KA7 4PQ
Tel: 01292 442511
Fax: 01292 442511
E-mail: doonbrae@aol.com

Entry No: 535   **Map no: 18**

You can sink into the sofas without worrying about creasing them; it is a beautiful 18th-century Scottish Georgian house, yet there's not a hint of formality. The sociable Dicksons are at ease here and so will you be. The sitting and dining rooms connect through a large arch and there are family pictures, rugs on wooden floors, a feng shui cabinet. In the bedrooms: a cast-iron bed, excellent furniture, elegant linen and masses of light and good books. There are 200 acres, a dog, cat, donkeys, and free-ranging hens. This excellent house gets better and better.

Rooms: 1 twin with private bathroom; 1 double, en suite (bath/shower). Cot available.

Price: £36 p.p. No single supp.

Meals: Breakfast until 10am; dinner, £20, may be available on request.

Closed: Christmas.

There are formal gardens, a small fishing loch, masses of rhododendrons and a large productive vegetable garden within the 20 acres that surround this former Victorian shooting lodge. It's a large, professionally-run house, but lots of books, some fine paintings and sculpture, and log fires lit for breakfast demonstrate a personal touch. Christopher is a classic car enthusiast; Mary is an excellent cook, using home produce. Bedrooms are large, bright, and well-furnished, with good rugs and the odd *chaise longue*. A Victorian billiard room with full-size table, too. *Children over 12 welcome.*

Rooms: 3 twins/doubles, all en suite (bath/shower).

Price: £30-£33 p.p. Single occ. £38.

Meals: Breakfast until 9.15am; packed lunch from £3.50; dinner, £17.50, by arrangement.

Closed: 1 November-Easter.

A75 Dumfries ring road for Stranraer. Through Crocketford to Springholm & right to Kirkpatrick Durham. Left at x-roads, after 0.8 miles, up drive on right by white lodge.

From Dalbeattie, south-east on B793. House 7 miles down this road on right. Turn right &, after 30 yds, left through gate posts.

Willie & Catriona Dickson
Chipperkyle
Kirkpatrick Durham
Castle Douglas
Dumfries & Galloway DG7 3EY
Tel: 01556 650223
Fax: 01556 650223
E-mail: dickson@chipperkyle.freeserve.co.uk

Christopher & Mary Broom-Smith
Auchenskeoch Lodge
By Dalbeattie
Dumfries & Galloway DG5 4PG
Tel: 01387 780277
Fax: 01387 780277
E-mail: brmsmth@aol.com
Web: www.auchenskeochlodge.com

Entry No: 536   Map no: 18

Entry No: 537   Map no: 18

You'd hardly believe that you are 30 minutes from Glasgow. The hamlet used to house the furniture makers of nearby Beith - each cottage is whitewashed and immaculate and there's absolute peace. Aileen loves her 1800s mini-manor and sharing the house and the garden; she's a Blue Badge guide and therefore full of excellent, original travel ideas. The bedroom is under the eaves with chintz poppy curtains and bedspread and views to garden and fields one way and to Loch Winnoch the other. Magazines and flowers, conservatory and drawing room, orchards and fields – a real retreat.

Rooms: 1 double, en suite (bath/shower); child's bed available.

Price: £25-£28 p.p. No single supp.

Meals: Breakfast times flexible. Dinner available locally.

Closed: Christmas & New Year.

Glasgow-Irvine, A737, bypass village of Howwood, sign on left to riding stables & B&B. Follow road through stables & farm. Signed, 2nd on left.

Aileen Biggart
Glenshian, Newton-of-Beltrees
By Loch Winnoch
Renfrewshire PA12 4JL
Tel: 01505 842823
Fax: 01505 842823
E-mail: sambiggart@aol.com
Web: www.aboutscotland.com/glasgow/glenshian.html

Entry No: 538   **Map no: 18**

"Too small for envy, for contempt too great" - the 17th-century motto is written above the door through which Robbie Burns entered when he came to stay. Knockhill is superbly authentic and architecturally impressive. Great stone stairs, carved oak furniture, lovely rugs, grandfather clocks , smooth grass tennis court and croquet lawn. The beamed and eaved attic room has a door that's 4 feet something high - your stoop is rewarded with long views. Grand farming feel and the Morgans are the easiest of hosts. "These are top people doing B&B in the very best way," says our inspector.

Rooms: 2 twins, 1 with private bath, 1 with private shower.

Price: £30-£35 p.p. No single supp.

Meals: Breakfast times flexible; dinner £23.

Closed: Christmas & New Year.

From M74 junc.19, B725 for Dalton for 1.5 miles. Right at x-roads to Lockerbie, 1 mile on, right at small stone lodge. House at top of long, unsurfaced drive.

Yda & Rupert Morgan
Knockhill
Lockerbie
Dumfries & Galloway DG11 1AW
Tel: 01576 300232
Fax: 01576 300818
E-mail: morganbellows@yahoo.co.uk

Entry No: 539   **Map no: 19**

In utterly quiet and peaceful surroundings overlooking the River Annan, this old sandstone house reveals, astonishingly, the remains of a medieval motte within its big walled garden. The house is ideally placed on the route halfway between deep south and far north - explore the ancient church or the wetlands bird sanctuary nearby. The bedrooms are big and pristine and so are the bathrooms. There is a warm family air to it all, and furniture is a mix of old comfort and old elegance. *Children over 10 welcome.*

Rooms: 1 double with private bath; 2 twins, both en suite (bath).

Price: £30-£32 p.p. Single supp. £5.

Meals: Breakfast times flexible; dinner £22. B.Y.O. wine.

Closed: Never.

The grandeur may be faded, but this former manse in stunning border country is holding its own. There's a lovely garden, your own drawing room with old pictures and log fire, comfortable bedrooms and some amazing floral wallpapers. Yours hosts are keen on country sports and, with notice, can arrange hunting or fishing. If you stay for dinner you will have good country food, usually locally raised. This is a smoking household and the bedrooms are only ever let to one party so you can make up your own rules. *Children, other than toddlers (sorry), welcome.*

Rooms: 2 twins, 1 single, let only to members of the same party, sharing private bathroom.

Price: £30 p.p.

Meals: Breakfast until 9.30am; dinner, from £17.50, by arrangement.

Closed: Occasionally.

A74 (M) junc. 17 to Lockerbie. B7076 to Johnstonebridge. 1st right 1.5 miles on & 100 yds on left over m-way bridge. After 1 mile on right at T-junc., then 2nd left to church. House next to church.

From A74M, junc. 20 onto B722 to Eaglesfield. 2nd left after 350 yds, signed Middlebie. There, house & gate are next to church.

Frank & Jane Pearson
Applegarth House
Lockerbie
Dumfries & Galloway DG11 1SX
Tel: 01387 810270
Fax: 01387 811701
E-mail: jane@applegarthtown.demon.co.uk

R.& U. Milne Home
Kirkside of Middlebie
Lockerbie
Dumfries & Galloway DG11 3JW
Tel: 01576 300204

Entry No: 540   **Map no: 19**

Entry No: 541   **Map no: 19**

Highland cattle graze contentedly as you drive up to the early 17th-century laird's house, the oldest in the parish. It has been done up recently to make it lighter and brighter, and elegant. You breakfast in the big kitchen at one large table and have your own sitting room with woodburning stove, tartan carpet, red sofa, leather chair and pine furniture. Dinner is served in the cosily elegant dining room. There are 60 acres of woodland and grazing, so you are undisturbed by the noise of the 20th century. It is a lovely house, in a superb setting, with a big welcome attached.

Rooms: 1 twin, 1 double (with extra bed), both with private bathroom (1 shower, 1 bath).

Price: £35-£40 p.p. Single supp. £10.

Meals: Breakfast until 9.30am; dinner including complimentary drinks, £22.50, by arrangement.

Closed: Never.

Purest Walter Scott: castles, abbeys, keeps, gardens, salmon and trout rivers - here are the wild, rolling Borders at their most romantically beautiful. The rooms at Ancrum Craig are part 18th century, part Victorian, and the views are stupendous, particularly from the bay-windowed, antique-furnished Gold Room. Johan will tell you all about the best walks, but don't dash off to explore until you've eaten Jill's sustaining Scottish breakfast with haggis; her smoked salmon and scrambled eggs are equally delicious.

Rooms: 2 doubles, 1 twin/double, all en suite (1 bath, 2 showers).

Price: £23-£25 p.p. Single supp. £12. Discount for longer stays.

Meals: Breakfast times flexible; walker's supper, from £9, by prior arrangement.

Closed: New Year.

From Hawick A698, right on A6088 signed Bonchester Bridge. Follow road into village (6 miles), sharp right-hand bend at foot of hill. After 100 yds, 1st turning on right before little bridge.

From Jedburgh, A68 for Edinburgh. Left after 3.5 miles to Ancrum. Fork left to Denholm before village. After 1.75 miles, right signed Lilliesleaf. Bear left, then left to Ancrum Craig.

Christopher & Jacqui McLean May
Hobsburn
Bonchester Bridge, Hawick
Scottish Borders TD9 8JW
Tel: 01450 860720
Fax: 01450 860330
E-mail: b+b@mcleanmay.com
Web: www.mcleanmay.com

Jill & Johan Hensens
Ancrum Craig
Ancrum, By Jedburgh
Scottish Borders TD8 6UN
Tel: 01835 830280
Fax: 01835 830259
E-mail: ancrumcraig@clara.net
Web: www.ancrumcraig.co.uk

Entry No: 542   Map no: 19

Entry No: 543   Map no: 19

How grand: a Virginia creeper-clad residence with a turret and a tower set in seven acres with views of the Cheviot Hills. But not too grand: there's no standing on ceremony here - this is a homely and comfortable place to be. Elizabeth is new to B&B, courteous and kind; Francis is a whizz with computers and runs courses for the over-fifties (why not join in?). Pastel bedrooms have quilted twin beds, smart dressing-tables and the occasional expected Scottish touch such as tartan drapes. Walkers and anglers are well catered for - there is a drying room.

Rooms: 3 twins, 1 with private bathroom, 2 sharing a bathroom.

Price: £29 p.p. £35 single supp.

Meals: Breakfast until 9.30am; packed lunch available (price on request); dinner £20; both by arrangement.

Closed: Christmas & New Year.

A 50-ft drawing-room with Venetian glass windows and Adamesque ceiling, Arts & Crafts carvings on the wood-panelled stairs and original cast radiators in the dining room... the small Georgian mansion with neo-Jacobean additions is full of historic surprises. One bedroom has a flash jacuzzi with gold basins to match; all come with their own grand balconies overlooking gardens and fields. Work up your appetite in hunting, shooting and fishing country: Joan is a brilliant cook (*Cordon Vert*) and her veg is organically home-grown.

Rooms: 1 double, 1 twin, both en suite; 1 double with private bathroom.

Price: From £27.50 p.p. No single supp.

Meals: Breakfast times flexible; packed lunch, £4.50 and dinner, from £16, by arrangement.

Closed: Never.

From Coldstream, take Guards Rd next to Esso garage for 3 miles until sign on left opposite house.

From Edinburgh A68 for Jedburgh. Left at Carfraemill, A697 for Duns. Left in Greenlaw, A6105 for Duns. There, pass Jim Clark Museum, & left at Preston-Grantshouse rd. House 600 yds on right.

Elizabeth & Francis Gradidge
Ruthven House
Coldstream
Berwickshire TD12 4JU
Tel: 01890 840771
Fax: 01890 840680
E-mail: gradidge@gradidge.worldonline.co.uk
Web: www.bordersovernight.co.uk

John & Joan Bimson
Wellfield House
Preston Road
Duns, Berwickshire TD11 3DZ
Tel: 01361 883189
Fax: 01361 883189
E-mail: john.bimson@virgin.net
Web: www.wellfieldhouse.com

Entry No: 544   **Map no: 19**

Entry No: 545   **Map no: 19**

Lucy's cooking is mouth-watering: kedgeree and waffles for breakfast, *Cordon Bleu* dishes by night, both served in a delightful, elegant dining room. A sense of solidity pervades this wide-corridored, high-ceilinged Victorian home, run by the charmingly down-to-earth Forrest family who've been here for years. Bedrooms are comfortable and full of lovely extras like fresh flowers, candles and, in one, an ancient teddy holding the bottled water. And there's so much to do: tennis in the garden, golf nearby, fishing, moorland walks and Edinburgh less than an hour away.

Rooms: 1 double, 1 twin, sharing private bathroom; 1 double with extra single bed, en suite (bath & shower).

Price: From £25 p.p. Single supp. by arrangement.

Meals: Breakfast times flexible; dinner from £15, by arrangement. B.Y.O. wine.

Closed: Never.

Early Victorian and creeper-clad - the Taylors moved to this old manse after they retired from farming. The rooms are large and bright, there is a fine cantilever staircase up from the hall, and the dining room's long windows frame good rural views. The big bedrooms, with shutters and long curtains, are large and comfortable, the bathrooms smart. The colourful walled garden, full of clematis, honeysuckle and roses, hides a small vegetable garden, orchard and ornamental pond. Beyond, fields rise and there is deep rural seclusion. Genuinely nice people and good, easy conversation. *Children over 12 welcome.*

Rooms: 1 twin, 1 double, both with private bathroom.

Price: From £25 p.p. No single supp.

Meals: Breakfast times flexible; dinner from £14.50, by arrangement.

Closed: Christmas & New Year.

From A1 north of Berwick, A6105 to Duns. There, A6112 & house is on left (3 miles on) before sharp corner.

From A1 towards Duns on B6438 for 5.5 miles. Left at Bonkyl church sign. On for 0.25 miles to church; house 2nd right through black gate.

Mrs Lucy Forrest
Preston Farmhouse
Preston Farm, Preston Duns
Berwickshire TD11 3TQ
Tel: 01361 882826
Fax: 01361 882066
E-mail: lucy@forrest4.freeserve.co.uk
Web: www.forrest-preston.co.uk

Libby & Martin Taylor
Kirkside House
Bonkyl
Nr. Duns
Berwickshire TD11 3RJ
Tel: 01361 884340
Fax: 01361 882273

Entry No: 546   **Map no: 19**

Entry No: 547   **Map no: 19**

Borders & Lowlands

A traditionally run organic farm producing wholesome milk from British Friesians and meat and wool from Scottish Mule ewes. There's a real back-to-nature approach with free-range hens providing the eggs for breakfast. Simple, comfortable rooms, bright from big windows, and everywhere an eccentric 1700s nooks-and-crannies mood prevails. From the family room you can see the old Border keeps and a spider web of stone walls. In nearby Melrose, beneath the Eildon Hills, Robert the Bruce's heart lies buried. A peaceful and romantic spot.

Rooms: 1 family with private bathroom; 1 double, en suite (shower).

Price: £23 p.p. Single supp. £5. Family room £55.

Meals: Breakfast usually 8.30am, but times flexible; packed lunch available; dinner from £12.

Closed: Never.

From Galashiels, A7 past Torwoodlea golf course & right to Langshaw. After 2 miles, right at T-junc., then left at Earlston sign in Langshaw. House is white, in trees, signposted at farm road.

Sheila & Martyn Bergius
Over Langshaw Farm
Galashiels
Selkirkshire TD1 2PE
Tel: 01896 860244
Fax: 01896 860244
Web: www.bergius@overlangshaw.fsnet.co.uk

Entry No: 548   **Map no: 19**

You can roam over 1,300 acres with sheep, cattle, horses and abundant wildlife. An excellent base for families: Arran, in Spring, encourages children to bottle-feed lambs. Rooms are comfortable, not grand, with silk flowers, patterned carpets and rugs and, in the bedrooms, wooden floors and reproduction furniture - but the surroundings are what you came for and the views will make your heart soar. Fishing, walking and pony-trekking are yours for the asking or you can relax in the walled garden. The silence at night is disturbed only by wildlife. Nearby is Lyne Fort, a major Roman encampment.

Rooms: 2 doubles, 1 twin, sharing 2 bathrooms.

Price: £18-£20 p.p. Single occ. £22.

Meals: Breakfast times flexible; packed lunch, from £3-£5 available. Dinner available locally.

Closed: Christmas Day.

4 miles west of Peebles on A72, signed on right-hand side of main road.

Arran & John Waddell
Lyne Farmhouse
Lyne Farm
Peebles
Peeblesshire EH45 8NR
Tel: 01721 740255
Fax: 01721 740255
E-mail: awaddell@farming.co.uk

Entry No: 549   **Map no: 19**

Beside the green in a Borders sheep-farming village, Skirling House is imbued from top to bottom with the spirit of the Scottish Arts and Crafts movement; it has innate grace of space and form in its one-room-thick layout, and gathers its beautiful gardens in a peaceful embrace. The harmony goes on inside - there's a study for you and soft colours and superb design are enhanced by Bob and Isobel, whose eye for complementary ancient and modern is acute. Sleep soundly in your bright, comfortable bedroom, and awake to stunning views.

Rooms: 1 twin, 3 doubles, all en suite.

Price: £35 p.p. Single supp £10. 5% discount for longer stays.

Meals: Breakfast 8-9.30am; dinner £22.

Closed: Christmas, January & February.

You'll be serenaded by the birds and the bees. The infectiously vibrant Carina and Jim have poured energy, affection and an artistic streak into their lovely 18th-century family home: Turkish rugs, ethnic cushions and intriguing knick-knacks everywhere. A comforting hubbub emanates from the kitchen - Carina is an excellent cook and you'll be chatting easily before you know it. With table-tennis, snooker and a trampoline in the garden, this is a great base for families, as well as for those looking for a country retreat. Glorious views, too.

Rooms: 1 double, 1 twin, both en suite (bath and shower, respectively).

Price: £30-£40 p.p.

Meals: Breakfast times flexible; lunch, packed lunch and dinner, by arrangement.

Closed: 20 December-6 January.

From Biggar, A702 for Edinburgh. Just outside Biggar, right on A72 for Skirling. Big wooden house on right opp. village green.

From Edinburgh A1 for Berwick-upon-Tweed. Left for East Linton, left again under r'way bridge & through village. After 0.5 miles, left for Markle. 1st white house on right.

Bob & Isobel Hunter
Skirling House
Skirling, By Biggar
Lanarkshire ML12 6HD
Tel: 01899 860274
Fax: 01899 860255
E-mail: enquiry@skirlinghouse.com
Web: www.skirlinghouse.com

Carina & Jim McGuinness
Markle House
East Linton
East Lothian
Tel: 01620 860570
Fax: 01620 860937
E-mail: mcguinness@marklehouse.fsnet.co.uk

Entry No: 550   **Map no: 19**

Entry No: 551   **Map no: 19**

Gwen has lavished a huge amount of time and love on her 1780s Georgian manse - bedrooms are light and airy and hung with generous swathes of fabric and easy chairs have pretty cushions. There are many original features such as fireplaces, arched glass and long, Georgian windows. The sea is two-minutes from the house and this is heaven for golfers - there are 18 courses within easy reach. There's a fascinating seabird centre close by, too, yet you are only a 30-minute drive from Edinburgh - regular trains will take you to the foot of the castle, too.

Rooms: 1 double, en suite (shower); 1 four-poster, en suite (bath/shower); 1 twin with private bathroom.

Price: £30-£40 p.p.

Meals: Breakfast times flexible. Restaurants in town.

Closed: Christmas & New Year.

From Edinburgh, A1 signed Berwick. Left onto A198, follow signs into North Berwick. Right into Station Rd signed 'The Law', to 1st x-roads, left into town centre; house on left behind wall.

Gwen & Jake Scott
The Glebe House
Law Road, North Berwick
East Lothian EH39 4PL
Tel: 01620 892608
Fax: 01620 892608
E-mail: j.a.scott@tesco.net
Web: www.aboutscotland.com/glebe/house html

Entry No: 552   **Map no: 19**

A Georgian farmhouse surrounded by 350 acres of undulating countryside - and so close to Edinburgh! The farm has won awards for conservation and Michael is deeply committed to the countryside. Barbara is a gifted hostess. Gardens are informal and pretty and you may roam on the farm or play tennis. On sunny days, breakfast is served in the lovely conservatory full of fragrant climbing geraniums and jasmine. Co-ordinated bedrooms with inspired use of fabric and colour, great views and lots of space. The coral drawing room with log fire is most striking.

Rooms: 2 doubles, both en suite (bath); 2 twins, 1 en suite (shower), 1 with private bathroom.

Price: £25-£30 p.p.

Meals: Breakfast times flexible. Dinner available locally.

Closed: Christmas.

From A1 at Haddington B6368 south signed Bolton & Humbie. 2.5 miles on through Bolton, at top of hill, fork left signed Eaglescairnie. Entrance 0.5 miles on left.

Barbara Williams
Eaglescairnie Mains
Gifford
Haddington
East Lothian EH41 4HN
Tel: 01620 810491
Fax: 01620 810491
E-mail: williams.eagles@btinternet.com

Entry No: 553   **Map no: 19**

It is spectacular, built in 1798 in classical Georgian proportions. The architectural elegance is inevitable, as are the Adam fireplace, the ornate plasterwork, the mahogany furniture, and, perhaps, even the grand piano. Bedrooms encourage indolence. White linen, rattan and mahogany, a four-poster, and a sofa in each one where you may recline. The 22-acre garden and the self-catering Coach House is another escape - and all so close to Edinburgh.

Rooms: 1 four-poster, en suite; 2 twins/king size, 1 with dressing room & bathroom en suite, 1 with private bathroom. Coach House self-catering or B&B for 4-6.

Price: £45-£50 p.p. Single supp. £20. Coach House; B&B for 4: £200 per night or self-catering for 4-6 from £600- £1200 p.w.

Meals: Breakfast times flexible; packed lunch, from £3-£5 and dinner, from £20-30, by arrangement.

Closed: Never.

A8 from Edinburgh. At large airport sign, immed. left to Gogarstone Rd. At end, right into Freeland Rd. Follow to end; sign for Ratho Hall 1.5 miles on. Take care crossing road to driveway.

Janet & Freddie Small
Ratho Hall
Baird Road, Ratho
Midlothian EH28 8QY
Tel: 0131 335 3333
Fax: 0131 335 3035
E-mail: ratho.hall@btinternet.com
Web: www.countrymansions.com

Entry No: 554   **Map no:** 19

Life here tends to centre around the kitchen table and the Aga - which is not to say that the dining room isn't peaceful, with its family paintings and country views, nor that the drawing room isn't inviting, with its log fire and comfy sofas. You'll get a big and totally relaxed welcome from the Westmacotts. Bedrooms are prettily decorated and kitted-out with comfort in mind - basins and bathrobes, for example. Only 10 minutes from Edinburgh airport with a train from nearby Dalmeny village to the city centre every half hour. Louise is happy to meet you from Dalmeny station.

Rooms: 2 twins/doubles, 1 double, 1 single all sharing a bathroom and separate wc.

Price: £25-£30 p.p. Single supp. £5.

Meals: Breakfast times flexible. Dinner available locally.

Closed: Christmas.

From lights in centre of Kirkliston, follow sign for Forth Rd Bridge (A8000) & continue at r'bout. Approx. 0.5 miles on, 1st right after Milton Farm. Down lane, over small bridge & right before cottages.

Louise & Michael Westmacott
Craigbrae
Kirkliston
By Edinburgh
West Lothian EH29 9EL
Tel: 0131 331 1205
Fax: 0131 319 1476
E-mail: westmacott@compuserve.com

Entry No: 555   **Map no:** 19

A setting that townies dream of – 170 traffic-free acres that wrap around the house, and majestic views. This is an excellent base for families, with sheep, horses and cows and masses of opportunity for fishing, walking, cycling and climbing. Your pine-clad, cathedral-roofed sitting room is sunny and south-facing and has a gallery landing with two single beds. Val, generous and enthusiastic, will collect you from the airport or the station; she has cooked professionally, so the food's great.

Rooms: Guest wing: 1 king-size, 2 singles, shower room and sitting area. House: 1 twin/double, en suite (bath).

Price: £30 p.p. (3 + nights, £25 p.p.) No single supp. Reductions for children.

Meals: Breakfast times flexible, by arrangement; packed lunch, from £3-5 and afternoon tea, from £3; dinner £20-£25; all by arrangement.

Closed: Rarely.

A81, 3 miles south of Aberfoyle. 0.5 miles north of Gartmore House, over River Forth & 1st private road to right. Look for house sign half way up. Drive to right of house beside pond.

Val Willis
The Barns of Shannochill
By Aberfoyle
The Trossachs
Stirlingshire FK8 3UZ
Tel: 01877 382878
Fax: 01877 382964
E-mail: shannochill@aol.com

Entry No: 556   **Map no: 23**

High on Edinburgh's most exalted Georgian escarpment, this eyrie mixes 19th-century elegance with Danish and Middle Eastern style. Brass beds, burnished pine floors and a vast hall with a stairway that floats regally above a magnificent sitting room; glimpse the Castle through the trees. Erlend, an award-winning travel writer, swapped the rigours of daily deadlines (he was a Scottish correspondent) for freelancing and advanced egg-scrambling. Breakfasts are a full Franco-Scottish affair with oak-smoked salmon and home-made Auvergne jam. The Cloustons will meet you from the train or take you on a tour. It's relaxed and fun.

Rooms: 1 twin with basin and private bathroom (Victorian bath & shower); 1 double with basin, with private shower next door.

Price: From £42.50 p.p. Single occ. £55.

Meals: Breakfast times flexible. Dinner available locally.

Closed: Hardly ever.

Heriot Row is parallel to Princes Street, 3 major blocks north.

Erlend & Hélène Clouston
41 Heriot Row
Edinburgh EH3 6ES
Tel: 0131 225 3113
Fax: 0131 225 3113
E-mail: erlendc@lineone.net

Entry No: 557   **Map no: 19**

Edinburgh

A treat to stay in a Victorian Edinburgh townhouse that remains a family home with original fireplaces, cornices and (working) shutters. Michele is Australian and a ceramicist, so visit her basement studio and enjoy the 'down under' artistic flair revealed throughout the house and the fascinating collection of antique and modern furniture, art and artefacts collected on her travels. Up the cupola-lit stairs to the guest rooms at the top – we fell for the doubles, with their multi-coloured bedspreads and views to the Pentland Hills. A warm and stylish city-centre retreat.

Rooms: 1 double, en suite (shower); 1 double, 1 twin sharing bathroom and separate wc.

Price: £35-£45 p.p. August £45-£55 p.p. Single occ. £45-£60.

Meals: Breakfast times flexible; dinner, £15-£25, on request.

Closed: Never.

On A8 from airport, at Haymarket Terrace, left at lights into Grosvenor St, then left into Crescent. Airport bus stops 1 block away. 5 minute walk to Princes St.

Michele Bills
17 Lansdowne Crescent
Edinburgh EH12 5EH
Tel: 0131 5384926
Fax: 0131 5384926
E-mail: billsmic@cableinet.co.uk
Web: www.aboutscotland.com/edin/lansdowne2.html

Entry No: 558   **Map no:** 19

Only the tick-tock of the grandfather clock disturbs the peace as you lounge in armchairs after breakfast with the papers, or discuss the cultural delights of the city with your friendly, multi-lingual hostess - Gillian is a blue-badge guide. Bedrooms (below stairs, looking onto an attractive patio garden) are decorated harmoniously in cerise and cream: Farrow and Ball paints and Nina Campbell fabrics are standard here. Scottish shortbread and books in the bedrooms, local artists' paintings on the walls and the Meadows opposite - a seductive city base indeed.

Rooms: 1 twin, en suite (bath/shower); 1 twin (with single room attached), en suite (bath/shower).

Price: From £32.50 p.p. From £40 p.p. during Edinburgh Festival.

Meals: Breakfast until 9am, July-August; flexible rest of the year. Dinner available locally.

Closed: 22-27 December.

From centre of Edinburgh (West End), Lothian Rd to Tollcross (clock) & Melville Drive. At 2nd major traffic lights, right into Argyle Place & immed. left into Fingal Place.

Gillian Charlton-Meyrick
2 Fingal Place
The Meadows
Edinburgh EH9 1JX
Tel: 0131 667 4436
Fax: 0131 667 4436
E-mail: bleish1936@aol.com

Entry No: 559   **Map no:** 19

The house is blessed with fine features: a cantilever staircase and cupola, a bow-walled dining room, spiral stairs that lead down to the basement where the guest rooms are. It's a rare find, too - an entire, undivided Georgian house, in a lovely terrace (1821) and so close to the city centre. Susie and Andrew have done everything well and the brightly coloured rooms are better kitted out than most poly-starred hotel rooms; the single, however, has no window. But the comfort here comes with a personal touch and with very nice hosts who can give you inside knowledge of this most beautiful of Scottish cities.

Rooms: 1 twin, 1 double, both en suite (shower); 1 single, en suite (bath).

Price: £35-£50 p.p.

Meals: Breakfast times flexible. Huge variety of restaurants close by.

Closed: Christmas.

Queensferry Road out of Edinburgh towards Forth Road Bridge. Travel 250 yds along Queensferry Street. Before Dean Bridge, bear left.

Andrew & Susie Hamilton
16 Lynedoch Place
Edinburgh EH3 7PY
Tel: 0131 225 5507
Fax: 0131 226 4185
E-mail: susie.lynedoch@btinternet.com

Entry No: 560   **Map no: 19**

American Clarissa has lost none of her enthusiasm for her adopted city. The house is handsome, the atmosphere is easy. From the sitting room you look onto pear tree and clematis and, in the distance, the rolling Pentland Hills. The terrace and south-facing garden are perfect for relaxation and reading. Guests have a study/sitting room - complete with log fire - to themselves and an apple-green painted bedroom with antique American four-poster bed. Fling open your shutters in the morning, then breakfast in the elegant dining room. Clarissa is involved in the arts and local events and can help plan your day.

Rooms: 1 double, en suite (bath); 1 double, with private bathroom.

Price: £30-£40 p.p. Single night supp. £5.

Meals: Breakfast times flexible. Dinner available locally.

Closed: 23-29 December.

From centre of Edinburgh, A702 south, signed Peebles. Pass Churchill Theatre (on left), to traffic lights. Albert Terrace 1st right after theatre.

Clarissa Notley
1 Albert Terrace
Edinburgh EH10 5EA
Tel: 0131 447 4491

Entry No: 561   **Map no: 19**

A 10-minute stroll through some of Europe's finest classical architecture is all that stands between you and the centre of Edinburgh. What a city base! The 1825 house is a showcase for Fiona's professional interior design talents. Impressive features - cantilevered staircase, marble fireplaces, double-barrelled cupola and soaring ceilings - sit with lavish design, designer fabric, real candle chandelier and four-poster or canopied beds. The self-contained flat is equally sumptuous.

Rooms: 2 doubles, 1 single, all en suite. Self-catering: 2 doubles in separate flat, both en suite.

Price: £50-£55 p.p. Self-catering £140 per night (3 nights minimum).

Meals: Breakfast times flexible. Great selection of restaurants nearby.

Closed: Christmas Day.

From Edinburgh, Queensferry Rd for Forth Rd Bridge. 3rd right after Dean Bridge into Dean Park Crescent, then 2nd right into Danube St.

Fiona Mitchell-Rose
7 Danube Street
Edinburgh EH4 1NN
Tel: 0131 332 2755
Fax: 0131 343 3648
E-mail: seven.danubestreet@virgin.net

Entry No: 562   **Map no: 19**

A huge Jacobean cupboard, a Georgian mosaic, a cantilevered staircase with cupola above: the entrance promises much and you won't be disappointed. You are the guest of a bright, easy-going, chatty hostess whose house is one of only 20 complete Georgian houses left in Edinburgh. A mere five minutes' walk from the city centre, yet many guest bedrooms have garden and sea views. It is large, yet the scale remains human and there are many homely touches. Some rooms have opulent drapes, some patchwork quilts; all have lovely linen.

Rooms: 1 triple, 1 twin, 3 doubles, 3 twins/doubles, 1 single, all en suite (bath &/or shower).

Price: £45-£60 p.p. Single supp. by arrangement.

Meals: Breakfast 8-9am Mon-Fri, 8.30-9.30am Sat-Sun. Dinner available locally.

Closed: Never.

Abercromby Place lies parallel to Queen Street just north of city centre in 'New Town'. Off-street parking.

Eirlys Lloyd
Abercromby House
17 Abercromby Place
Edinburgh EH3 6LB
Tel: 0131 557 8036
Fax: 0131 558 3453
E-mail: eirlys.lloyd@virgin.net
Web: www.abercrombyhouse.com

Entry No: 563   **Map no: 19**

For nearly 200 years, Annie's terraced fisherman's cottage has stood beside a salmon and trout river. Even today, you can catch your own breakfast in the river, and Annie - a professional cook who conjures up the most delicious breakfasts, including her own home-made mushroom scones, bread and marmalade - will prepare it for you. Bedrooms are fresh, airy and very comfortable and the whole cottage is full of light, flowers, books and original watercolours; there are two gorgeous retrievers, too. No wonder people keep coming back to visit. *Children over six welcome.*

Rooms: 1 double, en suite; 1 twin with large private bathroom (down narrow stairs).

Price: £20 p.p. Single supp. £25.

Meals: Breakfast until 9am. Good restaurants nearby.

Closed: Never.

From south A1, exit for Musselburgh. Through town & cross bridge. Eskside West 1st left. From Edinburgh, A199 (A1) to Musselburgh bridge. Eskside West on right, just before bridge.

Annie Deacon
53 Eskside West
Musselburgh
Edinburgh EH21 6RB
Tel: 0131 665 2875

Although you're within hailing distance of Edinburgh city centre, you can add a rural footnote to the metropolitan delights. The front door opens onto a mosaic-tiled entrance hall. From the bay-windowed breakfast room, light and airy and with original cornice and plasterwork, you look out over the garden; the patio catches the evening sun. Breakfasts are something special - Iola makes her own bread and jam and offers the full Scottish feast. Bedrooms are fresh, welcoming and blissfully quiet.

Rooms: 1 twin with private bathroom; 1 double with private shower.

Price: £28-£30 p.p. Ask about single supp.

Meals: Breakfast times flexible. Dinner available locally.

Closed: 23-26 December.

Enter Edinburgh on A702. 0.5 miles from bypass, fork right down Braid Road, after pedestrian crossing. House 0.5 miles on left after mini-r'bout. Free on-street parking.

Iola & Michael Fass
60 Braid Road
Morningside
Edinburgh EH10 6AL
Tel: 0131 446 9356
Fax: 0131 447 7367
E-mail: fass@dial.pipex.com

There are secrets sealed at Inveresk - from the heavy, long-locked safe to the still-hidden Roman tunnel. Two enormous bow-fronted, pine-floored rooms are in the tower. Built in 1596 on an ancient Roman site with Georgian and Victorian additions, Cromwell plotted his siege of Edinburgh Castle from the house. The dining and drawing rooms are huge and you can play the grand piano; panelling cloaks the hall and the wide 1643 staircase. Modern flower paintings adorn the bedrooms; a 19th-century Italian mahogany bed with matching wardrobe and washstand dominate the suite.

Rooms: 1 family en suite (shower); 1 double, 1 twin, both en suite (bath).

Price: From £35 p.p. Single supp. £5.

Meals: Breakfast 8.30am. Dinner available locally.

Closed: Never.

First and foremost it is a home - this Edwardian townhouse certainly feels friendly and easy - but it's big on comfort, too. Barbara goes the extra mile for you: beds are capacious, bathrobes are large and fluffy, curtains and pelmets elaborate, fireplaces are beautifully renovated and there's sherry on the dresser. Barbara is super (so is Poppy, the Cairn terrier!) and you may find it hard to leave. For breakfast, local sausages and bacon, Finnan haddock, kippers or omelette. Regular buses run to the centre and there are eating places within 10 minutes' walk.

Rooms: 2 doubles, en suite (bath & shower); 1 twin/double, en suite (shower).

Price: £37.50 p.p. Single supp. £12.50.

Meals: Breakfast times flexible. Dinner available locally.

Closed: Never.

From Edinburgh, A199 (A1) to Musselburgh. There, follow signs to Inveresk. At top of Inveresk Brae, sharp right into cul-de-sac. 2nd opening on right, opp. gates with GM on them, bear right past cottages to house.

Leave city by-pass at Straiton exit & follow A701 for City Centre until 1st r'bout. Take 2nd exit, Craigmiller Park, then 2nd left, Wilton Rd & 2nd right, Granby Rd. Free on-street parking.

Alice & John Chute
Inveresk House
3 Inveresk Village, Musselburgh
Edinburgh EH21 7UA
Tel: 0131 665 5855
Fax: 0131 665 0578
E-mail: chute.inveresk@btinternet.com
Web: www.btinternet.com/~chute.inveresk

Barbara Kellett
32 Granby Road
Edinburgh EH16 5NL
Tel: 0131 667 9078
Fax: 0131 668 1051
E-mail: barbara.kellett@virgin.net
Web: www.barbara-kellett.com

Entry No: 566   **Map no: 19**

Entry No: 567   **Map no: 19**

The fine, organic garden gives fruit, the river yields salmon, the moors provide game in winter. Likeable and energetic, the Grahams are an exceptionally welcoming family combining informality and luxury in peaceful, rural, central Scotland. Colin, a piper, is a trilingual tour guide while Fiona is a wine buff and talented cook (shortbread is always in good supply and ice-cream, jam and bread are home-made, too). Imaginative dinners are served in the conservatory with views to a floodlit Stirling Castle. The bedrooms have gigantic beds and generous, sunny bathrooms. You are 30 minutes from Gleneagles and Loch Lomond.

Rooms: 1 twin/double, en suite (bath & shower); 1 twin with private bath & shower.

Price: From £35-£38 p.p. Single supp. £15.

Meals: Breakfast 8.30-9am; dinner £25.

Closed: Never.

You will love Kippenross, a superb example of William Adam's Scottish Georgian country house architecture. It might be the fruit and flora of the Italian-inspired plasterwork in the duck-egg blue morning room that captivates you. It could be the polished and creaking mahogany staircase that springs from the oak-parqueted hall past ancestral portraits to the delicately printed Colefax and Fowler bedrooms. Or the stunning grounds, which are almost an arboretum, landscaped nearly 200 years ago; there are miles of river to splash and fish in, too.

Rooms: 1 twin with private shower; 2 twins, en suite (bath/shower).

Price: £39.50 p.p. Single supp. £10.

Meals: Breakfast times flexible; dinner, £24, by arrangement.

Closed: Never.

From M9, north, junc. 10 onto A84 towards Doune. After 5 miles, left on B826 towards Thornhill. Drive on left after 2.2 miles, turn right off farm drive.

From junc.11 of M9, B8033 towards Dunblane. Get in right hand lane & take 1st right across reservation to lodge. Keep on drive, over bridge, up hill to house.

Fiona & Colin Graham
Mackeanston House
Doune
Trossachs
Perthshire FK16 6AX
Tel: 01786 850213
Fax: 01786 850414
E-mail: mackean.house@cwcom.net

Sue & Patrick Stirling-Aird
Kippenross
Dunblane
Perthshire FK15 0LQ
Tel: 01786 824048
Fax: 01786 823124
E-mail: kippenross@hotmail.com

Entry No: 568   **Map no: 23**

Entry No: 569   **Map no: 23**

A lovely Georgian manse tragically burnt down in 1996 but rebuilt with great taste, elegance and style. Light wood predominates and rooms are warm with cornicing, thick carpets, combed ceilings, traditional bedding and lots of space. Bright and quirky Joanna and Duncan clearly enjoy the world of B&B, and the atmosphere is relaxed and informal. Guests eat in the wonderful country kitchen or in the conservatory overlooking a pretty walled garden with colourful borders. Under five miles from the motorway and 35 miles from Edinburgh.

Rooms: 1 twin, en suite (bath/shower); 1 twin with private bathroom.

Price: £28-£32 p.p. No single supp.

Meals: Breakfast times flexible; dinner from £15, by arrangement.

Closed: Christmas & New Year.

When Frances and Hamish first set eyes on Caplawhead it was derelict, but it stood among panoramic views - they couldn't resist. Now lovingly restored and seamlessly extended, the house has comfortable cottagey bedrooms, pristine shower rooms and an elegant drawing room with a little tower built especially to take in the view down the valley to the 'links' of the Forth. Ebullient and enthusiastic hosts - ask Hamish about all things Scottish and try Frances' fragrant jams and jellies. There are books, pictures and family antiques and pictures, but a Winnie the Pooh weathervane says it all. This is a fun place.

Rooms: 1 twin, 1 double, both with private shower.

Price: £25 p.p.

Meals: Breakfast times flexible. Good pubs and restaurants nearby.

Closed: Never.

From Edinburgh, cross Forth Road Bridge. Follow M90 to junc. 8. Through Glenfarg, then 1st right, signed Arngask. 1st house on right.

From M90, junc. 6, then A977 to Kincardine Bridge. 1 mile after The Crook of Devon, right to Rumbling Bridge & Crieff (A823). 1 mile on, house signed to right. At end of lane.

Joanna & Duncan Cameron
The Old Manse
Arngask
Glenfarg
Perthshire PH2 9QA
Tel: 01577 830394
Fax: 01577 830394

Frances & Hamish Lindsay
Caplawhead
Rumbling Bridge, By Yetts o' Muckhart
Nr Kinross
Perthshire KY13 0QD
Tel: 01259 781556
E-mail: hamish-frances@caplawhead.freeserve.co.uk

Entry No: 570   **Map no:** 23

Entry No: 571   **Map no:** 23

Expensive, but worth it. You will be spoiled - here is huge comfort, beautiful food and bathrooms and bedrooms to expand in. The approach sets the scene - a mile-long drive through wood and rhododendron leads you to formal gardens, exotic trees, ferny burn and waterfall. It is a surprising house (built in 1969) and the third to be built on this historic site; you can see the remains of earlier castles. The interior is magnificent, with elegant, generously furnished guest rooms. Your hosts are great fun and shooting and fishing can be arranged. *Children over 12 welcome.*

Rooms: 2 twins/doubles, en suite (bath/shower); 2 twins/doubles, en suite (bath).

Price: From £70 p.p. Single supp. £15-£70.

Meals: Breakfast until 9am; dinner, 3 courses, £30, with 24 hours' notice.

Closed: Christmas & New Year.

From M90 Broxden r'bout, A93 towards Perth for 1 mile, then sharp right onto B9112 for Dunning. After 2.7 miles, wrought-iron gates on right.

Derek & Angela Straker
Dupplin Castle
By Aberdalgie
Perth, Perthshire PH2 0PY
Tel: 01738 623224
Fax: 01738 444140
E-mail: dupplin@netcomuk.co.uk
Web: www.dupplin.co.uk

Entry No: 572   **Map no: 23**

Anne and David are natural hosts and enjoy sharing their newly renovated, traditional Scottish farmhouse overlooking the River Tay. Through their farm/livery stable yard runs the Coronation Walk used by the ancient Scottish kings en route from Falkland to Scone. Inside, dusky pink, cream and pale yellow work well with polished mahogany, while the scent of fresh flowers fills the rooms. Anne loves to cook using local produce and fruit and veg from the garden. The A90 (0.5 miles from the house) can be busy during the day but should not disturb you at night.

Rooms: 1 double, en suite (bath & shower); 1 twin, en suite (shower); 1 twin, en suite (bath).

Price: From £28 p.p. Single supp. £5.

Meals: Breakfast times flexible; dinner, £20, by arrangement.

Closed: Christmas & New Year.

From A90 Perth to Dundee road, take Kinfauns exit (NOT Kinfauns Castle). Drive up hill for 0.25 miles, left, & straight up hill to gates on left.

Anne & David MacLehose
Over Kinfauns
Perth
Perthshire PH2 7LD
Tel: 01738 860538
Fax: 01738 860803
E-mail: b&b@overkinfauns.co.uk
Web: www.overkinfauns.co.uk

Entry No: 573   **Map no: 23**

Sitting on the shoulder of Lucklawhill, this traditional stone-built cottage is part of a former community of smallholdings. The impressive conservatory has stunning views south over the Eden estuary to St Andrews. You can have afternoon tea here and Alison will bake cakes for you and serve her home-made jams. The furnishings and décor throughout reflect her many years spent in the far east. There's a sitting room with a woodburning stove and a door to the tranquil garden and terrace. In the bedrooms there are books, magazines and fresh flowers. Excellent value.

Rooms: 1 double, en suite (shower); 1 twin/double with private shower room.

Price: From £25 p.p.

Meals: Breakfast times flexible; packed lunch, £5 and dinner, 20, by arrangement.

Closed: Never.

Sit on the terrace and listen to numerous songbirds. Surprisingly, you are in the middle of St Andrew's, just ten minutes walk from the Royal and Ancient Golf Club. This tall, terraced house may be grey-stoned and traditional on the outside, but it has been decorated with a contemporary flourish by Jill. Gorgeous mosaic tables and showers, a stunning turquoise kitchen, and a bright conservatory. In the bedrooms, antique bedcovers and lovely linen and chintzes. Enchanting. Jill is easy, really friendly and generous. *Children over 12 welcome.*

Rooms: 1 twin, 1 double, both en suite (shower); 1 double with private bathroom.

Price: From £35 p.p. Single occ. £42.

Meals: Breakfast times flexible. Lunch & dinner available locally.

Closed: Never.

A914 to Balmullo. Through village heading north, & 0.25 miles on, hard left. Right at top of road; left at phone box.

Enter St Andrews on A917. Past Old Course Hotel. Right at 2nd mini r'bout then left through arch at 2nd mini r'bout. 250 yds on, right into Queens Gardens. Right at T-junc. House on left.

Alison Outlaw
Ashbank
Lucklawhill
Balmullo
Fife KY16 0BQ
Tel: 01334 870807
E-mail: alison.outlaw@talk21.com
Web: www.ashbank-standrews.co.uk

Jill Hardie
18 Queen's Terrace
St Andrews
Fife KY16 9QF
Tel: 01334 478849
Fax: 01334 470283
E-mail: jill_hardie@hotmail.com
Web: www.allaboutscotland.com

Entry No: 574   **Map no: 24**

Entry No: 575   **Map no: 24**

A long, tree-lined drive leads to an elegant farmhouse, good furniture, space, fun and a huge welcome. The double-ended drawing room has two large log fires, bow windows, pine floor and flowers from the garden. The farm runs down past tennis and croquet lawns almost to the Rock and Spindle beach, the views are spectacular, the coastline walks exhilarating, the cooking (by both hosts) excellent; they love to use local produce. They are easy hosts who know how to look after you. Come join the family.

Rooms: 1 twin, en suite (bath); 1 twin/double with private bathroom; 1 twin/double, en suite (shower).

Price: £28-£32 p.p. Single supp. £10.

Meals: Breakfast times flexible; dinner £25, by arrangement.

Closed: Never.

From St. Andrews, A917 for 2 miles towards Crail. Driveway in 1st line of trees on left after St. Andrews.

Sandy & Frippy Fyfe
Kinkell
St. Andrews
Fife KY16 8PN
Tel: 01334 472003
Fax: 01334 475248
E-mail: fyfe@kinkell.com
Web: www.kinkell.com

Entry No: 576   **Map no: 24**

Borrow a bicycle made for two (or one), take a packed lunch and explore; there are masses of birds and wildlife to spot, or you can wander dreamily amid the glorious profusion of the garden. Rosie, *Cordon Bleu* trained, loves cooking, using produce from her own garden. You eat in the sitting room of this converted 18th-century smithy; it has family paintings, antiques and a real pipe organ. No fear of night starvation, either - in the bedrooms, which have stencilled cornices, there are delicious home-made biscuits.

Rooms: 2 twins, en suite (1 shower, 1 bath/shower).

Price: From £25 p.p. Single supp. £5.

Meals: Breakfast times flexible; dinner, from £15, by arrangement.

Closed: Occasionally.

From St. Andrews, A917 for Crail. After 4 miles, ignore turning for Boarhills, & continue to small river. Over bridge; house 2nd on left.

Rosie & Keith Birkinshaw
Falside Smiddy
Boarhills
St. Andrews
Fife KY16 8PT
Tel: 01334 880479
E-mail: birk@falside.freeserve.co.uk

Entry No: 577   **Map no: 24**

"One of the prettiest houses in Scotland"? It is an historic, traditional country house set in lovely gardens and run by delightful people. The bedrooms are big and utterly charming and among the most comfortable that we have stayed in. Then there's a 170-acre private loch where birds can be watched and pike fished; a great organ halfway up the main stairs with air pumped from a separate building in the grounds; a 16th-century central building with wings added in 1780 to a design filched from Adam. So *much* of interest. Elegant furniture, lovely pictures and excellent bathrooms. *Children over 12 welcome.*

Rooms: 1 twin, 1 double, both en suite (1 bath, 1 bath/shower). Adjoining twin available for children sharing parents' bathroom.

Price: £35-£40 p.p. Single supp. £5.

Meals: Breakfast times flexible. Bistro nearby for dinner.

Closed: Christmas & New Year.

From Blairgowrie, onto A923 for Dunkeld. Look for sign saying 'Kinloch. Drive safely'; 1st entrance on left after sign.

Kenneth & Nicolette Lumsden
Marlee House
Kinloch
Blairgowrie
Perthshire PH10 6SD
Tel: 01250 884216

Entry No: 578   **Map no:** 23

The view from the circular balcony that rings the drawing room is simply stunning and the deep gorge provides fabulous walks. Nicky and Lachie battle to keep up with the needs of the vast, impressive home that has been in the family for five centuries and you, too, will forgive it any mustiness or dustiness. Staying here is a memorable experience. Nothing contrived, sterile or luxurious, but so much drama and intrigue that it could be a film set. Breakfast is served in the 18th-century dining room and you can use the Regency drawing room.

Rooms: 1 four-poster, en suite (bath); 1 twin with extra single, with private bathroom.

Price: £35 p.p. Single supp. £5.

Meals: Breakfast 8-9am. Dinner available locally.

Closed: 30 November-1 March.

From Blairgowrie, A93 towards Braemar for 2 miles. Just before end of 30mph limit, sharp right-hand bend, with drive on right. Follow drive for 1 mile.

Nicky & Lachie Rattray
Craighall Castle
Blairgowrie
Perthshire PH10 7JB
Tel: 01250 874749
Fax: 01250 874749
E-mail: lrattray@calinet.co.uk

Entry No: 579   **Map no:** 23

East Scotland

Ancient, historic and packed with interest, the house was begun as a tower in 1585 and added to until Victorian times and into the present century. Inside, it is delightfully old-fashioned, even a little threadbare in places but so much to compensate: beautiful plasterwork, marble busts, antiques, impressive staircase, open fires. Paul is a conservationist and writer and both he and Louise welcome with grace and humour and are generous in a naturally spontaneous way. You can roam freely on the estate with its parkland, woods and heather moorland.

Rooms: 1 four-poster with private bathroom; 1 double with shared bathroom. Further single available.

Price: £30-£35 p.p. No single supp.

Meals: Breakfast times flexible; dinner, £15-£20, by arrangement.

Closed: Christmas & New Year.

Boats are dangerous things, liable to turn over, slip below the waves, hit rocks or make you sick. So what a brilliant idea to provide you with a 'risk-free nautical accommodation experience' as it is described by the local Tourist Board (in their inimitable way). Having plied the North Sea for years as a fishing vessel, she - the boat - has come to a more dignified end than awaited her at the boat-breakers. Those of you with a sense of history will not mind the odd angles and unusual arrangements. Expect a hull of a breakfast. A very special plaice, indeed.

Rooms: 1 Neptune-sized hammock; seagull nest for smaller folk.

Price: Sole occupancy preferred.

Meals: Fishnet soup with buttered coast.

Closed: 1 August 2001.

From Blairgowrie, A926 to Kirriemuir. After 5 miles, left to Alyth. Through town on Airlie St. After 2.5 miles, round sharp left bend. Right into drive.

From coast of Angus, snorkel due east past oil rig to upturned boat, following palm trees on horizon. Appease Man O War at door with seaweed garland.

Paul & Louise Ramsay
Bamff House
Alyth, Blairgowrie
Perthshire PH11 8LF
Tel: 01828 632992
Fax: 01828 632992
E-mail: louiseramsay@bamff.demon.co.uk
Web: www.bamff.co.uk

Ivor Sunk
Shorley Knot
Upside Town
Angus HE1 PME
Tel: 0800 S0S0S0S
E-mail: runaground@fishandchips.com
Web: www.fishandchips.com

Entry No: 580   **Map no: 23**

Entry No: 581   **Map no: 24**

An 18th-century farm building halfway up a mountain: Lindsay has carried out award-winning renovation and is now working on the garden. Inside: patchwork bedspreads, blue and white Portuguese tiles, seagrass matting and a woodburning stove. You have your own kitchen, dining and sitting room, too, so you can self-cater (min. three days, and by arrangement) if you like. Lindsay is charming and loves nurturing her garden, her pets and her guests. Sit on the patio, tuck into her fruitcake, gaze at snow-capped mountain-to-loch views. The sunsets and walks are fabulous too. *Children over eight welcome.*

Rooms: 1 twin, 1 double sharing private bathroom and sitting room.

Price: £28 p.p. Single supp. £12.

Meals: Breakfast times flexible. Dinner, 3 courses, with wine, £20, by arrangement.

Closed: Christmas & New Year.

From A9 north of Pitlochry, take Killicrankie turning. Left onto B8019 for 8 miles to Loch Tummel Inn. House up forestry track on right, 0.75 miles on.

Lindsay Morison
Grenich Steading
Strathtummel
Pitlochry
Perthshire PH16 5RT
Tel: 01882 634332

Entry No: 582   **Map no:** 23

At the foot of Glenesk, this 18th-century house has a gorgeous setting. Your hosts are fun - John, with a twinkle in his eye, Valerie, lover of Labradors, adores a chat, and is charming and kind. Soft sofas, pretty lamps, robes in the bathroom – it's deliciously old-fashioned, stylish and cosy. Family photos sit alongside fine china and prints that hint at John's love of country pursuits. Valerie waves her wand in the kitchen, too: her fish, meat and game dishes are matched by fine wines (their son is in the trade), served in glasses that sparkle. A delightful place.

Rooms: 1 twin, en suite (shower); 1 twin with private bathroom (bath); 1 single with either shared or private bathroom.

Price: £30 p.p.

Meals: Breakfast until 9.30am. Dinner, by arrangement.

Closed: December 14-January 14.

From A90, B966 through Edzell, continue on towards Fettercairn. House just under 2 miles along, behind a beech hedge.

Valerie & John Smart
Woodmyre
Edzell
Brechin
Angus DD9 7UX
Tel: 01356 648416
Fax: 01356 648416
E-mail: smart@woodmyre.freeserve.co.uk

Entry No: 583   **Map no:** 24

"The people, the setting, the house, are just perfect," wrote our inspector. You might find David casting a line into the River Dee that flows behind the house, or Meg picking flowers for your room; they will stop it all to greet you and soon you'll be having tea on the terrace, maybe with binoculars in hand, following a kestrel or an eagle. Your room may be huge - two are - and full of fine furniture, fluffy bathrobes, fresh flowers and, maybe, a balcony. Bathrooms are exquisite with great views, too. There are so many places to visit and Meg seems to know them all.

Rooms: 1 twin/double, en suite (bath/shower); 1 twin/double (with balcony & dressing room); 1 double, with private shower rooms. Extra shower, too.

Price: £30-£40 p.p. No single supp.

Meals: Breakfast 8-9am; dinner, £22.50, by arrangement. Also available locally.

Closed: Rarely.

From Aboyne, A93 west towards Braemar. Just after 50 mph sign, left down Rhu-na-Haven Road. House 400 yds on, 4th gateway on right.

David & Meg White
Lys-na-Greyne House
Rhu-na-Haven Road
Aboyne
Aberdeenshire AB34 5JD
Tel: 013398 87397
Fax: 013398 86441
E-mail: dwhite7301@aol.com

Entry No: 584   **Map no: 24**

Offspring of the *original* Aberdeen Angus herd graze the 300 acres here and you can roam the same fertile, Don valley land. The handsome farmhouse has been in the family since 1762 and was completely redecorated three years ago, when the guest rooms were added. The décor is 'traditional country house' with family pieces, like hunting prints, Colefax fabrics and Farrow & Ball paints. Guests are treated very much as friends and your *Cordon Bleu*-trained hostess is happy to set dinner in the dining room or in the Aga-warmed kitchen. On the Aberdeen 'Castle Trail' and totally peaceful.

Rooms: 1 twin en suite (bath); 1 twin, 1 double sharing bath & shower room.

Price: From £28 p.p.

Meals: Breakfast times flexible; dinner, 3 courses, £20.

Closed: Occasionally.

20 miles from Aberdeen on A944 (towards Alford); through Tillyfourie, then left for Muir of Fowlis & Tough; after Tough 2nd farm drive on left, signed.

John & Veronica Evans-Freke
Lynturk Home Farm
Alford
Aberdeenshire AB33 8DU
Tel: 019755 62504
Fax: 019755 63517

Entry No: 585   **Map no: 24**

New life and comfort at this unusual Gordon castle. Lois is a West coast Gordon and has used bold, traditionally-inspired colour schemes (plenty of tartan) in the big Georgian guest rooms and fittingly old-fashioned bathrooms. The atmosphere is definitely 'castle' but without the chill (new central heating) or overly formal factors. Dinners are five-course and candlelit with plenty of good home-made and local food. Painting and bridge courses and Jacobite murder mystery weekends are part of the new order too. 30 acres of garden to roam, as the deer do - or settle for a game of croquet?

Rooms: 1 four-poster en suite (bath); 1 four-poster, 1 double, 2 singles sharing bathroom.

Price: £77.50 p.p. dinner, 5 courses and B&B.

Meals: Breakfast times flexible. Dinner included. Packed lunch by arrangement.

Closed: Never.

On B9023, 0.5 miles south of Cornhill.

Lois Breckon
Castle of Park
Cornhill
Aberdeenshire
Tel: 01466 751111
Fax: 01466 751111/751667
E-mail: booking@castleofpark.net
Web: www.castleofpark.net

Entry No: 586   **Map no:** 28

When the Minister lived here in the 1820s, he commissioned a builder to add a kitchen for the princely sum of £130. The views beyond the Blanches' eight and a half acres have changed little since then; still no other houses. Sensitively restored, spotless bedrooms are light and airy and Doreen thoughtfully lays out fruit and mineral water. The drawing room has a baby grand and stacks of books. Only an hour from Aberdeen airport and close enough for you to enjoy the little fishing villages of the Moray coast. Look out for the touches of exotica - the elephant lamps and a Burmese temple door. *Children by arrangement.*

Rooms: 1 double, en suite (shower); 1 twin, en suite (bath).

Price: £30 p.p. No single supp. £27.50 p.p. for two nights or more.

Meals: Breakfast times flexible; dinner, 3 courses, £20.

Closed: Occasionally.

From Keith, A95 towards Banff. After 3.5 miles, left signed Grange Church. Left again opposite church.

Doreen & Bill Blanche
Grange House
Grange
Keith
Banffshire AB55 6RY
Tel: 01542 870206
Fax: 01542 870206
E-mail: wd.blanche@zetnet.co.uk

Entry No: 587   **Map no:** 28

East Scotland

The Bishop of Spynie used to row across the lake to 'entertain' at Westfield House. There's stacks of history here, but John and Veronica have underplayed it and the result is a bright, elegant, easy place. John's family settled here in 1862 when the house was 300 years old and the solid oak staircase, hung with ancestral oils, sports a Maclean tartan carpet. Heavy, antique furniture sits with plump sofas and the bedrooms are fun - one is extremely pink - and have lots of books, old bedsteads and lovely views. You can play tennis, walk for miles and buy John's whisky - he grows the barley for it right here.

Rooms: 1 twin, en suite (bath); 1 twin with private bath & shower; 1 single with private bath.

Price: £30 p.p. No single supp.

Meals: Breakfast until 9.30am; dinner, 3 courses, £20, by arrangement.

Closed: Never.

From Elgin, A96 west for Forres & Inverness. After 2.5 miles, right onto B9013 for Burghead. After 1 mile, house signed right at x-roads. Continue to sign 'Westfield House & office'.

John & Veronica Maclean
Westfield House
Nr. Elgin
Moray IV30 8XL
Tel: 01343 547308
Fax: 01343 551340

Entry No: 588   **Map no: 27**

With listed buildings, a sense of history is usually assured; at this 1776 country mansion, history extends into the orchard where King Malcolm was murdered among the windfalls about 1,000 years ago. The stone staircase came from ruined Blervie castle. Paddy and Fiona, who know the area well, are still restoring; there are original doors and shutters, marble and carved wood fireplaces, antiques, antlers, guns, violins, huge painted four-posters. Large, ornate mirrors add sparkle. There's a sofa in the bedrooms, books and flowers. Magical, peaceful.

Rooms: 1 four-poster with single bed and private bathroom; 1 four-poster, en suite (bath).

Price: £35 p.p. No single supp.

Meals: Breakfast until 9.30am; dinner, 4 courses, £22.

Closed: Christmas & New Year.

From A96, to Forres. South at clocktower, straight across at r'bout & take B9010. Pass hospital & 1 mile on, left at Mains of Blervie sign. Right at farm.

Paddy & Fiona Meiklejohn
Blervie
By Forres
Moray IV36 2RH
Tel: 01309 672358
Fax: 01309 672358
E-mail: meiklejohn@btinternet.com

Entry No: 589   **Map no: 27**

Three generations of women live here - when we visited, the family dog had been painted partially pink. Built as a sporting lodge in the 19th century, Garramore sits in six acres, on the road to the Isles that was built to take Highland cattle to Lowland markets. This is a former youth hostel; you won't have to make your bed these days, but bedrooms are basic and unadorned; sofas have throws. Julia, who grew up on the island of Eigg, can help you make the most of this part of Scotland. The beach is two minutes' walk away.

Rooms: 1 family (double & single bed), 1 double, both en suite (bath); 1 twin with private shower room; 3 family (double & single bed) sharing separate shower and bathroom.

Price: £20-£28 p.p. Single occ. £30.

Meals: Breakfast times flexible; dinner, 3 courses, from £15-£25, May-Sept; rest of year, supper, from £12-£15, by arrangement.

Closed: Never.

From Fort William, A830 to Mallaig. Garramore approx. 3 miles past Arisaig & 1 mile before Morar.

Julia & Sophie Moore
Garramore House
South Morar
Nr. Mallaig
Inverness-shire PH40 4PD
Tel: 01687 450268
Fax: 01687 450268

Entry No: 590   **Map no: 22**

Loch Duich is sea-fed, so seals come close and if you're lucky you might even see a dolphin. The setting is dazzling - across the Loch sit the Five Sisters of Kintail mountains and the sitting room window frames the view perfectly. You can, if you wander the large garden (complete with burn), or follow the forest or loch walks, see pine martens and deer and even eagles. Dinner is equally interesting, with sushi and Scottish seafood a speciality. Rooms are plush yet uncluttered and Anne thoughtfully lays a tray with spring water, fresh fruit and biscuits. Skye, and its ferry, are easily reached.

Rooms: 2 twins/doubles with private bathrooms.

Price: £34-£38 p.p. Single supp. £12.

Meals: Breakfast times flexible; dinner, 4 courses table d'hôte, £28, by arrangement. B.Y.O. wine.

Closed: November-April. Can open by arrangement.

Down Glenshiel on A87, & left at Shiel Bridge to Letterfearn. Over bridge, & on for 1 mile. Right at next sign for Letterfearn. House 3 miles on left.

Anne Kempthorne
Duich House
Letterfearn
Glenshiel
Ross-shire IV40 8HS
Tel: 01599 555259
Fax: 01599 555259
E-mail: duich@cwcom.net

Entry No: 591   **Map no: 22**

You can only reach Skiary by boat or on foot. Enveloped in the wilds of Loch Hourn it is lost to the outside world. No electricity, no roads, no neighbours: just mountains, waterfalls (there is a burn and pool yards up the hill for swimming), otters in the loch, deer-feeding along the shoreline. The tiny, pine-lined cottage is the last inhabited dwelling of a once busy fishing village. You will be pampered, with 'hotties', early morning tea and log fires and wonderful meals are served in the lochside greenhouse dining room. John's ferry service for guests down and across the loch makes spectacular walking accessible from Skiary.

Rooms: 3 twins with shared bathroom.

Price: Half-board (B&B, packed lunch & dinner) £70 p.p.; full-board £425 p.p. per week.

Meals: Breakfast times flexible; packed lunch & dinner included. B.Y.O wine.

Closed: Mid-October-mid-March.

From Invergarry, A87 north; left after 5 miles to Kinloch Hourn. Continue for approx. 22 miles to Kinloch Hourn, at end of road, where hosts will meet you with boat.

John & Christina Everett
Skiary
Loch Hourn
By Invergarry
Highlands PH35 4HD
Tel: 01809 511214

A peaceful, no smoking home run by Margaret, a professional musician and James, a retired chemical engineer. It is a converted coach house and stables in the beautiful Great Glen that sit among 50 acres of rhododendron, woodland and superb trees in wild lochside grounds. There are lovely views of Loch Lochy and the surrounding mountains from the guest drawing room. Bedrooms are traditional, floral. Guests can walk to the private shingle beach on Loch Lochy - wild roe deer can often be seen. *Children over eight welcome.*

Rooms: 2 twins, en suite (1 with small shower room, 1 with bath). Further twin available.

Price: From £23-£25 p.p. Single supp. £10.

Meals: Breakfast 8.30am. Good restaurants in area.

Closed: Never.

From Spean Bridge, head north on A82. After 5 miles, house signed on left.

Margaret & James Cairns
Invergloy House
Spean Bridge
Inverness-shire PH34 4DY
Tel: 01397 712681
Fax: 01397 712681
E-mail: cairns@invergloy-house.co.uk
Web: www.invergloy-house.co.uk

On the hillside by the loch, here are great views and no noise. Ponder over breakfast as the boats drift by on Loch Linnhe, then ride the cable car to what seems to be the top of the world, climb Ben Nevis or bag a Munro before returning for a tot of whisky. It's hard to fault what the Campbells have done - everything is just so, from co-ordinated fabrics and wallpapers to the complementary sherry and carved four-poster and French oak bed. The silver gleams, the flowers are artfully arranged. Joan has faithfully kept to a Victorian theme.

Rooms: 2 doubles, both en suite (bath/shower); 2 doubles, both en suite (1 bath, 1 shower).

Price: £38-£46 p.p. Single occ. £70-£90.

Meals: Breakfast until 9am. Dinner available locally.

Closed: Mid-November-Easter.

What views! "The word 'breathtaking' is entirely appropriate," says our inspector. Loch Linnhe is 200 metres away and light floods in; there is wood outside and in, windows everywhere and the walls are white to reflect the sun. The daughter's modern art hangs above a classical marble fireplace in the sitting room. The dining room connects open-plan, with a good, simple, long oak table. Bedrooms are done in fresh apple greens, yellows and white with fresh flowers, books and views. The two-acre garden is 100% organic, fertilised by seaweed, the ponies and free-range chickens.

Rooms: 1 double, en suite (shower); 2 twins sharing bath & shower.

Price: £20-£25 p.p. Single supp. by arrangement.

Meals: Breakfast until 9.15am. Dinner available locally.

Closed: Christmas & New Year.

From Glasgow, A82 to Fort William. There, right up Ashburn Lane, next to Ashburn guesthouse. House on left at top.

From Oban north on A85, then A828. Continue up to village of Duror, then left, signed Cuil. House on left after 0.5 miles.

Joan & John Campbell
The Grange
Grange Road
Fort William
Inverness-shire PH33 6JF
Tel: 01397 705516
Fax: 01397 701595
E-mail: jcampbell@grangefortwilliam.com

Bridget & Hugh Allen
Druimgrianach
Cuil Bay
Duror
Argyll PA38 4DA
Tel: 01631 740286

Entry No: 594   **Map no: 22**

Entry No: 595   **Map no: 22**

Perfect peace, rare stillness, and nothing to jar the senses. The setting itself is healing and Earle and Stella, with their understated generosity and quiet concern for guests' comfort, fit the place perfectly. At bedtime you will find your covers turned down, a hot-water bottle inside, curtains drawn and the bedside light on; maximum care and minimum fuss. The hills of Glen Etive wrap around Loch Baile Mhic Chailen, in which the house almost paddles (you certainly can) and Glencoe can be seen in the distance. Food is beautifully presented and the bread is home-made; Stella is a wonderful cook. *Children by arrangement.*

Rooms: 1 twin, 1 double, both en suite (bath); 1 twin with private shower.

Price: £24-£32 p.p. No single supp.

Meals: Breakfast times flexible; dinner, 4 courses, £18.

Closed: Never.

14 miles north of Connel Bridge, 20 miles south of Ballachulish on A828, Oban/Fort William/Glencoe rd. At r'bout, continue along lochside rd (disregard bridge). Follow large white signs to Invercreran House Hotel. Cottage 1 mile on, on right.

Earle & Stella Broadbent
Lochside Cottage
Fasnacloich
Appin, Argyll PA38 4BJ
Tel: 01631 730216
Fax: 01631 730216
E-mail: broadbent@lochsidecottage.fsnet.co.uk
Web: www.lochsidecottage.fsnet.co.uk

Entry No: 596   **Map no: 22**

It's easy to see why Maria and Roger chose to build on this spot – a blissful corner of land with ancient birch trees and a burn that's deep enough to dive into. Building was a five-year labour of love and the resulting house a unique combination of wood, slate and stone, with verandas to the front and the rear. Bedrooms are well decorated and functional, the ground floor twin wheelchair-friendly; bathrooms are shiny and new. Expect a feast of home-grown, organic food at dinner: Maria is a terrific cook. Our inspector happily polished off his Simnel cake.

Rooms: 2 doubles, 1 twin, both en suite (shower).

Price: £30 p.p. Single supp. £15.

Meals: Breakfast times flexible; packed lunch £5; dinner including wine, £28.

Closed: October 15-December 31.

A82 from Glasgow to Crianlarich, then A85 to Taynuilt. Left to Kilchrenan for 6 miles on a single track road. House on left down hairpin drive.

Roger & Maria Soep
Roineabhal
Kilchrenan, Taynuilt
Argyll PA35 1HD
Tel: 01866 833207
Fax: 01866 833474
E-mail: maria@roineabhal.com
Web: www.roineabhal.com

Entry No: 597   **Map no: 22**

A 'Wee Free' church used to stand on the site – Rob and Sheila will tell you all about it; history is their delight. This is a delectable place to stay, a 19th-century manse in acres of peaceful woodland garden with the Isle of Bute nearby. Bedrooms have old family pieces and fine views: we liked the twin with the pink French wallpaper, antique brass beds and old desk (complete with writing paper). Your hosts are enormous fun – and very good cooks. The wooden-shuttered, book-lined dining room is an intimate setting for memorable meals.

Rooms: 1 twin, en suite (shower); 1 twin, 1 double sharing bathroom.

Price: £30 p.p. No single supp.

Meals: Breakfast times flexible; packed lunch £5; dinner, 3 courses, £20.

Closed: Never.

From Tarbet A83 to Cairndow. Before village, left on A815 to Strachur, then lochside for Dunoon; entrance 50 yds on right signed 'Free Church'. House on brow of hill.

Spoil yourself - a magnificent Victorian country seat in verdant gardens on the shores of Loch Fyne. And the gardens! Six acres of rhododendrons and specimen trees and 180ft-high Redwoods which, says David, are mere "babies". Nod at the stuffed Highland bull in the hall and sweep up the baronial stone stairway to your room - the doubles with the lavish and king-size *lits bateau* have garden-to-loch views. After a sumptuous dinner, head for the leather chairs beside the fire in the billiard room. There's a comfortable drawing room too. *Self-catering cottage available.*

Rooms: 3 doubles, 2 en suite, 1 with private bathroom.

Price: £35 p.p. Cottage for 2 from £195-£345 p.w.

Meals: Breakfast until 9.30am; dinner, 3 courses, £24.95.

Closed: Never.

From Lochgilphead, A83 towards Campbelltown; 3 miles to Ardrishaig. Over swing bridge; house is 1 mile on right.

Sheila & Rob Macpherson
The Old Manse
Strachur
Strachur
Argyll PA27 8DF
Tel: 01369 860247
E-mail: Sheila.Macpherson@cwcom.net

Kay & David Cameron Davies
Fascadale House
Ardrishaig, Lochgilphead
Argyll PA30 8EP
Tel: 01546 603845
Fax: 01546 602152
E-mail: info@fascadale.com
Web: www.fascadale.com

Entry No: 598   **Map no: 22**   **Entry No: 599**   **Map no: 22**

The closest thing to being on board ship while not on the high seas - every corner of Fernfield exudes Mike's passion for the sea. Perched above Crinan Harbour, with the most staggering views of the Western Isles, our inspector wrote: "A great place, 10 out of 10, and, perhaps, the best view in the book." The light, elegant upstairs drawing/dining room is a perfect vantage point - the sunset often stops dinner in its tracks. Delightfully pretty, spotless and comfortable bedrooms, and one bathroom has a huge stone bath. *Children over 12 welcome.*

Rooms: 1 double, en suite (bath); 1 double, 1 single sharing bathroom.

Price: £30-£32 p.p. Discount for 3 nights or more. No single supp. in rooms that share a bathroom.

Meals: Breakfast times flexible; packed lunch, by arrangement; dinner £22.

Closed: Christmas & New Year.

From Lochgilphead, A813 towards Oban. After 3 miles, B841 west towards Crinan. Pass sign to Crinan Harbour. Pass row of cottages. Take 1st driveway on left & fork left between wooden gates.

Michael & Monica Stewart
Fernfield
Crinan
Argyll PA31 8SW
Tel: 01546 830248
Fax: 01546 830282
E-mail: fernfield@easynet.co.uk

Entry No: 600   **Map no: 22**

Barbara and Hew are generous, kind people - they run a 400-acre hill farm but find time for real hospitality and for preparing delicious food, including shellfish from the Ardfern landings, and home-bakes. The views are stupendous; wander as you wish and admire. The house is elegantly white, the farm definitely working; yet the eye always comes to rest on the water and boats of Loch Craignish. The drawing room is the original 16th-century bothy with coved ceiling, four-foot-thick walls and log fire. Bedrooms are simple and the downstairs loo doubles as the library.

Rooms: 1 double, en suite (bath), with sitting room; 1 suite: 1 double, 2 singles let to one party with sitting room and bathroom.

Price: £34 p.p. No single supp.

Meals: Breakfast until 9am; lunch from £10; dinner £23-£35, on request.

Closed: 22 December-3 January; 4th week of August.

From A816, B8002 to Ardfern, & through village. 0.75 miles beyond church, you will see long white house on top of hill on right. Turn right by Heron's Cottage, up drive to Corranmor.

Hew & Barbara Service
Corranmor House
Ardfern
By Lochgilphead
Argyll PA31 8QN
Tel: 01852 500609
Fax: 01852 500609

Entry No: 601   **Map no: 22**

Robert wears his old-school, fishing-mad, gentleman's heart engagingly on his tweed sleeve. This 1960s lodge conceals a rich rococo interior of 18th-century style and comfort. He has dragged and ragged the walls to a warming vibrancy and is the perfect host - turning his gatherings into house parties. The pretty garden is terraced down to the River Awe and lies at the foot of two Munros. He'll gladly brave the evening's midges and take you to the barrage where the salmon leap or tell you of the west coast gardens to visit. The rooms are simply furnished, light and airy.

Rooms: 2 twins/doubles, 1 twin, all en suite (bath).

Price: £35 p.p. Single supp. £7.

Meals: Breakfast 8.15-9.15am; dinner £25.

Closed: Christmas & New Year

From A85 (Oban road), 23 miles west from Crianlarich. 1.5 miles after Awe Barrage, right signed 'Inverawe Fisheries' just before bridge. House 1st on left after high hedge. If you reach Taynuilt you have travelled 3 miles too far!

Robert Knight
Bridge of Awe Lodge
Taynuilt
Argyll PA35 1HT
Tel: 01866 822642
Fax: 01866 822510

Entry No: 602   **Map no: 22**

Excellent value and marvellous views. Climb up from the rugged coastline of fell and rocky outcrop and watch the sun set over Iona, Coll and Tiree; then turn round and see the heavenly red glow. People sail in just for John's cooking - the cranberry dining room is a welcoming place. The house, warm and simple, is perfect for the setting - the real star of this place. The water is crystal clear, seals - even dolphins or a whale - swim by. Eleanor works in her silversmithing workshop by day; both she and John are free spirits inhabiting a cheerful, cosy and eccentric enclave.

Rooms: 2 twins, 1 double sharing 2 bathrooms.

Price: From £16.50 p.p.

Meals: Breakfast until 9am; à la carte dinner in restaurant, from £10.

Closed: Rarely. Please check.

4 miles beyond Bunessan on road to Iona ferry, right to Kintra. After 1.5 miles, left down track & through iron gate. Cottage is on shore.

John & Eleanor Wagstaff
Red Bay Cottage
Deargphort
Fionnphort
Isle of Mull PA66 6BP
Tel: 01681 700396

Entry No: 603   **Map no: 21**

At the end of a windy lane, in the heart of epic Highland countryside, a home much loved by James, Christina and family. They are the third generation to live here, and the hub of the community. The house is comfortable without being imposing, an 1850 original with later add-ons, mostly clad in gleaming white wood. Christina is lively, down-to-earth, a great hostess. Wholesome, whole-hearted hospitality guaranteed - along with home-produced honey, fruit and veg from the garden. The three llamas add an exotic touch.

Rooms: 1 double (extra single bed), en suite (bath & shower); 1 twin en suite (shower).

Price: £25 p.p.

Meals: Breakfast until 9.30am; dinner £15.

Closed: Christmas & New Year.

Pine martins nested in the hedge last year - rare indeed. This former ferryman's house is small, welcoming, homely, informal, charming and just 50 yards from the River Spey where ospreys and otters fish. Explore the wonderful countryside or sit in the garden with a pot of tea. The sitting room is cosy with a woodburning stove and lots of books (no television). Elizabeth, who lived in the Sudan and is a keen traveller, appreciates delicious food: heathery honeycomb, home-made bread and preserves, herbs from the garden and fresh veg. A superb base for nature lovers and explorers. Good value, too.

Rooms: 1 double, 1 twin, 2 singles, all sharing 1 bathroom & 2 wcs.

Price: £21 p.p.

Meals: Breakfast times flexible; packed lunches £5, dinner £16. B.Y.O. wine.

Closed: Occasionally in winter.

North of Aviemore for 26 miles, left onto B851 signed Fort Augustus. Continue over bridge, through Inverarnie to Farr & past children's playground on left. House 2nd gate on left, after playground.

From B970, to Boat of Garten. House on left, just before River Spey. From A9, follow main road markings through village. Pass golf club & cross river.

James & Christina Murray
Farr Mains
Farr
Inverness
Inverness-shire IV2 6XB
Tel: 01808 521205
Fax: 01808 521466
E-mail: murray@calico.uk.net

Elizabeth Matthews
The Old Ferryman's House
Boat of Garten
Inverness-shire PH24 3BY
Tel: 01479 831370
Fax: 01479 831370

Entry No: 604   **Map no: 23**

Entry No: 605   **Map no: 23**

A cobbled courtyard wall shelters you from blustery winds and, beyond, there's a path to the pebbly Shuaineboist Sands where, in glorious isolation, you can take in the view to the Butt of Lewis. The modern bedrooms are pinkly squeezed under the eaves, flush with facilities. Downstairs, the sun circles the many-windowed library and its well-stuffed leather suite. John, who was born here, was a motorway cop and now he and Dorothy are Atlantic crofters and run the local post office. 'The food is excellent,' says our inspector, 'and the people wonderful.'

Rooms: 1 family/double, 2 twins, all en suite (shower) & use of shared bathroom.

Price: From £31-£35 p.p. Childen under 4 free, 4-12 half-price.

Meals: Breakfast 8.30am; dinner £18.

Closed: Rarely.

The sky envelops you; sea, lochs and views of distant isles surround you. The 300-year-old Tacksman's house is hidden down a bluebell-flanked private drive – and with what energy and enthusiasm it has been renovated. Marcus is restoring the 1.5-acre walled garden to its former glory - it now produces certified organic fruit and vegetables - and, within, Linda has created a luxurious retreat. There are wrap-around views in your bedroom and sitting room; both are bathed in an explosion of magnificent golden light at sunset. Fresh flowers, bathrobes and a heated floor in the shower room; you are spoiled. Popular with honeymooners, but use any excuse to come.

Rooms: 1 double, en suite (shower); 1 small twin with private bathroom.

Price: £40 p.p. Single occ. £50.

Meals: Breakfast times flexible. Dinner available locally.

Closed: Christmas & New Year.

20 miles from Stornoway, on A857 for Port of Ness. Signed left off main road in village, 0.5 miles on, by sea, on left.

Cross Skye Bridge; A87 north, through Broadford & Portree. At Borve, A850 (left fork) signed Dunvegan. Note Treaslane river and 2.4 miles on, gates & Gate Lodge. House 0.5 miles along drive.

John & Dorothy Russell
Galson Farm
South Galson
Isle of Lewis HS2 0SH
Tel: 01851 850492
Fax: 01851 850492
E-mail: galsonfarm@freeserve.com
Web: www.galsonfarm.freeserve.co.uk

Marcus & Linda Ridsdill-Smith
Lyndale House
Edinbane
Isle of Skye IV51 9PX
Tel: 01470 582329
E-mail: linda@lyndale.free-online.co.uk

Entry No: 606   **Map no: 25**

Entry No: 607   **Map no: 25**

In the 16th century the MacLeod chief of the day brought the King of Scotland to the top of Macleod's Table to show him the beauty of Skye. They roasted ox under the stars and the King was impressed - he couldn't fail to be. Time has not diminished that beauty. After a lifetime in the diplomatic service, Donald and Rosemary enjoy putting people at ease. Their former manse and garden is an oasis of comfort and charm encircled by mountains, sea and dramatic lochside beauty. Deeply comfortable beds, pretty china and linen and a warm atmosphere. Local produce and a range of home-made breads are a speciality. *Children by arrangement.*

Rooms: 2 twins/doubles, both en suite (bath/shower); 1 double with private bathroom.

Price: From £35 p.p. Single supp. £7.

Meals: Breakfast times flexible; dinner, 4 courses, £20.

Closed: Christmas & New Year.

Masses of thought has gone into this neat, professionally run house, yet Kate fills it with a personal friendliness. Her cooking is good; she uses whatever is fresh, local and best, and everything, including bread and the cake on your tea tray, is home-made. There are the expected splashes of tartan and Kate puts fresh flowers in the bedrooms along with fluffy towels and smellies in the bathroom. The whitewashed croft sits in a spectacular position - the sea is nearby and there are views to the An Teallach mountain range.

Rooms: 1 double, en suite (shower); 1 double, en suite (bath); 1 double with private shower room.

Price: B&B £30-£40 p.p.; Dinner, B&B £55-£65 p.p. Single supp. £5.

Meals: Breakfast until 9.30am; packed lunch £6; dinner, 4 courses, included (not Sundays).

Closed: November-March.

From Skye Bridge, follow signs for UIG to Sligachan Hotel. Left fork to Dunvegan (22 miles). There, left (just before bakery) signed Glendale. White house in trees after 0.75 miles.

From Inverness on A835 follow signs for Ullapool. Left 12 miles south of Ullapool onto A832 coastal route to Gairloch. 29 miles from this junction, house last on left in Laide.

Donald & Rosemary MacLeod
Kinlochfollart
By Dunvegan
Isle of Skye IV55 8WQ
Tel: 01470 521470
Fax: 01470 521740

Kate & Steve Macdonald
The Old Smiddy
Laide
Ross-shire IV22 2NB
Tel: 01445 731425
Fax: 01445 731696
E-mail: oldsmiddy@aol.com

Entry No: 608   Map no: 25

Entry No: 609   Map no: 26

Highlands & Islands

You have windows for walls in this lovely weatherboard house and stunning views of Loch Broom and the rolling hills beyond. You can scramble around the heather-covered headland, stroll to the private beach and, if you're hardy, swim. Anne is a great cook and she searches out the best local ingredients which she uses in simple, contemporary cooking. The dining room with French windows is connected to a huge sitting room with grand piano, books, CDs, a fire and a hint of the Orient. Super bedrooms with rattan furniture, wicker chairs, crisp duvets and great bathrooms.

Rooms: 1 double, 2 twins, all en suite (bath/shower).

Price: £35-£38 p.p. Single supp. £20.

Meals: Breakfast times flexible; packed lunch from £7.50; dinner, 4 courses, £25.

Closed: Christmas & New Year.

On outskirts of Ullapool from Inverness on A835, left immed. after 4th 40mph sign. Take cattle grid on right & left fork down to house.

Anne Holloway
Tanglewood House
Ullapool
Ross-shire IV26 2TB
Tel: 01854 612059
Fax: 01854 612059
E-mail: tanglewoodhouse@msn.com
Web: www.tanglewoodhouse.co.uk

Entry No: 610   **Map no: 26**

They know the land and its animals, the people and their ways, the geography and the history of their piece of Scotland. Caroline grew up here and Robert, who used to have Les Ambassadeurs, the Park Lane club, has adopted the place as his own; it would be hard to imagine them or their four dogs ever leaving. Staying here, you will be cared for - extra blankets, torches, wellingtons and rucksacks to borrow, home-grown veg and home-made bread freshly prepared for you - yet not fussed over. It is one of the homeliest of our houses. Two rooms are in the Manse and one in the pine-vaulted studio.

Rooms: Main house: 2 doubles with private bathrooms. Stable studio: 1 double, en suite (shower), suitable for partially mobile.

Price: £40 p.p. No single supp. 2% credit card charge.

Meals: Breakfast times flexible; dinner, 2-5 courses, £12-£25. B.Y.O. wine.

Closed: Occasionally.

From Inverness, A9 north. Cross Dornoch bridge. 14 miles on, A839 to Lairg. Cross small bridge in Rogart & sharp right-turn uphill, signed St Callan's church. House 1.5 miles on, on right, next to church.

Robert & Caroline Mills
St Callan's Manse
Rogart
Sutherland IV28 3XE
Tel: 01408 641363
Fax: 01408 641313
E-mail: stcallan@talk21.com

Entry No: 611   **Map no: 27**

A perfect synthesis of owners, house and countryside; the Robertsons are a young family - gentle and lively and utterly committed to this part of the world. The house was built as four cottages in the 1800s - in front, 100 acres of pasture and hardwood woodland roll down to the river Skiach where you can fish or swim in the pool where the waterfall lands. Views go on forever. In the house, gumboots by the door, deep sofas, open fires, rugs, pretty porcelain, long views and light flooding in.

Rooms: 2 twins, sharing bathroom.

Price: £25 p.p.

Meals: Breakfast times flexible; afternoon tea £3.50; dinner, 3 courses, £20.

Closed: Occasionally.

A stupendous, moated house, in the family since 1780. You get columns, a grand piano, big fireplaces, trophies, a snooker table, massive gilt mirrors, silver candelabras and Elizabeth who, in contrast to the grandness of her home, welcomes you in the friendliest way. Beautifully Georgian, the house sits in its own estate; there are 2.5 lochs to fish, wonderful walks, a boat and 1,000 acres of organically reared cattle. The manor – from the antler-bedecked billiard room to the Italian hand-painted and panelled drawing room to the huge, stately, four-poster room with its bearskin – generates a sense of life lived to the full. Superb.

Rooms: 2 doubles, both en suite (bath/shower); 1 four-poster, en suite (shower).

Price: £35 p.p.

Meals: Breakfast times flexible; dinner, 3 courses, £22.

Closed: Occasionally.

A9 north for Inverness for 12 miles. Left into Evanton & left again at village shop for Swordale. House at end of road, 3.5 miles on.

From Inverness, A96 for Nairn. After 9.5 miles right on B9090 through Cawdor. B9090 turns left for Nairn, but continue on B9101. Turn 1st right. House up drive.

Phiddy & Gordon Robertson
Fannyfield House
Swordale
Evanton
Ross-shire IV16 9XA
Tel: 01349 830520
Fax: 01349 830493
E-mail: gar.management.@quista.net

Elizabeth & Jamie Mackintosh-Walker
Geddes House
Nairn
Highlands IV12 5QX
Tel: 01667 452241
Fax: 01667 456707
E-mail: elizabeth@geddes55.freeserve.co.uk

Entry No: 612   **Map no: 27**

Entry No: 613   **Map no: 27**

Wales

Its smallness is not petty;
on the contrary, it is profound.

Jan Morris

One of very few Grade I-listed buildings in the country - this medieval manor possesses staggeringly ancient beauty. Underfloor heating warms the flagstones, the dining room is lit by candles in Tudor candlesticks and some of the stone window frames retain the original 1600 finger moulding. Bedrooms have dramatic mountain views and there is a fascinating herb and knot garden, plus a yew maze. A truly historic house, and conservation and commitment to the environment are evident everywhere - for example, all the soaps are handmade here to traditional recipes in a medieval still room. *Children over 12 welcome.*

Rooms: 1 twin/double, 1 double, 1 four-poster, all en suite (bath).

Price: From £40 p.p. Single supp. £20.

Meals: Breakfast 8.30-9am Mon-Sat; 9.30-10am Sun. Excellent pubs and restaurants nearby.

Closed: Never.

From Abergavenny north on A465. 5 miles on, left for Pantygelli. After 0.25 miles, follow signs to Penyclawdd Farm, pass this to buildings at top of track.

Julia Horton Evans
Penyclawdd Court
Llanfihangel Crucorney
Nr. Abergavenny, Monmouthshire NP7 7LB
Tel: 01873 890719
Fax: 01873 890848
E-mail: pyc@supanet.com
Web: www.1stmanorhouse.co.uk

Entry No: 614   **Map no: 9**

Rivers rush and castles and roman ruins stand proud in the magical Usk Valley. In 10 acres of parkland there are rare trees, shady lawns, lofty Wellingtonia, magnificent rhododendrons and a pool, too. The Countess' home has much to catch the eye: Indian embroidery in carved panels, by Flavia's grandmother, sketches by Flavia's grandfather (the Punch cartoonist) and deep sash windows with seats and lovely views. Bedrooms are large and quiet and the drawing room is Italianate with family portraits. No frills or fussiness, just a timeless, easy elegance that pervades the whole house.

Rooms: 1 double, 1 twin, both with private bathroom.

Price: £35 p.p.

Meals: Breakfast 8.30-9.30am. Dinner available locally.

Closed: Christmas & New Year.

On B4233 between Monmouth & Abergavenny. In Llanvapley look for drive with stone gateposts & white railings.

Countess Flavia Stampa Gruss
Llanvapley Court
Llanvapley
Nr. Abergavenny
Monmouthshire NP7 8SG
Tel: 01600 780250
Fax: 01600 780520

Entry No: 615   **Map no: 9**

The approach is majestic and the house, deep in countryside between England and Wales, meets all expectations; the Georgian, the Victorian and lines of the Welsh longhouse blend beautifully together. Surrounded by 140 acres of farmland, with gardens sloping down to a small lake and stream that meanders through the woodland, you'll find plenty to explore. There's a tennis court and a swimming pool, too. Lovely wallpapers and curtains, good linen and antique furniture in the large bedrooms and you breakfast in an upstairs gallery overlooking that lovely garden. The peace and the seclusion are soothing.

Rooms: 1 double, 1 twin, 1 family, all with private bathroom.

Price: £35 p.p. Single supp. £5.

Meals: Breakfast times flexible; dinner £17.50-£20, by arrangement.

Closed: December.

There is so much to recommend Stembridge: committed owner, organic food, luxurious bedrooms, beautiful surroundings, hot tub, pool, summer concerts and ballet in the garden... You can enrol on courses, too: singing, creative writing, photography. The mill is 17th century, the pond is still there, and brown trout and otters live in the stream. The chef worked with Raymond Blanc, so the food's excellent. You can self-cater or do B&B and children are welcome and can be be looked after, fed and entertained while you relax or learn. Perfect.

Rooms: 2 doubles/twins, en suite (bath/shower); 2 doubles, both with gallery floor with twin beds, both en suite (bath/shower).

Price: £65-70 p.p. Single supp. £30.

Meals: Breakfast times flexible; dinner £35.

Closed: Never.

B4295 Llanrhidian; on to Oldwalls. Take road past Greyhound pub in Oldwalls (pub on left). After 1 mile, downhill double bend; out of 2nd bend, look for house signed 50 yds on right.

Please ask for directions when booking.

Mrs Susan Inkin
Court St. Lawrence
Llangovan
Monmouth
Monmouthshire NP25 4BT
Tel: 01291 690279
Fax: 01291 690279

Francesca & Wendall James
Stembridge Mill
Stembridge
Gower SA3 1BT
Tel: 01792 391640
Fax: 01792 391640
E-mail: stembridge.mill@virgin.net
Web: www.stembridgemill.co.uk

Entry No: 616   Map no: 9

Entry No: 617   Map no: 2

Sandy beaches, white-crested waves, exhilarating surfing and cliff-top walks are all within minutes of the house. This used to be part of the Earls of Cawdors' estate, hence the Scottish influence in the architecture. You'll savour Emma's imaginative cooking using local ingredients and lobster feasts can be organised, too. 95% of food is organic and wines are, too. The beds, with good mattresses and linen, feel luxurious. Country sports can be arranged with notice and this is a good stop-off point for the Pembroke-Rosslare Ferry. There are two very attractive self-catering cottages available.

Rooms: 1 double, 1 twin, both with their own bathrooms. Two self-catering cottages, sleeping 5 and 4.

Price: £27 p.p. Self-catering from £350 p.w.

Meals: Breakfast until 10am; packed lunch available; dinner, 3 courses, £19.

Closed: Never.

From Pembroke, B4319 for Castlemartin. Approx. 6 miles on, Castlemartin village sign on left. At round stone wall (sheep pound) r'bout, left through village, past Welcome Inn on right. Drive on right.

Christopher & Emma Younghusband
The Old Rectory
Castlemartin
Pembrokeshire SA71 5HW
Tel: 01646 661677
Fax: 01646 661677

Entry No: 618   **Map no: 2**

The soft coo of pigeons, clucking of hens and grunts of contented pot-bellied pigs greet you at this mellow-stoned 1708 mansion at the foot of the Black Mountain. There is a stunning garden, a lovely crumbling dovecote and energetic Katy has hacked a path through a jungle of laurels and rhododendrons to a dark, cool, 25-foot-deep icehouse. Follow the river running through the estate to a spectacular waterfall. Indoors, the drawing room has a baby grand. Wallow in the bucolic sights and sounds of a passing pastoral age; you can even get married here.

Rooms: 1 double, 1 twin/double, both en suite (shower); 1 double with shared bathroom. Self-catering also available.

Price: From £22 p.p. Check for self-catering prices.

Meals: Breakfast times flexible; dinner, 3 courses, from £15, by arrangement.

Closed: November-February (except for large groups and self-catering).

From M4 to Pont Abraham services, 2nd exit marked Ammanford. There, left at 2nd set of lights. After 2 miles, 2nd right after Llandybie sign; house 1 mile up on right.

Katy & Carole Jenkins
Glynhir Mansion
Llandybie, Ammanford
Carmarthenshire SA18 2TD
Tel: 01269 850438
Fax: 01269 851275
E-mail: glynhir@glynhir.demon.co.uk
Web: www.theglynhirestate.com

Entry No: 619   **Map no: 8**

It is a cliché, but - hey, they built houses to last in those days. Were a bright young modern architect to come up with the idea of one central supporting structure, and make it work, the media would drivel. This structure has stood every test that Nature and Man have conspired to throw at it. Not a penny has ever been spent on maintenance. The roof is as sound now as it was long before the Celts tugged the Roman beard. The decision to do without windows was far-sighted - again, no maintenance. It may be uncomfortable and of little use to man or beast, but it satisfies our key criteria; it is unusual, interesting, attractive, and - it has soul.

Rooms: Nooks and shadows.

Price: 1 flint axe p.p. Scary sacrificial weekends available.

Meals: Breakfast is a mug of dew at sun up. Dinner, roast boar, assuming your resident Neolithic hunter strikes lucky.

Closed: Winter & Summer solstices and other pagan festivals.

From Carmarthen, left and up the nearest hill. At summit, realise it's the wrong hill, but you'll be able to see the one you should be on.

Stig of the Hump
Yr Dolmen
Carmarthenshire
Tel: 0800 10000BC
Fax: 0800 10000AD
E-mail: freeze@tombstodiefor.co.uk
Web: www.tombstodiefor.co.uk

Entry No: 620   **Map no: 8**

Near Dylan Thomas's Laugharne, this unassuming Georgian country house has its own water supply. You can stable your horse, play tennis and revel in 16 acres of beautiful grounds complete with pond and mature woodland; brilliant for bird-watching. Furnishing is traditional; rooms, including bathrooms, are big and light. The oak-floored sitting room has an open fire and French windows onto the walled garden. This place is convenient for the A40, good value and 15 minutes from the National Botanic Garden of Wales.

Rooms: 2 large doubles, 1 twin, all en suite.

Price: £22.50-£27.50 p.p. Single occ. £28-£35.

Meals: Breakfast times flexible; dinner, 3 courses, approx. £15, by arrangement. B.Y.O wine.

Closed: Never.

From Carmarthen A40 west. Right for Bancyfelin 4 miles on. After 0.5 miles, right into drive on brow of hill.

Cynthia & David Fernihough
Sarnau Mansion
Llysonnen Road
Bancyfelin
Carmarthenshire SA33 5DZ
Tel: 01267 211404
Fax: 01267 211404
E-mail: fernihough@sol405.force9.co.uk

Entry No: 621   **Map no: 8**

With a deft touch Sue, a professional interior decorator, has added individuality to this 200-year-old farmhouse. She is a very keen cook and her vegetarian dishes, with much organic fruit and vegetables, are exceptional. In the attractive dining room revel in good food and sparkling conversation and discuss country pursuits with Nick, followed by a game of billiards in the newly-restored hall. At the end of the day you sink into large, comfortable beds with embroidered sheets and at the beginning, contemplate the heart-healing views. Aberglasney and the National Botanic Gardens are nearby.

Rooms: 1 twin, 1 single, sharing private bathroom (let only to members of same party); 1 double, en suite (bath).

Price: £27.50 p.p. No single supp.

Meals: Breakfast times flexible; packed lunch £5; dinner, 3 courses, with wine and coffee, £15.

Closed: Christmas.

From Llandovery, A40 towards Llandeilo. At Llanwrda, right for Lampeter (A482). After 1 mile, 1st right past M H Evans. Over bridge & up hill; 1st left. House 1st on right.

Sue & Nick Thompson
Mount Pleasant Farm
Llanwrda
Carmarthenshire SA19 8AN
Tel: 01550 777537/777877
Fax: 01550 777537
E-mail: rivarevival@aol.com

Entry No: 622   **Map no: 8**

Carole and Allen who are devoted to conservation unfussily draw you into their home, cosy with warm, natural colours in paintings and woollen tapestries; they serve Welsh cakes on your arrival. Their organic farm is Soil Association-registered, so you will eat very well. Plentiful birdlife adds an audible welcome to Broniwan: tree-creepers, wrens and redstarts all nest in ivy covered walls or mature beech trees. There's a wonderful garden, views of the Preseli hills and the National Botanic Garden of Wales, and Aberglasney to visit.

Rooms: 1 double, en suite (shower); 1 double with private bath.

Price: £24-£26 p.p. No single supp. Reductions for longer stays.

Meals: Breakfast 8-9.30am, but can be flexible; packed lunch from £6; dinner £17; light supper £11.

Closed: Never.

From Aberaeron A487 for 6 miles towards Brynhoffnant. Left at B4334 to Rhydlewis; left at Post Office & shop, 1st lane on right, then 1st track on right.

Carole & Allen Jacobs
Broniwan
Rhydlewis
Llandysul
Ceredigion SA44 5PF
Tel: 01239 851261
Fax: 01239 851261
E-mail: broniwan@compuserve.com

Entry No: 623   **Map no: 8**

No wonder this was the Quay Master's house - the Cleddau Estuary laps against the garden wall and the views are spectacular. Boldly decorated in sympathy with its Georgian interior, the house is run with a certain humour by Philip; it's a relaxing and easy place to be. The Wights relish producing memorable food: their own wild smoked salmon, fishcakes made with local fish and much local and home-grown organic produce. Walk off the excesses along the miles of river footpaths to watch kingfishers, herons and shell ducks. There's a fine old-fashioned inn a minute's walk away.

Rooms: 1 twin with private bathroom; 1 double, en suite (shower); 1 four-poster, en suite (bath). Self-catering cottage for 4 with sea views.

Price: £25-£30 p.p. Single occ. £35. Cottage from £200 p.w.

Meals: Breakfast times flexible; packed lunch from £6; dinner £25.

Closed: Christmas.

From A477, right onto A4075. Left at garage selling 4x4s. House on left after 1.4 miles, just before bridge.

Philip Wight
Cresswell House
Cresswell Quay
Nr. Pembroke
Pembrokeshire SA68 0TE
Tel: 01646 651435
E-mail: phil@cresswellhouse.co.uk
Web: www.cresswellhouse.co.uk

Entry No: 624   **Map no:** 7

The setting is breathtaking: you could take your breakfast cup of coffee to the edge of the cliff and still drink it piping hot. Or you could simply admire the views from the sunshiny dining room. The '60s house is formal, traditional, colourful inside - fitted cupboards and very British, yet surprising. Bird-watching, seal-watching, fishing or just sunbathing - all are possible and the Pembrokeshire Coastal Path runs past the house. Jane and Anthony will give you lifts back from walks. From here it's easy to explore the bird sanctuary islands of Skomer, Skokholm and Ramsey. *Children over seven welcome.*

Rooms: 1 twin with conservatory, en suite (shower); 1 double, 1 single, both en suite (bath); 1 single, 1 double with private bathrooms.

Price: £24-£32 p.p.

Meals: Breakfast times flexible; dinner, 2 courses, £15, by arrangement; not July & August.

Closed: November-January.

From Haverfordwest, B4341, signed Broad Haven. Right at sea front, then up hill signed Nolton. House 1st on left.

Jane & Anthony Main
Lion Rock
Broad Haven, Haverfordwest
Pembrokeshire SA62 3JP
Tel: 01437 781645
Fax: 01437 781203
E-mail: lion.rock@btinternet.com
Web: www.jpmarketing.co.uk/lionrock

Entry No: 625   **Map no:** 7

An ancient bluebell wood pulsates with colour in the spring; wild flowers of all kinds bloom generously, and badgers lumber into the lovely garden to feed. This is an impressive, creeper-clad house, filled with family antiques, candles and crystal; one of the bedrooms has a fine, restored half-tester bed and both share a giant bathroom with a big Victorian washstand and wooden floor. There are fluffy bathrobes for you. Local produce for breakfast along with home-made jams and marmalades, fresh fruit and yogurt. The Pembrokeshire coastal path runs through the land.

Rooms: 1 half-tester and 1 twin, each with private bathroom. Let together only to members of same party.

Price: £25 p.p. No single supp.

Meals: Breakfast until 9.30am; packed lunch £5 by arrangement. Dinner available locally.

Closed: Mid-October-Easter.

The Flynns took on a huge project renovating a Georgian country house built on to an old Welsh farmhouse. They are energetic, fun and helpful. You can take a packed lunch on a walk and arrange to be collected, or hire bicycles - the house borders the National Park with its Coastal Path and unspoilt beaches. Equally you can do nothing more strenuous than play croquet or take tea on the lawn. There's stacks of room here with various barns and outbuildings, and there are plans to host arts and crafts courses. The large guest bedrooms in the main house all have small bathrooms and views over open countryside to the Irish Sea.

Rooms: 3 doubles, 2 twins, all en suite.

Price: £27.50-£40 p.p. Single occ. £35-£55.

Meals: Breakfast times flexible; packed lunch from £4. Good restaurants and pubs locally.

Closed: Never.

B4320 from Pembroke centre for Hundleton. After woods, house 1st on right.

From Fishguard A487. Right at Croesgoch x-roads, 6 miles from St David's. After 1 mile, left at Llanrhian x-roads. House on left, 0.5 miles on.

Mrs Ann Morris
Bowett Farm
Hundleton
Pembroke
Pembrokeshire SA71 5QS
Tel: 01646 683473

Caroline & Eric Flynn
Trevaccoon, Llanrhian
St. David's, Haverfordwest
Pembrokeshire SA62 6DP
Tel: 01348 831438
Fax: 01348 831438
E-mail: flynn@trevaccoon.co.uk
Web: www.trevaccoon.co.uk

Entry No: 626   Map no: 2

Entry No: 627   Map no: 7

Britain only has one Coastal National Park. The Old Vicarage is in it and the most challenging section of the path - a stunning bay and great cliffs - is just a mile away. Inland there are woodland walks and the Preseli Hills. Set in an acre of lawned gardens, the house is Edwardian, with books and family paintings and, best of all, the most glorious sunset views of the sea and total peace. Bedrooms - pink, green and yellow - are large and drink in the sea views. David and Patricia take enormous pride in their cooking and guests rave about the food.

Rooms: 2 doubles, 1 twin, all en suite (shower).

Price: £23-£30 p.p. Single supp. £10. Special breaks in low season.

Meals: Breakfast usually 8.30-9am; picnic lunches available; dinner, 3 courses, £18.

Closed: December, January & February.

From Cardigan bypass towards Cardigan at southern r'bout. Left by Eagle Inn to St. Dogmaels. Sharp right at end of High St to Moylegrove. There, 1st left to Glanrhyd, then up hill. House on right, past church.

Patricia & David Phillips
The Old Vicarage
Moylegrove, Nr. Cardigan
Pembrokeshire SA43 3BN
Tel: 01239 881231
Fax: 01239 881341
E-mail: stay@old-vic.co.uk
Web: www.old-vic.co.uk

Entry No: 628   Map no: 7

For 300 years praise has been heaped upon this unique estate overlooking the Towy Valley; Mandinam means 'untouched holy place'. Daniella and Marcus, an artist, are its guardians today: you'll stay as friends and are encouraged to enjoy the house and garden. Stay all day - and Daniella will prepare all your meals. Here are log fires, shutters, rich rugs on wooden floors; in the fields and woods, wildlife and wild flowers. The twin room in the ancient Coach House has a private terrace and woodburner. As you watch the sun go down before dinner you'll agree that this is secret and magical.

Rooms: 1 double with private bathroom in house; 1 twin in Coach House with private shower room.

Price: £75 p.p. per day full-board.

Meals: Breakfast times; all meals included.

Closed: November-March.

Halfway between Llandeilo and Llandovery on A40, turn off for Llangadog. There, left at Mace foodstore. 50 yds on, right for Myddfai. Past cemetery, 1st right for Llanddeusant. 1.5 miles on, see track through woods on left, House signed.

Daniella & Marcus Lampard
Mandinam
Llangadog
Carmarthenshire
Tel: 01550 777368
E-mail: info@mandinam.co.uk
Web: www.mandinam.co.uk

Entry No: 629   Map no: 8

A super 14th-century house reborn: Freddie has done a tremendous job and restored her 'Church of David Higher' in traditional country style. The house sits high up the River Towy - this is a designated SSSI and you can fish on the private stretch of water. Sink into the comfort of the house - brass beds, chintz, patchwork, terracotta walls and beams, surrounded by peace and tranquillity. The vegetable garden feeds Freddie's guests and two fine, new garden projects are nearby, Aberglasney and the National Botanical Garden of Wales.

Rooms: 2 doubles, en suite (bath); 1 twin with private bathroom. Self-catering cottage for 6 available.

Price: £28 p.p. Single occ. £40. Please ask for price of cottage.

Meals: Breakfast 8-9am, or by arrangement. Dinner £25.

Closed: Christmas.

B4300 from Carmarthen to Capel Dewi. Leaving village follow sign on left & down drive off main road.

Fredena Burns
Capel Dewi Uchaf Country House
Capel Dewi Road, Capel Dewi
Carmarthenshire
Tel: 01267 290799
Fax: 01267 290003
E-mail: uchaffarm@aol.com
Web: www.walescottageholidays.uk.com

Entry No: 630   **Map no: 8**

It's all there: croquet and boules, a piano upon which to tinkle, a jacuzzi for one of the bedrooms, log fires in the sitting rooms and acres of gardens to roam. The Brecon Beacons National Park is close and there are some ancient trees (e.g. magnolia) to sit and dream under. Inside, it is solid and traditional, rather than informal, almost luxurious: fitted carpets, antiques and modern furniture, big pelmeted floral curtains and perfect comfort, everything reliable, nothing out of place. It is impressive and terrific value.

Rooms: 1 family, 1 twin, both en suite (shower); 1 Master room, 1 West Wing double, both en suite (bath & shower); twin with jacuzzi room.

Price: From £22.50-£27.50 p.p. Single supp. £30-£35.

Meals: Breakfast 8-9am; packed lunch, £3-£5; dinner, by arrangement, £20.

Closed: Never.

From Abergavenny, A40 for Brecon & Crickhowell. Approx. 2 miles on, pass car sales garage on right & 200 yds on, a county sign. Next drive on right with lodge at gate.

Mrs Christina Jackson
Glangrwyney Court
Crickhowell
Powys NP8 1ES
Tel: 01873 811288
Fax: 01873 810317
E-mail: glangrwyne@aol.com
Web: www.walescountryhousebandb.com

Entry No: 631   **Map no: 9**

With views to Pen-y-Fan, the highest point of the Brecon Beacons, and next to the Monmouth and Brecon Canal, this 18th-century farmhouse has so much to offer the active. Canal boating is the Atkins' passion and they own, maintain and hire out their brightly-painted vessels. Canoes, mountain bikes and pony trekking are available locally. Freshly-painted bedrooms are simple, with new pine, and duvet covers and curtains patterned with small florals. Guests have their own wing of the house with a conservatory and a separate entrance and staircase. Delightful canal-side pubs nearby.

Rooms: 1 double, 1 twin, both en suite (bath); 2 doubles, both en suite (shower).

Price: £22.50 p.p. Single occ. £28.

Meals: Breakfast 8.30-9am. Dinner available locally.

Closed: End of October-mid-March.

From Abergavenny, A40 to Brecon. After 15 miles, left to Talybont-on-Usk, then right onto B4558 to Pencelli. Through Pencelli for 1 mile, over canal, then immedi. right. Signed.

Nicola & Bob Atkins
Cambrian Cruisers, Ty Newydd
Pencelli, Brecon
Powys LD3 7LJ
Tel: 01874 665315
Fax: 01874 665315
E-mail: cambrian@talk21.com
Web: www.cambriancruisers.co.uk/bandb

Entry No: 632   **Map no: 8**

Penpont is magnificent in its sweeping grounds on the River Usk and folded into the gentle Brecon Beacons' foothills. It has not a whiff of pretension yet a relaxed stateliness of its own: great one-table dining room, grand oak staircase and an oak-panelled drawing room. Large bedrooms (one with tapestried walls) have stacks of atmosphere. An early 19th-century conservatory and two Victorian walled gardens are under restoration and a maze is being nurtured. Overflow into tents (£5), show off on the tennis court, fly-fish on the Usk, borrow wellies and just walk - wonderful!

Rooms: 1 twin, en suite; 1 double with private shower room; 2 family & 2 private bathrooms. Self-contained north wing annexe sleeps 14 in 6 bedrooms.

Price: £30-£40 p.p. Children half price. Cot £5.

Meals: Breakfast times flexible, within reason! Dinner available locally (not walking distance).

Closed: Never.

From Brecon, west on A40 through Llanspyddid. Pass 2nd telephone kiosk on left. Entrance to house on right. (Approx. 4.5 miles from Brecon.)

Davina & Gavin Hogg
Penpont
Brecon
Powys LD3 8EU
Tel: 01874 636202
Fax: 01874 636202
E-mail: penpont@globalnomad.co.uk
Web: www.penpont.com

Entry No: 633   **Map no: 8**

A fascinating, medieval, cruck-built longhouse; it lured the McKays away from the rat race and they've been thankful ever since. Annie and John are knowledgeably restoring this former bishop's summer house to its original state, yet marking it with their distinctive and delightful personalities. Reached by bumpy, private access across farmland, it's utterly quiet. The atmosphere is relaxed and the arrangements flexible. One bedroom has a dramatic half-tester; the other has twin beds with plain black and yellow linen. Chickens, cats, goats, birds outside. Come once and you'll long to come back.

Rooms: 1 double, 1 family, both en suite (bath); 1 twin, with private shower.

Price: £19.50-£22.50 p.p. Family room £55.

Meals: Breakfast times flexible; dinner £9.50. B.Y.O. wine.

Closed: Christmas.

From Hay-on-Wye, A479 then A470 to Builth Wells. Through Lyswen, past forest on left, down hill. Next left for Trericket Mill, then immediate right & up hill. Pass farmhouse on right, straight on through gate across track to house.

Annie & John McKay
Hafod Y Garreg
Erwood
Builth Wells
Powys LD2 3TQ
Tel: 01982 560400

Entry No: 634   **Map no: 8**

The food is plentiful and truly delicious and the dining room has been created amid corn-milling machinery; B&B guests and campers can eat here together in the evening. The Grade II*-listed watermill has wood, flagstone, terracotta, woodburning stoves, comfortable chairs, simple pine bedrooms and a riverside garden. The bunkhouse and camping facilities in the old cider orchard give the mill an informal mood with a planet-friendly bias. A good base for exploring on foot, horseback, bicycle or canoe - lovers of the outdoors looking for simple, good value will be in heaven.

Rooms: 1 twin, 1 double, both en suite (Continental bath/shower); 1 double, en suite (shower).

Price: £21-£24 p.p. Single supp. £10.

Meals: Breakfast times flexible; dinner, 3 courses, £12.75; simple supper £5.50; both by arrangement.

Closed: Christmas & occasionally.

12 miles north of Brecon on A470. Mill set slightly back from road, on left, between Llyswen & Erwood.

Alistair & Nicky Legge
Trericket Mill Vegetarian Guesthouse
Erwood, Builth Wells
Powys LD2 3TQ
Tel: 01982 560312
Fax: 01982 560768
E-mail: mail@trericket.co.uk
Web: www.trericket.co.uk

Entry No: 635   **Map no: 8**

Free-standing baths, seagrass matting, white linen, wooden floors - it has a dash both of Shaker and Scandinavia. "It's 'cool', without the attitude," said our inspector. It's luxurious, too, and host and guests are tangibly happy and relaxed. Login (pronounced 'Lowgin') is 200 years old and has been nurtured and carefully restored by Charlotte and Richard; Charlotte, easy-going and kind, is a *Cordon Bleu* cook and professional caterer for private parties (the food is excellent); Richard, a wood carver, does guided fishing trips and walks. The house is on the A40, but the triple glazing *really* works!

Rooms: 1 double, 1 four-poster, both en suite (bath).

Price: £20-£25 p.p. Single supp. £10-£15.

Meals: Breakfast times flexible; packed lunch £4.50; light supper/dinner, £6-£15.

Closed: Never.

From Brecon, A40 towards Llandovery; 12 miles to Trecastle. House on right, signed.

Charlotte Roskill
Login House
Trecastle, Brecon
Powys LD3 8UP
Tel: 01874 638030
Fax: 01874 638005
E-mail: charlotteroskill@btconnect.com
Web: www.loginhouse.co.uk

Entry No: 636   Map no: 8

This is handsome Georgian on a vast scale with masses of light and space and not a whiff of cloying cosiness. The Morrows have brought new life to the old hall with great decorative flair. The drawing room has Italianate gilded ceilings and the bedrooms are decked out in a mix of period and contemporary; every piece of furniture is special. Duck-down duvets, oak floors, high ceilings, stone staircases, fruit in the rooms and good, fresh food with much garden produce. Ancient trees in the grounds and a vast walled garden. Pretty Berriew and Powys Castle are nearby.

Rooms: 2 twins/doubles, 6 doubles, 1 single, all en suite.

Price: £30-£52.50 p.p. Single occ. £45-£80.

Meals: Breakfast times flexible; dinner, 3-course set menu, £21.50 (not Mondays); hampers also available.

Closed: Sunday.

6 miles south of Welshpool on A483. Drive on right, 50 yds after Nags Head Hotel.

Tim & Nancy Morrow
Garthmyl Hall
Garthmyl
Montgomery
Powys SY15 6RS
Tel: 01686 640550
Fax: 01686 640609

Entry No: 637   Map no: 8

In a wide, open valley with steep woodland rising up behind the house and fine views that fall away from the terraced garden, it is the sort of retreat that has city dwellers vowing to leave for the country. The smell of woodsmoke completes the rural idyll as you sit by the inglenook fireplace in your own comfortably furnished, beamed sitting room. The bedrooms, with fresh flowers, are pretty and light, in pale blue and white. Jane is a professional *Cordon Bleu* chef, so meals will be good. Fishing, painting, pottery, golf and riding can be arranged. *Children by arrangement.*

Rooms: 1 double, 1 twin, both en suite (bath).

Price: From £25 p.p. Single supp. by arrangement.

Meals: Breakfast times flexible; packed lunch from £5; dinner, 2-4 courses, from £13.95-£20.95. B.Y.O. wine.

Closed: Never.

A487 from Machynlleth towards Dolgellau. Left onto B4405, through Abergynolwyn. 2nd farmhouse on right after 1 mile.

Mrs J. Howkins
Tan-y-Coed Isaf
Bryncrug, Tywyn
Gwynedd LL36 9UP
Tel: 01654 782639
Fax: 01654 782639
E-mail: tanhow@supanet.com
Web: smoothhound yuck

Entry No: 638   **Map no: 8**

There are two donkeys (Coppelia & Ophelia) in the garden, a self-catering cottage and a weeping ash that is over 140 years old. Pistyll Rhaeadr, Wales' highest waterfall, is just up the lane. In this superbly-preserved example of neo-Gothic architecture (1861), the hall is dominated by the oak staircase winding to the galleried landing full of pictures, the décor painstakingly restored. Beautiful shower rooms are totally up-to-date and from the bright sunny bedrooms, Sunflower, Orchid and Bluebell, you can see the bracken-gilt Berwyn Mountains. The work on their lovely garden goes on.

Rooms: 1 twin, 1 double, 1 family, all en suite (shower). Self-catering cottage sleeps 2.

Price: £22-£28 p.p. Single supp. £5.

Meals: Breakfast from 8.45am; packed lunch available on request. Dinner available locally.

Closed: Never.

12 miles west of Oswestry on B4396. In village, right after HSBC bank into Waterfall Street.

Karon & Ken Raines
Bron Heulog
Waterfall Street
Llanrhaeadr Y-M Mochnant
Powys SY10 0JX
Tel: 01691 780521
E-mail: kraines@enta.net
Web: www.kraines.enta.net

Entry No: 639   **Map no: 8**

It's a good mile down the hill to the gracious sweep of Cardigan Bay but it looks as though you could hurdle the wall and jump straight into it. Walkers will love Llwyndû, it's warm and earthy, generously simple, with bold colours on ancient stone walls, spiral stone stairways and inglenook fireplaces. Bedrooms are split between the main house and the granary; there are beams, good bathrooms and bunk beds for children. All this in four acres with pretty views up and down, cats, dogs and a horse that comes home for the holidays.

Rooms: 4 doubles (2 four-posters), 2 family, 1 twin, all en suite.

Price: £32-£38 p.p.

Meals: Breakfast times flexible; packed lunch £4-£5; dinner, 3 courses, from £17.95.

Closed: Occasionally in winter.

Our inspector's arrival was greeted by a toot from the driver of the light railway on his way to historic Bala. This old stone house is 1820s and a former vicarage; Bala Lake - Wales' largest - lies still and shimmering below. Bedroom views - of lake and mountains - are life-affirming. Bright, fresh and modern bedrooms with palatial bathroom and, downstairs, waxed pine, light colours and unfussy furnishings. Olwen is the kindest of hosts; she loves her cottage garden with its slate terrace, ponds and Welsh poppies - and people and poetry, too.

Rooms: 1 double, en suite (bath); 1 twin with private bathroom. Also self-catering cottage (2 bedrooms).

Price: From £22 p.p. No single supp. Cottage from £150-£390 per week.

Meals: Breakfast times flexible; packed lunch from £3. Restaurants available locally.

Closed: Never.

A496 north from Barmouth. Through Llanaber. After last house on left, Llwyndû signed on right.

Peter & Paula Thompson
Llwyndû Farmhouse and Restaurant
Llanaber, Barmouth
Gwynedd LL42 1RR
Tel: 01341 280144
Fax: 01341 281236
E-mail: intouch@llwyndu-farmhouse.co.uk
Web: www.llwyndu-farmhouse.co.uk

On entering Bala on A494, left & drive across head of lake. Right on B4403 to Llangower & cross bridge. Look for sign straight ahead.

Olwen Foreman
Plas Gower
Llangower, Bala
Gwynedd LL23 7BY
Tel: 01678 520431
Fax: 01678 520431
E-mail: olwen@plasgower.com
Web: www.plasgower.com

Entry No: 640   **Map no: 8**

Entry No: 641   **Map no: 8**

Gabrielle is brilliant at detail and knows what guests want. She ensures you have comfortable beds, the crispest linen, luxurious towels and super food and wine - maybe roast duck with rich plum sauce or lemon ice cream cake with hot gin blueberries... and has created a no-pressure environment in which to savour it all. Fresh flowers everywhere, good paintings, prints and family antiques, and so many beaches and mountains to explore. The house records go back to the 1600s. You can come and go as you please - guests often book for one night and stay for more.

Rooms: 2 twins, both en suite (bath); 2 doubles, both en suite (1 shower, 1 bath). Self-catering cottage, sleeps 6/7.

Price: £35 p.p. Single supp. £10-£15. Cottage £250-£500 p.w.

Meals: Breakfast 8-9.30am; packed lunch £5; dinner, 3 courses, £22.50, or light supper £17.50; by arrangement.

Closed: Christmas.

From Pwllheli, A499 to r'bout. Right onto A497 Nefyn/Boduan road after 3 miles. Left opposite church. House set back, on right.

Gabrielle & Roger Pollard
The Old Rectory
Boduan
Nr. Pwllheli
Gwynedd LL53 6DT
Tel: 01758 721519
Fax: 01758 721519

Welcoming dogs and Welsh air will soothe the weary traveller; so, too, will the mountain and river views and the Harmans who entertain guests without huge fuss. Rambling, 18th-century, slate-floored, the farm is in the most glorious setting with the River Dee rolling by at the bottom of the valley. Comfortable, antique furniture, old beams and simple, but delicious, food. Most vegetables come from the well-tended garden and you eat Aga cooking in the dining room off the kitchen. Guests have two sitting rooms. There is absolutely nothing here to ruffle you.

Rooms: 1 twin en suite (shower), 1 twin with private bathroom, plus 1 single available for members of same party willing to share bathroom.

Price: £22-£24 p.p.

Meals: Breakfast until 9.30am; packed lunch £3; dinner £11, by prior arrangement; B.Y.O. wine. Also available locally.

Closed: November-February.

From Shrewsbury, A5, right at lights in Llangollen. Over bridge & left onto A542, signed Ruthin. After 1.5 miles, left onto B5103 to Rhewl. On for 2.5 miles. Farm 400 yds on left after redbrick chapel, before Sun Inn.

Mary Harman
Dee Farm
Rhewl
Llangollen
Denbighshire LL20 7YT
Tel: 01978 861598
Fax: 01978 861598
E-mail: harman@activelives.co.uk

The 15th-century wattle-and-daub house and former cow byre sit in a glorious position. The typical, honey-coloured barn has been sensitively converted for guests, keeping its low sloping ceilings, beams and small windows; you can still see the outlines of the original thick stone walls. The sitting room looks over the Vale of Clwyd and your jolly hosts will drop and collect you from Offa's Dyke walks. Irene runs craft courses - textiles and paper-making, for example - ask her for details. Good value, too. *Self-catering possible. Children over 10 welcome.*

Rooms: 1 double, 1 triple, both en suite (shower).

Price: £20 p.p. Single occ. £22.

Meals: Breakfast times flexible; packed lunch £3.50. Supper available at nearby inn.

Closed: Never.

A494 east from Ruthin. Left opposite Griffin Hotel onto B5429. After 0.5 miles, right to Llangynhafal. After 2 miles, Esgairlygain signed on right about 100 yds past Plas Draw. House left of courtyard.

Irene Henderson
The Old Barn
Esgairlygain
Llangynhafal, Ruthin
Denbighshire LL15 1RT
Tel: 01824 704047
Fax: 01824 704047

Entry No: 644   **Map no: 8**

Nothing is frilled or flounced - befitting the Arts & Crafts style - but handsome architecture, panelling and solid furniture speak of fine values. The house has been in the family for 400 years and it traditions have changed with the times. A spring runs beneath the dining room and on a beam above the hall fireplace is carved *Aelwyd a gymhell* ('A welcoming hearth beckons'). Upstairs, the feel is fresh and more modern; beds are comfortable and towels are thick. A copper beech rustles in the west wind; views are to Offa's Dyke and there's not another house in sight.

Rooms: 1 double, 1 twin, both en suite (shower).

Price: £22-£25 p.p.

Meals: Breakfast times flexible; packed lunch £3; dinner £11.50, by arrangement.

Closed: Never.

From Chester, A55, then left onto B5122 for Caerwys. There, 1st right into High St. Right at end, continue 0.75 miles to x-roads & left, past camp, straight for 1 mile. House on left at sign.

Mrs Nest Price
Plas Penucha
Caerwys
Mold
Flintshire CH7 5BH
Tel: 01352 720210
Fax: 01352 720881

Entry No: 645   **Map no: 8**

A haven for musicians, walkers and those who love the simple life. Fresh air, birdsong, good conversation and hot scones for breakfast – could you want more? Alan is a pianist who might play after your (excellent) supper; Irish Ger plays the fiddle and is happy to talk. The small bedrooms in this long, low, wonky-floored granite cottage are whitewashed and fuss-free, personalised with cheerful rugs and friends' paintings. The bathroom is overlooked only by sheep, and there's a guests' sitting room with a woodburner. An atmospheric riverside retreat. *Children over 10 welcome*

Rooms: 1 double, 1 twin, 1 single, sharing bathroom.

Price: First night, £17 p.p. £15 p.p. thereafter.

Meals: Breakfast times flexible; packed lunch £3.50; dinner, £7.50-£10, by arrangement. B.Y.O. wine.

Closed: November-March.

From A5 B4406 through Penmachno. Left at The Eagles Pub. Follow road for 2 miles until 'S' bend sign; cottage left before bridge.

Ger Tunstall
Rhyd-y-Grô
Cwm Penmachno
Betws-y-Coed, Conwy LL24 0RB
Tel: 01690 760144
Fax: 01690 760144
E-mail: afonig@btinternet.com
Web: www.afonig.com

Entry No: 646   **Map no: 13**

Above you is the Little Orme with stunning views; below, across the main coast road, is the sweep of Llandudno Bay. And, inside, what a surprise! Patricia has given her passion for paint techniques full rein. The Marina Room is fresh yellow with a turquoise ceiling and a painted Neptune on the cupboards and she is constantly updating the colours and themes of the whole house; much of it has been recently refurbished. You have your own sitting room, bedrooms are double-glazed and the views are lovely. *Children over 12 welcome.*

Rooms: 1 double, 1 twin, en suite (shower); 1 double with private bathroom; 1 four-poster, en suite. Only 3 rooms let at one time.

Price: From £25 p.p. Single supp. £5 or half room charge.

Meals: Breakfast until 9am. Dinner available locally.

Closed: Mid-December-mid-January.

B5115 Llandudno/Colwyn coast road, (sea on left). Continue past turning for Bryn Y Bia on right. House on right.

Patricia Richards
Lympley Lodge
Craigside
Llandudno
Conwy
Tel: 01492 549304
E-mail: clive@lympleylodge.co.uk
Web: www.lympleylodge.co.uk

Entry No: 647   **Map no: 13**

Pure Elizabethan, magical and intriguing - Golden Grove was built by Sir Edward Morgan in 1580. The Queen Anne dogleg staircase, oak panelling and furniture are set off beautifully by the rich jewel colour schemes (the breakfast room is red, the dining room a subtle aquamarine). The two Anns are wonderful hosts - they serve breakfast from kitchens at each end of the morning room and the family foursome tend the formal garden, organic vegetable garden and nuttery and run a sheep farm as well as their relaxed B&B. Friendly, fascinating; worth the trip. *Children over 12 welcome.*

Rooms: 1 twin, 1 double, both with private bath & wc; 1 double, en suite (bath).

Price: £37 p.p. Single occ. £47.

Meals: Breakfast 8-9.30am; dinner £22. Pub food also available locally.

Closed: December & January.

Turn off A55 onto A5151 for Prestatyn. At Spar shop before Trelawnyd, turn right. Branch left immed. Over 1st x-roads & right at T-junction. Gates 170 yds on left.

Ann & Mervyn & Ann & Nigel Steele-Mortimer
Golden Grove
Llanasa, Nr. Holywell
Flintshire CH8 9NA
Tel: 01745 854452
Fax: 01745 854547
E-mail: golden.grove@lineone.net

Entry No: 648   **Map no: 14**

Church records show that the house was built in Elizabethan times with some later Victorian additions - it is beautiful and surrounded by bluebell woods. It also looks like something out of a fairytale and the two-acre terraced garden adds to the magic. Inside there are beams everywhere, open fires and lovely views across the valley from all the windows. The bedding is Egyptian cotton, the duvets are goose down and the towels huge and thick; there are bathtime goodies, too. Much of the food is organic and locally-grown and Charmian, who spent some years in Mallorca, often adds a Mediterranean touch to her cooking. *Children over eight welcome.*

Rooms: 1 twin/double, 1 double, both en suite (bath & shower).

Price: £37 p.p. Single occ. £47.

Meals: Breakfast 8-9.15am; packed lunch £5; dinner, 4-courses, £22.

Closed: Never.

From Mold A494 towards Ruthin. 300 yds past Rainbow Inn, left onto Maeshafn rd. 1 mile on, right at T-junc. into Maeshafn. Past phone box, left fork through woods; through gates & courtyard.

Charmian & Ted Spencer
Pentre Cerrig Mawr
Maeshafn, Nr Mold
Flintshire CH7 5LU
Tel: 01352 810607
Fax: 01352 810607
E-mail: pentre.cerrig@virgin.net
Web: www.pentrecerrigmawr.com

Entry No: 649   **Map no: 14**

Climbing the steps to the tower bedrooms, you get a real sense of adventure: the age and history permeate your skin as you discover mullioned windows, portraits, antique furniture and big beds. This is the only remaining fortified house on the border and it was built over 500 years ago by the family who occupy it now. The medieval dining hall in the tower displays the coat of arms and the family motto 'without God there is nothing'. Breakfast is taken at the library end of the large drawing room. All this, and four acres of formal gardens in which to dream.

Rooms: Tower: 1 double, en suite (bath); 1 double with private bathroom. Main house: 1 twin with private bathroom.

Price: £35 p.p. Single supp. £15.

Meals: Breakfast until 9am. Dinner available locally (within 2 miles).

Closed: 22 December-3 January.

To traffic lights in centre of Mold, turn into Wrexham road (B5444). After 0.7 miles, fork right into Nercwys. After 0.4 miles, entrance on right, through large black gates.

Charles & Wendy Wynne-Eyton
Tower
Nercwys
Mold
Flintshire CH7 4EW
Tel: 01352 700220
Fax: 01352 700220
E-mail: wynne.eyton@virgin.net

Entry No: 650   **Map no: 14**

"Unbelievable!". Our inspector was blown away by it. An incredible adventure from the moment you leave your car and are taken in the 4x4 vehicle along the cliffs to this isolated outpost on an RSPB Reserve. The old Fog House (a former signal station for Trinity House) is now converted into a bird-watching observatory. Philippa is a painter and will organise painting expeditions on request. She cares deeply about guests, and is generous with everything, food included. The bedrooms, part of the former keeper's quarters, are simple and attractive. Don't forget waterproofs and binoculars. *Advance booking essential.*

Rooms: 1 double next to private shower room; 1 twin, sharing private bathroom.

Price: £25 p.p. No single supp.

Meals: Breakfast times flexible; packed lunch £2.50; dinner including wine, £15.

Closed: November-March.

On Holyhead seafront, take upper road on left. After 2 bridges, Warden's House at Breakwater Country Park is on left. Phone to be collected. If coming by train or ferry, ring from station.

Philippa Jacobs
North Stack
c/o 4 Lower Park Street
Holyhead
Anglesey LL65 1DU
Tel: 01407 769715
Fax: 01407 761252

Entry No: 651   **Map no: 13**

Quick reference indices

Quick reference indices

Quick reference indices

Wales

South Wales • 615

West Wales • 619 • 622 • 623 • 625 • 626

Mid Wales • 637

North Wales • 641 • 646 • 651

CHILD-FRIENDLY
The owners of these houses welcome children of any age, but do discuss any special needs; cots and high chairs may not be available.

Bath & N.E. Somerset • 7 • 8 • 11 • 13 • 15 • 16

Berkshire • 18

Bristol • 21 • 22 • 23

Buckinghamshire • 24

Cambridgeshire • 26 • 28 • 31

Cheshire • 33 • 35 • 36

Cornwall • 37 • 43 • 45 • 50 • 55 • 58 • 59 • 61 • 62 • 64 • 66 • 67 • 76

Cumbria • 81 • 82 • 85 • 90

Derbyshire • 98 • 102

Devon • 106 • 107 • 108 • 113 • 115 • 117 • 118 • 125 • 126 • 131 • 138 • 139 • 140 • 145 • 146 • 148 • 149 • 151 • 152

Dorset • 158 • 159 • 161 • 162 • 164 • 170 • 172 • 176

Durham • 178 • 179

Essex • 182 • 184 • 185

Gloucestershire • 187 • 188 • 192 • 193 • 194 • 195 • 196 • 199 • 201 • 203 • 205 • 206 • 207 • 208 • 209

Hampshire • 214 • 216 • 222

Herefordshire • 228 • 232 • 233 • 237 • 238 • 240 • 241 • 242 • 243 • 245 • 247

Isle of Wight • 250

Kent • 253 • 254 • 257 • 261 • 263 • 268

Lincolnshire • 271 • 273 • 274 • 276 • 278

London • 281 • 284 • 289 • 290 • 292 • 303

Norfolk • 308 • 309 • 314 • 316 • 317 • 320 • 321 • 324 • 326

Northamptonshire •329

Northumberland • 331 • 332 • 335 • 339

Nottinghamshire • 341 • 342 • 343

Oxfordshire • 344 • 347 • 352 • 354 • 355

Shropshire • 360 • 365 • 367 • 372

Somerset • 376 • 377 • 380 • 382 • 383 • 386 • 395 • 396 • 398 • 403

Staffordshire • 405 • 407 • 409 • 410

Suffolk • 415 • 418 • 421 • 422 • 423 • 424 • 425 • 427 • 429 • 431 • 432 • 435

Surrey • 439 • 440 • 442 • 443 • 444 • 445

Sussex • 450 • 452 • 453 • 455 • 462

Quick reference indices

NO CAR?
These owners have told us that their B&B can be reached by public transport and/or that they are happy to collect you from the nearest bus or train station - please check when booking. (Other owners not on this list may be just as helpful, so do ask.)

Quick reference indices

GROWN

These owners use mostly organic ingredients, chemical-free, home-grown or locally-grown produce.

Quick reference indices

PETS WELCOME

The owners of these houses are happy to discuss the idea of your bringing your pet with you.

Quick reference indices

What is Alastair Sawday Publishing?

A dozen or more of us work in two converted barns on a farm near Bristol, close enough to the city for a bicycle ride and far enough for a silence broken only by horses and the occasional passage of a tractor. Some editors work in the countries they write about, e.g. France and Spain, others work from the UK but are based outside the office. We enjoy each other's company, celebrate every event possible, and work in an easy-going but committed environment.

These books owe their style and mood to Alastair's miscellaneous career and his interest in the community and the environment. He has taught overseas, worked with refugees, run development projects abroad, founded a travel company and several environmental organisations - many of which have flourished. There has been a slightly mad streak evident throughout, not least in his driving of a waste-paper-collection lorry for a year, the manning of stalls at impoverished jumble sales and the pursuit of causes long before they were considered sane.

Back to the travel company: trying to take his clients to eat and sleep in places that were not owned by corporations and assorted bandits he found dozens of very special places in France - farms, châteaux etc - a list that grew into the first book, *French Bed and Breakfast*. It was a celebration of 'real' places to stay and the remarkable people who run them.

The publishing company is based on the unexpected success of that first and rather whimsical French book. It started as a mild crusade, and there it stays - full of 'attitude', and the more appealing for it. For we still celebrate the unusual, the beautiful, the individual. We are passionate about rejecting the banal, the ugly, the pompous and the indifferent and we are passionate too about promoting the use of 'real' food. Alastair is a trustee of the Soil Association and keen to promote organic growing and consuming by owners and visitors.

It is a source of deep pleasure to us to have learned that there are many thousands of people who share our views. We are by no means alone in trumpeting the virtues of standing up to the destructive uniformity of so much of our culture.

We are building a company in which people and values matter. We love to hear of new friendships between those in the book and those using it, and to know that there are many people - among them farmers - who have been enabled to pursue their lives thanks to the extra income the book brings them.

www.specialplacestostay.com

Adrift on the unfathomable and often unnavigable sea of accommodation pages on the Internet, those who have discovered www.specialplacestostay.com have found it to be an island of reliability. Not only will you find a database full of honest, trustworthy, up-to-date information about over a thousand *Special Places to Stay* across Europe, but also:

- Direct links to the web sites of hundreds of places from the series
- Colourful, clickable, interactive maps
- The facility to make most bookings by email -
  even if you don't have email yourself
- Online purchasing of our books, securely and cheaply
- Regular, exclusive special offers on books from the whole series
- The latest news about future editions, new titles and new places
- The chance to participate in the evolution of both the guides
  and the site

The site is constantly evolving and is frequently updated. By the time you read this we will have introduced an online notice board for owners to use, where they can display special offers or forthcoming local events that might tempt you. We're expanding our European maps, adding more useful and interesting links, providing news, updates and special features that won't appear anywhere else but in our window on the world wide web.

Just as with our printed guides, your feedback counts, so when you've surfed all this and you still want more, let us know - this site has been planted with room to grow!

Russell Wilkinson, Web Editor
editor@specialplacestostay.com

Alastair Sawday
Special Places to Stay series

ITALY

BRITISH HOTELS, INNS AND OTHER PLACES

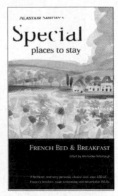

FRENCH BED & BREAKFAST

FRENCH HOTELS, INNS & OTHER PLACES

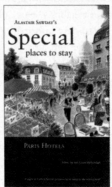

PARIS HOTELS

IRELAND

SPAIN

PORTUGAL

GARDEN BED & BREAKFAST

www.specialplacestostay.com

Order Form UK

All these books are available in major bookshops or you may order them direct. Post and packaging are FREE.

	Price	No. copies
Special Places to Stay: **Portugal**		
Edition 1	£8.95	
Special Places to Stay: **Spain**		
Edition 4	£11.95	
Special Places to Stay: **Ireland**		
Edition 3	£10.95	
Special Places to Stay: **Paris Hotels**		
Edition 3	£8.95	
Special Places to Stay: **Garden Bed & Breakfast**		
Edition 1	£10.95	
Special Places to Stay: **French Bed & Breakfast**		
Edition 7	£14.95	
Special Places to Stay: **British Hotels, Inns** and other places		
Edition 3	£11.95	
Special Places to Stay: **British Bed & Breakfast**		
Edition 6	£13.95	
Special Places to Stay: **French Hotels, Inns** and other places		
Edition 2	£11.95	
Special Places to Stay: **Italy**		
Edition 2	£11.95	
Special Places to Stay: **French Holiday Homes**		
Edition 1 (available January 2002)	£11.95	
The Little Earth Book	£5.99	

Please make cheques payable to: **Alastair Sawday Publishing**   **Total**

Please send cheques to: Alastair Sawday Publishing, The Home Farm Stables, Barrow Gurney, Bristol BS48 3RW. **For credit card orders call 01275 464891 or order directly from our website www.specialplacestostay.com**

Name:

Address:

Postcode:

Tel: Fax: BBB6

If you do not wish to receive mail from other companies, please tick the box ☐

Order Form USA

All these books are available at your local bookstore, or you may order direct. Allow two to three weeks for delivery.

	Price	No. copies
Special Places to Stay: Portugal		
Edition 1	$14.95	
Special Places to Stay: Ireland		
Edition 3	$17.95	
Special Places to Stay: Spain		
Edition 4	$19.95	
Special Places to Stay: Paris Hotels		
Edition 3	$14.95	
Special Places to Stay: French Hotels, Inns and other places		
Edition 2	$19.95	
Special Places to Stay: French Bed & Breakfast		
Edition 7	$19.95	
Special Places to Stay: Garden Bed & Breakfast		
Edition 1	$17.95	
Special Places to Stay: Italy		
Edition 2	$17.95	
Special Places to Stay: British Hotels, Inns and other places		
Edition 3	$17.95	

Shipping in the continental USA: $3.95 for one book,
$4.95 for two books, $5.95 for three or more books.
Outside continental USA, call (800) 243-0495 for prices.
For delivery to AK, CA, CO, CT, FL, GA, IL, IN, KS, MI, MN, MO, NE,
NM, NC, OK, SC, TN, TX, VA, and WA, please add appropriate sales tax.

Please make checks payable to: The Globe Pequot Press   **Total**

To order by phone with MasterCard or Visa: (800) 243-0495. 9a.m. to 5p.m.
EST; by fax: (800) 820-2329, 24 hours; through our web site:
www.globe-pequot.com; or by mail: The Globe Pequot Press, P.O. Box 480,
Guilford, CT 06437.

Name: Date:

Address:

Town:

State: Zip code:

Tel: Fax:

Report Form

Comments on existing entries and new discoveries.

If you have any comments on entries in this guide, please let us have them. If you have a favourite house, hotel, inn or other new discovery, not just in Britain, please let us know about it.

Book title: _____ Entry no: _____ Edition: _____

New recommendation ☐ Country: _____

Name of property: _____

Address: _____

_____

Postcode: _____

Tel: _____

Date of stay: _____

Comments: _____

_____

_____

_____

_____

From: _____

Address: _____

_____

Postcode: _____

Tel: _____

Please send the completed form to: **Alastair Sawday Publishing, The Home Farm Stables, Barrow Gurney, Bristol BS48 3RW** or go to www.specialplacestostay.com and click on contact.

Thank you.

Find out what happens to the food we eat and why organic is the more natural choice.

'The truth about food' - yours FREE when you join the Soil Association

If you care about the food you eat **_join the Soil Association today_** and add your voice to one of the fastest growing movements of our time. As a charity we urgently need your support to fund our campaigning work to help build a sustainable future for the British countryside.

Join today and you will receive

The truth about food, a fascinating 40 page full colour booklet which addresses many of the most pressing issues concerning the food we eat in the 21st century. ***Plus*** quarterly editions of our award winning magazine *Living Earth*. ***Plus*** £6 off your first year's membership

---

YES. I want to discover 'the truth about food' and save £6 off my first year's membership of the Soil Association

Registered Charity No. 206862

I enclose a cheque for a total of £18.00

OR/ Please debit my VISA/Mastercard/Access a total of £18.00

Card No. _____

Expiry Date _____ Issue Number (Switch only) _____

NAME _____

ADDRESS _____

_____ POSTCODE _____

Tick here if you do not want further appeal information ☐

**Return this coupon to: the Soil Association.
FREEPOST (BS4456) Bristol BS1 6ZY**

Index by surname

Index by surname

Index by surname

Index by surname

Index by surname

Index by surname

Index by place name

Index by place name

Index by place name

Index by place name